Approaches to Teaching Cervantes's *Don Quixote*

Second Edition

Approaches to Teaching
World Literature

For a complete listing of titles,
see the last pages of this book.

Approaches to Teaching Cervantes's *Don Quixote*

Second Edition

Edited by

James A. Parr

and

Lisa Vollendorf

Modern Language Association of America
New York　　2015

© 2015 by The Modern Language Association of America
All rights reserved
Printed in the United States of America

MLA and the MODERN LANGUAGE ASSOCIATION are trademarks
owned by the Modern Language Association of America.
For information about obtaining permission to reprint material from
MLA book publications, send your request by mail (see address below)
or e-mail (permissions@mla.org).

Library of Congress Cataloging-in-Publication Data
Approaches to teaching Cervantes's Don Quixote / edited by James A. Parr and
Lisa Vollendorf. — Second edition.
pages cm. — (Approaches to teaching world literature, ISSN 1059-1133 ; 134)
Includes bibliographical references and index.
ISBN 978-1-60329-187-3 (cloth : alk. paper) —
ISBN 978-1-60329-188-0 (pbk. : alk. paper) —
ISBN 978-1-60329-189-7 (EPUB) —
ISBN 978-1-60329-190-3 (Kindle)
1. Cervantes Saavedra, Miguel de, 1547–1616 — Study and teaching.
2. Cervantes Saavedra, Miguel de, 1547–1616. Don Quixote.
I. Parr, James A., 1936– editor.   II. Vollendorf, Lisa, editor.
PQ6344.A67 2014
863'.3 — dc23   2014042206

Approaches to Teaching World Literature 134
ISSN 1059-1133

Cover illustration of the paperback edition:
Don Quixote and Sancho on Their Way to Puerto Lápice, by José Moreno Carbonero.

Published by The Modern Language Association of America
26 Broadway, New York, NY 10004-1789
www.mla.org

CONTENTS

Classroom Contexts

PREFACE

In 1984, the Modern Language Association published Richard Bjornson's *Approaches to Teaching Cervantes'* Don Quixote. Essays on *Don Quixote* as funny, metafictional, and archetypal were balanced by reader-response and psychoanalytic approaches to the text. The volume was notable both for its ability to serve instructors over time as well as for its rootedness in literary criticism of the 1970s. The dramatic changes in literary theory, methodology, and pedagogy in the intervening years have changed the ways many students and scholars approach Cervantes's text. Where we used to speak of perspectivism, often illustrated through the *baciyelmo* (basin-helmet) episode, we are now more likely to speak of a negotiation of multiple perspectives on truth influenced by subject position, cultural identity, and political motivation. Reading *Don Quixote* solely as a funny book or as a novel that traces the Quixotization of Sancho in exchange for the Sanchification of Don Quixote no longer resonates with many readers, particularly those in cultural studies. As several essays in this second edition of the volume attest, today we continue to look for both literary and sociohistorical contextualization as critical to our understanding of the text, and we also bring different critical and pedagogical approaches to bear.

Despite changes in emphasis and orientation, our purpose is not to supplant the 1984 volume but to supplement it. The quality of the studies it contains is not at issue. Nor is their continuing usefulness. Why, then, does the volume need supplementing? In the late 1970s and early 1980s, structuralism had made slight inroads in Cervantes studies, while deconstruction was unknown. Questions of origins, framing, mise en abyme, and interarts theory had not entered the conversation. Roman Jakobson's classic communication model was ignored or thought to be irrelevant. Reader-response criticism was a novelty. Narratology was little known and even less practiced. More specifically, Cide Hamete was accepted as the frame narrator, intentionality remained largely unquestioned, Cervantes's point of view toward his protagonist was considered to be benign, generic bending and blending had not been explored, the notion of the dominant genre had not been introduced, and the Romantic approach remained ascendant. The mimetic received a great deal of attention, while diegesis was relegated to a subordinate position. Modern genre theory hardly entered the picture. The universe of discourse surrounding both theory and practice has changed enough since 1984 to merit a new collection of different approaches to teaching *Don Quixote*.

Whether teaching the entire novel or only excerpts, many of us now make connections with popular culture, film studies, Cervantine literary and artistic legacies throughout the world. We also rely more heavily on external resources in our teaching. *PowerPoint*, *Prezi*, course management systems, and the Internet make it possible to make Web sites, audio recordings, films, and the plastic arts part of the teaching and learning experience. Close reading of the text remains central, but the understanding and appreciation of that text can be greatly enhanced through technology and interdisciplinarity.

The digital revolution has changed our lives dramatically. Today's students are likely to have experience more in microblogging and writing wikis than in reading a long novel. In an age of quick-paced communication, it is both a privilege and a challenge to teach and study *Don Quixote de la Mancha*. The text's influence on world literature continues to reverberate and metamorphose with each new generation of writers. Over the centuries, countless visual artists and, more recently, filmmakers and multimedia creators have got into the act. Trinkets and sculptures of Don Quixote and Sancho Panza are sold in markets across Latin America and Spain. Their story—and likenesses—have been repurposed for Japanese anime, Chicano literature, and Broadway. Don Quixote has become the standard-bearer for those who act when no one else will; for those whose courage requires a dose of lunacy; for those who step out of the everyday and dare to dream, as the song goes, the impossible dream. Such is the inspiration we take from this timeless character that a *Google* search of *quixotic* in June 2014 produced more than 850,000 hits.

Don Quixote requires us to slow down, attend to detail, and allow our inboxes to fill as we read all 126 chapters. Reading the novel is a daunting task for students; yet they commit themselves to it with enthusiasm and energy. For many, especially those who already feel connected to Don Quixote and Sancho because of their cultural background or their personal history, reading the *Quixote* and discovering its complexities with a community of learners is a once-in-a-lifetime opportunity.

We hope that the essays in this volume will inspire *Quixote* instructors to experiment with new techniques and integrate new ideas into their teaching. We also hope that they will be motivated by the commitment to teaching literature, history, and culture that can be found in the pages that follow.

We thank the MLA for recognizing the need to provide an update to Bjornson's fine book, and we acknowledge his role in guiding *Quixote* instructors for nearly four decades. The insights of James C. Hatch, a senior acquisitions editor at the MLA, and Joseph Gibaldi, a former editor of the MLA series Approaches to Teaching World Literature, have immeasurably improved this volume. We could not have completed the project without the the support of the MLA director of Scholarly Communication, Kathleen Fitzpatrick, and the fine editing work of Michael Kandel. Finally, we are deeply grateful to the contributors of this volume for sharing their scholarly and pedagogical expertise. We already have integrated many of their creative ideas into our own *Quixote* courses.

Introduction

Don Quixote is one of the most influential texts of world literature. In 1997, a special issue of *Life* magazine included the publication of *Don Quixote* among the hundred most important events of the millennium ("*Don Quixote de la Mancha*"). The BBC reported on 7 May 2002 the results of a poll taken by the Norwegian Nobel Institute, in which a hundred of the world's leading authors were asked to list the ten works of fiction that they considered the "best and most central works of world literature." The BBC reported, "Leading authors have named [seventeenth-century] Spanish story *Don Quixote* as the best work of fiction ever written, ahead of works by Shakespeare, Tolstoy, and Dostoyevsky" ("*Don Quixote* Gets"). Cervantes's masterpiece received fifty percent more votes than the second-ranked work.

Such statements pique the curiosity of those who have not read *Don Quixote*; those who have do not need others to validate their love of the text. The adventures of Don Quixote and Sancho Panza—and the strategies used in the telling of that tale—have delighted and intrigued readers for centuries. Each time we teach a course or recommend the text to a friend, we are expanding the community of readers, inviting new interpretations and new understandings to come forward and be added to the mix. Every reader has a favorite episode or element. And with each passing decade the reading of the text may change as the reader's life story changes.

Published in 1605 (part 1) and 1615 (part 2) to immediate success, *El ingenioso hidalgo don Quixote de la Mancha* put Cervantes on the map as a European author of stature. Among the many accomplishments of *Don Quixote* we should note Cervantes's ability to express so many of the social and cultural changes that occurred in his lifetime and his ability to express them without being censured. Issues of race, ethnicity, religion, imperialism, class, and gender all surface, as do questions related to power and authority. His literary contributions are without parallel in his time. His feat of forging a new kind of literature out of all the genres and discursive styles available to him makes the text at once challenging and gratifying, a veritable treasure trove of literary, cultural, and historical references for readers who care to decipher its ambiguities.

Carroll Johnson's Don Quixote: *The Quest for Modern Fiction* (1990) recapitulates what many have said about irony and ambiguity in the text: "The ideological constraints imposed by [Cervantes's] society precluded the open expression or even the suggestion of dissent. Following Erasmus and doubtless his personal inclination as well, Cervantes adopted a rhetorical strategy based on pervasive and systematic irony. Ambiguity is the watchword" (10). On occasion, the irony of some episodes is so patent that the text leaves little room for ambiguity. Ambiguity may be embedded in an episode, a passage, or the words of a title, as in "ingenioso" and "mancha" in the festive 1605 title. The often complementary use of irony, ambiguity, and paradox explains why, after more than four hundred years, *Don Quixote* remains a tantalizingly elusive text. As with all fine literature, the more we read, the more questions we have. Cervantes's use of narrative voice, cultural commentary, characterization, and intertextuality become more, not less, complex with each reading.

In the United States and Canada, *Don Quixote de la Mancha* is taught in both Spanish and English, primarily in language programs and in comparative and world literature departments. In the second half of the twentieth century, it often was read and taught as a funny book (following certain British critics), as a text offering clearly universal archetypes (in the Jungian tradition), as an example of linguistic perspectivism (per Leo Spitzer), and as a work in dialogue with the chivalric tradition (per Daniel Eisenberg and Martín de Riquer). Yet, as the essays in this MLA volume attest, today instructors use the literary and sociocultural contexts of Cervantes's day to demonstrate the aesthetic innovation, literary complexity, and ideological tensions of his work. Most instructors consider authorial intention as an unknowable aspect of cultural production. Today we point students instead to the construction of truth, the societal portrait painted in the novel, and the navigation of changing ethnic and economic realities in Counter-Reformation Spain. We may interweave notions of class, gender, ethnicity, urbanity, modernity, politics, and religion into our classroom discussions. We draw heavily from Web, film, and digitally based materials to show students the legacy of *Don Quixote*.

A significant shift has occurred in modern language departments in the recent past: the integration of Latin American studies and, often, United States Latino or border studies into Spanish programs has resulted in a curricular overhaul that, in many instances, has marginalized *Don Quixote* in the undergraduate curriculum. Moreover, budgetary pressures and data-driven course scheduling have caused many institutions to suspend or permanently cut low-enrolled, nonessential courses. *Don Quixote* as a stand-alone monographic course has all too often fallen victim to these shifting realities. For this reason, and in an effort to preserve this cultural treasure for the next generation, our contributors provide pedagogical approaches to *Don Quixote* that can be adopted at different kinds of institutions and in a range of classes in both English and Spanish.

Volume Overview

This volume aims to assist instructors in many different institutional contexts. Its contributors hail from liberal arts colleges, large public universities, and both public and private research universities. Curricula, student demographics, and class size vary greatly among those institutions, but readers easily can glean ideas and adapt them to their own classroom needs.

The essays in the first section provide historical, literary, and cultural background that will contextualize the text for twenty-first-century students. The second section explores the narrative and formal elements in *Don Quixote*; its essays discuss narrative scaffolding, references to manuscript culture, reading as a trope, and the reverberations of the novel's devices in Latin American literature. Section 3 centers on the visual elements of the text; its essays discuss the visual aesthetic as a literary device and the use of the plastic arts and film in the *Quixote* classroom. The next section examines the benefits of bringing four different theoretical approaches to bear on pedagogical application. The final section deals with *Don Quixote* taught in courses for diverse student populations.

A common theme of the essays is the desire to make *Don Quixote* accessible and interesting. Some elements are immediately accessible to students — think of the physical humor of the Balm of Fierabrás or of the blanketing of Sancho (pt. 1, ch. 17) — but the combination of irony and ambiguity emphasized by Johnson and many others (e.g., Durán; Allen, *Don Quixote*) can pose obstacles to comprehension in the undergraduate classroom. Likewise, the historical nature of the text places many elements out of the reach of students unless we provide background information about the Spanish Empire, the Inquisition, the Moorish presence, and the printing press, to name but a few topics.

The best teachers know that the more new ideas and enthusiasm they bring to classes, the more students will respond with a willingness to learn. In this volume are pedagogical strategies and words of advice about teaching *Don Quixote*. We hope that its essays will inspire students and instructors alike to ask more questions, do more research, and to become lifelong fans of Cervantes's text.

The Instructors' Survey

More than fifty instructors responded to the survey on teaching *Don Quixote* distributed by the MLA in preparation for this volume. Instructors taught the text in monographic courses lasting one quarter, one semester, even one year. Others gave courses on *Don Quixote* and another major early modern text or other texts that followed in Cervantes's footsteps. Thematic and genre-based courses on the early modern and colonial Hispanic worlds might include excerpts from the *Quixote*: examples were courses on the Inquisition, the Spanish Empire, the *comedia nueva* of Lope de Vega. Comparative literature courses might include *Don Quixote* and readings from later texts that incorporated Cervantes's stylistic or thematic devices. In one such course, Quixotic Desire, *Madame Bovary, Death in Venice, Lolita,* and Kathy Acker's *Don Quixote* all made an appearance after students read excerpts from *Don Quixote*. Among the Spanish texts chosen by instructors, those edited by John Jay Allen (Cátedra), Luis Murillo (Castalia), and Tom Lathrop (Juan de la Cuesta) were commonly used. Affordability, availability, and accessibility were given by instructors as the three most important factors in their choice of edition. For courses taught in translation, the most commonly used translations were those by Edith Grossman and by Burton Raffel. Almost all the respondents who taught the course in

Spanish highlighted the difficulty of the language—both in terms of vocabulary and syntax—and many said that they encouraged students to consult English translations when needed. Every respondent who taught *Don Quixote* in English mentioned the importance of educating students about the art of translation and the question of what is lost or gained when certain words are chosen and others discarded. In this volume, Jonathan Thacker's "*Don Quixote* in English Translation" addresses these and other issues as they apply to the classroom.

Most courses on *Don Quixote* required at least some outside reading. Excerpts from fifteenth- and sixteenth-century texts such as *Cárcel de amor*, *Amadís de Gaula*, *La Diana*, *El Abencerraje*, and *Lazarillo de Tormes* were used. Because most courses involved response papers or longer research papers, students read at least a few historical and critical texts. Several respondents mentioned their reliance on Johnson's Don Quixote: *The Quest for Modern Fiction* to provide historical background. Johnson's work also encouraged students to think critically about the reading experience.

Many instructors began and ended their course with film versions of *Don Quixote*; others integrated film clips and Web sites into weekly class sessions. Some used the *Centro Virtual Cervantes* and other sites on a daily basis to call up digital editions of *Don Quixote* and to create a visual experience for students.

Many monographic courses culminated with a research paper in which students compared *Don Quixote* with related films, paintings, novels, or short stories. Such assignments often involved works inspired by Cervantes, such as Gustave Doré's engravings, Jorge Luis Borges's "Pierre Menard, autor del *Quijote*," and Miguel de Unamuno's *Niebla*. Many instructors encouraged students to analyze film or other art that utilized Cervantine strategies, such as those related to narrative authority, intertextuality, and the probing of truth versus fiction. Among films shown in class and used in such assignments, *Man of La Mancha*, TNT's version of *Don Quixote* (with John Lithgow), and *Lost in La Mancha* were frequently mentioned. Several survey respondents assigned Bruce Burningham's article on *Toy Story*, then asked students to watch that film and write a comparative analysis.

Regardless of the length, type, or language of the course, respondents unanimously agreed that students loved reading *Don Quixote*. The humor of the text was the reason given by nearly everyone, but the characters too received high marks from students. Questions of social justice and diversity as well as an issue that is central to the text and its main character—whether violence and sexuality in simulacra of reality (fiction then, film, digital games, and video now) can affect our lives—were of great interest to students and very relevant. Cervantes's complex representation of multiple perspectives on truth, sanity/insanity, and tolerance/intolerance provided an inexhaustible source for discussion, interpretation, and application to lived experience.

The challenges of teaching *Don Quixote* were felt to be significant. Most instructors valued connecting the text to its historical context as well as to their students personally. While many syllabi identified the demonstration of analytic reading skills as a student learning outcome, an implicit goal for many courses was that students learn to articulate in their own words what made *Don Quixote* such a famous text in world literature. Many instructors said that they had increased the use of the visual components of the text, but one respondent cautioned, "*Don Quixote* cannot be made into a movie; it is about the writing of a new . . . genre that critiques previous fiction as much as it co-opts the historical writings of the period."

Our respondents all agreed on one challenge: the language and length of *Don Quixote* made it a demanding text to read. The sheer bulk of the text was enough to frighten off even the most serious students at the start of a new academic quarter or semester. Numerous instructors reported that, although they taught heritage speakers of Spanish primarily, the language and length of the text were still barriers to student success. Others reported a problem that occurs in Spanish programs across the country: the disparities between native and nonnative speakers of Spanish tend to divide classes and leave the nonnative speakers behind. Yet instructors also said that allowing students to read in English translation when necessary mitigated this problem. Using Lathrop's edition also helped, since the footnotes and vocabulary explanations in English made the text more accessible.

Another frequently mentioned pedagogical challenge involved the contextualization of *Don Quixote*. Questions of prejudice and discrimination arose repeatedly as students read the text, and many respondents felt the need to provide historical context about the Inquisition, censorship, and nation building, while also reminding students that irony was an all-pervading strategy. It was no small task to teach them that many modern attitudes would be an anachronism in the seventeenth century and to help them understand what was innovative about *Don Quixote* in its day. The interpolated tales intrigued some students and confused others. Cervantes's manipulation of the narrative—and of the reader—disoriented them. Instead of merely asking if Don Quixote is hero or fool, crazy or sane, today's instructors were more likely to attend to the text's representation of Spain's ethnically diverse population or the depiction of the hereditary nobility in part 2. Notwithstanding the text's length, challenging language, and unfamiliar cultural context, Don Quixote and Sancho rarely failed to win students over.

Building a Quixote *Course*

The essays in this volume provide a wealth of strategies and ideas for teaching *Don Quixote* in secondary and higher educational contexts. Despite the diversity of approaches used by instructors across the country, survey respondents all identified the same two key components for successfully teaching *Don Quixote*: literary background and historical context. This agreement became our guiding principle, and in the overview that follows we give some aspects of the literary context and historical context that instructors might use to build their *Quixote* courses.

Formal and Aesthetic Aspects

The 1605 title, *El ingenioso hidalgo don Quixote* [now *Quijote*] *de la Mancha*, is a miniprologue, for it hints broadly at authorial point of view, thus serving to orient reader response. The irony and ludic manner we associate with Cervantes are apparent in the sequence and choice of words. The title within the title, *don*, calls attention to itself because it is located at the center and because it does not jibe with the two words that frame it. Hidalgos of Alonso Quijano's modest means were not entitled to use that honorific; further, *Quijote*, if we assume that name to be a reformulation of the character's true last name (Quijano [pt. 2, ch. 74]), should not be preceded by *don*, which is used only with first names. We might assume *Quijote* to be, or at least to function as, a given name in conjunction with *don*, but even so it would be a first name derived from a last name. Thus *don Quixote* inverts the time-honored, Old Christian process of naming, whereby first names gave rise over time to patronymics. (*Sancho* gave rise to *Sánchez*, or "son of Sancho"; *Rodrigo*, to *Rodríguez*; *Pero*, to *Pérez*; and so forth. Hence the humor of the name of the village priest, Pero Pérez, whose last name is a patronymic of his first name.)

However we approach *Quijote*, it stands out as an anomaly, freighted with irony. A *quijote* is the piece of defensive armor that protects the thigh. *Quijote* also contrasts implicitly with *Lanzarote* ("Lancelot"), that paragon of knights, whose name incorporates the offensive weapon par excellence, the lance. This literary resonance does not favor our knight. *Ingenioso* is ambiguous and ambivalent, suggesting a humoral imbalance (an excess of yellow bile or choler) and thus a tendency toward outbursts of anger and violence; but it also suggests a quick wit (*agudeza*) and a facility with words. The reference to origins, *de la Mancha*, points to a specific geographic area, the mid-south of Spain, but it may also suggest a spot or blemish (a *mancha*) on the family coat of arms (i.e., the blemish of Jewish or Moorish ancestry) or even that the character emerges from the spots of ink on the printed page. Whatever its source or original intent, the title is more playful and ironic than positive or straightforward. It is evident, even before we begin reading, that we will be dealing here with a mock hero, neither a hero like Lancelot nor an antihero like the *pícaro*.

The dominant themes of part 1 (1605) are literature, love, and chivalry, in approximately that order of importance. These themes nevertheless overlap and interpenetrate to such a degree that they are complementary if not inseparable. For instance, Don Quixote, aspiring to a life of chivalry, proceeds to emulate knights of yore, all of whom are fictional characters in the books he reads day and night. His adopted role is thus literature-inspired, and his somewhat servile imitation of literary models is a constant. His love of his fantastical lady,

Dulcinea, is also prompted by the literary world that has taken over his mind. He thus incorporates all three themes in his own person, in his attitudes and actions. There are, of course, mainly literary episodes, such as the scrutiny of his library in part 1, chapter 6; mainly chivalry episodes, illustrated in the windmill encounter and his farcical dubbing; and mainly love episodes, as in the interpolated stories of Dorotea, Cardenio, and the husband who was too curious for his own good. Joaquín Casalduero's 1949 treatment of this subject is still valuable.

Numerous thematic tensions are woven into the text. They arise from the pull between past and present, between history and fiction, between arms and letters, and between orality and literacy. In part 1, Don Quixote's quest imposes on the present a literature-inspired vision of an idyllic past. The attempt never succeeds, and thus the text underscores the futility of returning to the past. Occasionally, history is contrasted with fiction in terms of the relative merits of one over the other (the words in Spanish are *historia* and *poesía*), linking this tension to the larger theme of literature. A question implicitly raised is whether there is any appreciable difference between history and story, both of which can be rendered by the Spanish word *historia*. Don Quixote praises arms at the expense of letters, seemingly unaware that he owes his knightly identity to letters and that the stories of derring-do that are his vade mecum would not have reached him without that medium. Orality versus literacy is exemplified in the contrast between the two main characters, and it is masterfully illustrated at the beginning of part 2, chapter 44, where writing defers to orality for ultimate grounding. The tension is enhanced by having an editorial voice comment throughout in quasi-oral fashion, assuming obvious control in part 2, while the bulk of the story is attributed to a man of letters, a mock historian. This tension between showing and telling is sometimes almost palpable. Inside versus outside can be as complex as one chooses to make it. One might begin by explaining and giving examples of how the work bares its devices, calling attention to itself as artifact, making clear that what is happening is done with smoke and mirrors and is therefore not real. Here comparisons to contemporary works such as Velázquez's *Las meninas* and Lope de Vega's "Soneto de repente" would be appropriate. A complementary strategy might be to introduce Jacques Derrida's notion of framing, showing how frames that supposedly set apart the work of art are sometimes porous, even illusory. In Derrida's words, "il y a du cadre, mais le cadre n'existe pas" 'there is [a process of] framing, but the frame [as such] does not exist' (*Vérité* 93 [our trans.]). Like Velázquez, Cervantes is both inside and outside the work of art, and the presence of characters in both dimensions clearly transgresses the frame of his text.

Another crucial aesthetic aspect of *Don Quixote* is its Janus-like nature. Cervantes looks back (consciously) but also forward to our own time (as we can see when we look back). His work is a response to first-person narration, which he must have seen as a limited and limiting form of expression. The polemic with the first-person picaresque, particularly the 1599 best seller *Guzmán de Alfarache*, is patent albeit subtle. *Don Quixote* might not have materialized without the stimulus provided by Mateo Alemán's *Guzmán* in 1599 and 1604 (Alemán's part 2). Cervantes's text can be seen as a countergenre to a form that would not have allowed Cervantes the freedom to modulate discourse and experiment with it, a freedom that third-person narration offered. *Don Quixote* also resonates with more idealistic genres, such as pastoral and sentimental romances. Books of chivalry are the romance subgenre most obviously implicated, and many of its devices and narrative techniques are parodied, while other aspects are deftly appropriated. Cervantes's roots in drama are frequently discernible, while poetry, his first love as a writer, is especially evident. Ulrich Wicks gives an overview of Cervantes's generic antecedents in an essay on the picaresque. That *Don Quixote* anticipates both the realistic and self-conscious forms of the novel is ably sustained by Robert Alter.

The self-conscious use of rhetorical and stylistic devices is another hallmark of *Don Quixote*. It consistently troubles translators and also makes problematic the work's acceptance as a realistic novel. The most commonly used device is *fabla* (the term in Cervantes's day was *habla*; *fabla* has its roots in the Vulgar Latin *fabulari*). These archaisms are typical of the style of the medieval books of chivalry, and the protagonist through his obsessive reading has assimilated them. Other characters — for instance, Dorotea in her role as Princess Micomicona — may use archaisms to enter into Don Quixote's imaginary world. Sancho is able to reproduce his master's archaisms surprisingly well, and even the narrator's discourse on occasion becomes contaminated by *fabla*, thereby introducing into the work what we might call linguistic metalepsis. Notably, as the mock hero's zest for the quest diminishes, his use of archaism diminishes (Mancing, *Chivalric World*).

Other common devices used in part 1 are:

comic inversion of logic: "no sólo en España, pero en toda la Mancha" 'not only in Spain but throughout the length and breadth of La Mancha'
(1: 421 [ch. 30]; 274)[1]

juxtaposition of higher and lower registers — a procedure Cervantes may have assimilated from Ariosto's *Orlando Furioso* (see Gregory 23). An example is Don Quixote's poetic description of his first sortie, which is undermined immediately by the prosaic comment of the narrator.   (ch. 2)

paronomasia: "despeñar y despenar al amo," "a emboscar y a buscar" 'put my master out of his misery,' 'I took to the forest again to look for . . .'
(403 [ch. 28]; 259)

antanaclasis or zeugma: "con . . . salir del aposento mi doncella, yo dejé de serlo" 'and then my maid left, and I stopped being one'
(398 [ch. 28]; 255)

Caesarean *veni, vidi, vici*: "ella lloró, gimió y suspiró" 'wept, sighed, and moaned' (379 [ch. 27]; 236); "Besé la cruz, tomé los escudos, volvíme al terrado" 'I kissed the cross, I took the escudos, I went back to the roof terrace' (537 [ch. 40]; 371)

symmetrical bimembration: "triste y pensativo . . . imaginaciones y sospechas . . . sospechaba ni imaginaba . . . triste suceso y desventura" 'dejected and sunk in thought . . . suspicions and imaginings . . . the sad event and the misfortune' (379 [ch. 27]; 236); "y los *consejos y compañía* del maestro Elisabat *le fue y le fueron* de mucho *provecho y alivio* para poder llevar sus trabajos con *prudencia y paciencia*" 'and the advice and the company of Master Elisabat were of great benefit and comfort to her, to help her bear her trials with prudence and patience' (342 [ch. 25]; 205)

anaphora: "Allí fue el desear de la espada de Amadís . . . allí fue el maldecir de su fortuna . . . allí fue el exagerar . . . allí el acordarse . . . allí fue el llamar" 'And then he did wish for Amadís's sword . . . and then did he curse his ill fortune; dwell on how sorely his presence would be missed . . . call for his trusty squire' (580–81 [ch. 43]; 408)

apostrophe: "—¡Oh, mi señora Dulcinea del Toboso . . . !" 'O my lady Dulcinea del Toboso . . . !' (577 [ch. 43]; 405)

asyndeton: "lo habéis de creer, confesar, afirmar, jurar y defender" 'you must believe, confess, affirm, swear and uphold it' (141 [ch. 4]; 46)

polysyndeton: "y así, se iba al jardín de Zoraida . . . y le pedía fruta, y su padre se la daba . . . ; y aunque él quisiera hablar . . . y decille . . . " '[he would go] to Zoraida's villa and ask for fruit, and her father would give him some . . . and although he would have liked to speak to Zoraida . . . and tell her . . .' (545 [ch. 41]; 378 [trans. slightly modified])

synecdoche, as the relation of part to whole, illustrated in the main character in relation to a part of his armor, the *quijote* ("thigh guard")

Together, these stylistic devices show what is called in Spanish a *voluntad de estilo*, a will or conscious effort to go beyond straightforward expression. Some instances are a tour de force, suggesting the author's desire to create surprise and wonder in the reader. This attempt to arouse *admiratio* is typical of seventeenth-century Spanish writers and artists. Every other page of *Don Quixote* contains at least one word associated with that aesthetic impulse (e.g., *admirarse, maravillarse, suspenderse, pasmarse*).

An *idée reçue* of Cervantes studies has it that there occurs in the course of the two volumes a reciprocal influence of the two main characters of *Don*

Quixote. In Salvador de Madariaga's terms from the 1920s, this idea is known as the quixotization of Sancho and the sanchification of his master. While there are hints of such a process at work, we might more accurately say that the two characters are highly malleable and adaptive. Don Quixote can be witty and wise, or he can be insufferably pedantic, delusional, violent, and a risk to himself and others. Sancho can be asinine, obtuse, and cowardly, or he can be charming, clever, and even judicious. Sancho is the wise fool (*tontilisto*), his master the sane madman (*cuerdo-loco*). Both are cartoon-like in their malleability, in their contradictions, and in the fact that they can be pummeled mercilessly in one chapter and return as good as new in the next. This treatment of characters is typical of satire. Students should be reminded that our literary focus is on the process of characterization — how characters see themselves, how others see them, how the narrator presents them — and that we should not emulate that notoriously inept reader, our errant knight, by talking about the characters as though they had reality in themselves. Both authorial point of view and the characterization process are made manifest in the 1605 title, and the mock-heroic, playful tone established there remains in force throughout part 1.

The question of literary genre, as David Boruchoff explains in his contribution to this volume, is crucial for understanding *Don Quixote*. Part 1 is predominantly inverted romance coupled with Menippean satire in structure and with mild Horatian satire in manner and tone. In the prologue to part 2 and toward the end of that book, there are glimmers of the more caustic and personalized satire associated with Juvenal, in the negative references to the interloper Avellaneda. A convention of satire is that we must look outside the text to identify its target. Thus some sociohistorical information is essential. Cervantes draws on traditions of satire and romance that have their roots in antiquity, but he also draws on contemporary manifestations of these traditions in the picaresque, pastoral, sentimental, and Moorish forms of narrative. In both cases he illustrates the axiom that literature is made from other literature.

Although the two main characters are essentially the same in both parts, the supporting cast in 1615 differs considerably from that of 1605, and Don Quixote and Sancho appear in a different light in part 2. Don Quixote is a bit more subdued. He does not ordinarily take one thing for another, and his use of archaic diction (*fabla*) has virtually disappeared. Sancho is much more developed and has a larger role in 1615. Death becomes a leitmotif early in part 2, foreshadowing the knight's demise.

Regarding Sancho's enhanced role in part 2, Raymond Willis has suggested that the man rather than his master is the prototype for the modern novel. While the 1605 volume drew extensively on the books of chivalry, the 1615 volume draws heavily on part 1, and, when the author becomes aware of Avellaneda's spurious sequel of 1614, it begins to draw on that source also. Part 2 integrates interpolated stories much more seamlessly into the main plot. The mix of romance, novel, and satire continues, but one can discern both the realistic and the self-conscious novel in embryonic form. Some say that the work foreshadows the modern novel, others that it has more in common with self-conscious, postmodern narrative. It may be that the realistic novel is indebted primarily to the mimetic action of *Don Quixote*, whereas postmodern narrative owes more to the novel's diegetic domain.

Perspective — and perhaps perspectivism — is another central element of the text. Many readers assume that the point of view of an implied or inferred author is discernible in any narrative. They also assume that this perspective can be a valuable guide to the reader in reaching an understanding and appreciation of that text. The playful and mock-heroic point of view apparent in the 1605 title obtains in the prologue and opening chapters. It is modulated hardly at all in part 1, and the cumulative effect on the astute reader is ironic distancing from both the protagonist and the world he inhabits. Achievement of this detached vantage point — which we can assume that the author himself enjoys — is a prerequisite for the proper appreciation of his art. The protagonist and the second author are negative models as readers, on the mimetic and diegetic levels respectively, since both are gullible, overeager consumers. One might also take into account the ironic point of view toward an inferred reader — especially in the chapter headings — and toward characters such as the gentleman in the green greatcoat, the duke and duchess of part 2, and the pseudo-author Cide Hamete (also the second author of part 1, chapter 9). Note the decidedly more favorable presentation of several female characters, such as Maritornes, Marcela, Dorotea, Zoraida, and Ana Félix. Students' engagement with perspectivism can lead to intriguing discussions about points of view, relativism, and the power of discourse to shape a version of the truth.

Cultural and Historical Background

The relation between text and its social context is a major component of any *Quixote* course. As the contributions to this volume by Joan Cammarata, Cory Reed, Lisa Vollendorf, and Barbara Fuchs confirm, there are many cultural and historical facts that come to bear when *Don Quixote* is taught. Cervantes explores the shifting cultural realities of his time, forging a new kind of literature for the growing community of readers in the seventeenth century. As both Cammarata and Fuchs argue, students should have some exposure to the Hapsburg era, including the rise and decline of the empire and the role of the Inquisition in building the early modern nation-state. Students in North America generally understand the effect of colonialism on the Americas but have not considered its effect on Europe.

An overview of major events of the period will help students understand what it was like to live in Cervantes's time, characterized as it was by much change. Background should include the unification of Spain, the new nation's reliance on the Inquisition, and the inception of book culture and of humanism. Readers and reading, as Salvador Fajardo argues in this volume, lie at the heart of the text, so some time should be spent on the emerging book market, the importance of aural reading, and the slow increase of literacy in the period. The Counter-Reformation's influence on Cervantes should also be included: the emphasis on confession and its link to what presently we think of as autobiography shaped such diverse genres as the religious *vitae* ("lives") and the picaresque—exemplified, respectively, in Teresa de Ávila's *Libro de su vida* ("Book of Her Life") and *Lazarillo de Tormes. Don Quixote* subverts that tradition by providing only a slice of life: its first-person narrative omits the protagonist's origins; formative experiences; indeed, almost all his adult life.

Military and maritime culture both played a role in the shaping of the nation and of people's lives during the period. The struggle to maintain the empire on numerous fronts is dramatized in the surprising defeat of the Armada in 1588. That defeat shows students that the empire already was in decline when part 1 of *Don Quixote* was published. As the empire declined, those with aspirations and identities linked to the imperial enterprise—like Cervantes—found themselves in a world that was at once expanded and constricted.

The autobiographical specter looms large in the minds of uninitiated readers. Many students want to connect Cervantes's life and times with the text in ways that sometimes limit their ability to see beyond the biographical. For this reason, it is worth considering what they know before they come to class. They will have knowledge of Don Quixote and Sancho Panza—two of the most iconic characters in all of literature (they are sure to have seen statuettes and paintings of them)—and the windmill episode. If students do not know, they will soon learn that Cervantes was maimed in the Battle of Lepanto and held captive in Algiers. His possible converso background, his limited formal education, and his failed attempts to secure a post in the Americas also will be brought to the table. It is both challenging and rewarding to guide students toward balanced readings that consider the author's life and milieu but keep in mind the text and, where applicable, criticism about it.

Don Quixote navigates potentially controversial issues with dexterity. Muslims, conversos, Moriscos, and New and Old Christians intermingle in the text. Spain's mechanisms of justice, especially the Inquisition and the legal system, are called to our attention without being directly denounced. Through the Moorish characters, the text probes the human cost of the state policy of expulsion. All social classes (in both rural and urban settings) find a place in *Don Quixote*, and the highest-born nobles come out looking the worst. Women's changing roles are captured through characters who represent different social classes, positions, and personalities. The text makes one thing clear about the women: even if they have the ability to choose their paths, society gives them few options. As the adventures culminate in Barcelona with Don Quixote's defeat, one wonders whether urban, modern life has not played a role in his demise.

Regardless of what approach is taken, teaching *Don Quixote* offers the opportunity to spend time with a richly complex text. No two courses on the work will be the same, and no two instructors will agree on how best to teach the course. *Don Quixote* explores the shifting cultural realities of the early modern period and forges a new literary genre that speaks not only to Cervantes's contemporaries but also to the readers of today.

NOTE

[1] The Spanish edition cited is Allen's, the translation Rutherford's.

Part One

MATERIALS

The Instructor's Library

James A. Parr and Lisa Vollendorf

This section aims to aid instructors in choosing the editions and materials to use when they prepare to teach *Don Quixote*. In our overview of available editions in Spanish and English, we provide some guidance as to their advantages and disadvantages. We also discuss reference works, multiauthor volumes, monographs, and other critical studies on Cervantes and *Don Quixote* to orient instructors in the vast fields of Cervantine and early modern Spanish studies.

Reading Don Quixote *in Spanish*

For those who can read *Don Quixote* in Spanish, we recommend these editions, which are well executed, available, and affordable: John Jay Allen's (the publisher is Cátedra), Tom Lathrop's (Cervantes & Co.), Luis Murillo's (Castalia), Francisco Rico's (many editions; initially Crítica; Instituto Cervantes [1998]), and Salvador J. Fajardo and James A. Parr's (Pegasus).[1]

Allen's edition comes in two volumes, which are skillfully but not overly glossed. The thoughtful introductory essay provides an effective overview of Cervantes's life, the literature of his time, and the primary innovations of the text. Allen's "Prefacio post-centenario a la edición renovada y actualizada" ("Post-centenary Preface to the Renewed and Updated Edition") gives insight into some of the fundamental questions facing editors of the text today—for instance, the matter of fidelity to the first edition. Allen follows Rico in admitting modifications introduced in subsequent printings and editions. He points out that Rico followed Allen's lead (of 1977) in modernizing orthography, but Allen stops short of Rico's wholesale modernizing. He departs from Rico in not consigning to an appendix the two sections on the loss and recovery of Sancho's donkey. Allen's preface is instructive because it points to the decision-making processes involved in editorial work and draws students' attention to the fact that no two editions are alike.

Rico's editions do not adhere to the 1605 Juan de la Cuesta first edition and the original spelling. His description of his editorial decisions is interesting reading, as he discusses the process by which a manuscript makes it to press. The edition Rico prepared for the Real Academia Espanola's fourth centenary celebration of the text is now available online at *Centro Virtual Cervantes*. The extensive footnotes, several on every page, provide clarifications and interpretations. Some readers may find these notes intrusive, but the edition is useful because of its modernized spelling and the erudition that Rico and his collaborators bring to the text.

Fajardo and Parr's *El ingenioso hidalgo don Quixote de la Mancha* is guided by the principles of readability and teachability. Based on Allen's first edition, this version provides either a one-volume or two-volume paperback text that offers notes that are explanatory rather than interpretative, and everything is in Spanish. Specifically aimed at the North American higher-education market, the edition has a glossary, an introduction to usage of Cervantes's day, introductions to each part, and a concluding critical essay for each part. Lathrop's edition is idiosyncratic in places. Some may like the English-language footnotes, the cartoonish but clever illustrations, and the companion Don Quijote *Dictionary.* Lathrop modernized some spellings, but not all, on the basis of the Schevill-Bonilla edition. His footnotes define and clarify words and concepts and sometimes translate entire passages. Here the critical apparatus is at a minimum. The text has flaws, and students and instructors have been frustrated by its numerous printing errors. Like Fajardo and Parr's edition, Lathrop's is sold in the United States, so it can be purchased more quickly than editions produced in Spain or elsewhere. Editions by Allen, Fajardo and Parr, Murillo, and Rico are good choices for graduate and advanced undergraduate courses taken by heritage or native speakers of Spanish.[2] All four editions have been crafted with care, and all provide scholarly introductions and useful footnotes. Lathrop's edition, with notes and commentary in English, is more suited for undergraduate classes made up predominantly of anglophone students.

Explaining the differences among editions can be a helpful introduction to the editorial practices of Cervantes's day and our own. Graduate students in particular should know also that Rico's edition did not meet with universal acceptance. Florencio Sevilla Arroyo, who could likely point to as many printings of his edition (1994) as can Rico of his (1998), was especially acerbic (18). Sevilla Arroyo's edition for the Castalia Didáctica series might be considered for a class of predominantly heritage speakers of Spanish. In October 2012, Sevilla made available a text that adheres scrupulously to the first editions of 1605 and 1615, in an appealingly annotated and illustrated EPUB 3 format.

Reading Don Quixote *in English Translation*

As John Rutherford points out in a prefatory essay to the 2001 United States printing of his translation of *Don Quixote*, there are two major schools of thought on translation, the puritanical and the cavalier. He states that twentieth-century translations of Cervantes's novel remain largely in the "powerful puritan tradition" (Introduction xv), but Rutherford draws on both. This balanced approach is prudent. David Bellos writes, "A translation can't be right or wrong in the manner of a school quiz or a bank statement. A translation is more like a portrait in oils" (318). His assessment, like the philosophy expressed by Edith Grossman in *Why Translation Matters* (2010), defines the cavalier approach as one in which translators aspire to capture the spirit, style, and tone of the original work but do not intend to replicate that work precisely in a different language. But those who work with broad brushstrokes may compromise the meaning. One appears on the first page of Grossman's text, when the translator renders Alonso Quijano's greyhound (his "galgo corredor") as a racing dog rather than a hunting dog (113; 19). "Corredor" here means "for the chase." Grey-hounds were not raced for sport in that time and place; they were prized as hunting dogs, for their swift pursuit and capture of rabbits. A quick glance at *galgo* in Sebastían de Covarrubias, Julio Cejador, or the *Diccionario de autoridades* (roughly, "Authoritative Dictionary") clarifies the seventeenth-century definition.

Instructors who need to choose a translation of *Don Quixote* should assess which translation best meets the students' needs. They should also evalutate the edition's critical apparatus, and of course availability and price will play a role in their choice. Five translations now compete for instructors' and students' attention on the North American market. Charles Jarvis's translation was cor-rected and annotated by Edward C. Riley in 1992. Walter Starkie's translation was reissued in 2001 with Edward H. Friedman's introduction and updated bibliography. Others are by Burton Raffel (1995), Rutherford (2003), Gross-man (2003), and Lathrop (2005). Tobias Smollett's translation also is available in English (Cervantes, *History*), but his reliance on Jarvis makes his translation a less popular choice in most instances.[3]

Grossman and Raffel are chosen by many. Both these professional translators mirror the process described by Bellos: they aspire to a portrait in oils rather than to a precise rendering of the text. Raffel has modernized Cervantes's text into a relatively contemporary American English, replete with slang, which may have a certain appeal for undergraduate students but may at the same time distance readers from the original in important ways. Lathrop's translation, hav-ing an introduction and critical apparatus intended for anglophone college stu-dents, will appeal to instructors who work primarily with that audience.

The older translations—such as those by Jarvis (1742), John Ormsby (Cer-vantes, *Ingenious Gentleman* [1885]), J. M. Cohen (Cervantes, *Adventures* [1950]), and Samuel Putnam (1949)—offer students an opportunity to read the text as rendered into an English reflective of the various approaches to transla-tion that have existed over time. Generally speaking, a collation of these editions would be more appropriate for a course focused on the evolution of transla-tion theory than for one on *Don Quixote*. But instructors teaching *Don Quixote* and other world literature translated into English may well spend a significant amount of time on questions of translation. Bringing different translators' ver-sions of specific passages to bear on a classroom discussion can enlighten stu-dents who have not considered what it means to be unable to read an original text. In today's diverse classrooms, where often we have at least one Spanish speaker present, we also can rely on those who able to read the original Cervan-tine prose to help bring forward some of the challenges of translation. It helps to assign some translation theory in addition to assigning three or four different versions of an excerpt for students to read and study. Because most contact with *Don Quixote* in the English-speaking world has been through translation, we should all include some discussion of translation and cultural legacy in both hispanophone and anglophone traditions when we teach *Don Quixote*. Jonathan Thacker's essay in this volume, "*Don Quixote* in English Translation," takes up these and other issues in an effort to guide instructors and students through the difficult territory of reading the text in translation.

Reference Works

The sheer volume of scholarship on Cervantes and *Don Quixote* makes it impossible to do a comprehensive bibliographic review, but we suggest some publications that can help bring focus to that vast bibliography. Roberto González Echevarría's *Cervantes' Don Quixote: A Casebook* is one possible starting point for students and instructors interested in learning about some of the most important approaches to *Don Quixote* in the second half of the twentieth century. The book contains essays by Manuel Durán, Erich Auerbach, Ramón Menéndez Pidal, Georgina Dopico Black, E. C. Riley, Bruce W. Wardropper, Leo Spitzer, George Haley, and González Echevarría. Mariarosa Scaramuzza Vidoni's *Rileggere Cervantes: Antologia della critica recente* ("Rereading Cervantes: Anthology of Recent Criticism") stresses innovation more than tradition, giving samples of the work of Jean Canavaggio, Maurice Molho, Agustín Redondo, Michel Moner, Aurora Egido, José Manuel Martín Morán, Parr, and others. Early-twenty-first-century approaches are well represented in *USA Cervantes: 39 Cervantistas en Estados Unidos* (2009), edited by Black and Francisco Layna Ranz.

Among reference works that help instructors situate the text in the novelistic tradition is Harriet Turner and Adelaida López de Martínez's *The Cambridge Companion to the Spanish Novel from 1600 to the Present*, which contains numerous references to Cervantes and *Don Quixote* from various perspectives. Pablo Jauralde Pou, Delia Gavela, and Alique P. C. Rojo's *Diccionario filológico de literatura española: Siglo XVI* and *Diccionario filológico de literatura española: Siglo XVII* ("Philological Dictionary of Spanish Literature: Sixteenth Century and Seventeenth Century") can help students and instructors alike delve into the literary contexts of Cervantes's day. Anthony Cascardi's *Cambridge Companion to Cervantes* provides a noteworthy compilation of essays on Cervantes's contributions to narrative, drama, and the Hispanic literary tradition. Moreover, Cascardi's volume brings readers into the twenty-first century with essays on gender, culture, and the Americas.

Instructors also might refer students to Howard Mancing's two-volume *Cervantes Encyclopedia* and his *Cervantes's Don Quixote: A Reference Guide*, as well as to such dictionaries and encyclopedias as César Vidal Manzanares's *Enciclopedia del Quijote* and his *Diccionario del Quijote* ("A *Quixote* Encyclopedia" and "A *Quixote* Dictionary"), Jesús Abelleira Fernández's *Diccionario enciclopédico hermenéutico o auxiliar de lectura del Quijote* ("Encyclopedic and Hermeneutical Dictionary or Reading Aid for the *Quixote*"), and Juan Hernández Herrero's *Léxico español para lectores de* Don Quijote de la Mancha ("A Spanish Lexicon for Readers of *Don Quixote de la Mancha*"). Two essential dictionaries to which instructors should maintain ready access are the facsimiles of Covarrubias's *Tesoro de la lengua castellana o española* (1611; "Treasury of the Castilian or Spanish Language") and the three-volume *Diccionario de autoridades*, the first Royal Academy dictionary (1726–37), which, despite the dates, reflects usage of Cervantes's day. The most exhaustive study of the language of the *Quixote* is Cejador's voluminous critical-etymological concordance of 1905–06, the second volume of his monumental *La lengua de Cervantes* ("Cervantes's Language"), which was recently augmented and updated by Delfín Carbonell and Parr.

Such comprehensive, definition-focused books complement one's reading of *Don Quixote*, providing detailed information about Cervantes's life, times, use of language, and literary production as well as about modern scholarship on Cervantes.

Biographical Resources on Cervantes

Because there is so little information about the life of Cervantes, he poses a challenge to any biographer. Biographers can only speculate about why he never received permission to travel to the Americas and about how he was affected by the rise to fame of his archrival, Lope de Vega. Melveena McKendrick's *Cervantes* forges close links between the author's life and his desire to parody the literature of his time. Canavaggio's *Cervantes* and *Cervantes entre vida y creación* ("Cervantes between Life and Creation") are among the most informed biographical publications to date. His knowledge of Spain's early modern literature and history enrich every analysis. He refutes Rosa Rossi's theory—sometimes cited by students who have done their own biographical digging—that Cervantes was a homosexual converso. A fine study that brings in the material world surrounding the text is Donald McCrory's *No Ordinary Man: The Life and Times of Miguel de Cervantes*, while a meticulously documented and detailed chronological overview of the writer's life is *Vida de Miguel de Cervantes Saavedra* ("Life of Miguel de Cervantes Saavedra"), by Krzysztof Sliwa.

Other biographies that provide interesting material for historical and biographical discussions about Cervantes and his times are Manuel Fernández Álvarez's *Cervantes visto por un historiador* ("Cervantes Seen by a Historian") and F. J. Blasco Pascual's *Cervantes: Un hombre que escribe* ("Cervantes: A Man Who Writes"), which traces the emergence of Cervantes as a professional writer. Classic studies of Cervantes's life and times in Spanish are Ramón Menéndez Pidal's *De Cervantes y Lope de Vega* and Fernando Díaz-Plaja's *Cervantes (la desdichada vida de un triunfador)* ("Cervantes: The Unfortunate Life of a Triumphant Man").

Instructors should keep in mind that Cervantes, like other much-studied authors, has drawn innumerable speculations about such diverse topics as the biographical nature of his fiction, his sexuality, his religious identity, and his ethnic heritage. It is useful to incorporate a basic biographical sketch into classroom discussion and also have some biographical references available for those students interested in learning more about the author.

Critical Collections

The four hundredth anniversary of the publication of *Don Quixote*, part 2, in 2015 gave rise to many celebrations worldwide, much as the anniversary celebration of part 1 in 2005 did. Critical collections marking those celebrations later appeared on the book market and created a small boom in Cervantine scholarship at the beginning of the twenty-first century. One of the first and most elaborate commemorations was organized by Spain's Ministerio de Cultura in collaboration with the Sociedad Estatal de Conmemoraciones Culturales at the Fórum de Barcelona, 15–18 June 2004. The title of the two-volume set of proceedings, *El Quijote y el pensamiento moderno* ("The *Quixote* and Modern Thought"), indicates the ambitious focus of the sessions (Paz Gago and González Quirós). Among the invited speakers were Carme Riera, José Luis Abellán, Anthony Close, María Caterina Ruta, James A. Parr, Antonio Vilanova, and Eduardo Urbina.

Major commemorations were held in the United States—at Ohio State University; the University of New Mexico; the University of Texas; and the Graduate Center, City University of New York, to name a few. Among collections of essays that appeared were J. A. G. Ardila's *The Cervantean Heritage: Reception and Influence of Cervantes in Britain* and Darío Fernández-Morera and Michael Hanke's *Cervantes in the English-Speaking World: New Essays*, both of which analyze *Don Quixote* vis-à-vis the anglophone tradition. Julio Vélez-Sainz and Nieves Romero-Díaz's *Cervantes and/on/in the New World* and Gustavo Illades and James Iffland's *El* Quijote *desde América* ("The *Quixote* Seen from America") contextualize the text for twenty-first-century readers from the perspective of the Americas.

Among collections that brought new readings to bear on Cervantes's oeuvre, Frederick A. de Armas's *Ekphrasis in the Age of Cervantes* focuses on the visual aspects of *Don Quixote* and other early modern literature. Anne J. Cruz and Rosilie Hernández's *Women's Literacy in Early Modern Spain and the New World* provides historical analyses of women's education and reading practices in the period and so is important for our understanding of gendered readings of the novel. Egido's edited volume *Los rostros de Don Quijote: IV Centenario de la publicación de su primera parte* ("The Faces of *Don Quixote*: Fourth Centenary of the Publication of Part 1") includes an essay on the filmography of *Don Quixote*. José Manuel Sánchez Ron's edited volume *La ciencia y el* Quijote

("Science and the *Quixote*") brings readers up to date on technological and scientific advances that occurred in Cervantes's age and analyzes *Don Quixote* with some of those advances in mind.

John J. Allen and Patricia S. Finch's *Don Quijote en el arte y pensamiento de Occidente* ("*Don Quixote* in Western Art and Thought") situates the text in artistic and philosophical traditions in the West, while Eduardo Urbina and Jesús G. Maestro's Don Quixote *Illustrated* focuses on iconography and visual readings. Two noteworthy collections from the 1990s that continue to offer challenging readings of the text and also ground readers in the literary theory of the late twentieth century are Ruth Anthony El Saffar and Diana de Armas Wilson's *Quixotic Desire: Psychoanalytic Perspectives on Cervantes* and Anne J. Cruz and Carroll B. Johnson's *Cervantes and His Postmodern Constituencies.*

Finally, we would be remiss if we did not mention Harold Bloom's *Miguel de Cervantes,* a Modern Critical Views volume that includes pieces by writers and critics such as José Ortega y Gasset, Michel Foucault, Leo Spitzer, Jorge Luis Borges, and Juan Bautista Avalle-Arce. Bloom's volume offers readers the opportunity to read excerpts from important commentators who influenced the way *Don Quixote* was read in the second half of the twentieth century.

Critical Studies: Monographs on Literary and Artistic Traditions

For the past four hundred years, critics have been pondering the literary, social, and artistic contexts and legacy of *Don Quixote de la Mancha.* Classic studies of the work were written by Ortega y Gasset, Américo Castro, Joaquín Casalduero, Helmut Hatzfeld, Richard Predmore, and Leo Spitzer, among many others. These critics struggled with such issues as humor, nationalism, language, style, form, and meaning in *Don Quixote.* The questions they posed and answers they gave have had a lasting influence on the framing of inquiry for generations of scholars, such that most of the monographs discussed below acknowledge the influence of these critics. The classic treatment of Romantic influence on studies of *Don Quixote*, which prevailed for many decades and persists even today, is Anthony Close's *The Romantic Approach to* Don Quixote. Romantic studies are often referred to as soft, which is to say, in essence, soft on the main character. When Bloom asserts that "no writer has established a more intimate relation with his protagonist than Cervantes did" (*Western Canon* 148), he invites readers to contemplate the literary prowess and lasting legacy of *Don Quixote*. Instructors would do well to consult Bloom's chapter along with Johnson's Don Quixote: *The Quest for Modern Fiction*, a short text written for classroom use, as well as two books by James A. Parr, Don Quixote: *An Anatomy of Subversive Discourse* and Don Quixote: *A Touchstone for Literary Criticism*, which Félix Martínez Bonati has described as "a culmination of the hard approach" (243).

For studies on the literary context of Cervantes's day, Edward Dudley's *The Endless Text:* Don Quijote *and the Hermeneutics of Romance* traces the chivalric tradition in Western Europe, and Mancing's *The Chivalric World of* Don Quixote examines archaisms and formulaic chivalric discourse and their role in the characterization of Don Quixote. Two leading authorities on the books of chivalry in relation to Cervantes's text are Martín de Riquer and Daniel Eisenberg (*Romances*). Riquer's *Aproximación al* Quijote ("Approach to the *Quixote*") is an engaging vade mecum to the *Quixote*, highlighting identifiable allusions to the books of chivalry. Books of chivalry play a major role in Don Quixote's imagination as well as in his library, and Edward Baker's *La biblioteca de don Quijote* ("Don Quixote's Library") provides a comprehensive study of that library. Dominick Finello's *The Evolution of the Pastoral Novel in Early Modern Spain* is useful for understanding the literary context of the late sixteenth and early seventeenth centuries. De Armas's *Don Quixote among the Saracens* takes a new approach to questions of the embeddedness of culture and genre. In regard to genre, instructors might want to mention that Cervantes's first venture into prose fiction was a pastoral narrative, *La Galatea* (1585), and that his last lengthy narrative, *Persiles y Sigismunda* (1616), traces its generic pedigree to the Byzantine novel.

Edward H. Friedman has contextualized Cervantes's relation to realism in *Cervantes in the Middle: Realism and Reality in the Spanish Novel from* Lazarillo de Tormes *to* Niebla. Anthony J. Cascardi situates Cervantes as a political thinker in *Cervantes, Literature, and the Discourse of Politics*. Susan Byrne focuses on the relation between the law and history in her *Law and History in Cervantes'* Don Quixote. Michael E. Gerli's *Refiguring Authority: Reading, Writing, and Rewriting in Cervantes* gives readers an accessible yet erudite introduction to Cervantine encoding and decoding. Alberto Sánchez's *"Don Quijote, ciudadano del mundo" y otros ensayos cervantinos* ("'Don Quixote, Citizen of the World' and Other Cervantine Essays") contains a cogent overview of *Don Quixote* and its literary life in Spain over the centuries.

The complex narrative structure of *Don Quixote* continues to fascinate and perplex readers. Juan Bautista de Avalle-Arce's *Las novelas y sus narradores* ("Novels and Their Narrators"), although innocent of the insights of narratology, examines narrator reliability in Spanish literature and provides a modest introduction to some of the vexing questions about narration and narrators explored at length in *Don Quixote*. Anthony Close's *A Companion to* Don Quixote discusses the realism of the text. Mercedes Alcalá Galán's *Escritura desatada: Poéticas de la representación en Cervantes* ("Writing Untied: Poetics of Representation in Cervantes") analyzes the relation between life and art in Cervantes's work. Egido's *Cervantes y las puertas del sueño: Estudios sobre la* Galatea, el Quijote *y el* Persiles ("Cervantes and the Doors to Dreams: Studies on the *Galatea*, the *Quixote*, and the *Persiles*") remains important for its ability to inscribe the role of memory and dreams into our reading of *Don Quixote*. Luis Gómez Canseco's *El* Quijote, de Miguel de Cervantes ("The *Quixote* of Miguel de Cervantes"),

Charles Presberg's *Adventures in Paradox:* Don Quixote *and the Western Tradition*, Francisco Rico's *El texto del* Quijote: *Preliminares a una ecdótica del Siglo de Oro* ("The Text of the *Quixote*: Toward a Textual Criticism of the Golden Age"), Edward C. Riley's *La rara invención: Estudios sobre Cervantes y su posteridad literaria* ("Rare Invention: Studies on Cervantes and His Literary Legacy"), David Quint's *Cervantes's Novel of Modern Times: A New Reading of* Don Quijote, and Martín Morán's *Cervantes y el* Quijote: *Hacia la novela moderna* ("Cervantes and the *Quixote*: Toward the Modern Novel") stand out as significant contributions to Cervantine scholarship since the turn of the century. Georges Güntert has explored the contradictions of Cervantes's work with great erudition in *Cervantes: Narrador de un mundo desintegrado* ("Cervantes: Narrator of a Disintegrated World"). Also recommended are Francisco Vivar's richly informed *Don Quijote frente a los caballeros de los tiempos modernos* ("*Don Quixote* vis-à-vis Chivalric Heroes of Modern Times") and Redondo's influential *Otra manera de leer el* Quijote: *Historia, tradiciones culturales y literatura* ("Another Way to Read the *Quixote*: History, Cultural Traditions, and Literature"). *El* Quijote *desde el nacionalismo catalán, en torno al Tercer Centenario* ("The *Quixote* and Catalan Nationalism on the Eve of the Third Centenary"), by Carme Riera, a modern author, offers a fascinating take on the text from the perspective of a non- and perhaps even anti-Spanish nationalism that typified Cataluña around 1905.

Many thematic approaches to Cervantes can be found in the scholarly corpus. González Echevarría's *Love and the Law in Cervantes* takes up the legal context of Cervantes's day and provides illuminating readings on the relation between literature and the law in seventeenth-century Spain. Steven Hutchinson has two strongly argued books on Cervantes: *Cervantine Journeys* is structuralist in its orientation, while *Economía ética en Cervantes* ("Ethical Economics in Cervantes") offers an ethics-based reading of Cervantes's oeuvre. Joseph V. Ricapito, in *Consciousness and Truth in* Don Quijote *and Connected Essays*, brings an array of considerations to bear on his analyses of *Don Quixote,* including an examination of European and Arab influences. Two engaging readings of *Don Quixote* that are accessible to specialists and nonspecialists alike can be found in Emilio Martínez Mata's *Cervantes comenta el* Quijote ("Cervantes Comments on the *Quixote*") and in Ciriaco Morón Arroyo's *Para entender el* Quijote ("Understanding the *Quixote*").

Johnson's *Madness and Lust: A Psychoanalytical Approach to* Don Quijote, Ruth El Saffar's *Beyond Fiction: The Recovery of the Feminine in the Novels of Cervantes*, and Henry Sullivan's *Grotesque Purgatory* are classic—albeit highly debatable—Freudian, Jungian, and Lacanian analyses, in that order. José María Paz Gago's influential *Semiótica del* Quijote: *Teoría y práctica de la ficción narrativa* ("Semiotics of the *Quixote*: Theory and Practice of Narrative Fiction") brought a semiotician's view to the text. Another semiotic treatment is that of Ruth Fine in *Una lectura semiótico-narratológica del* Quijote *en el contexto del siglo de oro español* ("A Semiotic-Narratological Reading of the *Quixote* in the Context of the Spanish Golden Age").

Parr's Don Quixote*: An Anatomy of Subversive Discourse* puts forward the argument that *Don Quixote* is central to modern literary criticism; Parr also elaborates on narratology, point of view, characterization, and the dominant genre of the work. Parr's Don Quixote, *Don Juan, and Related Subjects: Form and Tradition in Spanish Literature, 1330–1630* deals with translations into English and the myth of origins and delves further into formal, psychological, and comparative aspects.

For those interested in visual culture, de Armas's *Quixotic Frescoes: Cervantes and Italian Renaissance Art* calls attention to the importance of the visual in Cervantes's masterpiece. José Manuel Lucía Megías's *Leer el* Quijote *en imágenes: Hacia una teoría de los modelos iconográficos* ("Reading the *Quixote* through Images: Toward a Theory of Iconographic Models") studies the iconographic legacy of the text over the centuries.

Critical Studies: Monographs on Sociocultural Contexts

Several monographs on *Don Quixote* and early modern Spain can provide helpful background on the society in which Cervantes lived and wrote. Anne J. Cruz's *Discourses of Poverty: Social Reform and the Picaresque Novel in Early Modern Spain* probes the socioeconomic realities of Spain's age of empire while also relating that analysis to the literary culture of the day. Johnson considers the material realities and their representations in *Cervantes and the Material World*. Carmen Bernis Madrazo's *El traje y los tipos sociales en el* Quijote ("Dress and Social Types in the *Quixote*") also might be of interest for those inclined to pursue the materiality of the text.

Students often express interest in learning more about women in the age of Cervantes. Overviews that give insight into women's economic, artistic, and cultural activity are Carolyn A. Nadeau's *Women of the Prologue: Imitation, Myth, and Magic in* Don Quixote I, Mary Elizabeth Perry's *Gender and Disorder in Early Modern Seville*, Allyson Poska's *Women and Authority in Early Modern Spain: The Peasants of Galicia*, and Lisa Vollendorf's *The Lives of Women: A New History of Inquisitional Spain*. Adrienne Laskier Martín's *An Erotic Philology of Golden Age Spain* and Sherry Velasco's *Lesbians in Early Modern Spain* explore eroticism from a gendered perspective and therefore provide an apparatus for considerations of sexuality. Georgina Dopico Black's *Perfect Wives, Other Women: Adultery and Inquisition in Early Modern Spain* examines sexuality in literature and society in the period.

The twenty-first century brought renewed attention to postcolonial studies and to Spain's imperial past. Barbara Fuchs's *Passing for Spain: Cervantes and the Fictions of Identity* is a monograph on Cervantes's work and times that highlights Spain's complex multiracial and imperial past. Christopher Brett Arredondo's *Quixotism, the Imaginative Denial of Spain's Loss of Empire* focuses on the imperial past. De Armas Wilson, in *Cervantes, the Novel, and the New World*, and Héctor Brioso Santos and José Montero Reguera, in *Cervantes y América* ("Cervantes and America"), turn our attention to the role played by the Americas in Cervantes's life and literary world.

The Arab presence in *Don Quixote* has been studied in María Antonia Garcés's attempt to engage trauma theory in *Cervantes in Algiers: A Captive's Tale*. Such a reading finds its complement in the broader focus on Hispano-Arab culture in Fuchs's *Exotic Nation: Maurophilia and the Construction of Early Modern Spain*, in Francisco Márquez Villanueva's *Moros, Moriscos y Turcos de Cervantes: Ensayos críticos* ("The Moors, Moriscos, and Turks of Cervantes: Critical Essays"), and in Perry's *The Handless Maiden: Moriscos and the Politics of Religion in Early Modern Spain*.

Numerous studies have traced the influence of Cervantes's work in a comparative context. William Childers's ambitious *Transnational Cervantes* explores the construction of meaning in Cervantes's work as a means of opening up that work to broader understandings of subaltern identities and non-Western art. Eric C. Graf's *Cervantes and Modernity* reads Cervantes's work as a launching pad for understanding multiculturalism and might suggest interesting points of departure for classroom discussions. George Mariscal engages with ideology in *Contradictory Subjects: Quevedo, Cervantes, and Seventeenth-Century Spanish Culture* when examining modernity and postmodernity and their relations to *Don Quixote*. Edwin Williamson's *Cervantes and the Modernists: The Question of Influence* is thought-provoking. Ian Watt views the protagonist as a precursor of modern individualism (*Myths of Modern Individualism:* Faust, Don Quijote, Don Juan *and* Robinson Crusoe). Javier Blasco, in *Cervantes, raro inventor* ("Cervantes: Unique Inventor"), considers how and why Cervantes is credited with writing a truly modern novel. José Montero Reguera's *Materiales del* Quijote: *La forja de un novelista* ("Materials of the *Quixote*: The Forging of a Novelist") does close textual reading to analyze the makings of a modern novel. Finally, three major critics who find Cervantes's conception of the novel unique are Martínez Bonati, in Don Quixote *and the Poetics of the Novel*; Stephen Gilman, in *The Novel according to Cervantes*; and Cesáreo Bandera, in *The Humble Story of Don Quixote: Reflections on the Birth of the Modern Novel*.

Don Quixote *on Film*

There are many film adaptations of *Don Quixote*, but few lend themselves to use in the classroom. One film that has served well as a complement to the text is Manuel Gutiérrez Aragón's El Quijote *de Miguel de Cervantes* ("The *Quixote* of Miguel de Cervantes") of 1990, produced for Televisión Española, with script by Camilo José Cela, a Nobel Prize–winning novelist. The two principal actors are Fernando Rey as Don Quixote and Alfredo Landa as Sancho. Both are excellent, as is their supporting cast. The film covers part 1 only.

Gutiérrez Aragón brought out a sequel in 2002, covering part 2 and titled *El caballero don Quijote* ("Don Quixote the Gentleman"). Juan Luis Galiardo played Don Quixote, and Carlos Iglesias played Sancho. The director wrote the script himself.

Both films are faithful to the spirit of the novel, given the considerable time constraints they work under. As would be expected, the interventions of the various narrators are not adequately captured in either film, although there is some attempt to dramatize the shift of narrative voices between chapters 8 and 9 of part 1 by introducing a figure who can only be Cervantes himself in the role of second author. Many scholars are not likely to subscribe to this reading, but it offers a plausible solution for a nonspecialized television audience.

A third adaptation, to which students relate remarkably well, since they have been exposed to cartoons on television from infancy, is the animated version of *Don Quixote*, produced for Televisión Española between 1970 and 1981, directed by Cruz Delgado. This version, covering both parts, reflects an important vein of critical commentary on Cervantes's original, which takes that text to be, in essence, a funny book. This vein is primarily British, stemming from the seminal work of Peter E. Russell; it privileges the reception the text almost certainly enjoyed by its first readers. One might dismiss this approach as too simple, but it may also be seen as an attempt to counter the Romantic readings of the novel (see esp. Close, *Romantic Approach*).

That the animated version was taken seriously by its producers and by Televisión Española is demonstrated by the facts that Manuel Criado de Val and Guillermo Díaz Plaja were contracted as consultants, another famous director (José Luis Berlanga) was actively involved, and the voice of Fernando Fernán Gómez, a well-known actor, was selected to give dignified and distinctive expression to the protagonist. Some aspects are directed more toward children, however. For example, Don Quixote's hunting dog and horse are humorous participants in the action.

The film of the musical *Man of La Mancha*, although based only tenuously on Cervantes's original, is nevertheless a great favorite of students. Very few of today's undergraduates are familiar with Dale Wasserman's Romantic fantasy, which has the advantage of being available in both English and Spanish. Two film versions in English that capture at least something of the original are the *Don Quixote* of Peter Yates, starring John Lithgow, Bob Hoskins, Vanessa Williams, and Isabella Rossellini, and *Monsignor Quixote*, an adaptation of Graham Greene's road novel starring Alec Guinness.

Film directors who adapted Cervantes's text to their idiosyncratic visions include Orson Welles (*Don Quixote*) and Terry Gilliam (*Lost in La Mancha*). There is an excellent Russian film, directed by Grigori Kozintsev (1957); a film starring Cantinflas (Mario Moreno), filmed in Mexico and titled *Un Quijote sin Mancha* (1969; "A Quixote without a Mancha"); an opera directed by Georg Wilhelm Pabst and starring Feodor Chaliapin (1933); and a film in Danish, *Don*

Quixote af Mancha, directed by Lau Lauritzen (1926) (for additional adaptations, see Payán; Hermosilla). Steven Ritz-Barr's puppet version of *Don Quixote* is available on DVD and offers a unique performance that resonates with the puppetry of Maese Pedro in Cervantes's text.

Introducing film into a literature course makes special demands on instructors. They may need special preparation to discuss technical aspects, such as camera manipulation—or perhaps some segments of the course could be team-taught with a colleague well versed in film theory. Barbara Simerka and Christopher Weimer's essay in this volume makes suggestions about how to incorporate film into a course, and a growing bibliography on the topic can help guide those interested in expanding their repertoire beyond films based on *Don Quixote* to include films whose themes and narrative techniques draw on the Cervantine tradition (see Burningham, *Tilting*).

Select Online Resources

Our students have been brought up on a steady dose of online gaming, social networking, and other device-supported communication, so we should expect that they will appreciate it when those media are used to complement the classroom experience. *Don Quixote*'s ubiquity can create fascinating opportunities for student projects that link the text to cultural and social phenomena, such as the Brazilian Projeto Quixote detailed in Rogelio Miñana's essay in this volume.[4] Creative appropriations of the characters, the story line, and the themes of Cervantes's text proliferate throughout the world, and many appear online. An assignment that allows students to focus on such appropriations and to consider their meaning can be a fruitful start to a course devoted entirely to *Don Quixote*: it encourages them to examine their own connections to Cervantes's beloved characters and prompts them to articulate their expectations about the novel they will be reading.

YouTube can be useful as an in-class tool, but instructors must know what they are looking for, as a general search of the site currently yields more than five thousand hits. But a casual search can help instructors get up to date on popular culture in a few quick strokes. *YouTube* has hundreds of excerpts from films, including those detailed in the film section above, that can be played in class or assigned to students for out of class viewing. Commonly taught films—including *Man of La Mancha, Lost in La Mancha*, the TNT version of *Don Quixote* (with John Lithgow), and Gutiérrez Aragón's *Don Quijote de la Mancha*—all can be found either in their entirety or excerpted on *YouTube*.

At least half a dozen professional or semiprofessional sites are extremely useful resources. *Centro Virtual Cervantes* provides a full online version of Francisco Rico's edition of *Don Quijote* (http://cvc.cervantes.es/literatura/clasicos /quijote/default.htm) along with an extensive bibliography and scholarly and cultural resources. The Cervantes Project at Texas A&M offers a multitude of links to electronic editions, images, iconography of Cervantes's texts, scholarly links, and a link to Eduardo Urbina's Cervantes Project Collection at the university's library (http://cervantes.tamu.edu/V2/CPI/index.html). The Biblioteca Virtual Miguel de Cervantes increasingly has online scholarly resources available for download. The Miguel de Cervantes site run by the Librería Cervantes in Oviedo provides information about the author's biography, bibliography, and artistic influence. That the journal *Cervantes: Bulletin of the Cervantes Society of America* is accessible via the Web makes it convenient for instructors to assign articles published in that venue and allows students direct access to a wealth of research on Cervantes. The Biblioteca Nacional de España has a beautifully designed *Quijote interactivo* site that includes a digital version of the text, videos, an interactive map of Don Quixote's travels, fragments from numerous chivalric novels, and other contextual information (http://quijote.bne.es/libro.html).

For those interested in visual culture, the *Banco de Imágenes del Quijote, 1605–1905* ("Image Bank"), sponsored by several cultural organizations and maintained at the Universidad Complutense de Madrid, has an amazing array of resources (http://www.qbi2005.com/). *Don Quijote de la Mancha en el cine* site, maintained by Enrique Martínez-Salanova Sánchez, is a treasure trove of information about films based on or related to *Don Quixote de la Mancha* (http://www.uhu.es/cine.educacion/cineyeducacion/donquijote.htm). The photographs, images, and bibliographic links available on William Thomas Little's site are a worthy addition to the rich resources available to instructors online (http://cla.calpoly.edu/~wlittle/). Many instructors take advantage of online dictionaries, such as the *Diccionario de la Real Academia Española* (http://rae.es/recursos/diccionarios/drae); others report using sites such as the *Molinos de Viento en La Mancha* (http://www.madridejos.net/Molinos/) to help students understand the material and physical worlds depicted in the text.

As the course on *Don Quixote* continues and students struggle to keep up with their reading, many turn to the Internet for voice recordings of the text. Instructors might consider giving students links to audio recordings and encourage them to listen—as most readers did in Cervantes's time—to a chapter or two. The rhythms of Cervantes's prose and of dialogue between Don Quixote and Sancho Panza are captured effectively in the Spanish-language audio version sponsored by the government of Aragón and posted at *Leer escuchando* (leerescuchando.net) and also in versions available on *Biblioteca Cervantes Virtual*. For classes taught in English, students can consult the audio version posted at *LibriVox*, where they can download the files or listen directly from the Internet.

The possibilities multiply as the online world grows and changes by the minute. As blogs, wikis, discussion groups, role-playing, and online collaboration make their way onto more syllabi, we will see our students and our colleagues adding to the resources that make teaching *Don Quixote* a personally and intellectually enriching experience.

Editions Used in This Volume

Spanish citations of *Don Quijote* are taken from John Jay Allen's Cátedra edition of 2009, unless otherwise indicated. The question of an English-language text is vexed, because of the various problems of and opinions about the translation. For the English translations, contributors quote from Edith Grossman and from John Rutherford and sometimes provide their own translations, as noted in the volume.

NOTES

[1] Fajardo and Parr's edition was last published in 2009.

[2] For a review that compares the Lathrop and Fajardo-Parr classroom editions, see Knotek.

[3] On Smollett's use of Jarvis's translation, see Allen, *"Traduttori,"* esp. 2.

[4] This São Paulo–based nonprofit organization seeks to get children off the streets and out of poverty (www.projetoquixote.org.br/).

Don Quixote in English Translation

Jonathan Thacker

Don Quixote reached England with remarkable speed. The accessions list of Oxford's Bodleian Library for 1605 records the arrival of part 1, the book probably having reached Oxford that summer, just a few months after its publication in Madrid (Michael 103–04).[1] The first recorded reference to the work outside Spain occurs in an English play;[2] and Thomas Shelton's version of part 1 predates any other foreign translation (Barrio Marco, "Proyección" 27–28). This translation was complete by 1607 but not published until 1612, and it was then revised and republished with Shelton's version of part 2 in 1620.[3] Such rapid translation of a Spanish text by a little-known writer would be impressive even today, but in fact there existed a strong (unreciprocated) tradition of Spanish-to-English translation through the sixteenth century, and there was ample expertise available to perform the task. Thus Shakespeare could have read Cervantes in translation before the end of his life, but Cervantes could not have read Shakespeare in Spanish.

The history of the reception of Cervantes's masterpiece in England — in theater, art, poetry, satire, and the novel — is a long one and replete with illustrious translators, adapters, imitators, and innovators. Two aspects of this afterlife that was granted to *Don Quixote* in the English-speaking world are particularly striking, because they carry an odd or counterintuitive truth. The first is that, however fortunate Spain might be to have begotten Miguel de Cervantes, his novel could be written in Spanish only once,[4] whereas it can be constantly rewritten and so reinvented in English and other languages. (Translators must cling to such aperçus when the world is generally against them.) The second is that until relatively recent times the work was influential more in English translation than in its original Spanish. *Don Quixote* was essential to the development of the novel particularly from the eighteenth century on, and many of the most important figures in the novel's evolution were writing (and largely reading) in English.[5]

When immersing themselves in *Don Quixote* in English over the centuries, then, readers have inevitably had their responses to the novel subtly or not so subtly molded by the version in their hands. Before we begin to look at the translations in detail, I mention two points, not unconnected, in the light of this influence. First, the philosophy of translating has changed from the early modern period to the twenty-first century. Early modern translators would freely add to the original text, distort it, or omit sections from it according to their own whims and their perception of their readers' desires or expectations. What may seem irreverence from the perspective of the modern day was the result of an attitude to translation that saw the practice as akin to imitation or emulation.[6] From what John Rutherford calls (not wholly pejoratively) this cavalier approach of Shelton and the early translators, who relied, of necessity, on their personal knowledge of Spanish, their wits, and their instincts and who had few reference tools available, translation practice moved toward expectations of a supposedly faithful rendering of a text, with *completeness* and *accuracy* as watchwords (Cervantes, *Don Quixote* [Rutherford] xiv).[7]

Recent translation theory argues that *fidelity*, *completeness*, and *accuracy* are relative terms—more, they are impossible goals, implying as they do that a text can be exactly re-presented in another language, with no change. Antoine Berman, a theorist and translator of Latin American literature into French, has shown how a version in a target language inevitably deforms the source text.[8] The translated text is a new creation, and translators, consciously or unconsciously, will have adopted the source text into their own linguistic and cultural norms—domesticated it, in current theoretical terminology.[9] Such domestication gave rise to few feelings of guilt or betrayal on the part of early translators of *Don Quixote*, as it was normal practice, perhaps never better expressed than by Perrot d'Ablancourt, a seventeenth-century French translator of Lucian: "[J]ust as in a beautiful face there is always something one would wish were not there, so in the best authors there are passages that one must touch up or lighten, especially when these things are done only to please" (qtd. in Worth-Stylianou 135). Shelton and his first followers certainly aimed to please. Then, in the later eighteenth and particularly the nineteenth century, there emerged a strong inclination to render a work accurately—that is, often with a word-for-word equivalence—a shift that came with a consequent disregard for the text's function (see Venuti 5–6). It is a paradox that translations produced in this way can be accurate in individual word choices and yet be wholly inaccurate in their insensitivity to tone (comic, parodic, tragic) or register (high, low). In the twentieth century, more translators began to play their role self-consciously: refusing to hide behind the myth of invisibility, a translator may, perhaps as a political statement or act, deliberately foreignize the target language, thus resisting "the ideological dominance of the target culture" (Munday 145).

Modern-day translators often feel a heavy responsibility on their shoulders; the accusation of treachery is never far from their mind. They cannot know the unconscious priorities and values behind all their choices, but many employ strategies of which they are well aware thanks to the burgeoning academic field of translation studies. The age of innocence is over, although it has to be said that the quality of a particular translation is by no means proportional to the level of the exponent's theoretical immersion.

The second point with regard to the history of *Don Quixote* in English is that the attitude of readers—in other words, the work's critical reception—has also changed considerably over time. This change is related more closely to literary movements and the zeitgeist than to specific issues of translation, though the movements and the zeitgeist are always intertwined with those issues. J. M. Cohen recognized as much in his 1962 overview of the translation of foreign works into English, when he opined that "every great book demands to be translated once a century, to suit the change in standards and taste of new generations, which differ radically from those of the past" (9).

Translators have tended to reflect in their versions the cultural view of the novel predominant in their time. In his seminal article on *Don Quixote* as a chiefly and unashamedly comic work, P. E. Russell writes, "There were some half-dozen excellent translations of *Don Quixote* published in England between 1612 and the end of the eighteenth century. I have not noticed anything about them which hints that their authors regarded this book as anything except a brilliantly funny book" (316).[10] The first translators did indeed find the book to be overwhelmingly funny. When the Romantics took a look at it anew, they saw in its protagonist an idealistic hero, unappreciated by the society around him, instead of a mad fool with lucid intervals, and translators accordingly served up to a new generation of readers a serious, heroic central figure, which is the one that predominates in artistic portrayals of the knight. In modern times, after the Romantic approach to *Don Quixote* was deconstructed by Russell, Anthony Close (*Romantic Approach*), and their followers and when a concomitant partial rehabilitation of the comic followed, there has been a shift back from dryness toward fun.

I deal briefly with these first translators, from Shelton, the novelist's coeval, to Tobias Smollett in 1755. They all obviously predate the development of the Romantic approach to *Don Quixote*, and so the tendency is, as Russell noted, to see the novel as comic, with its antiheroes' (or one might call them comic heroes) romance-induced madness and rustic stupidity primarily to be laughed at. Shelton's translation is of great interest and will give pleasure to students of early modern English literature, who have been schooled in the lexis and syntax of Shakespeare and his contemporaries. In part because the more flexible contemporary English does not balk at Cervantes's prolixity, Shelton's *Quixote* has greater fluidity than many modern attempts, which are prone to subdivide Cervantes's lengthy sentences and paragraphs. The translator emulates the changes in register so fundamental to the novel; he also mostly understands and tries to replicate the humor of the Spanish. Nevertheless, for some modern readers Shelton's version misses or misconstrues the author's parodic take on the chivalresque (Colahan 62) and "betrays a degree of haste and a lexical carelessness made worse by a faltering command of Cervantes's language" (Mayo and Ardila 54).

Mistranslations in Shelton's text are often due to superficial similarities between English and Spanish words, although many of the words Shelton used have changed in meaning, and so his version needs attentive reading today. On the plus side, he has the advantage of having lived (including for a time in Salamanca) in a world not unlike Cervantes's in terms of custom, dress, and general culture. This familiarity lends Shelton's prose a natural authority that later writers were unable to match, even when they corrected some of his mistranslations or misunderstandings. Perhaps for this reason his version was frequently reprinted, even into the twentieth century (see Rudder 137).[11]

The flavor of Shelton's style shows in this passage from part 2, chapter 4, as Sansón Carrasco and the knight continue to discuss the content of part 1:

> —¿Hay otra cosa que enmendar en esa leyenda, señor bachiller? —preguntó don Quijote.
> —Sí, debe de haber—respondió él—, pero ninguna debe de ser de la importancia de las ya referidas.
> —Y por ventura—dijo don Quijote—¿promete el autor segunda parte?
> —Sí promete . . .   (658)[12]

> "Is there aught else, Sir Bachelor," said Don Quixote, "to be mended in this legend?" "Yes, marry is there," said he; "but nothing so important as what hath been mentioned." "Perhaps the author promiseth a Second Part?" quoth Don Quixote. "He doth. . . ."
> (*History of Don Quixote* 2: 27)

The most recent modern English version renders this exchange as follows:

> "Is there anything else that needs correcting in that history, sir bachelor?" asked Don Quixote.

> "There must be something, but nothing can be as serious as the things already mentioned."

> "Does the author by any chance promise us a second part?" asked Don Quixote.

> "He does. . . ." (*Don Quixote* [Montgomery] 430)

Shelton is economical, often maintains the Spanish word order, and tends to stick to the closest phonological equivalent in English—for example, "mend" for *enmendar* and "legend" for *leyenda*. (These choices might indeed indicate occasional haste.) James Montgomery searches for a modern term equivalent to each of these Spanish words, "correct" and "history," aware from the results of decades of literary research that there are important differences among "history," "story," and "legend." But he then matches Shelton's archaic-sounding "Sir Bachelor," producing the odd, illogical mixture of styles that characterizes attempts to translate *Don Quixote* for the modern reader. Modern translators generally do not mimic the archaic verbal forms evident in Shelton's English: "hath," "promiseth," "quoth."

The second translation into English, by John Philips, nephew of Milton, was published in 1687 and has not since been edited (Rudder 137). It thus has little importance in the history of *Quixote* translation and is regarded in fact as "extraordinariamente infiel" (Rutherford, "Brevísima historia" 484; "extraordinarily unfaithful"). The most generous assessment of Philips's work views it as an interesting travesty, written on the assumption that the first translation into English was already known to the reader (Colahan 64). Philips frequently shortens and distorts the narrative (for example, he omits the first two short speeches of the extract given above), and much subtlety is lost. He adds realia from his own culture to augment Cervantes's text—an extreme form of domestication. An example is the stealing of Sancho's ass, as described in part 2, chapter 4. Sancho explains that he was propped up on poles by the thieves while asleep on his mount, which was then taken from under him. The translator has Sancho add, "or so it seems the country-fellow's Horse was stoll'n from under him in Barthemew-Fair" (*History of the Most Renowned Don Quixote* 310), a cultural reference clearly beyond the ken of the Spanish peasant. Philips's title page reads, *The History of the Most Renowned Don Quixote of Mancha: And His Trusty Squire Sancho Pancha*. The spelling quirks tend to be ironed out when the work is listed in bibliographies, but they are indicative of Philips's approach. That Sancho's family name does not always rhyme with *Mancha* in this translation indicates that consistency was less important to writer, publisher, and presumably readers than the comic thrust of the whole.

All three major eighteenth-century translations were more widely read as time passed, perhaps because the eighteenth century was an age that began to appreciate the novel at a deeper level (Candler Hayes 66). They are by Peter Motteux, published between 1700 and 1712, with a version revised by John Ozell appearing in 1719 (Cervantes, *Life*); by Charles Jarvis, originally spelled Jervas, in 1742 (*Don Quixote*); and by the novelist Smollett in 1755 (*History and Adventures*). The first was favored by readers as distinguished as W. H. Prescott and George Ticknor, the author of the three-volume *History of Spanish Literature*, published in the mid–nineteenth century. Ticknor found Motteux's translation too free but the best. It was Motteux's version that was published by Everyman's Library in 1906 and by Wordsworth Classics as recently as 1993 (Mayo and Ardila 55), although Jarvis's was also very frequently reprinted on both sides of the Atlantic, including in popular formats such as the Oxford World's Classics series, edited by E. C. Riley, in 1992.

Motteux was a French businessman and well-known translator of Rabelais. The extent of his role in the translation of the *Quixote* he published, ascribed originally to "various hands," is uncertain (Hopkins). He may have directed a team. Bertram Wolfe, in criticizing Motteux's version, lamented the translator's attempt to turn Cervantes into Rabelais and to sacrifice the subtlety for the belly laugh (Cervantes, *Don Quixote* [Putnam] x–xi). Henry Watts, one of the three late-nineteenth-century translators of *Don Quixote*, complains bitterly about Motteux's betrayal of Cervantes: "He tramples ruthlessly on all the delicate graces of the Spanish, blurring the native tints, decking the author with fancies not his own, loading false humour upon true, and producing something which is an outrage upon art and upon truth" (*Ingenious Gentleman* [Watts] 1: xx–xxi). These criticisms betray a new approach to translation, the attitude that the original text is sacrosanct. In the episode when Don Quixote sees and attacks the windmills (pt. 1, ch. 8), Watts's lexical choices are often very similar to Motteux's, but Watts does not allow himself the latitude Motteux takes in word order and looseness of expression. Thus Motteux's "This said, he clapped spurs to his horse Rozinante, without giving ear to his squire Sancho, who bawled out to him, and assured him that they were windmills, and no giants" (Cervantes, *Life* 1: 46) becomes in Watts "So saying he clapped spurs to Rozinante, his steed, without heeding the cries which Sancho Panza his squire uttered, warning him that those he was going to encounter were beyond all doubt windmills and not giants" (*Ingenious Gentleman* [Watts] 1: 101). At the start of this passage, Cervantes's "diciendo" (95) is rendered as "saying," not "said," and thereafter too Watts shows a distaste for Motteux's (hardly excessive) creative spirit.

Jarvis's version follows the text more closely word by word than do its predecessors but loses a great deal of the character and variety of the original Spanish. Sancho Panza emerges particularly poorly, since the contrast between his uncouth manner of speaking and his master's educated language is often effaced. In part 1, chapter 10, when Sancho advises his master to seek sanctuary from the Santa Hermandad, having freed the galley slaves, Jarvis has him declare, "Methinks, sir, it would not be amiss to retire to some church; for considering in what condition you have left your adversary, it is not improbable they may give notice of the fact to the Holy Brotherhood, and they may apprehend us: and in faith, if they do, before we get out of their clutches, we may chance to sweat for it" (*Don Quixote* [Jarvis] 1: 75). Shelton had rendered the passage thus: "Methinks, sir, that it will not be amiss to retire ourselves to some church; for according as that man is ill dight with whom you fought, I certainly persuade myself that they will give notice of the fact to the holy brotherhood, and they will seek to apprehend us, which, if they do, in good faith before we can get out of their claws I fear me we shall sweat for it" (*History of Don Quixote* 1: 65–66). Jarvis's translation begins as Shelton's does, and the striking similarity of the two demonstrates how one translator will often have another's version open on his or her desk. But Jarvis's register ("adversary," "improbable") undermines the linguistic ineptitude and ignorance of Sancho. (Quixote's sidekick misunderstands his master's use of the educated word "homicidio" [113] as "omecillos," meaning "grudge" or "hatred"—and preserving this clash of styles is essential to Cervantes's work.)[13] The general approbation of the accuracy of Jarvis has ignored the shortcomings in wit and imagination that are evident in his version. In Richard Hitchcock's words, "some of the sparkle of the original is lost in the sober and stilted style" ("Spanish Literature" 410).

Smollett's *Don Quixote* is readily available today thanks to its reissue in 1986 with an introduction by Carlos Fuentes. Smollett, a novelist, sees more clearly than Jarvis, a painter, Cervantes's literary modus operandi and in particular the comic effects at which Cervantes aimed. Smollett wrote a short preface outlining his objective in the translation: to "retain the spirit and ideas, without servilely adhering to the literal expression, of the original" (Cervantes, *History and*

Adventures 31). His version, although clearly influenced by Jarvis's translation, "tends to broaden the tone" and is "wordier in its solutions" (Terry 418). The accusation of plagiarism aimed at the novelist (most notably by John Ormsby in the nineteenth century but repeated in modern scholarship) has been vigorously and convincingly rejected (Candler Hayes 72; Hitchcock, "Spanish Literature" 410–11). Smollett's is the most readable today of the early translations,[14] though Montgomery complains that Cervantes's work is turned by Smollett into an English novel (xxxix), perhaps demonstrating that readability comes at the cost of domestication.

The late-Victorian period saw three new *Quixotes* emerge in England: versions by Alexander James Duffield, in 1881 (*Ingenious Knight*); by Ormsby, an Irishman, in 1885 (*Ingenious Gentleman*); and by Watts, in 1888. The first and last of these translators began as a team but disagreed and went their separate ways (McGrath, "Modern Translations" 76). As Cervantes's novel became a classic, scholarly editors and enthusiasts in Spain and England undertook a painstaking investigation of the text, its sources, and its contexts. One beneficial result of their effort was that new heights of equivalence were achieved by a fresh wave of translators. The cavalier era was over, and it was time to stop "making remarks instead of rendering words," as Duffield put it with reference to his predecessors (*Ingenious Knight* 1: xlv). Duffield confessed that he had been "making critical and historical notes" on *Don Quixote* for over twenty years but decided not to include them all in order to avoid the expansion of his edition from three volumes to six (lxi). His translation was heavily attacked by at least one anonymous reviewer of the day (Pym and Style 265) and has not been reissued since. The second of these Victorian *Quixotes*, Ormsby's, found most favor subsequently. Its accuracy attracted Kenneth Douglas and, after Douglas's death, Joseph R. Jones to overhaul it for publication by Norton in 1981, in an edition that introduced many North Americans to the novel and that remains popular with some *cervantistas*. In his preface to this edition, Jones calls Ormsby's original version "the first truly accurate English translation of Cervantes' great novel" and hesitates to point out its shortcomings. Nevertheless, these are neatly summed up a few lines later: "[W]here possible he [Ormsby, in 1885] follows the actual word order, translates very obscure words into their Elizabethan equivalents, carefully distinguishes among the forms of address . . . , and generally chooses to 'sacrifice' (as Putnam says) clarity and ease for accuracy" (*Ingenious Gentleman* [Ormsby] ix).[15]

Watts, who had also been working on his *Don Quixote* for twenty years (*Ingenious Gentleman* [Watts] 1: xliii), in his introduction sharply criticized the early translations, sparing only Shelton. Shelton was praised for his sound knowledge of Spanish and the "naïve felicity" he often achieved (xxii), but Watts's silence on his own immediate Victorian predecessors is pointed. Watts sets out the guiding principles of his translation at length in his prefatory remarks. He argues that "the duty of every translator is, as I hold, first to obliterate himself. The English is but the vesture in which the Castilian appears. It would be bad manners and worse taste to let the form within be disguised or dimmed by the clothing" (xxvi). His version is heavily footnoted so that readers can see the Spanish through the English, understand the text and context. He would have disapproved strongly of Rutherford's solution to the "homicidio" pun as an outrageous attempt to compete with Cervantes. But Watts's translation consistently gives the lie to his claim, among other claims, to have avoided archaism. Watts believes that "when Cervantes himself is speaking, the language is ever plain, clear, and graceful—his words, except when he intends to be jocose, or deliberately to wrap up his meaning, so simple that any peasant in Castile may understand him" (xxiii), yet Watts's quest for clarity blurs or homogenizes the deliberate variety (and frequent clash) of voices and poetic styles in Cervantes's Spanish. Despite producing a text that is copiously annotated and demonstrates clear understanding of the original (at the textual level), Watts was, like others of his time, affected by the well-established Romantic approach to the novel and its author, epitomized by Duffield's assertion that Cervantes was "at a time of great national frivolity, of all men the one most in earnest" (*Ingenious Knight* [Duffield] 1: xli).[16] Watts worries on his reader's behalf, for example, that Quixote's "most famous adventure . . . appears at first sight to be a little too extravagant" (*Ingenious Gentleman* [Watts] 1: 100) and proceeds to explain, in a footnote, how Spanish windmills were smaller than those of Kent or Sussex and therefore the would-be knight's lance could have reached their sails. Meanwhile the reader, unpreoccupied by precise measurements, is laughing at Quixote's wild description of a giant's arms being "of two leagues' length" (101).

Cohen, some years after translating *Don Quixote* himself, memorably opined that "the Victorians conferred on all works [that they translated] the brown varnish of antiquarianism" (10).[17] To put it another way, they were reluctant "to adopt a contemporary voice" (Pym and Style 266).

Today's expansion of narrative and translation theories throws a different light on how pre-twentieth-century English translators provided rationales for and defended their versions of *Don Quixote*. Nowadays scholars tend not to conflate voices in a novel so readily with its author's,[18] and the invisibility of the translator, advocated by Watts, is no longer held up as an ideal. Of recent translators, Rutherford best exemplifies a bolder approach to the text. He writes, "[W]e can regard the translator not as a passive reproducer of meanings or interlinguistic message-boy but as an active reader and creative rewriter of what he has read" ("Dangerous Don" 23). Such an attitude would have horrified the Victorians, but recent translators generally accept the theoretical impossibility of their task and engage in their own ways with the difficulties of translation that arise. The reviewers who discuss the modi operandi of the translators betray their own predilections in the process.

Before translation theories began to be seriously studied in the academy in the latter part of the twentieth century, other *Don Quixotes* appeared in North America and the United Kingdom. Although the versions of Samuel Putnam (1949), Cohen (1950), and Walter Starkie (1964) have been superseded by the five (six, if we include Ormsby-Douglas-Jones) versions to appear since the 1980s, the older versions had their admirers. Putnam, an American, gives his reason for undertaking the task anew—to produce a version "combining textual and linguistic fidelity with a readable prose" (*Don Quixote* [Putnam] xvi)—and remarks how useful to him was *Quixote* criticism written after the publication of translations before his. Daniel Eisenberg enthusiastically endorses Putnam's academic concern for establishing a trustworthy Spanish text from which to work; he contrasts Putnam's approach with the limitations of those of Cohen and Starkie ("Text" 104–06). But Arthur Terry finds that Putnam's modernized version reduces the rhetorical variety, producing "too even a register" (419).[19]

Cohen, a French scholar rather than a Hispanist, was invited by Penguin Books to render *Don Quixote* into English, and, thanks to this publisher's popularity, for several decades his version was most British readers' introduction to Cervantes's knight. Cohen did not use his own translations of much of the author's verse, anglicized names, all but dispensed with footnotes, and generally thought that the tale spoke for itself as "one of the best adventure stories in the world" (Cervantes, *Adventures* 20). Conjectures have been made about whether or to what extent Cohen had Jarvis's version to hand as he worked—and indeed many passages read as an updating of that eighteenth-century translation. Cohen himself admitted that his *Don Quixote* "[retained] a slightly archaic tone" (30). Terry dismisses Cohen's translation as the "Lowest Common Multiple of existing translations" (419). It is true that the story is there, but the life and humor are not. Starkie's *Don Quixote of la Mancha*, which appeared first as an abridged text in 1964 (and which continues to be printed as such—for example, in Signet Classics), is more readable than Cohen's but suffers from the same carelessness seen in Putnam. Although Montgomery considers Starkie's translation "haphazardly" done (xxxix), it is highly regarded by some; James Parr believes that it is one of the five translations worthy of serious attention (*Don Quixote, Don Juan*, ch. 1).[20]

The blandness and uniformity of the language, evident on every page of these mid-twentieth-century translations, is surprising, given the richness, variety, and virtuosity of the original Spanish. It may be that the translators lacked the talent to reproduce in English Cervantes's linguistic wealth and range of humor. It may also be that they were wary about departing too much from earlier English versions, their caution reducing the chance of a spark kindling. The growth of translation theory and the downplaying of the Romantic approach helped modern translators break free from this sense of confinement and rediscover the joy of creation evident in the earliest translators of Cervantes. An extensive discussion in the academy of the aesthetic, cultural, and even ethical issues raised by translation studies has been ongoing since the 1980s. This literature can help in deciding which English text should be chosen for students who have no Spanish.

Among the theoretical questions raised in the translation of *Don Quixote*, or of any classic work of literature, are

Should translators compete with Cervantes's genius, or should they resign themselves to the role of slavish imitator?

Is modernization or updating of the language justifiable, or should translators respect the period in which the text was written?

How does one render a register that is already archaic in an old text?

To what extent should translators consciously import or appropriate the story into their own culture—that is, domesticate it?

Should translators use footnotes to explain difficulties?

How much work should readers be expected to do in pursuing the meaning?

Should the culture of the original be embraced even if the English of the translation is affected by it (e.g., if the English becomes laced with foreign terms)?

Which text of the novel should translators use?

Is it important to render all the paratexts (mainly prefatory material)?

Should translators correct the original where it is inconsistent or explain it where it is ambiguous?

How readers respond to these questions will affect their attitude to a translation.

The five most recent English versions of *Don Quixote* are by Burton Raffel (1995), which supplanted the Ormsby-Douglas-Jones version in the influential Norton Critical Edition series in the United States; by Rutherford (2000, rev. 2003), which became the new Penguin translation; by Edith Grossman (2003); by Tom Lathrop (2005); and by Montgomery (2006). Recent times have seen a move toward American English versions of the novel. Grossman, a well-known translator of much modern Latin American literature, is also the first woman to have translated Cervantes's text.[21] Lathrop is the only editor of the Spanish text of *Don Quijote* to have ventured a translation. All five translators discuss their process of translation and the decisions they made in approaching the text.

Raffel is the only modern translator to replace *Don Quixote*'s traditional English *x* with the Spanish *j* (*jota*). His version is often praised: Terry finds attractive its economy and naturalness, its sensitivity to the language (especially Sancho's speech) and syntax of the original (419–20); Steven Wagschal begins his review by calling it a "magnificent achievement" (147). Raffel is harsh on all earlier translators, especially Cohen, accusing them of "not casual error but serious betrayal" of Cervantes ("Translating" 11), whom he places on a pedestal. The naturalness of Raffel's version is a drawback to some, however, who object to its being too colloquial and informal to the point of inelegance (Rutherford, "Brevísima historia" 489). Parr objects to Raffel's tendency to embellish (*Don Quixote, Don Juan* 29) and, along with other reviewers, finds errors and infelicities that detract from the whole. The modernization and Americanization to which Parr alludes in his criticism is striking, for example, in Raffel's translation of the contemporary Spanish *reales* into "dollars," even "dollar bills."[22] Raffel's practice of placing parenthetical explanations in the text (in addition to abundant footnotes) might disturb readers more.

When Quixote returns wounded from the first sally and asks to be taken to his bed, "Llévenme a mi lecho, y llámese, si fuere posible, a la sabia Urganda, que cure y cate de mis feridas" ("Take me to my bed and, if it's possible, call the wise Urganda to cure and tend to my wounds"), the housekeeper, in a bathetic outburst typical of the deflating humor aimed at the romances of chivalry, avers that they will be able to cure him "sin que venga esa hurgada" (*Don Quijote de la Mancha* 75 [pt. 1, ch. 5]). Performing the comic function that Sancho later will, she betrays her ignorance of the romances, turning Urganda la Desconocida ("Urganda the Unknown") from the *Amadís* cycle of romances into an *hurgada*. Raffel literally inserts the meaning, and we read the housekeeper's speech as, "You must get into bed, your grace, without calling on this Hurgada [*hurgada* = sexually well-used] and we'll get you well . . ." (*Don Quijote* [Raffel] 33). Rutherford manages to explain Spanish double meanings more elegantly, as in his references to Quijada and Quesada (and later Quijana) in the work's opening paragraph: "His surname's said to have been Quixada or Quesada (as if he were a jawbone, or a cheesecake)" (*Don Quixote* [Rutherford] 25). Rutherford renders the housekeeper's "hurgada" as "that there Ugandan woman" (51), alert to the comic function of the character's error and cleverly maintaining something of her mystified, insecure ignorance. He allows himself considerable creative freedom. Lathrop and Montgomery simply resort to a footnote (49; 40), and Grossman refers to "that gander woman" (*Don Quixote* [Grossman] 44), having changed Don Quixote's Spanish "la sabia Urganda" to "Uganda the Wise." Whether or not "Urganda" is a misprint in the Vintage edition, Grossman's play on words lacks comic force.

Rutherford, a British Hispanist and acclaimed translator of Leopoldo Alas's *La regenta*, is an accomplished defender of his own version of *Don Quixote*. He has set out in detail, in a number of pieces, how he approached the task, how long it took him, and his attitude to his predecessors and the odd successor (see Eisenberg, "Text"). His translator's introduction to the Penguin edition (Introduction xiv–xx), is the liveliest one ever written to *Don Quixote*. Rutherford raises important questions about translation, and his introduction should be read even by those who disagree with his approach or aspects of it. He sees the translator as an equal of the author, not as someone who "[grovels] at his feet" (xvi). Rutherford sought to avoid the worst and take the best from the cavalier and puritan traditions. He was aware that he could not be totally consistent in his version: the text's "otherness in time and in space," its "historicity and its foreignness" would always be evident (xix), even when he tried to make Sancho and Quixote speak "varieties of contemporary spoken English that men of their age and background would use today" (xviii).

Rutherford's belief that literary translation should be "subversive and dangerous" in nature ("Dangerous Don" 25) chimes with his broader attitude to literary texts expressed in this translator's preface:

> So the translation of *Don Quixote* does turn out to be logically impos-
> sible, after all. The translator must both make his text modern and keep
> it old, make it English and keep it Spanish. There can be no coherence
> or consistency. But this doesn't matter. All creative literature exists as a
> defiance of rational logic. There's nothing more illogical or irrational than
> a metaphor, saying that something is something else.
>
> (Introduction xx)

Those who have assessed Rutherford's version in print uniformly praise his textual knowledge and sensitivity to tone. Rutherford is, in Parr's words, the "best
at capturing ironic understatement and misstatement" (*Don Quixote, Don Juan*
24). He is also the first translator (now joined by Lathrop and Montgomery) to
have used the best modern edition of the original text, that by Francisco Rico
(Eisenberg, "Text" 107).

The sort of anachronism Rutherford embraces might seem too bold for the
purist. Yet there is less discussion in the academic community of his decision to
render Sancho's malapropism "Cide Hamete Berenjena" (645; a distortion of
Cide Hamete Benengeli, the narrative's fictitious author, into *berenjena* ["aubergine" or "eggplant"]) as a domesticating "Cide Hamete Brinjalcurry" ("Dangerous Don" 31–32) than of his British English. Lathrop, for example, is exercised
by "small beer," "aubergine," and "stone" (as a measure of weight) and fears that
Sancho has become "something other than a Spaniard" (Rev. of *The Ingenious
Hidalgo* 178). He also fails to pick up on the joke in the translation of "Pero
Grullo" as "Stan Streeson" (i.e., "stands to reason") in part 2, chapter 62. The absence of the various formal and informal terms of address (in Rutherford, they
merge into "you") is lamented by Lathrop, but Rutherford dismisses this worry,
attacking the absurd persistence of outdated pronouns such as "thou" and other
terms of address such as "your worship" or "your grace" (used to render the
Spanish "vuestra merced"). They were inappropriate, he argues, even when first
used by Motteux and Putnam. All other contemporary translators opt for "your
grace," which, as Rutherford recalls, "se emplea para dirigirse a duques, duque-
sas y arzobispos" ("Brevísima historia" 491; "is used for addressing dukes, duch-
esses, and archbishops") and is quite the wrong address in English for Sancho to
use for his master. Sancho's deference in English had become an unquestioned
feature of the work in translation, but Rutherford put the two men on a more
equal footing by avoiding the outdated and clumsy terms.

Grossman's version of Cervantes's novel spent some time near the top of the
best-seller lists in the United States. It took Grossman two years to complete the
translation, and it was the first of many she has undertaken to include footnotes. She began by refusing to look at others' attempts at rendering the novel
("Translator's Note" xviii). Like Rutherford, she decided that since Cervantes's
prose was modern Spanish in the author's day, she would use a modern English
idiom. She is not as consistent in this undertaking as Rutherford is, however, and
many reviewers have found her version less accurate and convincing than her

translations of modern fiction. That she is not a Golden Age specialist weighed against her in her choice of Spanish text (Lathrop, "Edith Grossman's Translation" 249). Eisenberg confirms that she is the "most textually ignorant of the modern translators" ("Text" 108), and her translation suffers somewhat as a result. Parr is more positive about Grossman's efforts, praising in particular her ability to find equivalents in English for the Spanish archaisms (*Don Quixote, Don Juan* 24); despite his reservations about her accuracy, he lists her among the best five translators of the novel into English.

Knowledge of the text of *Don Quixote* in Spanish led Lathrop to translate: he argues that others' versions "are frequently based on Spanish editions that have taken too many liberties with the original text, fixing perceived errors, changing chapter titles, even adding words" (*Don Quixote* [Lathrop] vii). He consulted many translations and took versions of the novel's poems from elsewhere instead of tackling the poems himself. His *Don Quixote* has been admired as "without a doubt the most aesthetically pleasing one to date," and his extensive use of footnotes—more than a thousand in total—was praised (McGrath, Rev. of *Don Quixote* [Lathrop] 216). But this editor-translator's maintaining of Cervantes's apparently deliberate errors has been questioned and is seen by some as idiosyncratic.[23] Lathrop's translation is reliable and readable, and the choice between it and Rutherford's for an anglophone reader may be a matter of taste. An example of their approaches to a speech made by the knight to his squire in part 2, chapter 3, demonstrates an essential difference between these contemporary Hispanist translators.

With Sansón Carrasco in attendance, Sancho, perhaps knowingly, undermines the bookish notion that his master has just explained to him of the head (i.e., the knight) suffering when any one of the limbs (i.e., Sancho) feels pain. Sensing that Sancho might be casting aspersions on his thirst for the fray, Don Quixote remarks:

> —Socarrón sois, Sancho—respondió don Quijote—. A fee que no os falta memoria cuando vos queréis tenerla.   (650)

Lathrop translates:

> "You're a jokester, Sancho," responded Don Quixote. "I swear your memory doesn't fail you when you want to remember something."   (532)

Rutherford opts for:

> "You are a sly dog, Sancho," replied Don Quixote. "I must say your memory works well enough when you want it to."   (505)

Two small but significant differences emerge. Lathrop remains closer to the Spanish in keeping the negative of "no os falta," while Rutherford characteristically finds a modern idiomatic phrase, "works well enough," and is content to shed the original formulation for wording that sounds close to what someone would say today. His "sly dog" also conveys more effectively than "jokester" the intimacy of the pair's relationship, which in part 2 becomes more knowing as they play elaborate games with each other and as each struggles to gain the upper hand.

The most recent translation of *Don Quixote*, by Montgomery, had a gestation period of twenty-six years. It is recommended highly by Michael McGrath in his review, although McGrath has reservations about occasionally archaic or stilted English. Like Rutherford, Montgomery knows the earlier translated versions of the novel. In his preface, he explains that he wants readers to "forget they are reading a translation." He aims to return the comedy, the wit, to a work that has suffered in the eyes of non-Spanish readers, being characterized as an "unfunny" comic novel (xl). That readers often do forget that they are reading a translated text is seen by many theorists as a problem: such unawareness can result from an ethically dubious process of domestication. Important to Montgomery is the sound of his version, for the reason that many of the first readers of the Spanish original heard the novel spoken instead of reading it silently to themselves (xlii). This idea is unusual among translators.

Modern scholars point out the inaccuracies of earlier English versions of the novel, yet mistranslations due to carelessness, poor judgment, or ignorance continue to affect modern-day versions. Although Lathrop and Rutherford maintain the highest levels of textual reliability, Montgomery's version does suffer from occasional infelicities. If we compare his few lines from the exchange between Sansón Carrasco and the knight (pt. 2, ch. 4) quoted above with the translation in Shelton's *History of Don Quixote of the Mancha*, we see that Montgomery prefers "history" to Shelton's "legend" for Cervantes's "leyenda" (2: 430 [ch. 27]; 658), but one might argue that neither adequately conveys the meaning of the original, "libro escrito para ser leído, lectura" (*Don Quijote* [Rico] 11n27; "book written to be read, reading"). Rutherford and Lathrop opt for "book" and "text," respectively (510; 538), clearly aware of the pitfalls of "history" or Shelton's "legend." Montgomery also omits "respondió él" completely in this section, having earlier in the chapter given an unassigned speech, usually (and more convincingly) ascribed to Don Quixote, to Sansón Carrasco (*Don Quixote* [Montgomery] 429).

When Cervantes ironically allowed Don Quixote a glimpse of his own future fame in part 2, chapter 3, with Sansón's assertion that "no ha de haber nación ni lengua donde no se traduzga" (648; "there's no language in the world into which it won't be translated"), it is doubtful that he expected that four hundred years later there would be nearly twenty full translations of his novel into English.

The choice of translation for a non-Spanish speaker is a subjective one. Some will be more comfortable with American than with British English; some will enjoy the flavor of an older English version; some will want a sense of the original Spanish through more literal translation or through frequent footnoting; some will not welcome commentary, preferring to lose themselves in the fiction, like the novel's protagonist; some will applaud the updating and domestication of Cervantes; some will deplore the intrusion of our times into a different historical and cultural context. As Eisenberg writes, "there is no one translation that will serve every purpose" ("Text" 120). Nevertheless, the profusion of versions from different periods, versions that have different goals and approaches, makes for a wonderfully rich translation history, from whose study much can be learned and taught.

NOTES

I am grateful to Jim Parr, Ian Michael, Stephen Boyd, and especially Martin Trew for reading and commenting on earlier drafts of this essay. My work also benefited from association with the research projects funded in Spain by MICINN (reference numbers FFI2011-23549 and CDS2009-00033).

[1] The details of the reference in the library's Benefactors' Register are provided in the first entry in Randall and Boswell (1–3).

[2] In George Wilkins's *The Miseries of Enforced Marriage*. See Barrio Marco, "Prólogo" 10.

[3] The extent of Shelton's involvement in the second part has been disputed. Lo Ré argues that Leonard Digges was responsible for the translation of part 2.

[4] Jorge Luis Borges playfully suggested otherwise in his short story "Pierre Menard, autor del *Quijote*."

[5] See, for example, Welsh, esp. 81. Henry Watts, a Victorian translator of the work, wrote, "Spain may have begotten the child, but England has been his foster-mother" (Cervantes, *Ingenious Gentleman* [Watts] xvi).

[6] Worth-Stylianou sees in some Renaissance translation a "paraphrastic approach, which can subsume translation within the realm of imitation" (129).

[7] The story of Don Quixote itself is—within the fiction of the novel—a translation from Arabic. Cervantes was himself well aware of the pitfalls of translating a foreign text, as is demonstrated by his famous analogy in part 2, chapter 62: a translation is like a Flemish tapestry viewed from the back.

[8] For further exploration of Berman's and others' theories of translation, see Munday 146–49; for salient texts on translation, see Venuti.

[9] The terms *foreignizing* and *domesticating* are common in translation studies today, being especially associated with the translation theorist Lawrence Venuti, but the ideas behind them were first set out by Friedrich Schleiermacher, a German theologian and philosopher, in an 1813 lecture.

[10] Rutherford states, "La aportación del traductor está en función de sus criterios y gustos personales, pero también de la interpretación que esté de moda cuando traduce" ("Brevísima historia" 482; "The translator is governed by his own views and personal preferences, but also by the interpretation in vogue when he translates").

[11] Rudder provides a convenient listing of the first and subsequent editions of *Don Quixote* translations into English, including their revision by others' hands and abridgements, selections, and adaptations of them (137–50). In 1950, when he published his own translation, J. M. Cohen called Shelton's the "best and raciest version . . . the nearest

to Cervantes in spirit" (11). I quote Shelton from the Navarre Society's edition published in London in 1923 in two volumes and listed by Rudder (137).

[12] Quotations from the Spanish text are taken from Rico's edition of *Don Quijote*.

[13] Shelton and Jarvis translate "omecillos" (113) as "Omicilles" and "omecils," respectively (66; 1: 76), and even Grossman, in her recent translation, uses an anglified version of the Spanish word (71), which is unlikely to be understood by the anglophone reader. The joke has become labored in the extreme in modern translations, since *homicide* is difficult to pun with. Only Rutherford, playing with "outrage" and "getting out of rages," brings it off (79).

[14] The reissue with Fuentes's introduction was reviewed by Hart; Allen, Rev. of *The Adventures*.

[15] On Ormsby, see also McGrath, "Modern Translations" 77.

[16] On the nineteenth-century approach to *Don Quixote*, heavily influenced by German Romanticism, see Close, *Romantic Approach*, esp. 41–57.

[17] Cohen refers specifically and interestingly to the Ormsby-Douglas-Jones translation of Cervantes's novel (29).

[18] The translator Burton Raffel does make the "segundo autor" mentioned in part 1, chapter 8, a first-person narrator, perhaps assuming that the voice belongs to Cervantes himself (*Don Quijote* [Raffel] 49). Most other modern translators avoid this pitfall, though Grossman and Ormsby-Douglas-Jones include footnotes that advise the reader that the "segundo autor" is Cervantes.

[19] Allen felt that Putnam missed or distorted much of the verbal irony of the work ("*Traduttori*").

[20] For further discussion of these three mid-twentieth-century translations, as well as the Ormsby-Douglas-Jones version, with teachers' responses to them, see Bjornson 8–10.

[21] Mary Smirke's version (1818) was apparently "pieced together" from other translations (Pym and Style 265).

[22] See also the review by Burch, as well as McGrath's various comments on Raffel's translation ("Tilting").

[23] See Eisenberg, "Text" 121. The study of the history of the book has thrown much light on these errors, which may not be errors; Rico, who engages critically with Lathrop's theories, explores them in depth, especially on 40–44.

Part Two

APPROACHES

Don Quixote: A Sociohistorical Compass

Joan F. Cammarata

While the objectives and content of courses on *Don Quixote* may differ, students benefit from appropriate historical and biographical information to situate their reading of the novel. In conjunction with the thematic and textual literary analyses performed in class, I encourage my students to look beyond the amusing adventures of Don Quixote and Sancho into Cervantes's revelations about the intellectual currents of seventeenth-century Spain.

One of the great innovations of Cervantes is that he replaces the escapist literature of chivalry with a literature that evaluates the cultural and historical reality of his world. That innovation can be understood only if it is contextualized in the social and political conflicts that the author personally knew. The challenge is to help students understand that *Don Quixote* relates as much to the literary and artistic trends of the day as it does to the sociocultural situation in which it was produced. The principal analysis in class of the novel focuses on literary aspects, but studying Cervantes's life and times brings richness to the reading experience that should be part of any course on the *Quixote*.

To identify the social issues integral to Cervantes's discourse, I provide students with a brief description of the historical events that preceded the *Quixote*. After the surrender of Granada (1492), which ended seven centuries of Moorish rule in Spain, the Catholic monarchs Ferdinand II of Aragon and Isabella I of Castile established their Royal Council in Castile to unify the land into a country where a uniform government, language, and religion prevailed. The first vernacular grammar book, Antonio de Nebrija's *Gramática castellana* (1492; "Grammar of the Castilian Language"), advanced Castilian as the official language of Spain. The religious spirit of the Reconquest shifted to the Christian unification of Spain achieved through the elimination of other religions. Jewish converts to Christianity who continued to live in Spain were known as conversos ("converts") or New Christians, and Muslim converts were identified as Moriscos ("Moors"). The Inquisition, adopted by the Catholic monarchs (1478), served as a powerful institution over several centuries to ensure Catholic orthodoxy and prevent heresy. These historical developments can be given through class lectures and supplemented by selected readings from John Edwards and William Prescott.[1]

In a society composed of New Christians and Old Christians, discrimination against converts was formalized in statutes of *limpieza de sangre*, which defined "purity of bloodline" as the absence of Jewish or Muslim converts in one's family for four generations. Students can review the origins and implications of these statutes in Albert Sicroff's comprehensive study.[2] Through the comments of Quixote's squire, Sancho, a laborer who consistently boasts of his status as an Old Christian, Cervantes voices the traditional dislike of converts:

> Y cuando otra cosa no tuviese sino el creer, como siempre creo, firme y verdaderamente en Dios y en todo aquello que tiene y cree la santa Iglesia Católica Romana, y el ser enemigo mortal, como lo soy, de los judíos, debían los historiadores tener misericordia de mí y tratarme bien en sus escritos.   (2: 91–92 [ch. 8])

> And even if I had nothing else, there is my belief, as I've always believed, firmly and truly, in God and in everything that is thought and believed by the Holy Roman Catholic Church, and there is my being, as I am, a mortal enemy of the Jews, and so the historians ought to take pity on me and treat me well in their writings.   (505)[3]

Students can be asked to consider to what extent hereditary membership in a particular ethnic or religious group determines outlook and aesthetic expression. Should Sancho's declaration of loyalty to the Church be understood as a device used by Cervantes to avoid inquisitorial scrutiny? The multivalent significance of Sancho's declaration becomes clear to students when they learn that Cervantes had numerous career frustrations and that some scholars believe him to be of Jewish descent.[4] Through the strategy of exclusion, aristocratic and ecclesiastical institutions barred the social advance of many by assigning resources only to those who provided certificates of purity of bloodline. Still others were denied privilege because they fell out of favor with the crown.

Cervantes expected honor and compensation because of his service to the crown in the battle against the Turks at Lepanto, in which his left hand was rendered permanently useless. For his distinguished service under Don Juan of Austria at Lepanto, Tunis, and La Goleta, he received letters of commendation that should have ensured his ransom when the galley *Sol* en route to Spain was captured by Muslim Berber corsairs and he was imprisoned. But after five years of prison in Algiers (1575–80), he and his brother Rodrigo were ransomed with his family's own money: there was no assistance from the crown. In Seville, Cervantes personally experienced Spain's demoralizing economy when he returned to a country that ignored the needs of many of its military veterans. He highlighted his sacrifices and military service in two written petitions for employment in the Americas (1582, 1590) to the Council of the Indies, only to have those petitions rejected. Unable to secure a bureaucratic position in the Americas or to earn a living from his writings, he worked as a commissary collecting provisions for the Armada (1587–89), with a meager income. He later became a tax collector (1595) and was temporarily jailed in Seville for irregularities in his accounts (1597).

Students interested in the particulars of Cervantes's life and times can consult the biographical works of William Byron, Donald McCrory, Jean Canavaggio (*Cervantes* [Armiño]), and Krzysztof Sliwa. The studies of María Antonia Garcés, Ottmar Hegyi, Alberto Sánchez ("Revisión"), and Alonso Zamora Vicente address Cervantes's captivity in Algiers and its effects on his writing.[5] Students will recognize that autobiographical elements contribute to Cervantes's creative world, but they should be reminded that a novel is neither autobiography nor history. They should consider to what extent a creative artist is governed by personal experience and to what extent that person transforms personal experience into art.

Information about Cervantes's experiences certainly helps students appreciate how his travels inspired the novel's varied cast of characters. Coming from every social condition, ranging from prostitutes to aristocrats, his characters are found on the roads and especially in the inns, social crossroads where different classes converge and interact.

Cervantes dedicates several lengthy chapters of part 1 of the *Quixote* to the captive's tale (chs. 39–40), a narration inspired by his five years of imprisonment in Algiers. Don Quixote's discourse on "arms and letters" (ch. 38), a preface to this tale, promotes Cervantes's view that soldiers deserve recognition because they risk their lives. The Christian captive, Ruy Pérez de Viedma, begins by describing his life with his father and two brothers, which gives the instructor an opportunity to explain to students the traditional career paths available to young men, "Iglesia, Mar o Casa Real" '[t]he Church, the sea, or the royal house' (1: 524 [ch. 39]; 335). Ruy describes his participation in the same historical battles in which Cervantes fought, then relates his capture and escape from Algiers, facilitated by a renegade, a label that requires explanation. Cervantes maintained his Christian faith in Algiers and awaited his release through ransom. But thousands of captives gained their liberty by converting to Islam; they became known as renegades, deniers of their faith. Almost half of Algiers, populated by Turks, Moors, and Jews, was composed of Turks by profession, *turcoples*, who were renegades newly converted to Islam to achieve their freedom (McCrory 93). Students often are surprised to discover that some cultural customs from Cervantes's lifetime endure to this day. The conversion to Islam as an option for the release of foreign hostages still exists in the twenty-first century, for example.[6]

Most students reading *Don Quixote* in Spanish programs probably have learned of Spain's glorious image as a world power in the sixteenth and seventeenth centuries, but they may not know that Spain's internal political and economic decline belied that image. The circumstances that resulted in poverty and hardship for Spain's inhabitants become clear to students through historical background readings in the general works of J. H. Elliott and of John Lynch and in the more specific studies of Geoffrey Parker and of Antonio Feros, which discuss Philip II's imperialism, the exodus to the Americas, the failure of the Spanish Armada, the inept government of Philip III relegated to the duke of Lerma, and the loss of agricultural and merchant classes in the 1609–14 expulsion of Moriscos. The Moriscos, living outside the cities and maintaining their dress, language, customs, and religious practices, were branded as a population that was incapable of assimilation into Spanish culture. Their ties to Spain's enemies, the Turks and Barbary pirates, and their desire for France and England to overthrow Spain made their presence a concern for national security.

This discussion prepares students for the Ricote episode of the *Quixote*, in which Cervantes criticizes his society's intolerance of the Moriscos and shows sympathy for their plight. Through Sancho's encounter with his long-lost neighbor, Ricote (pt. 2, ch. 54), who is a Morisco, students see how this group identifies itself as Christian, suffers in exile from its adopted homeland, experiences the hostility of Old Christians toward converts, and risks death to return in secret to the only home it ever knew. These issues are examined in the studies of Richard Hitchcock ("Cervantes"), Antonio Oliver, Ángel González Palencia, and Francisco Márquez Villanueva (*Moros, Personajes*, and "Problema"). Students can be asked to consider why it was dangerous for Cervantes to show compassion toward Moriscos and why Ricote affirms that the crown was justified in ordering the expulsion: "Finalmente, con justa razón fuimos castigados con la pena del destierro, blanda y suave al parecer de algunos, pero al nuestro, la más terrible que se nos podía dar" 'In short, it was just and reasonable for us to be chastised with the punishment of exile: lenient and mild, according to some, but for us it was the most terrible one we could have received' (481; 813). What was it like for Spain's inhabitants to live under the Inquisition, and are there comparable societies in the world today? For further study on the Inquisition, students can consult Henry Kamen (*Spanish Inquisition*).

The ubiquity of the Inquisition manifests itself in the language of the scrutiny of Don Quixote's library (pt. 1, ch. 6), conducted by Pero Pérez, a curate, and Nicolás, a barber, language that parallels that of the Inquisition's tribunal reviews. Don Quixote's niece tells the curate that all the books could have been burned, to which he responds assuringly, "[Y] a fee que no se pase el día de mañana sin que dellos no se haga acto público y sean condenados al fuego" '[A]nd by my faith, no later than tomorrow we will have a public proceeding, and they will be condemned to the flames' (1: 148 [ch.5]; 44). Students often find it remarkable that many of the books that Cervantes chose to save from the flames still form part of our literary canon.

The quixotic concepts of justice, liberty, and social empowerment provide the stimulus for student discussions of class structure. Cervantes's personal quest for justice in an unjust world finds expression in Quixote's well-known discourse on the golden age (pt. 1, ch. 11). In a critical commentary on societal ills, Cervantes describes the social conditions that will engender equitable political and social realms. Students might compare this vision of an ideal society with that of Thomas More's *Utopia* (1516).

Students might also consider how social class functions in the relationships between Cervantes's characters. The punishment of the young Andrés is only one example of social injustice predicated on class. Juan Haldudo the Rich, Andrés's master, dramatizes that no legal recourse exists for the poor in Cervantes's social world (pt. 1, ch. 4). Quixote's creation of a personal norm for justice does not coincide with that of Spain's juridical system, as when Quixote frees the criminals condemned as galley slaves: he considers their sentence excessive for crimes they described euphemistically (ch. 22). Cervantes advocates freedom for all regardless of social station. Is his opinion that women have the right to choose their own husbands (e.g., Marcela, Dorotea, Lucinda, and Zoraida) progressive or feminist?

Social stratification affected Spain's increasingly capitalistic environment. Students have the opportunity to explore seventeenth-century views on social status and compare them to their own ideas. Sancho often takes pride in his Christian lineage, claiming to be in the same group as "los que tienen sobre el alma cuatro dedos de enjundia de cristianos viejos como yo los tengo" 'those who have in their souls a little of the spirit of the Old Christians, like me' (2: 65 [ch. 4]; 484). He is unconcerned about overstepping boundaries in his ambition to purchase a title of high rank: ". . . que yo cristiano viejo soy, y para ser conde esto me basta" '. . . for I am an Old Christian, and that alone is enough for me to be a count' (1: 303 [ch. 21]; 161). The Spanish crown, generating revenue by selling titles, indeed favored Old Christians in such transactions.

How did Spanish capitalism affect the infrastructure of Cervantes's society? In this era of rising mercantilism, other sources of economic status available to Sancho were the ownership of manufactured goods and rights over the labor of others. In the past, only the aristocracy held this power, but with the emergence of *censos*, agricultural investments, even Sancho, in considering his adventures as a squire, dreams of this avenue to a secure income and an easy life: ". . . y el Diablo me pone ante los ojos . . . un talego lleno de doblones, que me parece que a cada paso le toco con la mano . . . y lo llevo a mi casa, y echo censos, y fundo rentas, y vivo como un príncipe" '. . . and the devil places before my eyes . . . a sack filled with *doblones*, and at every step I take I seem to touch it with my hand, and put my arms around it, and take it to my house, and hold mortgages, and collect rents, and live like a prince' (2: 131–32 [ch. 13]; 535). Through the desire of the lower classes to live like nobles and rise in public esteem by obtaining titles, Cervantes acknowledges the decline of the old social order and the growing power of money to change one's status.

Cervantes advocates a new order in which honor is no longer the patrimony of noble lineage but is the right of all individuals of merit. Quixote advises Sancho that as governor he should judge people according to their virtue, ". . . porque la sangre se hereda, y la virtud se aquista y la virtud vale por sí sola lo que la sangre no vale" '. . . because blood is inherited, and virtue is acquired, and virtue in and of itself has a value that blood does not' (2: 377 [ch. 42]; 731). Numerous passages in the text probe the possibility that an equitable society can be based on worth and not on distinctions of class, lineage, and power. As Sancho himself says, "no hay sino encomendarnos a Dios, y dejar correr la suerte por donde mejor lo encaminare" '. . . and when the lord we serve sees this, he'll have to reward us, each according to his merits' (1: 303 [ch. 21]; 157).

Cervantes's criticism of the Spanish class system is most evident in part 2 of the *Quixote*, where the duke and duchess exemplify aristocrats who treat the subordinate classes — Don Quixote representing the hidalgos, Sancho representing the peasants — with cruelty, mockery, and inhumanity. What determines a group's status in society, and how has that determination changed over time? For Cervantes, the aristocratic class is defined by its prestige and capital, not by virtue. Don Quixote and Sancho demonstrate the qualities that their aristocratic hosts lack. The series of humiliations that Sancho endures in his successful governorship, which is based on honesty and simple wisdom, illustrates the model of the aristocracy's domination of the working class. Cervantes's belief that effective government requires good people, a timeless concept and one that students endorse, is a condemnation of Spain's political and judicial system in the hands of a corrupt nobility, in a closed framework of lineage and favoritism.

The historical, political, and social circumstances integral to Cervantes's discourse are not immediately obvious to students, so some explanation by the instructor is needed. Students can also consult general studies on Spain in Cervantes's time by Marcelin Defourneaux, Antonio Domínguez Ortiz, Manuel Fernández Álvarez (*Sociedad*), Manuel Rivero Rodríguez, and Javier Salazar Rincón. Students, in conjunction with their literary textual analysis, should be guided through the circumstances of Cervantes's personal life and the real social issues denoted throughout his fictitious world. This interdisciplinary approach sparks critical evaluations, especially for students who are studying these issues in other courses. Many come to their reading of the text with some awareness of Don Quixote and Sancho through popular culture, but after our class discussions that explore the extraliterary aspects of the novel, they become more critical readers of this rich narrative.

NOTES

[1] Students can enhance their knowledge of the political trajectory of Spain's unification by reading Edwards, *Spain* (ch. 3, "The New Inquisition"; ch. 6, "Christians Jews and Muslims") and *Ferdinand* (ch. 4, "Defenders of the Faith"). They may further consult Prescott (ch. 6, "The Internal Administration of Castile"; ch. 7, "Establishment of the Modern Inquisition"; ch. 15, "The Expulsion of the Jews from Spain"; ch. 17, "Castilian Literature-Cultivation of the Court . . ."; and ch. 24, "Rising in the Alpuxarras . . . Edict against the Moors").

[2] Those who consult Sicroff should focus on chapter 1 of his book to situate the genesis of the conflict, "Los orígenes del problema judeo-cristiano en España en el siglo XV," and on chapter 7 to review the ramifications of the statutes, "Conclusión: Algunos aspectos de España bajo el régimen de los estatutos de limpieza de sangre." Fascinating studies on Spain's multicultural society are Fuchs, *Exotic Nation* and *Passing*.

[3] All citations and references to *Don Quijote* are taken from John Jay Allen's Spanish edition. All citations and references in English are taken from Edith Grossman's translation.

[4] If documentary evidence of Cervantes's Jewish ancestry ever existed, it was likely destroyed. We know that his paternal great-grandfather worked as a cloth merchant, a trade of New Christians, and that his paternal grandmother's family engaged in professions associated with New Christians: apothecaries, merchants, and doctors. For discussion of Cervantes's marginal status in society, see Castro, *Pensamiento*; Gilman, *Spain*; Durán.

[5] Cervantes weaves his life experiences as a captive into the life stories of the characters in his plays *El trato de Argel*, *Los baños de Argel*, and *La gran sultana* and in his exemplary novel *El amante liberal*.

[6] Students might find relevant a *New York Times* article about two journalists taken hostage in Gaza on 14 August 2006. When a demand for the release of Muslim prisoners was not met, the group insisted that the two men pay a ransom, convert to Islam, or be killed. The journalists were released 28 August after publicly converting to Islam (Erlanger).

Cervantes and the Invention of the Polyphonic Novel: Teaching the *Quixote* of 1605

David A. Boruchoff

This essay draws on my experience in teaching the complete *Don Quixote* in the context of a full-year seminar in Spanish on the works of Miguel de Cervantes for a group of sixteen to twenty advanced undergraduates and the occasional MA or PhD student. Despite its value as a summation of the principal currents in early modern literature, such a course is an uncommon luxury in academia today. Nevertheless, I have had the opportunity to offer it some fifteen times in the past twenty-two years, always with modifications to suit the needs and preparation of the students at hand, that is, the extent to which they are conversant in literary history and theory. I also regularly teach Cervantes's novel in English translation in a larger, one-semester course and the *Quixote* of 1605 (aka part 1 or *El ingenioso hidalgo*) as the capstone to a graduate seminar titled Literature and Society in Renaissance Spain.

No doubt many other instructors have experienced the changes that have occurred during my career. I can no longer expect undergraduate students to have completed a survey of medieval and Renaissance Castilian literature before they take my seminar. Indeed, many do not arrive familiar with the genres, themes, conceits, rhetorical devices, and social and religious values that inform the writings of Cervantes and his generation. Moreover, the anthologies now commonly in use are ever more inadequate for charting the continuity of social, artistic, religious, and intellectual topoi—and thus ill-suited to identify innovation and creativity—leaving students with little sense of what was orthodox or commonplace, for example, or even of the ideal of feminine beauty popularized by Petrarch and Garcilaso de la Vega, and reused more polemically and critically by Luis de Góngora, Francisco de Quevedo, and Cervantes.

Because my seminar serves as a pre-1700 requirement for undergraduate students in Hispanic studies, its primary foci are the text of Cervantes's novel, the construction of the novel as a work of art, and the often uneasy, if not self-conscious, position of Cervantes's novel at the crossroads of traditional and modern forms of thought, life, and literature. Cervantes was an uncommonly perspicacious and critical reader, unwilling to employ literary, intellectual, or social conventions without also noting their conventionality. This authorial practice made explicit the tensions between art and reality; between social, political, or religious norms (honor, patriotism, gender roles, *limpieza de sangre* ["purity of blood"]) and higher, spiritual, or moral values (virtue, truth, faith, friendship, equity); and between individual desires and collective or communal obligations. Cervantes was careful to rethink and rework his literary models, so that what may at first appear conventional—because of the presence of stock characters, situations, gestures, and modes of expression—is in the final analysis often antithetical to the intent and worldview of his precursors, making his texts innovative in both their approach and didactic intention, and thus ontologically different. In sum, Cervantes used topoi and stereotypes to challenge tradition whenever tradition was rooted in superficial or ephemeral concerns.

An attentive reading of Cervantes's works or those of the mid-sixteenth-century novelists with whom Cervantes was conversant is all that students need to understand the issues and currents at play. This is not to say that recent theoretical models have no role in my teaching. Rather, I seek to use them (as well as other models from classical, medieval, and early modern times) as tools instead of making them the focus of discussion. In this way, students come to appreciate Renaissance literature on its own terms. Whereas my seminar for masters and doctoral students builds up to the grand theory of part 1 of *Don Quixote* by examining the more limited pretensions of Garci Rodríguez de Montalvo's *Amadís de Gaula* (1508) and the several kinds of novel that all first appeared in Spain within the space of a very few years—*Lazarillo de Tormes* (1554), *Viaje de Turquía* (1557), Jorge de Montemayor's *La Diana* (1559), and *El Abencerraje* (c. 1560)—the undergraduate course uses Cervantes's works alone to identify the themes, actors, scenarios, narrative techniques, and moral or political aims of picaresque, pastoral, chivalric,[1] and Moorish (or, more correctly, Mediterranean captivity) fiction.

In the first semester of this course, we therefore read *La Galatea*, three or four *Novelas ejemplares* (usually including *Rinconete y Cortadillo* and *La ilustre fregona*), and *La gran sultana* or *Los baños de Argel* before examining the *Quixote* of 1605, so that, although the narrator and others (inside and outside the text) claim that the *Quixote* of 1605 is a parody or *invectiva* ("vituperation") of *libros de caballerías*, we see that Cervantes in fact draws on a variety of essentially modern genres, treats them critically, and weaves them into something new: a polyphonic or multivoiced novel.[2]

Students in my full-year undergraduate course are usually more open to this inductive approach to the *Quixote* of 1605 than are those in my graduate seminar or the course in English translation, perhaps because the latter two groups tend to have a stronger notion of what the novel would eventually become than of what it was in Cervantes's time and place. These students often arrive with a background in recent literary and cultural theory and few or no readings in pre-Romantic fiction. For this, some assert that *Don Quixote* is "so incredibly postmodern," whereas those in my full-year course can be brought more easily to comprehend that it is instead merely modern and that a characteristic of modernity is always to seek new ways to be modern. It is out of fashion in academia not to foreground theoretical models and instead try to derive the reader response to (or readerly understanding of) Cervantes and his contemporaries from texts of the period. Nevertheless, in my experience students become more proficient modern readers if they first learn to read through other, older eyes. To this end, I insist that we treat the *Quixote* of 1605 as a point of arrival and transition rather than solely as a point of departure.

I have elsewhere argued that the critical sensibilities and understanding of early modern literature now in common use are a legacy of the analytic tools and taxonomies developed first in the dialecticism of Hegel and then in the writings on the forms and evolution of history and genre of the Romantics. As a result, *Don Quixote* was and is still called the first novel because it was the first to display all the features expected of a novel in these later times. For many critics today, any work predating *Don Quixote* is necessarily something other than a novel; to name such a prenovelistic work, other terms, such as *romance*, were invented or adapted (Boruchoff, "Poetry" 275–76). Although Cervantes and his contemporaries both in Spain and abroad used a different vocabulary, one based on Aristotle's poetics—in which *poesía* signified fiction, and novels were called *libros*, *mentiras*, and *patrañas* ("books, lies, and falsehoods"), if not vain, useless, and pestilent occupations—it is evident that early modern writers and readers had an understanding of the novel as a distinct genre, albeit in the guise of one-dimensional and predominantly one-voiced narratives, such as those from the 1550s mentioned above. I want my students to appreciate this hallmark of early modernity, in which the practices of writing and reading outpaced critical vocabulary, so they might grasp the nature, scope, and significance of Cervantes's contributions to the development of the novel and of literature in general.

Cervantes's critical engagement with genre, and more broadly with social and literary conventions, becomes evident to students by first reading *La Galatea*, *Rinconete y Cortadillo*, and *La ilustre fregona*. Cervantes points up the capacity of language, especially first-person discourse, to impress and mislead, even as he repudiates the environmental and genetic determinism typical of the picaresque. In the despair of socially decorous pastoral lovers in *La Galatea* and the ostensibly perfect yet morally unsettling solutions put forth at the end of various of his exemplary novels, we see the high price of deference to the debased concept of honor that held sway in his time. As a result, when we turn to *Don Quixote*, students readily grasp that the tale of Marcela and Grisóstomo is essentially pastoral in inspiration, whereas that of the *capitán cautivo* ("captive captain") draws on the Moorish novel for its setting and actors to acclaim, without as much sentimentality, a set of ideals that surmount political, cultural, and sectarian difference, indeed calling into question what it means to be a good Spaniard and Christian. Even more, we see how models are adapted to new uses and insights.

These preliminary readings help us appreciate how creativity operates in the *Quixote* of 1605. For example, when Don Quixote encounters a band of goatherds, he associates their rustic reality with the ideal pastoral constructs of philosophy and art and launches into a discourse on the *edad de oro* ("golden age"), in which *zagalejas*, young shepherdesses, could wander the countryside on their own, without the unnatural adornments of modern times and without fear for their safety or reputation. This transformation wrought by the imagination of Don Quixote in turn spawns another on the part of the author, who follows with the self-consciously pastoral tale of two youths who become shepherds in dress alone, having been born to wealth, social standing, and the benefits of formal education: "aquel famoso pastor estudiante" 'that famous student-shepherd' Grisóstomo and the incompliant object of his affections, Marcela (1: 201 [ch. 12]).[3] Departing from the common practice of pastoral fiction, Cervantes supplies an experiential—that is, realistic—basis for the knowledge, talents, and freedom from want inexplicably shown by his literary shepherds. Furthermore, Marcela defies a broader set of artistic conventions (common to both pastoral and courtly literature) by refusing to be objectified and idealized and by using rational arguments to deconstruct the conventional and disdainful portrait of independent women that Grisóstomo and his friends present in their writings and speech, calling her a "fiero basilisco" 'fierce basilisk' (223 [ch. 14]) and "esquiva hermosa ingrata" 'coy, ungrateful beauty' (226). This associative process in the construction of Cervantes's novel continues as unrequited, pastoral love gives way to the quasi-human passion of Don Quixote's horse, Rocinante (pt. 1, ch. 15), the tryst of the serving girl Maritornes and the muleteer (ch. 16), and the concurrent chivalric fantasies of Don Quixote (ch. 16). The *Quixote* of 1605 is especially rich in such associative sequences, which provide insight into the inner workings of its composition, from the juxtaposed loves and penitences of Don Quixote and Cardenio to the similarly ill-advised obsessions of Cardenio and of Anselmo in "El curioso impertinente" (pt. 1, chs. 33–36), and the sundry ways in which personal interests conflict with social expectations in the entwined lives and tales of Cardenio, Dorotea, Lucinda, and Fernando.[4]

By addressing the *Quixote* of 1605 from this angle of how it engages, redeems—irony and parody aspire, after all, not simply to tear down but also to purify—and conjoins a series of modern genres that are usually held to be antithetical, insofar as some (*libros de caballerías*, pastoral novels, and Moorish novels) are said to be idealistic and others (the picaresque novel) to be realistic and moreover anti-idealistic, we see that a novelistic coherence both superintends and transcends the episodic structure or *sarta de relatos* ("string of tales") of traditional narrative, something that the deficient readers of part 1, who are figured as actors in part 2, patently fail to comprehend.

To facilitate this experimentation, Cervantes first shatters authorial authority, that is, the confidence instinctively given to the narrative voice as a reliable and omniscient force coming from within the author himself. In Don Quixote's second sally, beginning in part 1, chapter 7, a Moorish historian (Cide Hamete Benengeli), an amateur Morisco translator (found by chance in the marketplace of Toledo), and a nameless second author (whose opinions and habits humanize and therefore deauthorize him) all intervene between the action and the reader, creating not only distance but also doubt in regard to the truth of history. Lives are not merely told, as in the mainly one-voiced novels of the 1550s, but also

retold from different perspectives and with diverse intentions. In addition, because Sancho Panza is made the ostensible voice of reality, Don Quixote's claims
are opposed not to an impersonal authorial truth but to the more particular, and
often self-interested, words of another actor in the text. It is not by chance that
the narrators of the novels that emerged in Spain in the mid–sixteenth century
were, in whole or part, the protagonists themselves.

Thus, even as Cervantes systematically fragments the formal and ideological
homogeneity that Georg Lukács attributes to epic (34) and the monologic unity
that Mikhail Bakhtin attributes to the novel before Dostoevsky (but should instead attribute to all premodern writing), we see that there is a unity of another
sort in *Don Quixote*. This fundamental trait of all novels, both before and after
Cervantes, allows the hero to reveal his innate attributes, as in epic, and, more
important, calls attention to how his experiences transform him in some essential way.

The first readers of the *Quixote* of 1605 witnessed the development not only
of Don Quixote and Sancho but also of the novel itself. Don Quixote and Sancho continually change in the course of the novel, as does the reader's understanding of the novel as a genre. If in the beginning one sees Don Quixote as
an idealist and Sancho as a realist, in opposition to each other, and thinks that
the work's raison d'être is to stage a series of conflicts between Don Quixote's
dreams and his physical circumstances (or between art and life, ancient and
modern times, or any other fixed entities in a similarly Manichaean paradigm),
it eventually becomes apparent that the deeper structure and concerns of the
novel are otherwise.

For as the canon from Toledo notes (speaking of *libros de caballerías*), the
novel affords a "largo y espacioso campo por donde sin empacho alguno pudi-
ese correr la pluma" 'large and spacious field through which the pen might run
without constraint' (1: 620 [ch. 47]), so that a writer may treat a broad assort-
ment of themes and characters in all sort of modes (epic, lyric, tragic, comic).
By the time that the canon formulates these insights in his abstruse Aristotelian
terminology, calling agreement and harmony forms of beauty, and dispropor-
tion and depravity forms of ugliness, the attentive reader has already come to
see how Cervantes draws on extant forms of fiction to enhance the beautiful
and strip away the ugly to attain the poetic ideal of combined instruction and
entertainment.[5] In reworking genres such as the pastoral novel, the *Quixote* of
1605 does not merely attend to the artistic flaws that Cervantes or his characters
point out in the course of his works.[6] It also addresses a more essential moral de-
ficiency: that pastoral protagonists are normally absolved of the obligation that
all human beings have, which is to find a solution to their troubles by availing
themselves of their reason and free will.[7] Cervantes would explicitly redress this
problematic feature of pastoral literature in his own fictions. Inasmuch as the
revision of other genres in the *Quixote* of 1605 is guided by the same coherent
set of artistic and moral principles, the result of combining these genres is not
a chimera or hodgepodge but instead a polyphonic novel: one in which distinct

modes of discourse serve a collective critical purpose. Because of such changes to fictions traditionally despised as useless or pernicious, all three censors of the *Quixote* of 1615 praised Cervantes's novel for this difficult achievement and for enfolding the castigation of faults within the delight of wit in order to attract those readers most in need of correction (see Boruchoff, "Cervantes").

To bring these developments into focus, I usually ask students to write an essay explaining how two characters in part 1 (excluding Don Quixote and Sancho) intervene after chapter 20 to alter not only the course and nature of the action but also the idea that the reader of 1605 might have had of the novel as a literary genre. I ask them to think empirically about the work before the appearance of these characters and to consider how these characters open new formal and critical possibilities for the novel as it was imagined by Cervantes.

This appreciation of Cervantes's achievement is deepened by the response of the actors figured in the *Quixote* of 1615. While Sansón Carrasco presents a picture of part 1 based on its first chapters alone—citing only the windmills, the fulling mills, the armies of goats and sheep, the dead body, the galley slaves, and the fight with the Basque, in other words citing Don Quixote's armed exploits only as far as chapter 22—and dismisses the *Curioso impertinente* as having nothing to do with the history of Don Quixote (pt. 2, ch. 3), the duke and duchess illustrate the consequence of this blinkered reading of Cervantes's novel as a funny book grounded in physical encounters alone, one designed to entertain but not edify, when they cruelly treat its heroes as comic playthings. In contrast, Don Quixote underscores the moral and Christian values that have always guided his endeavor. Reprising his address on the golden age, he reminds the priest and barber, and thus the reader, at the outset of the *Quixote* of 1615 that knight-errantry is necessary to redress the evils wrought by the dissipation of modern society (ch. 1). Chiding his niece, he also contrasts knights-errant and courtiers, stating that virtue and self-sacrifice trump lineage and comfort and should thus be more greatly esteemed (ch. 6). He concludes, in terms reminiscent of his speech on arms and letters (pt. 1, chs. 37–38), that he is inclined by nature to follow the narrow and laborious path of Mars, "y por él tengo de ir a pesar de todo el mundo" 'and I must go down it, despite the whole world' in order to attain the life "que no tendrá fin" 'that will have no end' (78 [pt. 2, ch. 6]). This obviously Christian formulation of chivalric endeavor continues as Don Quixote and Sancho depart home with a discussion of the distinction between *fama gloriosa* and *vanagloria* ("true glory" and "false glory"), a discussion that equates knights-errant and saints and culminates in Don Quixote's astute remark that "no todos podemos ser frailes, y muchos son los caminos por donde lleva Dios a los suyos al cielo; religión es la caballería, caballeros santos hay en la gloria" 'we cannot all be friars, and there are many paths by which God leads his own to heaven; chivalry is a religion, and there are sainted knights in glory' (95 [ch. 8]).

Because these assertions appear at the start of part 2, one cannot help but see them as Cervantes's response to the improper way that part 1 was read: as a work of entertainment alone and not also of instruction. The equation of knight-errantry and Christian endeavor continues throughout the *Quixote* of 1615. At the table of the duke and duchess, Don Quixote answers the cleric's disapproval of his profession by asking in pointedly apostolic conceits, "¿Por ventura es asunto vano o es tiempo mal gastado el que se gasta en vagar por el mundo, no buscando los regalos dél, sino las asperezas por donde los buenos suben al asiento de la inmortalidad?" 'Is it perchance a vain pursuit or time misspent to wander the world seeking, not its pleasures but the rough patches by way of which the good ascend to the seat of immortality?' (297 [ch. 32]). On leaving the castle, he calls Saints George, Martin, James, and Paul "los mejores andantes que tuvo la milicia divina" 'the best knights-errant that the divine militia possessed' and "de los más valientes santos y caballeros que tuvo el mundo y que tiene agora el cielo" 'among the bravest saints and knights that the world once had and now heaven has' (507 [ch. 58]). One must conclude that Cervantes's intention is now to censure not the faults of earlier fiction but the inability of modern readers to grasp the nature of the modern novel. This conclusion, facilitated in the design of my course by studying the *Quixote* of 1605 in the first semester and the *Quixote* of 1615 in the second, further highlights Cervantes's importance as a transitional figure at the dawn of early modernity. For if, in the *Quixote* of 1605, innovation was inspired by a retrospective gaze on the mainly single-voiced novels of the mid–sixteenth century, in the *Quixote* of 1615 Cervantes instead looks to the future, confident in the multivoiced novel that would henceforth prevail.

NOTES

[1] The term *chivalric* may be misleading in that the fictions at issue recount *caballerías* ("deeds performed by a knight"), while paying little attention to the institution of chivalry (*la caballería*), which was already passé at the end of the sixteenth century, save for its affinities to broader political and social ideals. I therefore refer in what follows to Don Quixote's readings as *libros de caballerías*, using the Spanish term alone.

[2] *Rinconete y Cortadillo* and *La ilustre fregona* are read to bring into focus Cervantes's critical engagement with picaresque fiction, the Counter-Reformation doctrine of free will, and the theme of freedom more generally, issues that I examine in "Free Will, the Picaresque." *La gran sultana* and *Los baños de Argel* instead illustrate the conditions and concerns of Mediterranean captivity literature. The English titles *The Illustrious Kitchen-Maid* or *The Illustrious Scullery-Maid*, conventionally given to *La ilustre fregona*, are inaccurate. The verb *fregar* has the broader sense of "to scour," for which a *fregona* is a cleaning or scrubwoman in general. Because the character in question does not in fact scrub anything, this appellation is ironic, as is the adjective *ilustre*, a term reserved not simply for famous personages, but for the highborn. *Los baños de Argel*, normally translated as *The Baths of Algiers* or *The Bagnios of Algiers*, refers to the enclosures in which the Moors of North Africa confined their captives, especially those captives who might bring a large ransom. To Spanish Christians of Cervantes's time, neither *bath* nor *bagnio* conveys the same narrow and decidedly menacing sense of the original term.

3 All translations of primary sources cited in this essay are my own. One should note that Grisóstomo's motive for becoming a shepherd (to pursue his beloved) is socially more acceptable than that of Marcela, who instead seeks to delay or escape marriage and be free.

4 This associative method is still at work, although less conspicuous, in the *Quixote* of 1615. In chapters 18–21, the sonnet about Pyramus and Thisbe, by Don Diego's son, is followed by the tale of Basilio and Quiteria, which explicitly recalls "los ya olvidados amores de Píramo y Tisbe" 'the now forgotten love of Pyramus and Thisbe' (186 [pt. 2, ch. 19]) even as it inverts the tragic ending of Ovid's fable. Whereas suicide brings Pyramus and Thisbe together in death, the feigned suicide of Basilio unites him with Quiteria in marriage.

5 This ideal is famously set forth by Horace in *Ars poetica*, lines 343–44: "omne tulit punctum qui miscuit utile dulci, / lectorem delectando pariterque monendo" 'he who mingles the useful with the sweet wins every vote, / equally delighting and admonishing the reader.'

6 The *Quixote* of 1605 provides a biographical rationale for the learning evident in the poetry and speech of Grisóstomo, Marcela, and their fellow shepherds. Cervantes concedes in the prologue to *La Galatea* that true shepherds "pocas veces se levantan a más que a tratar cosas del campo, y esto con su acostumbrada llaneza" 'rarely rise to treating anything more than country matters, and this with their habitual plainness.' However, he continues, in both classical and modern works of fiction, many shepherds "lo eran sólo en el hábito" 'were [shepherds] only in dress' (158). Similar observations about the inverisimilitude of pastoral conventions are expressed by Berganza in *El coloquio de los perros* (*Novelas ejemplares* 2: 307–09). The criticism directed at *La Diana* in chapter 6 of the *Quixote* of 1605 is different. The presence of "la sabia Felicia y . . . la agua encantada" 'the wisewoman Felicia . . . and the enchanted water' (157 [pt. 1, ch. 6]) is a moral rather than artistic concern, insofar as it exempts other actors in Montemayor's novel from the duty to resolve their own problems (Boruchoff, "Free Will, Beauty").

7 On Cervantes's response in *La Galatea* and the *Quixote* of 1605 to the moral faults of pastoral fiction, see Boruchoff, "Free Will, Beauty."

Scientific and Technological Imagery in *Don Quixote*

Cory A. Reed

Technological imagery and references to science, pervasive in *Don Quixote*, evidence Cervantes's appreciation of the seventeenth century as a time of profound epistemological change. For teachers, the many images of science and technology in the novel present an opportunity to discuss the *Quixote* in the context of social tension and crisis, enriching the understanding of the novel's historical background while also encouraging comparisons with the role of technology as an agent of progress in our time. Don Quixote, a madman who seeks to live his life according to the code of a fictional system of medieval knighthood (based on the chivalric romances he reads), cannot comprehend aspects of the modern world that do not correspond to his outdated conception of society. Cervantes employs technology, scientific innovation, and the related concept of *ingenio* (the celebration of human ingenuity and of the creative imagination) as metaphors for modernity that force the protagonist to face the fact that he is an anachronism.

The iconic adventure of the windmills (pt. 1, ch. 8) is so well known that it has come to define the essence of the quixotic. Students, when polled on what comes to mind when they first think of *Don Quixote*, invariably point to this episode whether or not they have read the book. The protagonist's violent encounter with the revolving mechanical arms of the windmills resonates with students: it demonstrates the hero's disastrous attempt to imitate escapist, chivalric fiction; it comments on the illusory nature of reality and human perception; and it establishes the conflict of worldviews of Don Quixote and Sancho Panza that drives their relationship as the story progresses. On a level less familiar to students, the adventure depicts a battle between the would-be knight and a type of modern technology that represents not only the mundane, capitalistic values unknown to him but also the beginnings of what would later be called the scientific revolution—roughly speaking, the period of scientific and technological advancement and the rise of empiricism throughout Europe beginning in the early modern period (Shapin 2–3).

The encounter with the windmills contrasts an outmoded, scholastic worldview that localizes truth in the written word with a worldview that assumes an empirical basis for what exists. Don Quixote, who lives in and through the books he reads, relies on their textual authority for his interpretation of the events that shape his daily life. For him, truth is determined by the printed word, and his selection of literary fiction as his primary reference creates the confusion of fantasy and reality that characterizes his madness. Sancho Panza defends the actual world of sixteenth- and seventeenth-century Spain, a world of windmills, artillery, fulling mills, printing presses, mechanical contraptions, and political and economic systems that have neither precedent nor explanation in chivalric literature. Lost in a world of long ago that never existed, the anachronistic knight meets obstacles at every turn as he pursues his noble project of reviving the science "de la caballería" 'of knight errantry' (2: 177 [ch. 18]; 570) and the preindustrial, utopian golden age.

Cervantes composed his novel while Spain, like Don Quixote, was struggling with the inconsistencies of a text-based, scholastic understanding of the world and fighting the inevitable forward march of empiricism and modernity. The new Copernican cosmology's challenge to the geocentric universe, the rise of humanism, the development of mechanics, and the modern nation-state's consolidation of political power all informed not only Don Quixote's world but also the changing reality of seventeenth-century Spain. Historians and literary scholars identify the end of the sixteenth century as a transition between the glory days of the Spanish Empire and the period of decadence to follow (Maravall, *Culture* 19–53; Elliott 221). José María López Piñero describes the last decades of the sixteenth century as a period of tension between receptivity to new ideas and self-conscious closure, culminating in the triumph of a conservative and reactionary Counter-Reformation mentality (19). By the beginning of the seventeenth century, Spanish thought increasingly looked to the past, ignoring modern advancements while Europe forged ahead with its scientific revolution (23). Like Don Quixote, Spain took a deliberate step back.

Thomas S. Kuhn describes epistemic change as a paradigm shift. For Kuhn, a paradigm is a system of accepted theories and practices designated as normative in a given era (10). When the tenets of normal science can no longer explain observable phenomena, the crisis that results is resolved by either the amplification of the normal science or the emergence of a new paradigm and a battle over its acceptance (84). The scientific revolution was a paradigm shift in its reordering of thinking, the mechanization of nature and knowledge, the rise of empiricism to replace scholasticism, the destruction of Aristotelian cosmology, and the application of methodical approaches to nearly all fields of human endeavor. The philosophical, political, and spiritual ramifications of these developments contributed to the intellectual change that was openly debated in Cervantes's time and resisted by Counter-Reformation conservatism.

Don Quixote cannot comprehend the change at first but then gradually accedes to the modern world, learning "tocar las apariencias con la mano para dar lugar al desengaño" 'to touch appearances with one's hand to avoid being deceived' (2: 117 [ch. 11]; 523–24) as he relinquishes the medieval episteme he fought to revive. He begins as a one-dimensional parody of the medieval knight, out of place in a new world, but as the novel progresses, he increasingly embodies the conflict between medieval and modern. Along this path of transition, his confrontations with machines become turning points in the development of his character.

References to science and technology are too numerous in *Don Quixote* to list in this essay, but the three interdependent episodes that involve milling are among the most accessible to students and can be used to illustrate the overall movement of Don Quixote's character from *engañado* ("deceived by illusory appearances") to *desengañado* ("undeceived"), from madman to frustrated idealist, from certainty to self-doubt and ultimate disillusionment. The adventure of the windmills, the episode of the *batanes* (pt. 1, ch. 20; "fulling mills," water wheels retrofitted with hammers to flatten textiles), and the water mills of the enchanted boat adventure (pt. 2, ch. 29) outline his paradigm shift as he comes to realize that his chivalric model cannot explain the modern world. His original belief system (as expressed during the adventure of the windmills) develops tension between vision and empirical reality (the *batanes* episode) and finally articulates a crisis that demonstrates the necessity of a paradigm change to account for new phenomena (the enchanted boat adventure). The windmill technology shows how his view of the world is antiquated even though he persists in holding to it. In the episode of the fulling mills, he does not hallucinate but recognizes the impersonal functioning of modern machinery; indeed, he makes an explicit comparison with the windmills episode in an attempt to assert the validity of his views even after the inadequacy of his actions becomes apparent. By the end of the enchanted boat episode, machinery marks his complete frustration with the "máquinas y trazas" 'tricks and deceptions' of the modern world (2: 279 [ch. 29]; 652) and the impossibility of addressing modern complexity through his chivalric model.

In the windmills adventure, technology defeats the knight when the passive machine, having no connection to either providence or heroism, literally turns him and his medieval worldview upside down. Windmills, machines built for the purpose of grinding grain for sale in the marketplace, represent not only modern technology and its mechanization of the natural environment but also the capitalism that burgeoned throughout Europe during the early modern period. The specific type of windmill in this episode, with a rotating cap and tilting arm alignment designed to capture prevailing winds, was an improvement on earlier models and among the most modern machines known to Cervantes. In short, windmills were the high tech of the sixteenth century. By defeating the hapless knight, they dramatize the ascendancy of the modern over the medieval, of capitalism over feudalism, and of empiricism over fiction. The windmill, an icon of the modern world that Don Quixote desperately will try to understand throughout the novel, is one of its purest symbols of the paradigm shift.

The episode of the windmills shows how Don Quixote in his madness interprets reality according to the rules of chivalric fiction and refuses to learn from his mistakes. One result of a paradigm in crisis is that any data that do not conform to the prevailing belief system are ignored or disregarded as irrelevant (Kuhn 84). Don Quixote's comment to Sancho, "que no estás cursado en esto de las aventuras" '. . . thou art not well-versed in the matter of adventures' (1: 166

[ch. 8]; 58), exemplifies this behavior. Instead of recognizing that his theoretical premises need to be reevaluated, Don Quixote explains contradictory data in terms of the preexisting model.

Don Quixote's second encounter with technology, during the adventure of the *batanes*, demonstrates Kuhn's second point, that continued acquaintance with anomalies gradually leads to awareness of the model's inadequacies, even when no new paradigm is yet available to replace it (76). This episode contains "seis jayanes" 'six giants' (1: 289 [ch. 20]; 151) and lofty claims of chivalric destiny. In dialogue with the windmills adventure, it indicates the beginning of a change in the knight's engagement with the modern world. Experience creates a crisis in his fantastical episteme for the first time, and Don Quixote is forced to acknowledge what his senses report to him. He speaks of the importance of experience, calling it "la madre de las ciencias todas" 'the mother of all knowledge' (1: 293 [ch. 21]; 153), and begins to recognize the challenge that the modern world presents to his revival of the golden age, a project that Sancho mocks at the end of this chapter. In part 2 of the novel, Don Quixote further develops this recognition of the importance of experience, concluding that it is necessary "to touch appearances with one's hand to avoid being deceived."

In the third episode involving milling technology, the adventure of the enchanted boat, Don Quixote takes a significant step toward *desengaño*, in that he resigns himself to defeat at the hands of modernity. He expresses frustration with his chivalric paradigm, now expressed in his belief that he is caught between two enchanters at odds with each other. He concludes that the world itself is a series of opposing forces that render him helpless: "Dios lo remedie; que todo este mundo es máquinas y trazas, contrarias unas de otras. Yo no puedo más" 'God help us, for the entire world is nothing but tricks and deceptions opposing one another. I can do no more' (2: 279 [ch. 29]; 652). Faced with the complexity of the changing world around him, he retreats into fantasy once again, only to find that it too is inadequate. He is saying, in effect, "I give up." This episode, involving the oldest form of milling technology, begins the final breakdown of his paradigm, as he realizes that he can no longer explain the world in chivalric terms. From this point, we see a worn and introspective Don Quixote who is repeatedly abused and defeated by those around him, and eventually, in the final chapter, he renounces chivalry on his deathbed.

Don Quixote's path toward disillusionment is paved with many encounters with technology. Some examples are his ongoing diatribe against the evils of artillery, most notably during his speech on arms and letters (pt. 1, chs. 27–38). Condemning the "maldita(s) máquina(s)" and "endemoniados instrumentos de la artillería" 'damned machine(s)' and 'diabolical instruments of artillery' (1: 521 [ch. 38]; 352) responsible for the demise of knights-errant, Don Quixote advances a common opinion in an age when technological advancement outpaces the rest of society: that machines and technology are inherently evil and can bring about the downfall of civilized existence or traditional norms. In his depiction of artillery as a "diabólica invención" 'diabolical invention' (521; 352), he raises a question that students recognize as relevant to their time: What is the role of technology when it surpasses our moral ability to evaluate it?

Don Quixote has numerous adventures, mostly in part 2, with ingenious mechanical contraptions, including the theatrical *tramoyas* ("stage machinery") of the puppeteer Maese Pedro (ch. 26); Clavileño, a mechanical horse whose imaginary flight is narrated in the context of flaws in the medieval conception of cosmology (ch. 41); and a speaking automaton in the adventure of the enchanted head (a representation of a renaissance *lusus scientiae*, a parlor joke based on scientific or technical knowledge [ch. 62]). Each of these machines, in its own way, deconstructs Don Quixote's belief system for the reader, reducing its key elements, such as enchantment, to technological innovation and human *ingenio*. These adventures celebrate a festive attitude toward human ingenuity while articulating an elusive connection between deceit and artful illusion that comments on how truth is revealed through fiction (Reed 193, 212). Don Quixote's final encounter with a printing press in the urban center of Barcelona reveals that books themselves, the authoritative source of truth in his chivalric world, are produced for a consumer market in which the written word is now dependent on modern technology for its dissemination.

By the end of part 2, Don Quixote realizes that experience and observation are keys to understanding the empirical world and that there is no place for him in that world. Cervantes articulates an epistemological contrast between conflicting eras, in part through the use of technological images as metaphors of change. The protagonist's confrontations with various machines depict a time of modernization in which Spain, like Don Quixote, was struggling with the inconsistencies of a text-based, scholastic understanding of the world and resisting the inevitable embrace of empiricism and modernity.

NOTE

The English translation of *Don Quixote* used is by Edith Grossman.

Reading Gender in *Don Quixote*

Lisa Vollendorf

In part 1, chapter 13, of *Don Quixote*, approximately one hundred pages into the knight's adventures, the shepherdess Marcela stands on a hilltop and proclaims, "Yo nací libre, y para poder vivir libre escogí la soledad de los campos" 'I was born free, and in order to live free I chose the solitude of the countryside' (224; 99). Her rejection of marital, sexual, and gender norms awakens readers to the implications and intricacies of Cervantes's depiction of social control. Until this point, many students enjoy *Don Quixote* but do not connect personally to the text. Demographics and social context likely account for the connection: women earn more than half of all bachelor's degrees in the United States today, and majors in the humanities draw a disproportionate percentage of those women. Because many urban universities have experienced a significant increase in Hispanic enrollments, *Quixote* classrooms might be as high as 90% Latina. But all of us, men and women, live in an age informed by the civil rights and women's rights battles of the 1960s and 1970s. Marcela's struggle with marriage and gender expectations therefore speaks to students with a force that perhaps is unprecedented in the history of higher education.

As instructors of *Don Quixote*, we have the opportunity to educate students about the wealth of historical, cultural, and literary topics woven into the text and to bring recent knowledge about seventeenth-century Iberia to the *Quixote* classroom. We therefore have the opportunity to teach Cervantes's novel differently, taking advantage of the rich body of scholarship on women, gender, and cultural minorities in early modern Spain now available; and to learn from our students in the process.[1]

A word of caution is merited here: *Don Quixote* offers so many possibilities for interpretation that I take particular pains not to privilege gendered analyses in the classroom. Nonetheless, undergraduate and graduate students often ask if Cervantes was a feminist. Who but a feminist could depict women's plights with such sympathy? Their reasoning echoes that of many scholars. Fanny Rubio, a Spanish author, identified numerous characters (in particular, Marcela and Zoraida) as modern, prefeminist women (xvii–xxiii). Yet recent research on early modern Spain has shown that what matters is not whether certain people in the period were feminist but how women and men responded to the complex forces that shaped early modern Iberia. Asking this broader question has radically altered our understanding of gender issues in the period.

Perhaps more than any other literary piece from early modern Spain, *Don Quixote* represents the rapidly shifting roles of women. Ambitious in its depiction of that change — and of society's response — the *Quixote* integrates gender, class, religion, and ethnicity into its fabric. We now understand that, at the time Cervantes wrote, the shift to a mercantile economy, the Counter-Reformation emphasis on convent foundation, and the wealth brought in by an empire in full swing made women more active in economic, cultural, and political spheres. Women inserted themselves into traditionally male fields: wealthy women became influential patrons of religion and the arts, some widows inherited men's guild memberships, and single women ran printing presses in Salamanca and other cities. The increase of convents was accompanied by the founding by women of numerous schools for girls. But women also continued to earn their living as they had for centuries, working as midwives, sex workers, farmers, community counselors, and vendors.[2]

Instructors can benefit from exposing students to emerging knowledge about women in early modern Spain. That knowledge, when brought to bear on discussions about all aspects of the text, will help students appreciate Cervantes's deeply thoughtful engagement with his rapidly changing society.

Gender in Don Quixote

Don Quixote has been read in many different ways over the centuries. The most prominent gendered reading of the text from the past few decades is to see Don Quixote as a middle-aged gentleman unable to meet the social expectations placed on him. Proponents of this reading include Carroll Johnson, whose psychoanalytic *Madness and Lust* highlighted the woebegone knight's sublimated sexuality and his inability to live the normal life of a hidalgo in seventeenth-century, honor-obsessed Spain.

The text offers numerous examples of frustrated masculinity. In the first chapter, we learn that a hidalgo of La Mancha hunts wild game—as would be expected—yet lacks an elegant estate, a wife, and children. Although a bachelor, Don Quixote advises others about marriage and gives an exegesis on inner and outer beauty while explaining Altisidora's behavior to Sancho (2: 510 [ch. 58]; 836). The theme of marriage and children is woven into Don Quixote's adventure primarily through Sancho and his family, but it also emerges several times as an important failing of the protagonist. The second priest becomes so irritated with Don Quixote that he explicitly makes the connection between family and a man's appropriate place in the world:

> Andad enhorabuena, y en tal se os diga: volveos a vuestra casas, y criad vuestros hijos, si los tenéis, y curad de vuestra hacienda, y dejad de andar vagando por el mundo, papando viento y dando que reír a cuantos os conocen y no conocen.   (2: 295 [ch. 31])

> Go now in peace, and in peace I shall say to you: return to your home, and rear your children, if you have any, and tend to your estate, and stop wandering the world and wasting your time and being a laughingstock to all who know you and all who do not.   (665)

Normative masculinity for a hidalgo dictates that Don Quixote have an estate and a family to attend to.

After Sancho has left for his long-promised governorship, Don Quixote sits alone in his room at the ducal palace and laments his ripped green stockings. The narrative voice of Cide Hamete Benengeli intrudes here:

> ¡Miserable del bien nacido que va dando pistos a su honra, comiendo mal y a puerta cerrada, haciendo hipócrita al palillo de dientes con que sale a la calle después de no haber comido cosa que le obligue a limpiárselos! ¡Miserable de aquel, digo, que tiene la honra espantadiza . . . !
> (2: 391 [ch. 44])

> How wretched is the wellborn man who nurtures his honor by eating badly, behind a closed door, playing the hypocrite with the toothpick he wields when he goes out after not having eaten anything that would oblige him to clean his teeth! How wretched is he, I say, who is apprehensive about his honor. . . .   (742)

Benengeli's comment reminds readers of the pressures faced by Don Quixote vis-à-vis social class: the quest for the ever-elusive Dulcinea is accompanied by Alonso Quijano's meager home life.

This focus on masculinity is complemented by women's concerns in part 1 as Marcela and other female characters assert their independence and deal with compromised positions. Numerous characters address the pressure to marry that faces both men and women, for example. Whereas the second priest at the ducal palace demands that Don Quixote return home to attend to his wife and children, if he has any (pt. 1, ch. 34), Dorotea and Lucinda seek redress through marriage for the wrongs men have done to them. By leading students to read these and other episodes with an eye to gender norms, we deepen their understanding of the text's engagement with the social control that defined the early modern period and help them decipher the critiques embedded in the representations of the priest, the barber, the housekeeper, and the niece, all of whom act to control Alonso Quijano and contain the madcap adventures of Don Quixote.

Scholarship on masculinity and male identity has far outpaced critical attention to women and femininity. Exceptions to this rule are articles on some of the prominent female characters: the intriguingly independent Marcela (Jehenson), the assertive Teresa Panza (Ciallella), the elusive Aldonza Lorenzo (Langle de Paz), and the enigmatic Muslim convert Zoraida (Brownlee, "Zoraida's White Hand"; Fuchs, *Passing* 68; Garcés 182–232; Johnson, *Cervantes* 71–92). Readings of the feminine (Cruz, "Cervantes"; El Saffar, *Beyond Fiction*), of feminist allegiances with Cervantes (Cruz, "Cervantes"), and of cultural anxieties about gender (Martín, "Maritornes"; Velasco, *Lesbians* and "*Marimachos*") have framed feminist approaches to the text.

Yet women have generally not been a focal point of Cervantine criticism. Often they are analyzed as ancillary characters vis-à-vis their relationships with Don Quixote or Sancho. But when we raise awareness about gender in *Don Quixote,* we equip students to understand the text's broader theme of how social control affected individuals and groups in the early modern period.

Women in a Changing Society: Literacy and Economic Activity

Relation to the written word links many of the complex representations of women in the text. One of the finest examples of a female character whose relation to literature defines her life choices is Marcela. A female double to Alonso Quijano, she escapes social control by enacting a literary identity. The text never explicitly states that Marcela chose the pastoral life on the basis of texts she had read (or heard read), so it is possible that she saw no other option outside the convent or marriage. Regardless of the character's consciousness of the literary nature of her choice, readers in Cervantes's time understood that by living alone in the hills as a shepherdess she was positioned somewhere between literature and life.

Marcela's connection to literature highlights women's role as readers and points to the intensified relation to the written word that women enjoyed in Cervantes's lifetime. Research on literacy has changed our understanding dramatically in recent years, for we now know that reading and writing were taught as separate skills and also that women's ability to read or write may have reached forty percent in some urban areas and may have been completely absent in some rural areas (Cátedra and Rojo 42–43; Baranda Leturio 17–33). Pedro Cátedra and Anastasio Rojo's work on wills and inventories of expenses shows that families of lower social ranks paid for the education of girls, albeit less than what they paid to educate boys, and suggests that such an investment gave young women access to better jobs and more advantageous marriages (58–61). The historians have uncovered evidence that some women could read but not sign their names, others had literacy skills that allowed them to keep the books for family businesses, and still others earned their living as teachers of girls (59–63). Along with the proliferation of women writers in Spain after Teresa de Ávila's texts were popularized in the late sixteenth century, such data suggest that female literacy may have been a marriage-making tool among the lower and merchant classes and that the education of girls was more widespread than previously believed (Vollendorf 169–86). Anne J. Cruz and Rosilie Hernández's *Women's Literacy in Early Modern Spain and the New World* expands methodologies for examining women's relation to the written word through examinations of book dedications, libraries, convent culture, literary texts, and the visual arts.

Cervantes has many literate female characters, including the niece, Marcela, Lucinda, Dorotea, Zoraida, Camila, and the duchess. Women's illiteracy is connected primarily to the lower classes. That the housekeeper, Teresa Panza, and

Aldonza Lorenzo do not know how to read or write marks them as outsiders in a novel based on novels. Most characters have access to the written word, as people did in the early seventeenth century. Dependent on the literate men and women around them, the illiterate characters (including Teresa and Maritornes) hear letters and literature read aloud. Some ask others to write letters on their behalf, as in the comic epistolary exchanges between Teresa and the duchess in part 2. For many readers, the funniest exchange of letters is that between Sancho and Teresa, two illiterate characters whose mediated written conversation provides insight into class aspirations and spousal negotiations.

The descriptions of the stronger-than-an-ox Aldonza Lorenzo and of Teresa Panza as an active partner in her marriage to Sancho resonate with recent research on rural women in early modern Spain. Allyson Poska's work on women in Galicia, for instance, concludes that rural women in that area of high emigration to the Americas found themselves in the position of being strong participants in the economic and domestic spheres. The Galician evidence suggests that women made and broke partner allegiances with relative ease, shunned traditional marriage as overly restrictive, and played a major role in local economies. Poska opines that Galicia's society may well have been matriarchal (1–21). Note that Teresa Panza simply informs Sancho about her choice of husband for their daughter. She also emphatically states her opposition to Sancho's social-climbing tendencies, urging him to stay home rather than try to become a governor and marry Sanchica off to someone of higher status. And, like most other women of her social standing, she cannot read the letters delivered to her. By exposing students to research about rural women and asking them to consider the representation of Teresa as a headstrong, equal partner in her marriage to Sancho, we can help them probe both the stereotypes and social changes in the text.

Cervantes also embeds in *Don Quixote* women's newly complicated position in the populations forced to convert to Catholicism. The captive's tale (pt. 1, chs. 39–42) highlights the participation of the Algerian Zoraida, whose servant purportedly taught her about Catholicism and prompted her conversion. Zoraida is the first subaltern, non-Christian woman of the text. Her betrayal of her father enables the captive's escape to Spain, where she undergoes a radical transformation. On her home territory, Zoraida is a wealthy, articulate woman in charge of her destiny, but in Spain she speaks no Spanish and joins the population of Muslim converts to Christianity. Cervantes's inscription of the uncertain fate of the Moriscos, more specifically of the Moriscas, finds its echo in part 2 of *Don Quixote*, which, published six years after the 1609 expulsion of the Moriscos, repeatedly references the effects of that expulsion on individuals and on the nation. The Moorish character Ricote returns with Christian pilgrims to claim his buried treasure. Ricote's appearance as a wine-drinking convert from Islam is complicated by his insistence that his daughter and wife are actually true Christians, which intimates that he is not. Ricote's daughter, Ana Félix, appears later in the novel and is reunited with her father (pt. 2, ch. 56). The most interesting aspect of the reunification of Catholic and Islamic Spain is Ana Félix's union with the Christian captive Don Gregorio. This episode draws parallels with the first captive's union with the Muslim Zoraida and also relates to the roles played by some Moriscas both in keeping their family traditions alive and in helping persecuted families survive (Perry, *Handless Maiden* 1–18).[3] The emphasis on religious conversion in Zoraida's tale contrasts sharply with Ana Félix's devotion to family in ways that could provoke interesting classroom discussion about the choices faced by early modern Muslims in an age of religious intolerance. We might argue that the Ana Félix story affirms the need for unification of the country by integrating the expelled. At the same time, it acknowledges the role of women in the cultural survival of the convert populations.

Women and Gender in Don Quixote

A focus on women and gender in *Don Quixote* reveals that Cervantes masterfully weaves Spain's homogenizing impulses into his text in ways that make explicit the pressure of that homogenization on individuals and groups. Because research shows women's active participation in the economic, cultural, religious, and political workings of early modern Spain, it is clear that Cervantes had a keen understanding of that participation and included it in his representation of Spanish society. For example, he refers frequently to Aldonza Lorenzo (whom Sancho calls the best salter of pork in all of La Mancha [pt. 1, ch. 9]); to the innkeeper's wife, who runs the family business; and to the sex business of Maritornes. On the cultural front, we see women represented as consumers of culture (principally as readers) and as producers of culture (as seen in the enactments of pastoral and other literary identities by Marcela and Dorotea). On the political front, the duchess's intellectual prowess and orchestration of events resonates with research on powerful aristocratic women who exerted great political influence and engaged in patronage (such as María de Guevara and the Mendoza women).[4]

The focus on women's history in the early modern period has led to new understandings of that rapidly changing time. As instructors, we should bring that new knowledge to bear on our students' interpretations of the text. We may never be able to answer the question of whether Cervantes was a feminist, but we can invite our students to consider the rich engagement with issues of gender and social control that appear in *Don Quixote*.

NOTES

I wish to thank Barbara Simerka and James A. Parr for their insightful comments on this essay. The English translation of *Don Quixote* used in this essay is by Edith Grossman.

[1] Data on the gender divide in higher education vary, but the National Center for Education Statistics shows that in 2013 women received 57% of all bachelor degrees (*Degrees*). Marklein noted in 2010 that some experts predict a rise to 59%. Also see Pollard.

[2] In the late 1980s and early 1990s, numerous studies focused on women's participation in the economies and literary cultures of early modern Spain. Among them were Electa Arenal and Stacey Schlau's *Untold Sisters*; Mary Elizabeth Perry's *Gender and Disorder in Early Modern Seville*; Magdalena Sánchez's *The Empress, the Queen, and the Nun*; and Alison Weber's *Teresa of Ávila and the Rhetoric of Femininity*. Those studies laid the groundwork for later scholarship—for example, Elizabeth Lehfeldt's *Religious Women in Golden Age Spain*; Allyson Poska's *Women and Authority in Early Modern Spain*; Nieves Romero-Díaz's *Nueva nobleza, nueva novela*; Sherry Velasco's *Lesbians in Early Modern Spain*; and Lisa Vollendorf's *The Lives of Women*.

[3] Recent scholarship, probing the connection between the rise of intolerance toward Judaism and Islam on the Peninsula and women's changing roles in the affected populations, suggests that women in both groups, conversos and Morsicos, worked to protect cultural and religious traditions (Perry, *The Handless Maiden*; Starr-LeBeau).

[4] Nieves Romero-Díaz provides a fine synthesis of aristocratic women's influence in early modern Spain in her translation of María de Guevara's *Warnings to the Kings* (*Warnings* 1–49).

Spain and the Moors

Barbara Fuchs

From its narrative voice to its generic intertexts to the fantasies of its protagonist, *Don Quixote* engages with the problem of Spain's Moorishness at every level. Through a multifaceted engagement, the text considers the place of Moors within Spain in the violent and tragic aftermath of the fall of Granada. Cervantes thus crafts a variety of literary responses to the pressing political problem of Morisco assimilation in the period.

Over the course of the sixteenth century, Spain tried with mixed success to assimilate the Moriscos (or *nuevos convertidos de moros*, Muslims who had been forcibly converted to Christianity) and their descendants, while ostracizing their culture and language. The years immediately after the fall of Granada in 1492 were particularly uncertain. The guarantees of religious freedom offered to the Muslims at their surrender were quickly violated by the Spanish victors, and the ensuing revolts became a justification for more repressive measures. By 1502, a royal decree stipulating that all inhabitants of Castile must be Christians had voided the terms stipulated at Granada as well as older protections for the various Mudéjar communities of Castile (Harvey, *Muslims* 21–22). The culturally sensitive approach to proselytism favored by Archbishop Hernando de Talavera, who advocated preaching in Arabic, was replaced by a far more militant approach under Inquisitor General Archbishop Francisco de Cisneros. Muslims soon gave up their violent resistance to the conversions and instead turned increasingly to the covert practice of Islam. An important fatwa issued in Oran in 1504 offered guidance for devout Muslims on how to live as forced converts, through dissimulation and an internalized faith (60–64). By 1526, the Kingdom of Aragon had joined Castile in forcing Muslims to convert. As L. P. Harvey points out, "After 1526 there were certainly many Muslims in Spain, but they all had to be *crypto*-Muslims, and the public profession of faith (*idhan*), an act of such crucial importance in Islam, could no longer be heard in the land" (101).

From the 1520s through the 1560s, legislation against Moriscos was softened by means of bribes, as Muslims agreed to accept baptism and pay a heavy tax so that they could postpone scrutiny by the Inquisition into the real measure of their conversion. This accommodation became increasingly fragile as the century wore on, and Old Christians grew skeptical about any progress in the assimilation of the Moriscos. As the earlier accords expired, the crown passed ever more repressive legislation against Morisco cultural practices, including even the use of Arabic and Moorish names. This time, Morisco leaders were unable to secure postponement, and the legislation led to a violent uprising in the mountains of the Alpujarras (1568–71), which was put down only after heavy fighting and widespread destruction. The defeated were in many cases enslaved, and all Moriscos from Granada, with the exception of a very few noble families, were forcibly resettled throughout Castile.

Scholars disagree on the degree of assimilation that was achieved through acculturation and intermarriage during this period. Irrespective of the degree, the recalcitrant, devious Morisco became a reviled stereotype and an easy target for polemicists who argued that Moriscos, given their insincere faith, posed a religious threat to Christians and a military threat to Spain as a fifth column for the Ottomans, while multiplying dangerously because they neither went to war nor entered monasteries. In 1609, after decades of debating what it regarded as the Morisco problem, the crown finally decreed the expulsion from the Peninsula of what was now at least nominally a Christian minority of Muslim ancestry. This move met with strong disapproval from the Vatican. The expulsions, which extended to 1614, caused untold suffering and economic disruption. Cervantes's writing career, and in particular the second part of *Don Quixote* (1615), thus coincides quite closely with the years of greatest strife over the Moriscos and their place in Spain.

Yet however fraught Spain's relation to the last Moriscos on its soil, and despite the legal repression they suffered, Iberia was inextricably connected to Moors and Moorishness. Well into the sixteenth century, Spain was perceived by European travelers as a Moorish nation. And in an important sense it was: language, dress, food, architecture, gardens — all evinced the enduring traces of the culture of Al-Andalus in the Peninsula and could not be legislated away. In many cases, Moorish culture was not even recognized as such by Spaniards — it was simply local tradition — and it required the foreign gaze to stigmatize it as other. Toward the end of part 2 of *Don Quixote*, the hidalgo gives Sancho a lesson on Arabic etymology that establishes both his recognition of its place within Spanish and its ordinariness. From *alhombras* to *borceguíes*, Arabic names the stuff of everyday life. While Arabic had been forbidden in the 1560s as part of the wholesale repression of Moriscos, Arabic-derived Spanish could not be purged, and much of the material culture it named endured unproblematically.

The quotidian presence of Moriscos and of Arabic is part of the joke when in part 1, chapter 9, of the novel the primary narrator must find an Arabic translator for the old papers that he buys in the Alcaná market:

> . . . vile con caracteres que conocí ser arábigos. Y puesto que aunque los conocía no los sabía leer, anduve mirando si parecía por allí algún morisco aljamiado que los leyese, y no fue muy dificultoso hallar intérprete semejante, pues aunque le buscara de otra mejor y más antigua lengua, le hallara.
> (179)

> . . . I saw that it was written in characters I knew to be Arabic. And since I recognized but could not read it, I looked around to see if some Morisco who knew Castilian, and could read it for me, was in the vicinity, and it was not very difficult to find this kind of interpreter, for even if I had sought a speaker of a better and older language, I would have found him.   (67)

Speakers of both Arabic and Hebrew abound in the marketplace, whatever the official rhetoric about Spain's exclusive adherence to Christianity, and the translation of an Arabic manuscript in Toledo poses no difficulty.

From the moment the Morisco translator reveals that the old papers are really the *History of Don Quixote of La Mancha, Written by Cide Hamete Benengeli,* the entire text becomes colored by the problem of Christian-Muslim relations and the accommodation of Moorishness in Spain. The original narrator's first thought is that Cide Hamete will pass silently over Don Quixote's greatest deeds, in an effort to diminish the achievements of his natural enemy. But of course the conceit is that there is no Quixote beyond Benengeli's, and the Arabic author's frequent interjections, particularly in part 2, only exacerbate the feeling of ontological uncertainty. Benengeli invokes Allah, swears as a Catholic Christian, and generally reminds the reader repeatedly of the conditions under which this tale is being told.

Beyond the games with authorship, however, the very genre that Cervantes parodies reveals the particular closeness between Spain and the Moors. A Spanish knight of romance, Cervantes suggests, could never occupy the same position vis-à-vis a Muslim enemy as did other Europeans. While the Moors were the traditional enemies in the so-called Reconquest of southern Iberia, that protracted struggle also featured many instances of Christians allying with Moors for specific purposes. Such alliances feature prominently in the foundational narratives of the great heroes Cid Ruy Díaz de Vivar and Bernardo del Carpio. When Cervantes pokes fun at the genre of chivalric romance, then, he also ironizes Spain's traditionally marginal position in relation to Christian Europe. It becomes clear from Don Quixote's first musings on his chivalric models that Spain does not fit neatly in a chivalric paradigm:

> Decía él que el Cid Ruy Díaz había sido muy buen caballero, pero que no tenía que ver con el Caballero de la Ardiente Espada, que de solo un revés había partido por medio dos fieros y descomunales gigantes. Mejor estaba con Bernardo del Carpio, porque en Roncesvalles había muerto a Roldán el encantado, valiéndose de la industria de Hércules, cuando ahogó a Anteo, el hijo de la Tierra, entre los brazos.   (1: 116 [ch. 1])

> He would say that El Cid Ruy Díaz had been a very good knight but could not compare to Amadís, the Knight of the Blazing Sword, who with a single backstroke cut two ferocious and colossal giants in half. He was fonder of Bernardo del Carpio because at Roncesvalles he had killed the enchanted Roland by availing himself of the tactic of Hercules when he crushed Antaeus, the son of Earth, in his arms.   (21)

The historical Cid pales beside a romance *caballero*, but the really interesting figure here is Bernardo, supposed slayer of Roland in a myth that cannot be shared by other European nations. Bernardo is a national hero for the Spanish precisely because he vanquishes the great French paladin when France invades the Peninsula. The Spanish Bernardo thus stands in for Roland's Saracen enemy, in a striking local departure from the *matière de France*. In the struggle against the invading Franks, Spain occupies the space of the religious and ethnic other. As Spain's heroes, both the Cid and Bernardo complicate any simple division between Moors and Christians: both heroes forge pragmatic alliances with Moors. From these first fantasies, then, the text foregrounds the complexity of imagining a chivalric Spain in contradistinction to the Moors.

Cervantes also engages the genre of Maurophilia, the idealizing novels and ballads of lovelorn Moors and their ladies that featured Moors themselves as exemplary knights and lovers. This hugely popular genre, whose most famous examples are the anonymous novella *El Abencerraje* (1561, 1562, 1565), the ballads known collectively as the *romancero morisco*, and Ginés Pérez de Hita's historical romance *Guerras civiles de Granada* (1595; "Civil Wars of Grenada"), paradoxically flourished even as Moriscos were increasingly persecuted. Its highly romanticized vision of Moors provided a strong counterpart to the ostracism of their contemporary descendants and underscored the valorization of Moors and Moorishness in the Spanish imaginary. This valorization is apparent on the first, comically foreshortened sally of Don Quixote, when he is beaten by an irate muledriver and resorts to fantasy to console himself. His chivalric imagination accommodates what at first glance seems a contradiction: the hidalgo first fancies himself the knight Valdovinos, from the *romance* of the Marqués of Mantua, based on Carolingian legends. A moment later, however, he forgets Valdovinos and instead imagines himself the Moor Abindarráez, from the wildly popular *Abencerraje*, which Don Quixote would have read as part of Montemayor's pastoral *Diana* (1562). As the text of *Don Quixote* reminds us, in the novella Abindarráez is captured by the Christian Rodrigo de Narváez, whose generosity toward his lovelorn prisoner, whom he releases so Abindarráez can marry Jarifa, leads to a lifelong friendship among the three. Abindarráez is a worthy model both as a knight and as a lover. The small detail that he is a Moor does not seem to trouble Don Quixote at all. As this double identification suggests, a Spanish knight may occupy contradictory subject positions, shifting from a Carolingian knight to the Moorish knight who would have been his historical foe. Only Spain's intense imaginative engagement with Moors, however idealized, makes such contradictory identification possible.

These broader considerations will, I hope, demonstrate that the Moorish material in *Don Quixote* is hardly limited to the captive's tale, a supposedly exotic and extraneous supplement to the main story but instead absolutely intrinsic to the text. Two episodes, however, are explicitly concerned with the place of these intimate others within Spain. The first is the famous narrative of captivity and redemption in part 1, chapter 37 and following, in which the soldier Ruy Pérez de Viedma relates the story of his imprisonment in Algiers and his escape with a rich and beautiful Moorish woman Zoraida. A figure of romance who also serves the practical purpose of providing the funds for the escape, Zoraida claims to be a secret Christian desperate to reach Spain. The episode is striking in two respects. First, Cervantes paints a highly sympathetic portrait of the Moorish woman and her father, Agí Morato. Negative portrayal is reserved instead for the Turks, the colonial masters of Algiers, an Ottoman protectorate in the period. Thus a distinction is established between familiar, unthreatening Moors and menacing Turks. Second, and more important, the narrative takes Zoraida to Spain, and her story, though inconclusive, suggests that she will be admitted into the Christian faith and the Spanish polity as the captive's wife or protégée. Cervantes thus harnesses the resources of romance and Maurophilia to tackle the pressing contemporary problem of Morisco assimilation. If the exotic Zoraida (who insists on being called María at the inn) can find a place in Spain as a New Christian, whatever her ethnic and cultural differences, then surely Spain should be able to find room for its most proximate Moors, the Moriscos whose ancestors had in many cases been converted generations earlier. With the highly romanticized vision of a Moor who wishes devoutly to become a Christian, then, Cervantes rebukes those who emphasized the essential otherness of the Moriscos among them.

The second episode that makes the Moorish theme explicit is the story of the Morisco Ricote and his daughter Ana Félix, which appears in part 2, published immediately after the expulsions. When Sancho ignominiously abandons the *ínsula* he had so hoped to govern, he runs into a group of German pilgrims, one of whom greets him effusively and reveals himself as Sancho's former neighbor, the Morisco Ricote. After sharing a convivial meal including ham bones and wine, Ricote fills Sancho in on his adventures. While he praises the prudence of the legislation that expelled from Spain the purported snake in its bosom, he speaks movingly of how the Moriscos long for Spain, the only country they have ever known. But the ordinariness of the encounter is more eloquent than Ricote's speech: Ricote is effectively invisible to Sancho until he reveals himself—that is, he could presumably pass as an Old (Iberian) Christian just as he passes as a German; he speaks pure Castilian, does not abide by any dietary law that would separate him from Sancho, and seems essentially assimilated, though not particularly interested in any religion.

As if to make Ricote's story more powerful, Cervantes adds, a few chapters later, Ricote's daughter, a sympathetic figure who, unlike her father, is a true Christian. Ana Félix is introduced in spectacular circumstances: the dangerous young corsair captain attacking ships near Barcelona turns out to be a cross-dressed, fully Christian Morisca. Her story places the plight of the Moriscos at the very center of the text, as she relates the pain of the expulsion and her frustrated romance with an Old Christian, Don Gregorio. Cervantes once again mobilizes the sympathies of literary Maurophilia to convey the enormity of expelling good Christians who are as Spanish as they can be, whatever their ethnicity. He underscores the distinction between culture and religion, recalling, as in part 1, the pervasiveness of Arabic in Spain, in this case by making Ana's lover, Don Gregorio, a speaker of Arabic. After a series of fascinating adventures,

Ricote and Ana Félix are urged to stay in Barcelona while their noble protectors plead for them at court. And there Cervantes leaves them, long-term house guests of the viceroy and other Catalonian nobles, in an ending whose very inconclusiveness signals the enduring and fraught relation of Spain to its Moorish heritage (Fuchs, *Passing* 43–45).

Cervantes's treatment of Moriscos in *Don Quixote* is strikingly sympathetic, but there are moments elsewhere in his oeuvre that problematize this tolerance. We need to see Cervantes's portrayals in the complex context of Spain's treatment of Muslims, Moriscos, and Moorish culture in the period. The range extends from religious intolerance and political banishment to the idealizations of literary Maurophilia, all constructed against the messy reality of a material culture profoundly marked by the heritage of Al-Andalus.

NOTE

The English translation of *Don Quixote* used in this essay is by Edith Grossman.

Approaching Diegesis: Telling, Transmission, and Authority

James A. Parr

A unique adventure awaits the discerning student of *Don Quixote*, not only in the mimetic plot, which centers on the knight and his squire, but also in the diegetic plot, which features an impressive cast of characters who tell the story: an inferred author, a dramatized author, contrasting first and second pseudo-authors, a dominant editorial voice, a Morisco mock historian, an editorializing translator, character narrators, a quill pen that gains a voice of its own.[1] All this narrating takes place in a found manuscript that contains other found manuscripts and whose transmission is suspect, since the recording relied on word of mouth or translation or both.

The diegetic domain centers on the finding, assembling, sequencing, narrating, and transmitting of the mimetic action. It also presents some of the same tensions among the players that we find in that action. The diegetic-mimetic relation is especially important in the matter of literacy versus orality, personified on the mimetic level in the knight (literacy) and in his squire (orality), and in the tension between the editorial voice, representing orality, and Cide Hamete Benengeli, who represents the medium of writing. The mimetic and diegetic plots both employ the quest motif. The quest in the diegesis is for narrative authority, which is elusive at best and ultimately undermined irreparably, not unlike Don Quixote's futile attempt to reclaim a golden age or to disenchant his fantastical lady in the world of mimesis.

Perhaps the most important link between the two complementary plots involves masking and role-playing. Don Quixote himself plays a role, as do Dorotea, when she pretends to be a princess in distress, and Sansón Carrasco. The masking culminates, qua carnival, in the charades performed by the minions of the duke and duchess. We can challenge students to find and identify all the di-egetic masks Cervantes uses to tell his story. We should make it clear that, while the author is not the narrator, he does assume several personae in the form of pseudo-authors, editors, and narrators. If students are to appreciate his aesthetic achievement, they need to understand the relations and interactions among these carnivalesque masks that he dons and discards, particularly in part 1.

As the reading proceeds, students will see that the carnival atmosphere is pronounced in the telling of part 1 and in the showing of part 2. That is, there are more narrative masks involved in part 1, whereas only the editorial voice, translator, and Cide Hamete are implicated in the telling and transmission of part 2.

Close reading and attention to form underpin my approach. To orient students to the kind of scrutiny expected of them, I always devote much of the first class session, whether graduate or undergraduate, to a detailed analysis of the full 1605 title: *El ingenioso hidalgo don Quijote de la Mancha*.

We are then ready to move forward with the threshold structures (*umbrales, seuils*), focusing largely on the role of the dramatized author of the prologue, on self-consciousness, on what the Russian formalists called baring the device, and on the complementarity of mimesis and diegesis. By the end of the first week of an undergraduate class, we are into the text proper, usually chapters 1–3. I ask students to find evidence of the festive tone—a corollary of diegesis—that is maintained throughout the paratexts and on into the body of the work.

Students need more guidance with the diegetic than with the mimetic, because diegetic concepts are often new to them. Another connection we can make between the two plots is to talk about motivated and unmotivated players. Just as students need to seek out textual evidence of Alonso Quijano's motivation for setting out on his adventures and of Sancho's motivation for accompanying his master, so will they need to consider the motivations of the first and second authors (chs. 1–9), as well as that of the mock historian and third pseudo-author, Cide Hamete.

Attention to the layering of narrative voices is important for a close reading of the text. Our first pseudo-author is also the first narrator of record. Despite José María Paz Gago's protestations to the contrary, I believe that this surrogate functions as both narrator and pseudo-author. He addresses us as an editor-compiler and occasional commentator on the mimetic action. His source material includes oral tradition, other written versions of the story, and the annals of La Mancha. He collates all this into a kind of critical edition of the knight's story. He is self-conscious about his role in preparing the definitive version, at times describing the process of establishing the sequence of events rather than getting on with the telling. This conscientious attention to detail would seem to certify his commitment and authority—that is, until we reach the end of chapter 8 and discover that he has abdicated. Why would he abort such a promising beginning?

The answer may lie in his less-than-charitable attitude toward the knight. How many narrators can we recall who speak of their protagonist as brainless and call his high-sounding discourse nonsense (1: 25 [ch. 2])? This soon-to-be "discarded voice," as George Haley has described him, already undermined that discourse two paragraphs before by laconic and contrastive understatement: when the knight offers a description of his progress on horseback across the plains of Montiel, in the verbose and esoteric rhetoric of his beloved books of chivalry, the narrator comments, prosaically and dismissively, "Y era la verdad que por él caminaba" 'And it was true that this was where he was riding' (25; 31). Such bombast is relegated to a kind of narrative limbo that Gerald Prince calls the disnarrated ("Disnarrated").

At the end of chapter 8, between the interventions of the first and second pseudo-authors, an unannounced editorial voice facilitates the transition from one to the other. This voice will test the close reading abilities of students, for some may pass over it without noticing and others innocently conflate it with the next speaker, the second author. This is the first instance of narrative metalepsis in the book — that is, the surprising transgression of a different narrative voice into territory thought to belong to another. We are caught off-guard: the first narrative voice, which we assumed until now to be our frame narrator, is demoted to subordinate status, for this new extradiegetic speaker obviously knows more and speaks with greater authority. His knowledge of matters to be related in the next chapter affords him an Olympian perspective not in evidence before. Cervantes is parodying similar strategies of the books of chivalry but will soon go beyond that in his experiment with narrative technique.

A highly motivated second author narrates in chapter 9 the adventure of his miniquest in Toledo and makes available to us a found manuscript, which miraculously picks up and continues the story. He contracts to have the "caracteres . . . arábigos" 'Arabic characters' (65; 74; plausibly a transliteration of Spanish into Arabic script, as Carroll Johnson proposed ["Virtual *Don Quixote*"]) rendered into more readily legible vernacular characters by someone of dubious qualifications, whose haste and cut-rate fee may increase our suspicions about the manuscript's reliability. The second author is the counterpart of Alonso Quijano at the diegetic level, for he reads uncritically, identifying unduly with fictional characters and displaying no sense of aesthetic distance. He fails to grasp the irony and negativity of the process of characterization that has unfolded until now. He is presented in an unflattering light (because of his ethnic bias, simpleminded anecdote about virginal mothers, indiscriminate reading habits, and unfounded enthusiasm), so it strains credibility to think he could be the designated editorial voice for all that follows. I would suggest that the overarching editorial voice, the one that appeared between the first and second pseudo-author, appeared earlier, at the end of chapter 8, and that it will resurface, through a subtle instance of metalepsis, at the very threshold of the translation. This editor will come into his own in part 2, as will the metalepsis we begin to associate with him.

I situate the transition from second author to the embedded but dominant editorial voice in the "Good God!" that appears unexpectedly—and incongruously, coming from a follower of Islam: "¡Válame Dios . . . !" 'By God . . .' (2: 68 [ch. 9];77). Cide Hamete's proper mode of expression is found in part 2, chapter 8, in his "Blessed be Allah!" repetitions (501; 532). He refers to the divinity not as God but Allah. We seem to have here a Christian presence asserting itself from within what is presented as the writing of a follower of another faith, which introduces a tension between Islam and Christianity into the diegesis and also reasserts the knowledgeable editorial voice that surfaced first at the end of part 1, chapter 8. This tension is confirmed in part 2, chapter 63, where an overtly Christian voice emanates from Cide Hamete's translated manuscript, allying itself with the Christian naval forces ("nuestras galeras" 'our ships' [855; 919]) that are in combat with Turkish pirates. Being of the same faith as the Turks, Cide Hamete would hardly express solidarity with the Christians. Given the role of this dominant but intermittent editor-narrator, who is sometimes covert, sometimes overt in the ordering of the discourse, I often refer to him as the supernarrator.

In summary: Cervantes shifts to an extradiegetic (frame) narrator at the end of part 1, chapter 8, demoting and dismissing the first author, and he reaffirms that voice in the next chapter, again using metalepsis, thereby eclipsing and effectively eliminating the second author. Patterning preempts proximity; the recurrence of metalepsis trumps the more recent presence of the second author. This same extradiegetic editorial voice launches part 2 with "Cuenta Cide Hamete Benengeli en la segunda parte desta historia . . ." 'Cide Hamete Benengeli recounts in the second part of this history . . .' (2: 459 [ch. 1]; 487). What was tentative and experimental in part 1 becomes protocol in part 2, as the supernarrator is given overt control of the narration.

The reader's task is made even more interesting by considering that each narrator, extradiegetic and intradiegetic, addresses a different interlocutor, a different narratee. Students will need to configure these narratees on the basis of the manner and tone of each narrator. The narratee is a mental construct, an inference by the reader, just as the authorial presence that takes shape as we progress through the text is also inferred; thus the apt designator for this ubiquitous but concealed presence is the inferred author. Students can be asked to describe each of the several narratees according to the attitudes, language, and tone evident in the discourse of the sender of the message (each narrator). A quick reference to Roman Jakobson's classic communication model, adapted to literary texts, will be helpful here. The customary assumption of complicity and shared perspective between sender and inferred receiver makes it clear that the first and second authors address very different narratees.

E. C. Riley describes Cide Hamete as an example of total inverisimilitude (*Cervantes's Theory* 330). I would add that the inverisimilitude is a consequence especially of that narrator's questionable motivation. It is hard to believe that a Morisco who is clearly aligned with another faith and culture would bother to recount the misadventures of an ungainly, aging, Christian hidalgo of very modest means from a nondescript village in a backwater region of an inhospitable land—inhospitable particularly after the expulsion of the Moriscos between 1609 and 1614. What is Cide Hamete doing in Spain in 1615? What reason could he possibly have to tell this story? As a text speaker, albeit a marginalized and embedded one, situated perhaps at the intraintradiegetic level, he would surely qualify as an unmotivated narrator par excellence.

It would seem that Cervantes set himself the challenge of making a mock hero appeal to an audience and that, to increase the challenge of not alienating that audience, he had the hero's misadventures recounted by sometimes antagonistic, at best indifferent, narrators and pseudo-authors. The unperceptive reader (who in Cervantes's day would have been called the *lector vulgar*) will not understand or appreciate this self-assumed challenge, but the readers we hope to form under our tutelage may rise to the occasion.

Cide Hamete is not a text speaker but a text writer. He represents writing. Two other pseudo-authors precede him, but his is the most serious and sustained effort at recording words and deeds within the world of the book. So although he is miscast as a narrator, he may well have something to say as a writer. Or it may be that his mere presence, as chronicler in residence, communicates something significant.

In part 1, he is completely dispensable, is indeed an afterthought, as José Manuel Martín Morán maintains (El Quijote 67). Cide Hamete is mentioned only five times in part 1, between chapters 9 and 27, and never again by name after chapter 27. He is therefore a late addition to the 1605 volume; he is not a narrator; and his role, restricted to the internal parts 2 and 3, is largely the structural one of providing transitions between them and between a couple of chapters in that frame (84). This observation is a salutary corrective to some prenarratological perceptions of his role and importance. It seems likely that Cervantes again inserted the Muslim historian strategically, and much more frequently, throughout part 2, this time in response to the appropriation by Avellaneda, to counter Avellaneda's historian, Alisolán, reclaiming Cervantes's intellectual property in the process.

The narrative levels of Gérard Genette help us ascertain Cide Hamete's relative position: Cide Hamete's discourse is framed by those of two filtering intermediaries—namely, the translator and the supernarrator. On the other hand, we can now see the importance of Cide Hamete as a personification of writing that is both a supplement to orality and a means of indiscriminate dissemination. Although he is a marginal figure in the diegesis of the text, his emblematic presence and his role in the dangerous deferral inherent in the supplement called writing are rich and suggestive indeed (see Derrida, *Writing*).

The metadiegetic level of narration is assigned to those characters who recount their personal histories, such as Dorotea, Cardenio, and the captive. The extradiegetic and intradiegetic levels frame their discourse. The narrator of "El curioso impertinente" 'Ill-Advised Curiosity' (pt. 1, chs. 33–36) is unique, for he is not a character in the mimetic plot, and his moral voice and apostrophizing of characters set him apart, situating him on an intradiegetic level entirely his own.

Students will need to think about the roles of the various narrators in relation to the transmission of dramatized action and in relation to one another; of the authority with which each may be said to speak; of the inferred interlocutor of each; of narrative metalepsis; of ways in which one text speaker may subvert the authority of another; and, finally, of a possible hierarchy of narrative authority. They will also need to take into account Cide Hamete and the fact that these stories are all assumed to be part of his translated manuscript. As we proceed through the text, I frequently ask, "Who is speaking in this passage and with what relative authority? Is this speaker undermined by irony or by other narrators?"[2]

There is another side of the coin: disnarration. Students should be alerted to the possibility that a certain style may be introduced only to be supplanted by another, never to reappear, unless momentarily as parody. Don Quixote's paean to his first sortie is a perfect example. Then there are the subcategories of the unnarrated (ellipsis) and the unnarratable (insignificant details that do not merit our attention—for instance, when a character sneezes, hiccups, scratches, yawns, or heeds the call of nature). A remarkable juxtaposition of these two subcategories is found in part 2, chapter 60:

> . . . en más de seis días no le sucedió cosa digna de ponerse en escritura, al cabo de los cuales, . . . le tomó la noche entre unas espesas encinas o alcornoques; que en esto no guarda la puntalidad Cide Hamete que en otras cosas suele. (829)

> . . . for more than six days nothing happened, nothing at least worth writing about; and at the end of that time . . . night overtook him in a dense copse of evergreen oaks or cork-oaks—on this point Cide Hamete isn't as meticulous as usual. (891)

The conversations and events of six entire days are consigned to the unnarrated, while the focus shifts to the unnarratable, to a gratuitous detail about the kind of trees encountered, all of which is rendered tongue in cheek, of course. Nor is one commentator's unnarrated necessarily another's: although the translator arbitrarily suppresses the description of Don Diego de Miranda's house in part 2, chapter 18, his editorial decision is belated, because Don Quixote has just focalized it for us in some detail.

A related dimension is the tension between orality and literacy, personified respectively in the squire and his master at the mimetic level and in the supernarrator and Cide Hamete at the diegetic level. A remarkable instance of this dichotomy, one that nevertheless underscores the complementarity of orality and literacy, is the beginning of part 2, chapter 44: "Dicen que en el propio original desta historia see lee que . . ." 'It is said that in the original manuscript of this history one reads that . . .' (718; 776). Here literacy defers to orality and seeks grounding and ultimate authorization in that primary form of expression. Throughout part 2, the text defers frequently to primary orality for grounding; in part 1, grounding is generally sought in other written records. It is important to show students that the authority of writing, both secular and sacred, is implicitly called into question by Cervantes's text. In particular, the text parodies the transmission of such materials, via oral tradition and translation, casting doubt on the accuracy and authority of this and other more foundational scriptures (cf. López Baralt).

The foreignness of Cide Hamete is highly appropriate, for he embodies an alienated medium of expression that has traditionally been suspect, since Plato at least. Don Quixote's relation to the object that informs him is similar, in the sense that there is a remarkable complementarity between this piece of defensive armor, the thigh guard (*quijote*), and the region of the body it substantially protects (the genital area) and the passive, defensive posture of the knight in relation to sexuality. Cide Hamete is a part of a larger whole, writing; Don Quixote is a whole character closely connected to a much smaller but not insignificant part, the *quijote*. Cide Hamete is a writer, Don Quixote a reader, yet they are mirror images of each other and of the processes of encoding and decoding texts.

They also have in common an uncertain origin. We know little of Don Quixote's life before the age of fifty, and we know nothing of Cide Hamete's formation, place of origin, or vital statistics. They belong to two very different cultures of the book—the Qur'an and the Bible, Islam and Christianity—but converge in the variegated and diverse culture of Cervantes's polyphonic bible of humanity.

Attention to the diegetic domain affords an enhanced appreciation of Cervantes's aesthetic achievement and a heightened awareness of how Cervantes anticipates in his praxis significant theoretical and literary concerns of our day, such as narrative authority and orality versus literacy, made manifest specifically through narratology and deconstruction. Above all, Cervantes loosens the hold that fiction, history, and scripture may have on naive readers by implicitly questioning the modes of transmission, and thus the narrative authority, of all three.

NOTES

The edition of *Don Quixote* used in this essay is by Fajardo and Parr; translations are by Rutherford.

[1] Concise and authoritative definitions of the narratological terms used in this essay can be found in Gerald Prince's *Dictionary of Narratology*. I use *diegesis* throughout in its ancient and pristine sense of telling in contrast to showing (i.e., mimesis).

[2] Perspectives on the diegetic range from the simplistic to the highly technical. Claiming to apply Occam's razor, Howard Mancing eschews the customary distinction between

author and narrator, maintaining that the author deploys only one narrator, himself ("Cervantes"). See my response to this reading ("On Narration"). At the other extreme, José María Paz Gago and Ruth Fine both invite us into the more esoteric realms of semiotics and narratology. Fine also emphasizes the importance of metalepsis and pseudo-diegesis. Brian D. Patrick dissects key aspects of these two studies in a probing essay in *Letras Hispanas*. My preference is to avoid either extreme.

Reading the Missing Manuscript:
Teaching Textual Materiality in *Don Quixote*

Patricia W. Manning

Interactions with handwritten artifacts are passé for many student readers of the *Quixote*; these textual consumers are more familiar with the abbreviated codes of the text message than with the ethos of the handwritten note. Notwithstanding this unfamiliarity with paper-based forms, our students are often astute interpreters of the products of our material culture, readily able to distinguish the latest version of an electronic gadget from an earlier one. For these skilled analysts of goods in the twenty-first century, the material details of the *Quixote* form a useful connection to the study of the cultural circumstances of seventeenth-century Spain.

A number of the material elements of the *Quixote*'s parody of chivalric romances, such as the eponymous character's age and the conditions of his armor and steed, are obvious to novice readers, but the text's more subtle engagement with the conventions of manuscript culture frequently requires an instructor's guidance. As Claire Kramsch explains, one of the greatest interpretative challenges facing readers of a work produced outside their own cultural circumstances "is less the internal cohesion of the text than the cultural coherence of the discourse" (59). While the narrative complexities of the *Quixote* challenge students' interpretative abilities, oftentimes the importance of quotidian details of seventeenth-century textual life prove the most difficult element for students to grasp.

Handwritten texts in seventeenth-century Spain possessed a distinct cultural code that is almost entirely unfamiliar to twenty-first-century students. Long after Gutenberg's invention of the printing press, texts continued to circulate in handwritten form. Both types of distribution survived well into the seventeenth century (Bouza 16–17). Certain genres, such as "collections of letters, spiritual meditations, and poetry from academies," circulated in handwritten form to limit readership to a selected few (21). Like the domestic objects ably interpreted by scholars such as Lisa Jardine, Ann Rosalind Jones and Peter Stallybrass, and Raffaella Sarti, textual artifacts also attest to the status of their producers and intended consumers through elements such as the quality of the lettering, illustrations, and the material on which the artifacts were written or printed.

Manuscripts produced in many different circumstances play a prominent role in the *Quixote*'s plot line, since characters read a variety of works written by hand. This essay, offering an approach to teaching manuscript culture in the *Quixote*, focuses on one such work, the artifact attributed to Cide Hamete Benengeli and found in part 1, chapter 9. Its discovery in the Alcaná de Toledo parodies the trope of the unearthed foreign manuscript in chivalric romances by including a wealth of details about the social and economic circumstances surrounding the *Quixote*'s source. In addition, this episode forms part of a larger parody: characters throughout the *Quixote* misinterpret handwritten texts because they do not properly parse the contextual clues offered by them. By analyzing the physical forms of manuscripts throughout Cervantes's novel, students confront what Sam Wineburg terms "the distant past — a past less distant from us in time than in its modes of thought and social organization" (6–7). By moving beyond the facile connections between the past and present that according to Wineburg distort our interpretations of history (5–6), students develop "mature historical thought" that engages in critical thinking (5; see ix).

According to Wilbert J. McKeachie's research, certain conditions encourage the process of thinking critically: "Learning to think usually begins by (1) bringing order out of chaos, (2) discovering uncovered ideas, and (3) developing strategies while avoiding jumping to conclusions" (McKeachie and Gibbs 328). Since handwritten texts figure in both parts of the *Quixote*, the interpretation of them forms a consistent theme to help students evaluate the actions of the characters in the novel. Moreover, since handwritten matter is involved in many of the most ambiguous passages of the *Quixote*, a critical approach to the evaluation of that matter may lead students to original interpretations.

For students without physical access to manuscripts, the Internet supplies a wealth of examples to attune them to the significance of the details of handwritten products that will be read in the *Quixote*. The Web sites of the Lessing J. Rosenwald and Jay I. Kislak collections at the United States Library of Congress feature a number of digital images from manuscripts, including full-color illuminations (in the Rosenwald collection, at www.loc.gov/rr/rarebook /rosenwald.html) and digital copies of historical correspondence, such as letters from Hernán Cortés and Philip II (in the Kislak collection, at www.loc.gov/rr /rarebook/kislak.html). These documents allow students to study the functions of illuminations in manuscripts and the types of texts that tended to be illustrated. The Portal de Archivos Españoles (PARES) offers a rotating selection of digitized texts from a number of Spain's archives, including many examples of more informal handwritten notations (http://pares.mcu.es/). For those teaching the *Quixote* in English, the Beinecke Rare Book and Manuscript Library's Web and *Flickr* pages (http://beinecke.library.yale.edu/digitallibrary/paleography .html and www.flickr.com/photos/brbl/) present digital facsimiles of a number of manuscripts composed in English. Although most undergraduates lack the paleographic skills to read these documents in much detail, they get a sense of the types of errors that appear in hand-copied works and of the effort required to decipher informally penned communications.

After his source runs out in the midst of the battle between Don Quixote and the Basque in part 1, chapter 8, the second author visits the Alcaná market in Toledo, where he finds "unos cartapacios y papeles viejos . . . llevado desta mi natural inclinación, tomé un cartapacio de los que el muchacho vendía, y vile con caracteres que conocí ser arábigos" 'some notebooks and old papers . . . ; I was moved by my natural inclinations to pick up one of the volumes the boy was selling, and I saw that it was written in characters I knew to be Arabic' (1: 179; 67).

Lest there be any doubt about the handwritten nature of this collection of papers, according to the *Diccionario de autoridades*, a "cartapacio" is a "book or notebook of white [i.e., blank] paper in which one notes what one observes, reading or reflecting" (1: 203). Thus the truncated adventures of the Manchegan knight continue in a blank book filled with a handwritten text. Most students need background information to understand the significance of this datum.

In contrast to the romances of chivalry, in which often fabulous adventures uncover manuscripts that are in nonnative languages and have no connection to the cultural circumstances that produced them (Eisenberg, *Romances* 124–27; Johnson, "Phantom Pre-texts" 179–80), Benengeli's work comes to light in a recognizable setting that evokes Spain's fading cultural diversity. As E. C. Graf and María Rosa Menocal both observe, this scene occurs in the Jewish quarter of Toledo, long after any officially Jewish residents of Spain remained (Graf, "Pomegranate" 45–50; Menocal 253–54). Moreover, the market in Toledo is identified by a word based on the Arabic term for market (Graf, "When an Arab" 77; Menocal 255). The virtual tours of this part of Toledo at *Toledo es otra historia* (the site, not available now, is archived at https://archive.org/web) give students a sense of the shifting cultural boundaries evident in the buildings of this quarter of the town. A number of later references to this manuscript, including Benengeli's treatment of his pen in part 2, chapter 74, which Luce López Baralt interprets in Qur'anic terms (506), reinforce these connections to Islamic culture.

The setting is painstakingly detailed but not the manuscript itself. We learn from the second author that the text uses Arabic characters but do not know the language in which it is composed. Although there are two schools of thought as to whether the text was penned in Arabic (e.g., Harvey, "*Moro Aljamiado*" 66) or *aljamía*, a form of Spanish written in Arabic letters (e.g., Johnson, "Phantom Pre-texts" 191; Menocal 259–60), to my mind the narrative's imprecision concerning the language of composition is quite telling. We get the sense that it is best not to reveal too much about the language lest one be denounced to the Inquisition. According to rule 4 of the Spanish Inquisition's 1583 index of prohibited books, all works that propagated Jewish or Islamic doctrines were forbidden (Martínez de Bujanda 818). Amidst ever increasing levels of restrictions against the ethnically Arabic population, as Henry Kamen notes, when inquisitors came across texts in Arabic lettering, even when these officials could not read them to determine their content, they tended to decide that the volumes were Qur'ans and seize them (*Spanish Inquisition* 218).

Since the extent of the finder's knowledge is limited to his recognition of Arabic characters, the finder searches for a translator: "[A]nduve mirando si parecía por allí algún morisco aljamiado que los leyese, y no fue muy dificultoso hallar intérprete semejante" 'I looked around to see if some Morisco who knew

Castilian, and could read it for me, was in the vicinity' (1: 179 [ch. 9]; 67). As Luis Andrés Murillo observes in his edition of *Don Quixote*, such an encounter with a Morisco likely would have proved rather difficult by 1605 (Cervantes, *Ingenioso hidalgo* [Murillo] 1: 142n16). Given the continuing suppression of elements of Arabic culture and the forced resettlement of the Morisco population after the rebellion in the Alpujarras, it stretches credulity that a Morisco would readily identify himself as a reader of Arabic script to a stranger. Rafael Benítez Sánchez-Blanco's research of *relaciones de causas* ("summaries of inquisitorial trials") from the Toledo tribunal of the Inquisition indicates that prosecution of Moriscos represented 20.5% of the cases brought to this tribunal between 1601 and 1605 (733), so the danger in being identified as part of this community was quite real. This context explains why the manuscript attributed to Benengeli is so devalued that it is offered for sale to a silk merchant (179; 67)—perhaps as raw material for rag production, as Menocal suggests (255), or as "food for" silkworms, as Carroll B. Johnson proposes (*Cervantes* 6). It also helps explain the second author's evasiveness about describing the translator or manuscript in detail.

In immediately searching for an interpreter to decipher the manuscript, the second author breaks with an established element of reading protocol that began in handwritten works and continued in printed texts. Nonreaders used images to make guesses about the content of a work (Huot 7), and readers used illustrations to guide them in processing the text (Chartier 5). The second author does not begin with the first folder of the handwritten text, the manuscript's image of Don Quixote, Rocinante, Sancho, and the Basque Don Sancho de Azpetia: "Estaba en el primero cartapacio pintada muy al natural la batalla de don Quijote con el vizcaíno" 'In the first notebook there was a very realistic depiction of the battle of Don Quixote with the Basque' (180; 68). The image, which could have explained the work's content to one who does not know the Arabic alphabet, is discovered only after the Morisco translator reads aloud the marginalia referring to Dulcinea's remarkable abilities in the salting of pork (179–80; 68).

Like many consumers of handwritten texts in the *Quixote*, the second author fails to process this contextual evidence once he discovers it. He does not see the parodic valence of the Basque's self-defense using a pillow (180; 68). This error leads to a more substantial interpretative problem: as Charles D. Presberg argues, the second author truly believes that Don Quixote is "*nothing but* a noble, heroic knight" (120; see 170–79). For the reader familiar with print culture in sixteenth-century Spain, the second author's gaffe is even more humorous. According to Ana María G. Laguna, the Toledo manuscript parodies the frontispiece to *Le chevalier délibéré* ("The Determined Knight"), a chivalric text translated into Spanish by Charles V and an associate (45–47). It is evident to students who have studied manuscripts that the second author's limited description of the technical details of how the image was made, scant mention of its artistic style, and lack of any reference to its coloration do not jibe with the prominence of illuminations in handwritten works. Learners wonder if the second author's treatment of the illustration is abbreviated to draw attention away from his error.

If the second author's report of the particulars of the formatting of the handwritten text in part 1, chapter 9, is sparse, other manuscripts in the *Quixote* are depicted in more detail. For example, we learn that Cardenio's writings are composed in "un librillo de memoria" 'diary' (1: 320 [ch. 23]; 175), and the first sonnet in the diary that Don Quixote sees is "en él escrito, como en borrador, aunque de muy buena letra" 'in a kind of rough draft, though written in a very fine hand' (321; 175). Although this description marks the text as personal musings, Don Quixote ignores the private format of Cardenio's memoir and incorporates Cardenio's trials into his own adventures. Later in part 1, the handwritten "[n]ovela del curioso impertinente" 'novel of the Man Who Was Recklessly Curious' (1: 443 [ch. 32]; 272) is rendered "de muy buena letra" 'such a fine hand' (271). Given the costliness of a high-quality copy, "a fine hand" suggests an upper-class origin. These more precise descriptions make students think more about the second author's motives for revealing so little about the format of the found manuscript.

Issues relating to the physical presentation and consumption of handwritten texts reappear throughout both parts of the *Quixote*. In part 1, other manuscripts follow the pattern established by the text unearthed in the Alcaná de Toledo and often appear in interruptions in the chivalric plot line, such as the reading of the handwritten "[n]ovela del curioso impertinente" at Juan Palomeque's inn while Don Quixote slumbers. In part 2, manuscripts appear in more complex situations. These handwritten artifacts often evoke an alternative text or social context within an invented chivalric adventure, as in the correspondence exchanged during Sancho's governorship (for these letters, see chs. 47, 50–52).

The interpretative ethos of manuscript culture also provides a framework for understanding puzzling aspects of the *Quixote*'s narrative technique. In part 1, chapter 9, it becomes clear that the handwritten version contains several details that the imprint omits, like the visual depiction and the marginal commentary about Dulcinea mentioned earlier. According to Thomas A. Lathrop, this suppression of information raises questions about the "reliab[ility]" of the work (Introduction [1-vol. ed.] xxvii). Whereas print culture responds to such suppression with suspicion, manuscript culture tends to be more tolerant of a scribe's editorial decisions. For example, José Manuel Lucía Megías finds that a seventeenth-century scribe revised and retitled an already existing chivalric tale that circulated in manuscript form instead of faithfully copying the original version (*De los libros* 202). A similar level of comfort with emendations seems to be at work in the transfer of the manuscript found in the Alcaná de Toledo into the imprint that we read. Lathrop has interpreted the many temporal and spatial misalignments and continuity problems in the *Quixote* as a deliberate facet of the novel's imitation of the equally error-prone printed chivalric texts ("Contradictions" 298). The textual difficulties in the *Quixote* imitate not only the pretense of chivalric romances that they are based on manuscripts but also the inconsistencies found in handwritten matter (see Baena; Martín Morán, *El Quijote*).

Moving beyond the focus on handwritten products as a scaffold to organize the reading of the *Quixote*, this approach introduces students to current issues in the field of manuscript studies, such as the differing opinions of Pedro Cátedra and Fernando Bouza concerning whether short printed texts, like *pliegos sueltos* ("broadsheets"), or manuscripts were the preferred format for those learning to read (Cátedra 90, 151; Bouza 34). In this manner, the *Quixote* becomes not a masterpiece whose interpretation has been established by experts but a text awaiting new interpretations.

NOTE

The English translation of *Don Quixote* used in this essay is by Edith Grossman. All other translations from Spanish are mine, unless otherwise indicated.

eaders and Reading *in Don Quixote*

Salvador Fajardo

The function of reading is absolutely central to *Don Quixote*. The novel is populated by readers both sophisticated and naive. Hence, in my teaching—I usually teach the novel in a seminar for senior undergraduates or for graduates—I focus on it as a reader's guide: it guides its own reading but also the reading of all texts—in particular of authoritative texts. Recent experience has taught me, however, that reading practice must be thoroughly contextualized, that students at all levels need historical and cultural background to read the book profitably.

In the first three-hour class session, I give a broad cultural overview of the period (inns, roads and travel, typical foods, etc.) and address the issue of readers and reading in early modern Spain.[1] The prevalent culture was still mostly oral, the population having an illiteracy rate of eighty percent. Books were expensive—part 1 of *Don Quixote* would have cost a reader then between $75 and $100 in current American terms—and by common standards Don Quixote's library was exceptionally extensive. People who owned books were more likely to have a library like that of the knight in the green coat in part 2, who says he has about six dozen books, mostly devotional or historical, and no romances of chivalry. For these reasons, and perhaps because reading habits had been formed by the reading of devotional literature, books were read and reread, not consumed as we consume popular fiction today. Readers returned to their books often, dipping into them to read passages again and again, perhaps even using these books as manuals for their own expression, as models for writing letters and even for certain kinds of behavior.[2] I apply the next two hours to a reading of the prologue to part 1, focusing on the reading strategies that it calls for and addressing the issue of authorial authority. Thereafter, I try to limit my interventions in the class to redirecting discussion when redirection is needed, clarifying concrete details about the cultural or literary tradition, and pointing out important issues that might otherwise be bypassed.

A readerly approach to the novel emphasizes the practice of reading, which *Don Quixote* incorporates as both plot and theme. Most students respond positively to this emphasis. I suggest one central area of interest in each assigned reading segment, and from that area our discussion may branch out into adjacent portions of the text. Because we maintain our attention to the reading of a specific narrative strand, our experience will not be diluted by the manifold suggestiveness of the episodes—we can deal with that aspect later. For the first assignment, which usually covers chapters 1–9 of part 1, I ask that special attention be paid to how the narrative voice addresses the reader and describes action.

Don Quixote responds equally well to recent and traditional analytic methodologies. On the first day of class, I distribute a bibliography that incorporates theoretical work about reading practice and about cultural issues that will provide helpful background for our engagement with the text. Among items that I typically include in this list are, for the reading process, *Rereading*, by Matei Călinescu, and the still useful collection *The Reader in the Text*, by Susan Suleiman and Inge Crosman; for historical and cultural background, *Daily Life in Spain in the Golden Age*, by Marcelin Defourneaux, which is full of fascinating information, and *Imperial Spain, 1469–1716*, by J. H. Elliott, which retains its usefulness, though Henry Kamen's *Empire* has superseded it to some degree.

The novel itself constructs a model reader from its very first pages. Aspects of modern rhetorical analysis have proved useful, but careful reading remains our goal. Starting with the second class session, each reading is introduced by a student who serves as guide to our discussion. The other students are asked to bring to class three questions, issues, or problems that their own reading has suggested. I also ask students to write a journal of their interaction with the text. The journal often turns out to be the most difficult task: like Don Quixote, they find it easier to focus on the story than on the reading process. It takes time for them to be able to reflect on their readerly responses. Usually they need guidance in differentiating the diegesis (the telling of the story) from the mimesis (the representation proper, or the story told). After they realize how the power of mimesis tends to veil the text's diegetic component, they have a better understanding of their task, both in their journal and in class deliberations. Our method rests on gauging how we read against how readers in the novel read mimetically (such as Don Quixote, the priest, Sansón Carrasco, the duke, and the duchess) and diegetically (various editorial and authorial personae). The self-training of the journal can be useful. Journal writing over time makes students receptive to the tone of the narrative voice at the diegetic level and, in the mimesis proper, to the kinds of qualifiers a narrator uses to describe actions and attitudes. I also encourage students to think about how the sequencing of events affects the reading experience. For example, does a mad action become less mad in our mind if it is followed by a wise discourse or exchange, or does a wise discourse or exchange become less wise if it is followed by a mad action? How does our knowledge of a character affect our response to comments about that character made by a narrator, by other characters, and by the readers in the text? A student journal, if taken seriously, can be as valuable as class discussion for student learning. For that reason, I try to read the journals at least twice in a semester. Usually, after my first reading, I need to steer students away from plot summary and toward self-conscious reading.

Considering how the text's strategies affect readers and thinking of our reading as an actualizing process respond to the text's questioning of our habits of abstraction and imagination. Of course, readers' responses are sometimes counterintuitive and surprising. When and as soon as they surface, they should become the occasion for class discussion with minimal intervention by the instructor. My view is that, if a reading experience is to have a truly formative effect, instructors should resist imposing their own opinions.

Reflection on reading practice allows us to see more clearly a novel's strategies of distancing and disclosure.[3] For instance, we will ask, What is the role of the frequent narrative interruptions? How do they change our perception of narrative authority? How does the narrative frame function in the road adventures and in the interpolated stories? Questions of this nature lead us to a scrutiny of the novel's overall rhetorical disposition on three interrelated fronts:

1. *Don Quixote* as representation and communication: What kind of worldview does it dispense? How does it dispense it? When is the text ironic or satirical, mimetic or parodic?
2. *Don Quixote* as response: How does the text respond to the literary-cultural traditions of its day? to those of our own?
3. *Don Quixote* as guide: How does the text capture the reader? How does it form the reader?

Items 2 and 3 will form the constant background to our discussions, but item 3 will be their theme. An issue of equal importance is how reading is embedded in the book. Moving from the inside out, so to speak, or from the mimesis to the diegesis, we can identify four distinct levels. The first is that of the readers in the text, especially of Don Quixote, whose exchange of the *algo* of *hidalgo*—namely, "possessions, land"—for books transforms him into a *hijo de libros* ("son of books"). I ask students to consider what kind of reader Don Quixote is.

Many other readers are represented in the text. The first two are the priest and the barber, whose reading skills enter into play in part 1, chapter 6. In the last chapters of part 1, the canon garners enough information about Don Quixote's imprisonment in the wooden cart to make his reading of the character's situation close to ours. In part 2, we encounter Avellaneda in the prologue, Sansón Carrasco at the beginning, later the duke and duchess and others who have at least some knowledge of who Don Quixote and Sancho are.

The next set of readers—the second level—belongs to the diegesis proper. The first reader (leaving aside the prologues) is the narrator of chapters 1–8 of part 1. In chapter 8, other readers-commentators appear and complicate our engagement with the text. An editor links the abrupt ending of chapter 8 with the reader-author's good fortune in finding the Arabic manuscript; from the editor we learn that the first author is an Arab historian named Cide Hamete Benengeli, and the views of this historian's translator will come into play intermittently. The editor is assumed responsible for the division of the book into chapters and for their titles.[4]

This editor introduces a third, more abstract level: issues of form and framing. In general, the reader's sense of order and understanding corresponds to the narrator's control and authority. In *Don Quixote*, that sense interacts with the establishing and questioning of authorial authority. Because formal issues are also readerly issues, part of the text's persuasive force, we must pay attention to broad formal patterns: in part 1, the prologue provides an outer frame; chapters 6 and 47–52 of part 1 constitute inner frames. In part 2, the prologue also provides an outer frame; the first five chapters and chapter 72–74 constitute inner frames.

The fourth level of engagement is the detail of our reflective reading practice, detail that is generated by the text. The outward movement away from the mimetic ground of the book ends outside its covers and in us. If we respond to the text as aware readers, we will understand how the undermining of representational authority (through the multiplication of authors and other metafictional devices) places the final authority in us.

We should keep in mind that we are asking readers to consider an aspect of the text that frequently eludes them. To accustom students to the kind of attention they must exercise, I ask them to reflect on the beginning of part 1, especially the title and the paratexts—in other words, to identify what belongs to the inside world of the text and what belongs to its outside world. I ask how the tone of the introductory material prepares readers. In the first paragraph of the text proper, I ask students to discern mimetic and diegetic components and, in the diegesis, what interpellates those components. Mimesis and diegesis are immediately intermixed in chapter 1, which begins, "En un lugar de la Mancha, de cuyo nombre no quiero acordarme, no ha mucho tiempo que vivía un hidalgo . . . " 'In a village in La Mancha, the name of which I cannot quite recall, there lived not long ago one of those country gentlemen . . .' (1: 113; 25). I ask students to note the difference between the text's past and the 1605 reader's past. The paragraph continues with a description of clothing, eating habits, and household. These details introduce such topics as the hierarchy of description and the birth of the hero yet also raise various questions of a textual nature: How is the sense of reality transmitted? How much description is necessary to generate this sense? What operates in the amount of description necessary to create a world in a work of fiction?

Paragraph 1 ends with the issue of Don Quixote's original name, which is pure diegesis and gives us occasion to discuss the author's tone, interests, and role. I ask the students to consider the use of the modifier "our" for "story" and also the "truth" that is invoked in the statement that concludes the first paragraph of chapter 1: "Pero esto importa poco a nuestro cuento; basta que en la narración dél no se salga un punto de la verdad" 'But this doesn't matter much, as far as our story's concerned, provided that the narrator doesn't stray one inch from the truth' (114; 25). Sensitivity to narrative tone, in this passage as in many, will help students train themselves to read.

The prologue provides the theory—a reader's guide—for the entire first part. It is a prolepsis, first in the rhetorical sense of the word, as the anticipation of an objection, in this case the reader's forthcoming objections to the book's esthetic flaws; second in the formal sense, as a preview of important structural components of the book. This framing text is itself framed in that the speaker addresses a present reader, narrates his past conversation with a friend, and addresses the reader again in the conclusion. The beginning and final addresses may be considered the frame that contains the story of the friend's intervention. The game of the prologue is to seduce the idle reader by placing him at the apex of an ironic triangle aimed by the speaker at the common reader, who would prefer a prologue full of learned references. The speaker's implicit addressee is the idle reader, and the object of the speaker's irony is the common reader. The friend then replaces the common reader as object of irony, while the idle reader remains the irony's recipient.

As John J. Allen noted some time ago, when the friend enters and says that he can resolve the author's problem of not being able to write a prologue for the book, the author's response is ironic both in tone—the response is over-stated—and substance, in that we, the addressees, are familiar with the issues that have produced this writer's block (*Don Quixote* 37–38). When we return to the opening frame, now closed in the prologue's conclusion, the speaker approves and includes the friend's words. The insightful reader understands that these words become part of the prologue not because they add authority to it but, on the contrary, because they have been deprived of authority by the friend, who points out their uselessness. As we read the prologue's closing remarks, we are told how relieved we will be to find so sincere and uncomplicated a story as that of the famous Don Quixote of la Mancha, considered by the inhabitants of the district of Montiel to be the most valiant and chastely enamored knight in recent memory, and of the equally famous Sancho Panza, his squire. Readers will naturally step back from their engagement with this speaker, who appears to accept the historical reality of the double protagonist, the knight and his squire. This severing of the speaker → reader link places the responsibility of interpretation squarely on our readers' shoulders.

An awareness of how the speaker of the prologue operates prepares us for the problematization of the author function that occurs in part 1, chapter 8. The division of authorial responsibility among several reader-author figures in that chapter invites us to question the very notion of authorial authority—or at least not to assume it. We become attentive to the changes in authorial tone and to the intrusions by the various voices that accompany us on our readerly journey.

Most texts create a persona of their author, and they also create a persona of the reader. As we advance through this nine-hundred-page book, our reading is modulated not only by all its metafictional components but also by its purely fictional ones, such as our growing intimacy with its characters. This intimacy, our sensitivity to the text's solicitations and narrative tone, and our awareness of our readerly responsibilities allow us to measure our understanding against that of the book's various mimetic and diegetic interpreters. We are led to be critical of the book's ethos—that is, the persuasive power that can be attributed to the speaker, or narrator, at any given time. For example, at the end of book 2, chapter 29, the narrator says that Don Quixote and Sancho "(v)olvieron a sus bestias, y a ser bestias" 'returned to their animals, and to being animals' (279; 687), projecting an ethos that most readers, who have now accompanied Don Quixote and Sancho for six hundred pages, will find too harsh. Readers then need to reflect on why such a strong statement is made at this time. The statement may cast suspicion on the kind of guidance they will receive from this narrator in the upcoming episodes. At least it suggests that they remain aware of the narrator's hand. Issues of ethos help us reflect on the transformation of the protagonist's identity through his adventures, whose telling invites us to reflect as well on the adventure of our reading.

NOTES

The English translation of *Don Quixote* used in this essay is by John Rutherford.

[1] Chevalier gives a good overview of reading practice and libraries.

[2] The renting of books was common. Reading aloud, as in Juan Palomeque's inn (part 1, chs. 33–35), was also common practice. Most libraries had between forty and three hundred books. That of Diego Hurtado de Mendoza (1675), a grandee, held 453 books; that of Ferdinand of Aragon, duke of Calabria (1550), held 795 (Chevalier 31–36).

[3] This topic has been addressed by El Saffar (*Distance*).

[4] Parr has done the most extensive analysis of the game of authorship (Don Quixote: An Anatomy).

Reading *Don Quixote* in the Americas

William Childers

Reading is a transformative act, both in the sense that it changes us, but also insofar as we remake the text according to our own needs. To go too far in either direction, though, results in a sterile encounter. In the one case, we are too passive, seeking only to uncover some ready-made wisdom deposited in a text by the author; in the other, too cavalier in our willingness to have the text mean whatever is most comfortable for us, too ready to ascribe to it what we already think. Finding the balance between these two extremes makes reading a profoundly pleasurable and life-enriching activity, in which the books we read become building blocks for an individuated self and a singular way of understanding the world.

Few books lend themselves more completely to this reciprocal process than *Don Quixote*. The coherence and at the same time the radical ambiguity of its central theme, the loose complexity of its composition, and the extraordinary range of its sudden shifts of emotion all combine to propel even the unaccustomed reader into an active role. Yet a book whose setting is so unfamiliar, so distant from our time, compels a certain respect for whatever shards we think we glimpse of the author's intentions. Of course, no one reads *Don Quixote* entirely free of preconceptions, whether these derive from general expectations about the novelistic genre, or from images specifically referring to the madman of La Mancha, generated on Broadway or in Hollywood. The dialectic of reading is constrained, then, not only by the text itself and the reader's mind, but also by the interpretive community or communities to which the reader belongs.

One approach that foregrounds this complex process of meaning construction is to have students examine ways in which *Don Quixote* has been read in particular historical and geographical settings. By reading, as it were, over the shoulder of novelists who have appropriated Cervantes's work, students experience others' creative struggles to understand and reshape *Don Quixote*. The crucial unit of analysis for this approach is the overall strategy of appropriation used by authors over time. Such a strategy encompasses elements of plot, character, theme, and style carried over from Cervantes as well as the way these are transformed by their context in the new work. Any discussion of the strategy also must take into account the principal features of *Don Quixote* that were not incorporated into the new work. Such critical engagement requires students to consider historical circumstances conditioning specific authors' reading/ rewriting. This in turn can make students' own interpretations bolder and more self-reflexive.

Of course, *strategy* implies intention. To begin with, we ascribe intention to Cervantes's own strategic appropriation of other texts. Is he simply parodying chivalric romance or, beyond the literary target, poking fun at heroism itself? Novelists appropriating *Don Quixote* construct a model of Cervantes's intention suited to their purposes, and we in turn have to develop a model to understand theirs. Exploring this textual hall of mirrors, where multiple intentions reflect one another, offers an ideal occasion for students to consider their own mental construction of the author in the reading process. Another question that arises concerning intentionality is whether we must always imagine the appropriating author *consciously* engaged in a strategic dialogue with Cervantes's text. Not necessarily. Given its prominence in the novelistic tradition, we can assume some minimal familiarity with *Don Quixote* on the part of any serious novelist. We can therefore choose to posit an unconscious strategy where an overt one is absent. The intertextuality also may be mediated by other texts that engage Cervantes more directly. In fact, a strategy can become institutionalized, so that it ceases to be the product of any individual writer's intention, conscious or otherwise. For example, in the nineteenth-century novel, elimination of the comic dimension of the hero and the multigeneric nature of Cervantes's work enabled the appropriation of quixotic figures within the paradigm of psychological realism. Here one can speak of a collective strategy, adopted with greater or lesser degrees of awareness by different novelists. Although these issues are difficult to resolve, students should be encouraged to grapple with questions about authorial intent.

My experience with a group of undergraduates in an upper-level general education course (open to juniors and seniors in any major) showed me the effectiveness of having each student read a novel inspired by *Don Quixote* and discuss the author's strategy of appropriation with the class. Organizing these presentations into panels based on coordinates of time and place gave the ensuing discussion coherence and dynamism. But the course I taught at Brooklyn College in fall 2008 was too ambitious and diffuse. Students read European authors, including Tobias Smollett, Laurence Sterne, Charlotte Lennox, Charles Dickens, Stendhal, Gustave Flaubert, Miguel de Unamuno, and Graham Greene, as well as many of the Latin American and North American writers mentioned in this article. A narrower focus, either geographical or historical, would have been more appropriate. One useful frame reads *Don Quixote* in the context of its reception in the Americas. Appropriations of Cervantes on this side of the Atlantic all share the common necessity of adapting a European text to the postcolonial condition of our hemisphere. But they also fall conveniently into two contrasting blocks: Anglo-American versus Latin American. Given the presence of both of these cultural traditions in the contemporary United States, this way of framing *Don Quixote* highlights its current relevance to students in this country to a degree that other approaches do not.

A major challenge this approach must address is that students do not readily perceive strategies of appropriation. For most undergraduates, the concept will be alien to their existing habits of reading. They tend to conceive of a work of literature as an author's original creation ex nihilo, and to the extent that they are familiar with any intertextual approach to literature, they will most likely be accustomed to thinking of the relation of one text to another in terms of the influence of the earlier author on the later one. But the concept of influence does not do justice to the range of ways in which later novelists situate themselves vis-à-vis Cervantes, and it implies a dependent relation that in the context of postcolonial literatures could smack of cultural imperialism.

At the outset, then, it is crucial to adequately introduce students to the notion of strategic appropriation. Of course, this presupposes knowledge of *Don Quixote* itself, which ideally would be achieved in a previous course focused exclusively on Cervantes's novel. Since a year-long course is most likely impractical, a third of the course or more may need to be devoted to reading the original work; this is the occasion in which to establish a repertoire of characteristics of Cervantes's text from which any writer making use of it will have had to select. One of the major questions all novelists appropriating Cervantes confront is the complex array of comedic effects in the work. *Don Quixote* is a funny book, yes, but is its humor primarily parody of other literary genres, social satire, ideological critique, or carnivalesque laughter? The role of irony and humor within the work and the degree to which these effects are considered essential features can go a long way toward differentiating such appropriations as, say, *Moby-Dick*, *Tom Sawyer*, and *One Hundred Years of Solitude*. This question is intimately tied to the larger issue of the purpose(s) of the work, ranging from mere entertainment through a critique of literary practice to social and political reform; and of course, by extension, to the attitude toward the central, quixotic character(s). Does the author merely make fun of the protagonist, or is there an element of ambivalence, such as most readers perceive in Cervantes's original? Another feature that varies greatly is the way other authors make use of (or choose to ignore) the bold metafictional play with multiple narrators, self-reflexive irony, and unreliability. This manifests itself in writers as diverse as Ana Castillo, Paul Auster, or Junot Díaz, giving ample room for distinguishing one from another. The point of such analysis is not simply to list the features of Cervantes's text that one or another author uses but to elaborate from that bundle of features an articulate explanation of an author's overall strategy.

Ultimately, the best way for students to learn to recognize strategies of appropriation is by means of models brief enough to be read by everyone and discussed in class. I have found Washington Irving's "The Legend of Sleepy Hollow" and Jorge Luis Borges's "Pierre Menard, Author of *Don Quixote*" to be two valuable examples that illustrate very different techniques of appropriation, each of which lends itself to a definite historical and geographical explanation. Irving's story of Ichabod Crane is pedagogically useful on several levels; certain passages patterned on *Don Quixote* are hard to miss, but more subtle parallels of style and tone, such as the playful references to oral tradition that ironically undercut narrative authority, will not be immediately evident to all students, and therefore can be explored in class. Irving's purposes in turning to Cervantes are likewise multiple. The Hispanophilia of the author of *Tales of the Alhambra* is well known; in the postcolonial context in which he wrote, the Spanish tradition serves to displace British cultural dominance. At the same time, Irving appropriates Cervantes's nuanced combination of parody and satire to poke gentle fun at New England's Puritan tradition, through the superstitious schoolmaster's reading of Cotton Mather's *History of New England Witchcraft*. *Don Quixote* thus serves Irving extremely well in his particular time and place, and the parallels are remarkably rich. The point, then, is not simply to chalk up "The Legend of Sleepy Hollow" as one more instance of Cervantes's "influence," but to understand how a certain way of adapting aspects of *Don Quixote* to his own historical circumstances served Irving's purposes as he initiated a literary tradition independent of Britain.

Borges's "Pierre Menard," on the other hand, responding to his quite different postcolonial situation, displaces the obligatory Spanish classic by means of French modernism. Especially when read alongside Roberto González Echevarría's insightful "Cervantes and the Modern Latin American Narrative," which, focusing on Borges and Alejo Carpentier, emphasizes the productive power for Latin American writers of Cide Hamete Benengeli and the undermining of narrative authority in Cervantes generally, "Pierre Menard" establishes a baseline for distinguishing between Latin American and Anglo-American appropriations. Much more so than their North American counterparts, upon liberation the former Spanish colonies found themselves plunged almost immediately into "Third World" neocolonial status, where they still remain, for the most part. Thus Borges's preference for the most aggressive aspects of Cervantes's experimentation, combined with the disavowal of the Spanish literary tradition enacted by ascribing *Don Quixote* to a twentieth-century French writer, provides a powerful example of a decolonizing strategy that has important implications for all Latin American novelists.

So *Don Quixote* can be read as a vehicle for dialogue across cultural and linguistic traditions throughout the Americas. One effective way of organizing such a course is to place students into groups by geographical areas according to the novels they choose—for example, the Caribbean, the Deep South, Mexico and the Southwest, or the Southern Cone. The appendix to this essay provides a list of suggested novels for these purposes. Differentiation into periods might provide an even better basis for comparison, since there are common elements uniting nineteenth-century writers that cut across geographical distribution. So, for example, one group could be assigned the nineteenth century, in a comparative context, studying such authors as Irving, José Fernández de Lizardi, Mark Twain, and Juan Montalvo. It might be useful to place Borges together with Anglo-American writers who seem to have learned by his example, such as Kathy Acker and Paul Auster. Or one could juxtapose novels where a certain thematic similarity makes itself felt: *The Great Gatsby* and *Bodega Dreams* represent one such pair; *As I Lay Dying* and *The Death of Artemio Cruz* are another.

Such a course implicitly aims at mapping the reception of *Don Quixote*. Though students' presentations and the ensuing discussions should flesh out the map, some bare-bones orientation in an informal lecture format is probably needed. A number of existing studies already contribute to developing this topographic understanding. Timothy Reiss, in his essay "Caribbean Knights" (in *Against Autonomy*), associates "Quijote" with a dialectic of historical rooted-ness and forgetting that serves as a prelude to setting forth anew, freed of the oppressive burden of the past. Reiss sees this paradigm as characteristic of both Cervantes's masterpiece and West Indian narratives in English, Spanish, and French. In *The Southern Inheritors of* Don Quixote, Monserrat Ginés ties fas-cination with the mad knight to the "Lost Cause" of the antebellum South. Fur-ther, she perceptively links the ambivalence between nostalgia for the past and ridicule of the anachronistic element in Southern culture found in such novel-ists as William Faulkner, Eudora Welty, and Walker Percy to the persistence of premodern, traditional agricultural communities at a time when more modern social forms of individualism and class mobility had long since gained ground in the more industrialized North. (For Faulkner's relation to Cervantes in particu-lar, see Manuel Broncano's study.) Taken together, these arguments set up one axis for the reception of *Don Quixote*, in the area of the Americas where colonial plantations relied on African slave labor. In this part of the world, ridicule of a petty nobleman's dreams of reviving chivalry (and presumably feudalism) inevi-tably evokes the colonial legacy and the difficult transition to modernity.

Beyond this core region of the Caribbean and southeastern United States, the legacy of colonialism makes itself felt in the reception of *Don Quixote* in other ways. In the southwestern United States, Chicano writers, due to their own colonial and neocolonial legacies, have understood Don Quixote as a figure of resistance to Anglo-American cultural imperialism (Childers, *Transnational Cervantes* 194–222). In "On the Marvelous Real in America," the prologue to *The Kingdom of this World*, Carpentier first put forward the notion that early modern Spain shares with much of postcolonial Latin America a cultural hy-bridity of Western rationalism with other worldviews. He found this hybridity at work in the ambivalent play with the marvelous in *Don Quixote* and other Cervantine works, as well as in the widespread novelistic practice known as magical realism, found in a triangle extending from Mexico to the Antilles in the east and the Andes in the south (Carpentier; Childers, *Transnational Cervantes* 44–79). As one moves further north or south, however—to the northeastern United States, for example, or the Southern Cone of South America—the re-ception of *Don Quixote* seems to change, focusing less on collective issues of identity and the burdens of the past and more on individual alienation and the *mise en abîme* of the self mirrored in its endlessly refracted representations. This is not to say, however, that novelists in the Americas ever entirely escape their postcolonial condition; only that it becomes more attenuated, more mixed with familiar European themes, as one moves further away from the tropics in either direction.

A topographic model of this sort need not be conceptualized as purely static, that is, as if each author corresponded to a single point permanently fixed on a grid. Authors' lives and careers form trajectories, resulting in subtle combina-tions of previously established strategies. Thus John Kennedy Toole, a native of New Orleans, began to work on his quixotic-carnivalesque *Confederacy of Dunces* while stationed in Puerto Rico in the Army (Nevils and Hardy 93–138), and his novel indeed combines elements of the "Southern inheritors" paradigm with a comic vision closer in spirit to the reception of *Don Quixote* in the Caribbean. More recently, in *The Brief Wondrous Life of Oscar Wao*, Díaz, a Dominican-born writer raised in New Jersey, combines a novel of alienation worthy of J. D. Salinger with a Latin American dictator novel. Moreover, Díaz does this by means of a quixotic character who appears to be modeled on Ignatius J. Reilly, the protagonist of *Confederacy of Dunces*, while employing a narrative technique reminiscent of Cervantes's play with multiple sources and ironically juxtaposed layers that undermine the stability of narrative authority. As far as the appropriation of *Don Quixote* is concerned, then, Díaz's novel perfectly straddles the Anglo-American and Latin American traditions, confirming, in the complexity of its trajectory, the validity of the configuration we have been examining (Childers, "*Don Quijote*").

I offer this free-wheeling topography not as a definitive map of ways of reading *Don Quixote* but rather as a provisional sketch, in the hope that it will give those interested in employing a reception-based approach something concrete with which to grapple—and perhaps something to reject in favor of an entirely different picture. Of course, there can never be a definitive map of possible interpretations, but the broad model I sketch here can chart constellations of appropriating strategies in a way that makes it appear that their distribution in space and time is anything but arbitrary. Among existing studies that can help to further clarify Cervantes's relation to the Americas, Diana de Armas Wilson's *Cervantes, the Novel, and the New World* stands out, as do Héctor Brioso Santos and José Montero Reguera's *Cervantes y América*, Frederick Viña's anthology *Don Quijote: Meditaciones hispanoamericanas*, and Luis Correa-Díaz's *Cervantes y América, Cervantes en las Américas*. My "Baroque Quixote" reads *Don Quixote* in the context of Latin American colonial chronicles.

The approach described in this essay is discussed as the basis for a semester-long undergraduate general education or comparative literature survey course taught in English, but it could also be used as part of a larger course—a final project or presentation, for example, might be devoted to the mapping of strategies of appropriation. I append a list of texts that lend themselves to inclusion, all but three of which (*La Quijotita, Capítulos que se le olvidaron a Cervantes*, and *Don Quijote en Yanquilandia*) are available in complete English translation. If the approach is used in a course taught in Spanish, it would make sense to place less emphasis on the United States and include instances of deliberate appropriation of Cervantes in Spanish Peninsular literature, such as texts by Benito Pérez Galdós, Miguel de Unamuno (*Niebla*), Azorín (*La ruta de Don Quijote*), Juan Goytisolo (*La reivindicación del Conde don Julián*), or Carmen Martín Gaite (*La Reina de las Nieves*).

For a semester-long course devoted to Cervantes, this approach, whether used as the central focus of the course or a separate final project, introduces an element of variety that students find attractive. Examining appropriations is a stimulating way of raising the rather esoteric-sounding issue of Cervantes's place in literary history, and does so in a way that makes the seemingly abstract theoretical question directly compelling. The approach also raises fundamental concerns about authorial intent that students will not easily elude, since although they may not know Cervantes's intentions, they can see certain ways of construing his meaning reflected clearly in the work of other authors who took their inspiration from his masterpiece.

APPENDIX
SUGGESTED TEXTS FOR A COURSE ON THE RECEPTION
OF *DON QUIXOTE* IN THE AMERICAS

When students receive this list, they should also be allowed to choose a novel not included in it, subject to instructor approval. The texts here are listed chronologically by their first date of publication.

Latin American

Fernández de Lizardi, José Joaquín. *La Quijotita y su prima: Historia muy cierta con apariencias de novela*. 1819. (*The Little Quixotess and Her Cousin: A Very Certain Story That Looks like a Novel.*)

Montalvo, Juan. *Capítulos que se le olvidaron a Cervantes*. 1895.

Azuela, Mariano. *Los de abajo*. 1915. (*The Underdogs.*)

Polar, J. M. *Don Quijote en Yanquilandia*. 1925.

Borges, Jorge Luis. "Pierre Menard, autor del *Quijote*." 1939. ("Pierre Menard, Author of *Don Quixote*.")

Carpentier, Alejo. *El reino de este mundo*. 1949. (*The Kingdom of This World.*)

Fuentes, Carlos. *La muerte de Artemio Cruz*. 1962. (*The Death of Artemio Cruz.*)

Arenas, Reinaldo. *El mundo alucinante*. 1966. (*Hallucinations.*)

García Márquez, Gabriel. *Cien años de soledad*. 1967. (*One Hundred Years of Solitude.*)

Roa Bastos, Augusto. *Yo, el supremo*. 1974. (*I, the Supreme.*)

Mutis, Alvaro. *Empresas y tribulaciones de Maqroll el Gaviero*. 1995. (*The Adventures and Misadventures of Maqroll.*)

Allende, Isabel. *Hija de la fortuna*. 1999 (*Daughter of Fortune.*)

Anglo-American

Irving, Washington. "The Legend of Sleepy Hollow." 1820.

Melville, Herman. *Moby-Dick*. 1851.

Twain, Mark. *The Adventures of Tom Sawyer.* 1876.

————. *The Adventures of Huckleberry Finn*. 1884.

Fitzgerald, F. Scott. *The Great Gatsby*. 1925.

Faulkner, William. *As I Lay Dying*. 1930.
———. *Absalom, Absalom!* 1937.
———. *The Wild Palms*. 1939.
Toole, John Kennedy. *A Confederacy of Dunces*. 1980.
Auster, Paul. *City of Glass*. 1985.
Acker, Kathy. *Don Quixote, Which Was a Dream*. 1986.

Chicano-Latino

Venegas, Daniel. *Las aventuras de don Chipote*. 1928. (*The Adventures of Don Chipote*.)
Arias, Ron. *The Road to Tamazunchale*. 1975.
Castillo, Ana. *The Mixquiahuala Letters*. 1986.
———. *So Far from God*. 1993.
González, Genaro. *The Quixote Cult*. 1998.
Quiñonez, Ernesto. *Bodega Dreams*. 2000.
Stavans, Ilan. Spanglish translation of *Don Quixote*, part 1, chapter 1, in *Spanglish: The Making of a New American Language*. 2003.
Díaz, Junot. *The Brief Wondrous Life of Oscar Wao*. 2007.

Windmills of the Mind:
The Devilish Devices of *Don Quixote*,
Part 1, Chapter 8

Frederick A. de Armas

The episode of the windmills/giants is as devilish as Don Quixote thinks it is. For this reason, it is important for understanding the entire text of *Don Quixote*. The episode's simplicity and verbal economy cleverly hide numerous traps and call for the participation of an active reader. If knights of old must guard against the ambushes of their enemies, the reader must learn to be wary of Cervantes. Studying this episode gives us a glimpse of the treacherous nature of his text. The transformations perceived by the knight are both surprising and appropriate. Are the giants giants of the mind? What is their significance? In class discussion, we can consider the uses of metaphor, metamorphosis, mnemonics, imitation, ekphrasis, technology, infernal inventions and invitations, and the importance of the early modern reader's visual and literary points of reference.

I usually arrive in class with the text, relevant books of criticism, and some illustrations. If the class is small or a seminar, I pass around the books of criticism, which I will discuss in some depth. Undergraduate students enjoy thumbing through these and often ask questions about a particular critical approach.[1] I show the illustrations to both graduate and undergraduate students. In a larger course, I will use *PowerPoint* to project these images. In order to get the class ready for participation and debate, I ask, Why is the adventure of the windmills, which occupies just a few pages, often taken to represent this entire novel? I show the two illustrations by Gustave Doré dealing with the episode. Many of the students' answers reflect those that have been given by critics:

The episode is a perfect example of the knight's excessive imagination.

It is the first adventure with both Don Quixote and Sancho; thus we have two different perspectives on what happens.

It can be easily visualized. The size of the windmills suggests the height of giants; the arms of giants suggest the sails of windmills.

It is possibly the only instance in the novel where the transformation breaks the boundary between animate and inanimate.

Windmills were recently introduced in La Mancha. The knight is therefore fighting against technology.

Windmills, according to other critics, actually existed in La Mancha since the Middle Ages but were seen as keeping wheat from the poor or pumping water away from the fields.   (Weiner 125; Reichenberger 29)

The episode symbolizes the battle of the weak against powerful forces or institutions.

It may have to do with Spain's wars in the Low Countries.

The sails of the windmill recall the power of Fortune.

(Ziolkowski 885)

Windmills of the mind reflected the fluctuations of thought and so might allude to the knight's madness. In discussing this connection, I show students Velázquez's painting of the jester Calabazas with a pinwheel in his left hand and remind them that, like the windmill, the pinwheel can signify simplemindedness or insanity.

(Redondo, *Otra manera* 333; see Greer)

Many of these interpretations can be applied to the novel as a whole — for example, the knight's excessive imagination, the relationship between Don Quixote and Sancho, the role of technology, the political and religious connotations of the novel, the relation between wisdom and madness.

I ask the students if they think that the comparison of windmills with giants is apt and show them an illustration from Teodoro Miciano's edition in which both windmills and giants appear (Dorn 28). Is Don Quixote truly mad, or are his giants a way to look at reality metaphorically? His *ingenio* ("wit") is one that prefers metaphors to similes or analogies. For the knight, one subject is not like another; it is the other. Here he follows Aristotle's *Poetics*, where metaphor "consists in giving the thing a name that belongs to something else" (1457b). This new name creates not similarity but identity: a metaphor's assertiveness forces the reader to consider either the interaction or confrontation of the two elements. Thus windmills are giants or confronted by giants, large beings who swing their arms violently.[2] Windmills do not menace, but the metaphor alters the knight's mind. His constant reading has collapsed differences, turning the metaphor into the very visual reality of menacing giants. The madness that overcomes him has its roots in the rhetorical devices of the works he reads. Collapsing the two terms as in a metaphor turns him into a poet-madman who views the world around him in a new way. Reading has thus led to the creation of new (visual) images.

I ask the students to recall the beginning of chapter 2 in order to understand metaphor as an ever-present device in the novel. We look back at the passage describing the problem encountered by the knight as he sallies forth: because he has engaged in no chivalric feats, his arms are unadorned; they are "armas blancas" 'blank arms' (1: 120; 24). He decides to clean them so that they become whiter than ermine. This is no mere figure of speech. The knight must know that the ermine is a creature of royalty and heraldry. The story that the ermine, when encircled in mud, "would prefer to be captured rather than to sully itself while trying to escape" (Rowland 74) was to be found in emblems and dictionaries of the Renaissance and early modern period (Covarrubias 146). I show the class images that link royalty to the ermine.[3] The act of making his arms white as an ermine grants Don Quixote, through figuration, the status he lacks. He eliminates the *as* and believes that his arms and shield now embody this heraldic device. Metaphor has become problematized, since the shield is not an ermine but has the image of an ermine. In this rhetorical somersault, the knight has gone from metaphor to allusive ekphrasis (ekphrasis is the description of an art object in the text). Each of Don Quixote's adventures can be considered a work of fiction that stems from his mind. They often emerge from metaphor and turn into visual images that are then written down by the mysterious and conflicted Arab historian Cide Hamete Benengeli.[4]

Nothing is simple, though the prose style appears plain and the narrative uncomplicated. It is possible that Cervantes, through the knight's fictional transformations, may be seeking to imitate an antique and authoritative text.[5] After asking the class which classical authors they have discovered in Cervantes's novel (there are many interesting replies, from Vergil to Lucan, from Plato to Horace), I have them turn to the burlesque poems that introduce it, poems ascribed to fictional characters. Students discover that Cervantes fashions himself as "nuestro español Ovidio" 'the Ovid of our Spain' (1: 108; 12). The wondrous transformations that take place in the novel, starting with the rustic Sancho who becomes a knight's squire, are thus linked to one of the classical texts most cited in the early modern period, the *Metamorphoses*. So another way to view the novel is through the lens of Ovid, whose many metamorphoses are not so removed from metaphor. Metamorphosis shows the process of transformation of one subject into another. In addition, metamorphoses are at the heart of the mythical, according to Leonard Barkan:

> But in the image of magical transformation there is always the mystery of the divine embedded in the real, the natural, the quotidian. Once metamorphosis has been perceived in that way, it emerges as not merely one element in myth but rather at the heart of myth itself. For a mythic view of the universe depends upon seeing the divine in the familiar.   (18)

Once again, we have an aggressive conflation of different subjects, of the divine and the quotidian.

In Cervantes's novel, both Don Quixote and Sancho transform themselves by taking on new roles. The knight, followed by his squire, also travels through a rural landscape that he molds through his metaphoric, metamorphic, visual, and mythic thinking process. An Ovidian universe is being renewed in these adventures, albeit mediated by the romances of chivalry. Cervantes and his knight thus enter into a conversation with the ancients. Ovid himself recast ancient tales into new forms, in his *Metamorphoses*. Cervantes delegates authority for most transformations to his crazed knight, creating a kind of dialectic imitation in which Don Quixote seeks to make a better world just as the modern text seeks to surpass the ancient through a new vision of the world. Yet the ancient text also struggles to assert its presence in the narrative.[6] Thus metamorphosis does not fully point to the mythical, unless the knight's madness is taken as Plato's *furor poeticus*, a type of divine inspiration that suffuses the world with a new Ovidian magic. Yet Raphael, in his fresco depicting Poetry, has this figure hold a sign that reads, "Numine afflatur"—to be moved by wind or by the numinous (Beck). Cervantes may be giving a nod to this platonic concept, when Don Quixote sees windmills and, moved by the numinous to become a poet of the imagination, transforms them into giants.

I remind the class that during the Renaissance many of the translations from Ovid were profusely illustrated. These illustrations had more than one purpose. According to William E. Engels, illustrations from Ovid's text, such as those found in George Sandys's translation of 1640, were "'road maps' linking key episodes so one could find his way and later recall key 'places'" (55). In other words, the visual images were mnemonic aids for the reader-viewer. I explain to the class that during this time period, the art of memory was very important and that treatises stressed that one of the easiest ways to memorize was to imagine a painting. The metamorphoses in Ovid's book can be easily recalled since they describe amazing and visually appealing transformations. I ask the class to think of Cervantes's novel as a new way to write of transformations. His images, as visually striking as those in Ovid, are therefore equally easy to remember. I pick one of the fifteen illustrations from Ovid and ask the class to establish connections between it and a transformation in Cervantes's text. What would a Cervantine road map look like? Discussion will usually show students one of the main differences between Ovid and Cervantes. Transformations in Ovid usually move downward—that is, from a divine, semidivine, or human figure to the animal and plant world; in Cervantes, they move upward, from inns to castles, from prostitutes to ladies. I then ask students to find exceptions to these generalizations in both Ovid and Cervantes.

There is yet another way of viewing these adventures. The knight may also be an artist, a painter. Is Don Quixote painting his own vision on the canvas of reality? Sight, after all, is foregrounded in most episodes. Ian Watt notes a threefold structure in them: "a visual stimulus, a misinterpretation of the stimulus by Quixote in terms of his chivalric compulsions; a realistic correction by Sancho Panza . . ." (*Myths* 64). The idea of the knight as painter takes us from metaphor, metamorphosis, mnemonics, and Ovidian road maps to ekphrasis. In ancient rhetoric, ekphrasis was a break in a narrative to describe an object—often an art object. But this rhetorical device itself metamorphosed over time. Writers might not describe but simply allude to an art object (allusive ekphrasis), or they might take a painting and make it into a dynamic scene (dramatic ekphrasis).[7] I remind the class that we experienced a clash between these two types of ekphrasis in a previous episode. When Don Quixote discovers Andrés without a shirt, tied to a tree and enduring the lashings of his master, the youth at one point refers to his punishment as that of Saint Bartholomew, who was flayed alive (1: 138 [ch. 4]; 37). This allusive ekphrasis to the many paintings of the saint clashes with the scene taking place. Bartholomew was an older man when his flaying occurred, whereas Andrés is around fifteen; Bartholomew's tormentor used a knife to take off his skin, whereas Andrés is just being lashed. Thus the dramatic ekphrasis viewed by Don Quixote contrasts with the allusive ekphrasis provided by Andrés.

The question of ekphrasis is even more complex in the windmills episode. Given the many illustrations of this episode, the uninitiated reader would expect a lengthy description, an extended ekphrasis. All we are told is that the knight and his squire "descubrieron treinta o cuarenta molinos de viento que hay en aquel campo" 'saw thirty or forty windmills found in that countryside' (166; 58). The lack of detail is remarkable, a kind of ellipsis that leaves it up to the reader to imagine these windmills. The metamorphosis of them into giants is equally terse. Don Quixote tells Sancho, "La ventura va guiando nuestras cosas mejor de lo que acertáramos a desear; porque ves allí, amigo Sancho Panza, donde se descubren treinta, o pocos más, desaforados gigantes, con quien pienso hacer batalla y quitarles a todos las vidas" 'Good fortune is guiding our affairs better than we could have desired, for there you see, friend Sancho Panza, thirty or more enormous giants with whom I intend to do battle and whose lives I intend to take' (166; 58). Sancho (and the reader) are told to look, yet the giants are not described, except for the adjective "desaforados" 'enormous.' The transformation in itself is what astounds, which is a creation of the knight's imagination, thus an ur-ekphrasis, for an art object has come from the character's mind.

I remind the students that Ovid most often uses metamorphosis as part of the natural world. We recall transformations of Acteon into a stag; Aretusa into a spring; Adonis, Hyacinth, and Narcissus into flowers; Atalanta and Hipomenes into lions; Cyparissus into a cypress; Daphne into a laurel tree. Cervantes's novel usually follows Ovid in that beings are transformed into other beings—prostitutes into ladies, herds of sheep into armies, and so on. Cervantes's inanimate objects become other inanimate objects: inns, for example, turn into castles. But both Ovid and Cervantes sometimes break these rules. Ovid's metamorphoses can turn a woman to stone and bring a stone to life. Anaxarete, accused by her lover of having a heart of stone, is turned into a statue when she gazes at her dead suitor. When Pygmalion falls in love with a statue he has made and appeals to Venus at her festival, the ivory maiden comes to life. These transformations that break the boundary between the animate and the inanimate are related to the power of love. Cervantes challenges Ovid. His Anaxarete, Marcela, does not turn to stone when viewing the dead Grisóstomo. By telling others that his death was not her fault, she pleads for liberty in love. In the episode of the windmills, the transformation of inanimate into animate causes not love but hatred. These differences between Ovid and Cervantes show students that Cervantes was engaged in a conversation and contest with the classical authors of Greece and Rome as well as with the artists of the Italian Renaissance. In the process, students learn to read a text as a cultural response that imitates, appropriates, converts, and subverts images and ideas.

If Don Quixote is an artist who reinvents the reality around him, his creations are not always beautiful and enticing. He shows both sides of the artist, the inspired bard who perceives beauty, harmony, and the return of a golden age but also the melancholy painter who has nightmarish visions.[8] We do not have a true ekphrasis with the windmills. Sancho in his response to his master describes not them but their technology: ". . . y lo que en ellos parecen brazos son las aspas, que, volteadas del viento, hacen andar la piedra del molino" '. . . and what looks like their arms are the sails that are turned by the wind and make the grindstone move' (166; 58). Don Quixote proceeds to battle the new invention. This introduction of technology in place of ekphrasis reminds us that the ancients were fascinated with the animation of statues. Daedalus is said to have created statues that could talk and even walk, and Hephaestus was reputed to have created automata.[9] I ask the class, Is Ovid providing a mythical underpinning to technology? And is Cervantes taking this technology and mythologizing it? After all, he refers to the ancient gigantic creature Briareus (168; 59). Briareus is a devilish creature who is described in Dante's *Purgatorio* and inhabits the deepest pit of hell in Dante's *Inferno*. Is Don Quixote's melancholy mind invaded by beings from the netherworld?

The purgatorial and infernal aspects of the episode come to culmination when the knight is defeated. Revealing to us that an evil enchanter has turned the giants into windmills, he excises and exorcises his own metaphor. Evil powers prevent him from seeing the reality of his chivalric quest. But Sancho has the last word: he tells the knight that the knight carries windmills in his mind. The windmill was an image for madness, as seen in the Velázquez painting of Calabazas. The whirling of the sails is like the rush of disconnected thoughts.

As a concluding exercise, I show the class an image of the fresco in the Hall of Giants at the Palazzo del Te in Mantua, one of the most fantastic and frightening creations of the Italian Renaissance (Hartt 1: 153). The gods watch in horror as Jupiter destroys the giants who have rebelled against the Olympian deities and are ascending to the heavens. The arms and heads of giants floating among rocks could well have provided a model for the conflation of giant with stone (windmills) in Cervantes's novel. The strong winds that are pictured as blowing across the painting may also indicate how the giant/windmill is activated in Don Quixote. And Briareus shows his demonic presence in Giulio Romano's fresco. Jupiter destroys the giants, but Don Quixote is unable to contain his demonic inventions. They whirl in his mind like the wind that sweeps through Romano's gigantomachia, like the wind that turns windmills.

The buffeting winds of the episode have taken us from metaphor to metamorphosis to mimesis (imitation) to mnemonics to ekphrasis to madness. What are we to make of the windmills of the mind? Don Quixote, tilting at windmills, demonstrates how thin is the line between genius and madness and has us view in extraordinary ways the world—its objects, people, and ideas. We are stronger because of this feeble knight. The text gently endows the reader with the ability to see and to read in new ways. Even as Don Quixote fails in his enterprises, he challenges others to reconsider long-held ideas and to embrace the winds of change. For this reason, we turn to him in this modern world of constant change.

NOTES

The English translation of *Don Quixote* used in this essay is by Edith Grossman.

[1] For the windmills adventure I bring critical works by Barkan; Engels; Parr, *Don Quixote: An Anatomy*; Redondo, *Otra manera*; Richards; Watt, *Myths*; and Yates.

[2] For I. A. Richards, the image and the idea are given equal value in metaphor, since metaphor is "a transaction between contexts" (95). Richards points to a metaphor's interactions and its use to facilitate comprehension, but George Whalley prefers the term "confrontation" (494).

[3] There is a famous portrait of Elizabeth with an ermine at her side. The animal wears a collar in the form of a crown, which is "expressive of both the triumph of her reformed imperial rule and of her personal triumph as a chaste Petrarchan heroine" (Yates 114).

[4] On the many narrative levels in the novel and on the role of the metanarrator and of Cide Hamete, see Parr, *Don Quijote: An Anatomy*.

[5] For some critics, the prologue represents a rejection of the authority of the word, of *auctoritas*. But Cervantes is merely mocking those who use authority to make themselves authoritative—in this, he may be referring to Lope de Vega. Imitation of the classics or of religious texts, to be truly authoritative, must be subtle, disguised (see de Armas, *Cervantes* 1–15).

[6] According to Greene, we move to dialectic imitation when there is a current of mutual aggression as the modern text exposes the "vulnerability" of its model "while exposing itself to the subtext's potential aggression" (45).

[7] For a discussion of the different types of ekphrasis, see de Armas, *Quixotic Frescoes* 11–12.

[8] Teresa Soufas shows that in the ranks of the melancholy of Spanish Golden Age literature are the malcontent, the mad, the tortured, and the criminal.

[9] For Cervantes's uses of technology, see Jaksic; Weiner; and de Armas, *Quixotic Frescoes* 134–52.

Teaching *Don Quixote* through Images

Carmen García de la Rasilla

"Yo apostaré, dijo Sancho, que antes de mucho tiempo no ha de haber bode-gón, venta ni mesón, o tienda de barbero, donde no ande pintada la historia de nuestras hazañas" ' "I'll wager," said Sancho, "that before long there won't be a tavern, an inn, a hostelry, or a barbershop where the history of our deeds isn't painted" ' (2: 618 [ch. 71]; 923). Sancho's intuition proved to be visionary and true. Images of Don Quixote and his adventures, alone or in the company of his squire, proliferated in the centuries that followed the publication of the novel in the form of book illustrations, paintings, statues, and innumerable household objects and souvenirs.

As Edward C. Riley observed, the iconographic success of Cervantes's novel has no precedent in the history of literature. Unlike other famous literary char-acters, Don Quixote is an icon instantly recognized even by those who have not read a line of the book (*"Don Quixote"* 107–08). In fact, it would be dif-ficult to find statuettes of Oedipus, T-shirts with the image of Tartuffe, or soup dishes with Lady Macbeth, but objects of all sorts constantly reproduce Don Quixote's image. The long tradition of illustrations has made *Don Quixote* a text that constantly reminds us of its visual nature. Consequently, a pedagogi-cal consideration of the text's visual dimension and iconographic history merits consideration as one approach to teaching the novel.

Such an approach to *Don Quixote* may help make the complex Cervantine narrative more accessible to a young audience schooled in modern visual cul-ture. Close attention to the images generated by the text can elicit immediate empathy towards a character who, like students themselves, is interested in vi-sual constructions of the world. Similarly, an analysis of the visual components of *Don Quixote* can help students appreciate the masterful use of the written word to paint a complex fictional world.

The text's visual appeal constitutes one of the bases of modern narrative, for Don Quixote's visions are the raison d'être of his adventures and the spur of the novel's dynamics. As Roberto González Echevarría has noted, "*El Quijote* es la novela de la visión y de las visiones de su protagonista. Numerosas aventuras comienzan cuando el hidalgo y su escudero ven acercarse a alguien o algo, y culminan cuando cada uno ve una cosa diferente" 'The *Quixote* is the novel of the visual and of its protagonist's visions. Many adventures begin when the hidalgo and his squire see someone or something approaching and culminate when each sees a different thing' (*"Don Quijote"* 109; my trans.). It is no coinci-dence, then, that artists such as Gustave Doré or Salvador Dalí, who understood the visual language of the mind, chose to illustrate those imaginary moments of the story dominated by Don Quixote's paranoiac visions, such as the adventure of the windmills, the battle with a flock of sheep, the episode of the penitents, or the incident with the wineskins (see García de la Rasilla).

Among other topics, a course using this focus can revolve around three crucial subjects: (a) the analysis of the image of Don Quixote as an icon instantly recognized and even as a visual or media phenomenon that has become independent from the novel; (b) the Cervantine subject of *ut pictura poesis*—that is, the ekphrastic character of a narrative that reveals a double text, the written one and the visual and imaginary; and (c) the long tradition of *Don Quixote*'s iconographic exegesis as a reflection on historical perspectivism in reading, and as a testimony of its vitality and growth as a text constantly rewritten through evolving graphic interpretations. In sum, this essay will be useful for those instructors wishing to develop an interdisciplinary course on *Don Quixote*, as well as for those interested in teaching the exegesis and representation of the novel attempted by its illustrators throughout various historical periods and in diverse cultural circumstances, while an analysis of the text's pictorial dimension should offer insights into the suggestiveness of its complex narrative.

On the first day of class, students can be encouraged to confront their own image of Don Quixote and inquire how they can visually identify the famous character almost instantly even when they have not read the novel. This paradoxical situation can be an excellent opportunity to engage readers in the discovery of the literary and cultural mechanisms responsible for that phenomenon. In addition, students can discuss the need and role of illustrations and whether images complement or advance the written text. Donald W. Bleznick has highlighted the relationship between powerful archetypal appeal of the icon and noted that "Cervantes depicts the psyche's journey from the primordial pool of the unconscious to a higher level of consciousness and knowledge" (98). The studies of some major critics, such as Mikhail Bakhtin (*Rabelais*) and Francisco Márquez Villanueva (*Fuentes*), may help students understand the influence of archetypal figures such as those of Carnival (a fat, gluttonous man) and Lent (a thin, austere woman)—as depicted by Brueghel the Elder in his *Battle between Carnival and Lent* of 1559 (www.pieter-bruegel-the-elder.org/The-Battle-between-Lent-and-Carnival-large.html)—in the physical and psychological formation of Cervantes's characters.

However, it is also true that Cervantes humanized those rather abstract medieval figures and incarnated them in Don Quixote and Sancho through the use of realistic details drawn from popular beliefs and from the medical lore of his time (González Echevarría, *"Don Quijote"* 113). In fact, the construction of the image of Cervantes's famous characters may be traced to notions of physiognomy that circulated in Golden Age Spain closely related with well-established models of correspondence between body and mind. Julio Caro Baroja's *Historia de la fisiognómica: El rostro y el carácter* ("History of Physiognamy: Countenance and Personality"), as well as M. Herrero García's article "Los rasgos físicos y el carácter según los textos españoles del siglo XVII" ("Physical Traits and Personality in Seventeenth-Century Spanish Texts") and Agustín Redondo's edited volume *Le corp dans la société espagnole des XVIème et XVIIème siècles* ("The Body in Sixteenth- and Seventeenth-Century Spanish Society") are valuable sources for a historicist understanding of Cervantes's depiction of Don Quixote and Sancho. Students interested in psychology and perceptions of the body may also explore visual parallels with modern constitutional psychology and the cultural presence in Western and other civilizations of behavioral and intellectual expectations and assumptions based on physical appearance, as they operate in the novel's iconography.

In their study of the two protagonists, Redondo ("Tradición" and "Personaje") and Monique Joly have revealed how other pairs of carnivalesque and comic figures popular in Cervantes's day helped to mold the Manchegan knight and his squire. This parallel between Ganassa, a thin man, and Bottarga, a fat man, may become an excellent point of departure to highlight the fact that much of the popular success of Don Quixote and Sancho, as was the case with Ganassa and Bottarga, hinges on their being a comic double act. This trope of an odd pair in dialogue has both a distinguished ancestry and a long progeny. Thus students may be given individual assignments to explore its classical roots in the works of Roman playwrights such as Terence and Plautus and its role as a model for other canonic literary couples such as Mr. Pickwick and Sam Weller, Frodo and Sam Gamgee, Sherlock Holmes and Dr. Watson, and even for comedic duos such as Laurel and Hardy and Abbott and Costello, not to mention robots such as C3PO and R2D2 of *Star Wars* (Riley, "*Don Quixote*" 109–10). Students may well recognize other favorite literary, filmic, or TV couples whose comic look, personality, motivations and actions may have been colored by Don Quixote and Sancho, and analyze those common elements that come into play in their humorous appearance and interaction.

As a first step to approach the figures of the knight and his squire in the text, I ask students to look into specific chapters (I would recommend beginning with the prologue and chapters 1, 2, and 9 of part 1) and to find the precise lines that depict both characters.[1] Students generally realize that Cervantes's physical descriptions are brief and fairly sporadic. But how, then, did Cervantes manage to draw in a few brushstrokes such powerful and suggestive images? In their search for the pertinent descriptive passages students usually obtain different results as some references to Don Quixote and Sancho are subtly embedded in the text and thus may elude them. For instance, this is what generally happens when they read, "Iba Sancho Panza sobre su jumento como un patriarca con sus alforjas y su bota, y con mucho deseo de verse ya gobernador de la ínsula que su amo le había prometido" 'Sancho Panza rode on his donkey like a patriarch, with his saddlebags, and his wineskin, and a great desire to see himself governor of the *ínsula* his master had promised him' (1: 164 [ch. 7]; 56). Although at first sight this presentation offers no specifics regarding the squire's body or temper, a more analytic reading reveals an incisive and metonymic description of Sancho's sense of self-assurance and naïveté when the narrator points to his almost constant preoccupation with food and drink. Just as Pablo Picasso's emblematic and minimalist painting of Don Quixote and Sancho manages to convey with remarkable economy of details the iconic dimension and power of this literary couple (see Mallén), so Cervantes depicts with sparse but highly suggestive and scattered strokes two of the most interesting characters in world literature.

Students should also be asked to analyze and explain how Cervantes applies this "minimalist" technique to entire episodes, as is the case with perhaps one of the most famous and visually powerful passages in the novel: the adventure of the windmills. Again, we may ask students to write or discuss the iconic projection of this adventure, considering above all its conciseness and brief narrative architecture. Riley points out that the visual appeal of the scene can be found in its ties to Don Quixote's personal perspective, as well as his idealism, militancy, and capriciousness. That is, the scene underscores the qualities that inform the quixotic myth: "To contemplate the picture of Don Quixote tilting at a windmill is to grasp the sense of that 'familiar adjective' quixotic" (*"Don Quixote"* 115).

In other words, Cervantes constructed such a compelling popular icon in large part by tightly connecting Don Quixote's physical image with his psychological and spiritual qualities, whether he is found reading in his library or engaged in action or battle. Entire scenarios of the novel's most familiar episodes function as props for the development of his image. The construction of the image is then the result of a system of resonances that includes visual and non-visual aspects or elements and that often operates as follows: (1) the description of a few physical details; (2) the presence of objects that belong to or surround the two heroes, and that are evocative or symbolic of their psychological and spiritual personality and social status; (3) the confirmation of their qualities and personalities through their monologues, dialogues, interaction with other characters and involvement in specific actions and adventures.

The quixotic image is thus a complex synthesis of physical, psychological, spiritual, intellectual, and social traits that reflect and inform one another while projecting themselves onto the narrated scene or action. The adventure of the windmills with its aftermath provides instructors with a useful example of this visual dynamic. Students may be asked to search for what Jorge Luis Borges considered an essential asset of an enduring literary character, the memorable and symbolic or emblematic situation or object (*Prólogos* 119). Epitomized by his buckler and spear, windmills, the emaciated horse, and the Castilian plains, the image of Don Quixote lends itself to a variety of interpretative approaches, from the psychological to the social, and students often profit from an analysis of the historical and cultural implications of such iconic props.

The text's remarkable imagistic fertility should provide a fine opportunity to approach the ekphrastic component of the novel—that is, its use of words to depict images for the mind. Ekphrasis (from the Greek *ekphrazein*, meaning to tell in full) is an ancient artistic technique that consists of using words to create visual representations. This literary technique, dating back to Homer (the shield of Achilles in book 18 of *The Iliad*), led in the classical era to a fruitful discussion of the similarities and connections between the plastic arts and the written text that has lasted into modern times. As an exercise students may discuss Don Quixote's preoccupation with his literary image and to what extent his concerns were confirmed by the profusion of images that have deviated from the Cervantine icon. Cervantes addresses this subject of *ut pictura poesis* (Horace 490 [lines 361–65]; "as is painting, so is poetry") directly when Don Quixote expresses his preoccupation with the distorted image presented in Alonso Fernández de Avellaneda's unauthorized sequel (pt. 2, ch. 72).

The historicist approach of Frederick de Armas provides instructors with a very valuable insight into Cervantes's transformation of this tradition, what de Armas calls "the magic of the ur-ekphrasis"—that is, "the creation of an art object in the character's mind. And this imagination has as one of its functions to foreground the imaginative qualities of the text itself" ("Simple Magic" 18). I use the surrealist illustrations of a popular modern artist, Salvador Dalí, to explain how this "magic ur-ekphrasis" works. The Spanish painter depicts how Don Quixote visualizes in his mind a detailed obsessive image that produces a paranoiac interpretation of the external world and propels the consequent narrated adventures. In one of his prints Dalí literally opens Don Quixote's head to expose his paranoiac imagination at work (he is confronting a giant/windmill). Instructors may use the ekphrastic relationship between the written and visual aspects to ask students to consider and analyze other dichotomies and parallels, such as its dual nature as a novel of chivalry and a parody, and the protagonist's role as hero and antihero.

The ekphrastic (or pictorial) nature of the novel is behind an impressive iconographic production that may enable careful readers to see "what is absent or negated by the words in the text," as Eduardo Urbina points out (27). It will also allow them to observe and contextualize in historical terms the reception and reinterpretation of *Don Quixote* throughout the centuries. From the myriad of images available, instructors may choose the most famous, seminal, or influential to illuminate how every period has produced its own pictorial exegesis of the novel. according to specific cultural parameters and historical situations. For instance, the illustrations of Gaspar Bouttats (Brussels, 1662) are a possible point of departure for a discussion of seventeenth-century comic and carnivalesque conceptions of the text, while a hundred years later those by John Vanderbank, influenced by the spirit of the Enlightenment, present a very different perspective and elevate the previously denigrated and ridiculed image of Don Quixote while rescuing the novel for the intellectual elite. Historical periods, however, should not be taken monolithically, and students should also be able to appreciate interpretative discrepancies within eras. For instance, two late-eighteenth-century illustrators, William Hogarth and Francisco de Goya, both produced unorthodox illustrations of the novel that were rejected by the cultural establishment of the time. Their pictorial reading, identified with the knight's imaginative and sentimental perspective, foreshadowed the Romantic view of *Don Quixote* immortalized by Doré in the nineteenth century. Doré, like Goya, explored Don Quixote's paranoiac imagination and reflected the inner turmoil of the Romantic hero torn by the contradictions between his interior world and exterior reality.

The pioneering study of Juan Givanel Mas y Gaziel and more recent examinations by specialists such as Urbina, John J. Allen and Patricia S. Finch, Rachel Schmidt, Patrick Lenaghan, Enrique Mallén, or Stephen Miller, provide useful insights to teach the iconography of the *Quixote* from a variety of perspectives. Instructors may decide to focus on predominant models, such as responses offered by specific periods and cultural trends (the baroque era, the Romantic movement, realism and naturalism, modernism, postmodernism, etc.) or to provide an entire panorama of the novel's pictorial exegesis. I ask my students to compare the interpretation of artists from diverse centuries or artistic movements, and to explain their different pictorial views as a result of the interaction of three factors: the graphic demands or suggestions of the novel, the artist's personal style and development, and the specific cultural or historical circumstances of the period. Although quite challenging, this will often prove a useful technique with which to demonstrate the long reach of this novel beyond its moment, to connect with student interests in particular historical eras (for instance, contemporary America) and ultimately as a vehicle to discuss the special nature of texts canonized as classics.

José Manuel Lucía Megías's theory of "lectura coetánea" (*Leer* 39–64; "coetaneous reading") may be applied to the analysis of the different valorizations of the novel suggested by the evolution of quixotic illustration during the early modern and modern eras. Students could be asked to explain or discover which aspects of the novel have been elevated to graphic status and which have been dismissed or less frequently illustrated. More than studying those "universal" and classical images of Don Quixote and Sancho, depicted to transmit a close reading of the text, Lucía Megías focuses on models that have adapted *Don Quixote* and its imagery to the specifics of particular nationalities, cultures, or ethnicities (15–38).[2]

Present-day student audiences may find the internet an essential tool to manage the massive iconographic production generated by *Don Quixote*. The World Wide Web can be a crucial source for any investigation of the dimension, scope, and contemporary interest in the graphic aspects of Cervantes's novel. Directed by Eduardo Urbina, the "Cervantes Project" presents a general iconography of the work of Cervantes (http://cervantes.tamu.edu/V2/CPI/index.html) while the *Don Quixote* Exhibit displays translations and illustrations of the novel from the collection of the George Peabody Library and contains links to other useful sites (http://quixote.mse.jhu.edu/).

Finally, instructors interested in the modern graphic resonance of *Don Quixote* might wish to engage their class in a discussion of the theory and practice of commodification and their implications for the contemporary tourist industry in Spain and other Hispanic societies. The contemporary trade in quixotic products and images, evidenced in the thousands of Quixotes represented on ceramics, T-shirts, postcards, stamps, matchbooks, calendars, and all kinds of strange and extravagant objects and publications known as ephemera, can now be studied thanks to the database elaborated by the University of Castilla–La Mancha.

Using this tool, and as a final exercise in the appraisal of the graphic aspects of the book, the instructor could ask the class whether commodification helps to spread acquaintance with the novel and turn nonreaders toward the *Quixote* or actually cancels or subverts any possible cultural objective associated with the images of the hidalgo and his squire. Can a text as graphically fertile and suggestive as *Don Quixote* ultimately be undermined by the commercialization of its imagistic possibilities in today's globalized and leisure-oriented economy? In other words, has Don Quixote been beaten again by the image-seeking merchants of Toledo? In this manner, the course, like the novel itself, comes to a close by returning to the questions raised at the beginning.

NOTES

I wish to thank Professor Fernando González de León for his valuable suggestions and input concerning this essay. The English translation of *Don Quixote* used in this essay is by Edith Grossman.

[1] In addition to using Lathrop's Don Quijote *Dictionary* for a definition of the objects, arms, and pieces of clothing that configure the look of the knight and his squire, Givanel's classic *Historia gráfica de Cervantes y del* Quijote ("Graphic History of Cervantes and *Don Quixote*") offers a compendium of Cervantes's descriptions of the Manchegan hero and includes photographs of relevant contemporary items.

[2] To approach the *Quixotes* produced in the United States, for example, would be especially appealing for an American student audience. One may ask the class to discuss whether the various illustrated editions published in this country from the mid–nineteenth century to the present have denaturalized or recontextualized the novel by transforming or morphing the hidalgo and his squire into popular myths fighting in the United States, living in the twentieth century, traveling in balloons or by car, and even appearing in Mickey Mouse or Donald Duck cartoons. It would be fascinating to compare these depictions with other nations' versions of *Don Quixote*, each of which enacts its own iconographic program of cultural appropriation of the novel and the myth.

Don Quixote and Postmodern Film

Barbara Simerka and Christopher Weimer

When teaching texts from previous eras, we seek to engage students by identifying convergences among societies that are widely separated in time, yet we must also provide guidance to avoid anachronistic projections of present-day values. Long before the rise of cultural studies, traditional humanists presented canonical Renaissance texts as universal works because of a sense that the view of humanity in those texts anticipated the modern Western construct of the autonomous, democratic individual. Although notions of universal values have been challenged and new models for comparing historical moments have come into use, scholars continue to explore the reasons that sixteenth-century European culture appears to us as a refraction of society today. The term *early modern* has arisen in recent decades in order to accommodate new formulations of Renaissance cultures, which emphasize particular homologies with our current postmodern epistemology. We use the metaphor of refraction (as opposed to reflection) in order to engage students in a productive comparative analysis of the two cultural moments. In this essay, we delineate our tactics for using popular contemporary film in order to facilitate student understanding of the primary epistemological and narrative convergences between early modern and postmodern poetics, and also to develop student competence in comparative historical analysis.

To introduce Cervantes's cultural and intellectual milieu, we present key concepts from Stephen Greenblatt's *Renaissance Self-Fashioning*. Greenblatt conceptualizes the early modern and the postmodern in relation to modernity, a relation that the terms themselves indicate. The two eras serve as bridges leading to and from modernity: the early modern marks the formation of the modern, the postmodern the dissolution of the modern. Greenblatt asserts, "[W]e sense that we are situated at the close of the cultural movement initiated in the Renaissance and that the places in which our social and psychological world seems to be creaking apart are these structural joints visible when it was first constructed" (174–75). To prepare students for comparisons of the Cervantine novel to recent films, we foreground the heightened sense shared by inhabitants of each cultural moment that both the individual self and reality are ephemeral, "a construct, a thing made, as temporary, time-conditioned and contingent" (174). Next we present students with an overview of postmodernism, such as can be found in the first chapter of Linda Hutcheon's *The Poetics of Postmodernism*. We provide a reading guide with questions designed to help students identify connections between Greenblatt's formulation of the early modern and Hutcheon's postmodern paradigm. We emphasize passages that point to key convergences: early and postmodern texts alike are concerned with "an ironic reworking" of popular cultural texts of the past and with presenting startling juxtapositions of opposing genres that serve to demystify the process of narration itself (Hutcheon, *Poetics* 5). Both also employ unreliable narration and commit "radical" transgressions of the boundary between art and life (116).

Students may also read the introduction to Robert Alter's *Partial Magic*. Alter depicts *Don Quixote* as a text "that systematically flaunts its own condition of artifice and that by so doing probes into the problematic relationship between real-seeming artifice and reality" (x). He sees Don Quixote's visit to the publishing house in Barcelona as Cervantes's forceful reminder that "Don Quixote himself is no more than the product of the very processes he observes." Significantly, Alter also compares this textual moment's effect to "the cinematic device that has recently been put to such abundant and various use in which cameras, klieg lights, costumes, and props obtrude into the filmed scene" (4). Although Alter's book defines itself as studying the self-reflexive rather than the postmodern novel, his observations are clearly applicable. In this essay, using the frameworks provided by Greenblatt, Hutcheon, and Alter, we compare *Don Quixote* with three films: *Melinda and Melinda* (2004), *Stranger than Fiction* (2006), and *Nurse Betty* (2000).[1]

Reflexivity and Genre in Don Quixote *and* Melinda and Melinda

We first consider the deliberate and self-conscious scrutiny of how generic norms shape reader and viewer expectations in *Don Quixote,* part 1, and Woody Allen's *Melinda and Melinda.* Using James Parr's model of part 1 as an "anatomy" (Don Quixote: *An Anatomy*), we explore with the students how the text and the film similarly manipulate multiple narrative genres to lay bare and problematize the norms of those genres. A central feature of *Don Quixote's* part 1 is its incorporation of the many popular literary genres of Cervantes's era, among them the pastoral, Morisco narrative, the exemplary novel, the picaresque—and, most important, of course, the chivalric romance. Don Quixote and Sancho's adventures can even be read as a frame tale in the tradition of Boccaccio's *Decameron,* offering a deconstruction of chivalric norms even as it encloses numerous intertextual reworkings and parodies. Placing this aspect of the work in the tradition of Menippean satire's wide-ranging, "free-form structure," Parr argues that *Don Quixote* is "a self-conscious, subversive anatomy" and "a self-conscious and self-questioning text" resembling less the realist novel than "more modern (perhaps postmodern) narrative" (Don Quixote: *A Touchstone* 161).[2]

In the interpolated tales, as well as in the pseudo-chivalric misadventures, Cervantes reworks and reinscribes popular fictional genres in ways that both invert and subvert familiar tropes, ideas, and techniques. Thus readers who anticipate various conventions have surprises in store for them. Very few of Don Quixote's adventures successfully adhere to the chivalric template he tries so hard to impose on the world around him. The gap between his expectations and his lived reality lays bare the lack of verisimilitude in his favored genre. Similarly, the women of pastoral tales are not supposed to defend their independence as Marcela does, nor is Zoraida's relationship with the Spanish captain typical of captivity narratives. Genres in *Don Quixote* are deliberately, intrinsically unstable, calling attention to themselves by misleading and confounding expectations.

Keeping in mind the self-reflexive aspects of the interpolated tales in part 1, students can begin to explore postmodern parody through analysis of examples from popular culture. We begin with discussion of *The Simpsons*, for in nearly every episode of it Matt Groening deconstructs the generic norms of such bourgeois family comedies as *The Brady Bunch* and *Family Ties*. Students may expand this discussion by pointing to animated series like *South Park* and *Family Guy*, which push the ironic cartoon envelope even beyond Groening's innovations. Technology allows students to capture short sequences from Web sites, which they then present in class. We ask them to compare the tactics that *Don Quixote* and the three animated programs use to scrutinize genre codes in their respective cultural moments. We also discuss specifically the early modern cultural fantasies implied by the pastoral and chivalric genres as well as the phenomenon of entertainment fiction, in juxtaposition with the postmodern phenomena of idealized family comedy and television as cultural narrative.

Students can also find the violation of genre expectations in film; often they will point to misleading trailers or actors who deviate from their stock characters. This analysis paves the way for our consideration of *Melinda and Melinda*, which is structured as a Boccaccian frame tale of four New Yorkers enjoying an after-dinner conversation. Two of them, Sy and Max, are playwrights, one known for his romantic comedies and the other for his serious dramas. We show the opening scenes, in which their friend Al relates a real-life anecdote about a woman, Melinda, whose unexpected arrival disrupted a small dinner party. Each playwright presents his vision of Melinda's arrival: Sy's is comic, Max's dramatic. Both scenarios employ well-worn plot devices and thus create generic expectations in the viewers. After watching, students are asked to identify similarly well-worn films or television programs and predict, on the basis of their expectations, how both stories will unfold. The dramatic Melinda's account of her cross-country bus journey to flee a controlling, abusive husband immediately puts her story in the tradition of cinematic women in jeopardy, such as Julia Roberts's protagonist in *Sleeping with the Enemy* and countless heroines of made-for-television movies on the Lifetime network—women attempting to escape their pasts and remake their lives. On the comic side, unexpected intrusions by eccentric neighbors have been a staple of television comedies for decades: this Melinda is clearly a relative of Ed Norton from *The Honeymooners* and Kramer from *Seinfeld*. More important, she is also a variation on the figure of the zany, unpredictable woman whose arrival disrupts the uneventful existence of an inhibited man. Students familiar with Allen's film comedies from

Annie Hall onward might recognize the self-reflexivity at work here in addition to the conscious manipulation of audience expectations.

After both these story lines develop—the dramatic Melinda's blossoming romance with a talented pianist, the comic Melinda's growing fascination for her married upstairs neighbor—the students' viewing of the film can again be interrupted for a discussion of how the stories continue to adhere to or diverge from the initial generic expectations. At the end of the film, when both stories are concluded, we pay special attention to the dialogue between the two playwrights. Sy and Max discuss the generic norms associated with their imagined plays, dissecting how each play both conforms to and frustrates the norms of romantic comedy and serious drama. Both Cervantes and Allen thus offer reflexive frame narratives that foreground and demystify questions of generic codes.

"All the World's a [Sound] Stage": Art and Reality *in* Don Quixote *and* Stranger than Fiction

Even the briefest summary of *Stranger than Fiction* immediately invites students to offer a Cervantine reading of the film. The incredible, life-altering experiences of Harold Crick, an unremarkable IRS auditor, begin one morning when he unexpectedly hears a voice that narrates and comments on his every action. Harold's sudden knowledge that he is a character in an unseen author's fictional universe is soon followed by the voice's revelation that Harold's death is imminent—thus launching Harold on a quest to find his narrator and beg for a rewritten ending before it is too late. Worse still for the prospects of Harold's long-term survival, he already owes his ongoing existence only to the inability of Karen Eiffel, the morose, chain-smoking author of the novel in progress entitled *Death and Taxes* and the creator of its protagonist, Harold Crick, to resolve her acute case of writer's block and decide by exactly which brutal means Harold will meet his untimely demise. As in *Don Quixote*, then, students face a text that lays bare the processes, norms, and difficulties of authorship and textual production even as its embedding of one narrative in another questions the very possibility of distinguishing between reality and fiction, between individuals and their textual representations.

As their respective tales begin, neither Alonso Quijano nor Harold Crick could be said to have led a noteworthy life. We invite students to compare the first chapter of Cervantes's book 1 with the opening sequence of the film, in which Harold counts out the seconds it takes him to complete his unvarying morning routine. When each character comes to conceive of himself as a narrated subject, the monotony comes to an end. The hidalgo, as a result of his progressive book-based loss of sanity, dons his armor, sallies forth on Rocinante from his unnamed village, and begins imagining how some future *sabio* ("sage" or "scholar") will narrate his forthcoming adventures. It therefore comes as no surprise to Alonso Quijano in part 2 of the novel when Sancho informs him that, according to Sansón Carrasco, their adventures have appeared in print. For the hidalgo, no reward can be greater than to find himself the subject of narration. Lacking both Alonso Quijano's desire for eternal renown and his belief in enchanters, Harold Crick reacts very differently to the discovery of his fictional status. On first hearing his narrator describe him brushing his teeth, he examines his toothbrush and his whole bathroom to find the source of the voice. He shouts, "Who just said, 'Harold counted brushstrokes'? And how do you know I'm counting brushstrokes?!" Receiving no answer, he resigns himself to the voice's presence, but it becomes a continual distraction to him, causing him to miss his bus, to lose his concentration at work, and to ask other people if they can hear the voice describing his actions and thoughts. The two protagonists respond differently to the fact of their being narrated, but in each work this discovery serves to blur the border between representation and reality. To highlight the experience of ontological vertigo, we compare Don Quixote's encounter with Don Álvaro Tarfe and the scene in which Harold confronts his author. One also might mention Augusto's audience with his author, Miguel de Unamuno, in *Niebla* (1913; *Mist*), where Augusto is informed that he cannot commit suicide because his author forbids it (*Mist* 293).

Students in our classes have explored this ontological motif as it appears in a wide variety of popular films, such as *Fight Club* and *The Truman Show*. Even Disney has recognized the appeal of the metafictional theme, which is incorporated in *Enchanted*, where fairy tale characters arrive in contemporary New York City, and in the made-for-cable tween film *Read It and Weep*, where a teenage novelist's protagonist and alter ego comes to life. Students might also read Jean Baudrillard's study of the PBS reality television series *An American Family* as an example of the blurring of the line between the real and the fictional. Students update their findings through their exploration of this now ubiquitous narrative form. Comparative study helps them delineate a continuum from the fictional to the scripted and formulaic to the simulacrum of spontaneity. Such probing of the uncertain boundary between character and person, life and art, is central to both early modern and postmodern reflexivity.

Narrative and Technology in Don Quixote *and* Nurse Betty

Anxiety about new technologies of entertainment narrative mark both the early modern and postmodern as moments of transition. Cervantes's self-reflexive exploration of how the first century of print narrative affected Spanish society parallels current theoretical and cinematic depictions of visual technologies. We introduce students to present-day media theory through readings or lectures. Walter Ong's *Orality and Literary* offers an excellent point of departure: Ong sees the printing press as the paradigm that allowed early modern culture to represent itself in an entirely new way; at the same time, the press circulated new modes of being and thought that helped transform that culture (ch. 5).

Fredric Jameson's *Postmodernism* asserts that visual media were a major factor in determining twentieth-century cultural production, especially in the postmodern era (ch. 3).

The proliferation of books, which provides the opportunity for repeated individual consumption, is a core concern in *Don Quixote*. Ong and B. W. Ife have both noted that the private ownership of words made possible by the printing press transforms the manner in which stories are experienced. The first chapter makes clear that it is the act of solitary reading that has dried up Alonso Quijano's brain and destroyed his ability to distinguish between reality and fiction. Print culture also degrades the quality of narratives in circulation. The seemingly inexhaustible stream of new books that inundates the protagonist with narratives in a single and predictable generic convention leads to his obsession. He must sell parcels of land to keep up with all the available texts. The lack of merit in these books is demonstrated when the priest and barber, evaluating their friend's library, burn almost all the chivalric novels except the original volumes of *Amadís* and *Orlando*. In the 1615 volume, the criticism of unimaginative sequels is more acute, for Cervantes is compelled to prove the inferiority of the rival Avellaneda text. Students enjoy exploring the irony that, in order to reach his target audience, Cervantes employs the very same form of entertainment narrative that he criticizes.

Nurse Betty foregrounds the role of technology in the proliferation and resultant deterioration of narrative entertainment. In this film, the insipid and repetitive nature of televised soap opera is exacerbated by the use of a new device, the VCR, which permits the recording of a program for multiple viewings. Only a decade after the film's release, the VCR appears nearly as Jurassic to students as the books that so concerned the early modern era. Paradoxically, the experience of this recent technological change gives them an understanding of the historical gap between the early modern and the postmodern. Students also keep us up-to-date on the latest narrative devices, Web-based and portable, and share with us the anxieties expressed by their parents about the decline of quality and the unhealthiness of immersion.

Betty, a smart young woman who dropped out of nursing school in order to marry, now regrets both her choice of spouse and her job at a diner. Devotion to a television soap opera that takes place in a hospital and features a handsome and sensitive doctor offers a form of escape, picturing the ideal career and mate she could have had, similar to Alonso Quijano's retreat into chivalric narrative.

In one scene, Betty turns away from the verbal abuse heaped on her by her husband, Del, in order to immerse herself in the soap opera universe. After she retreats to the den to watch a VHS tape, two men enter her kitchen; they are hit men who have been sent because Del cheated a drug syndicate. After her husband is killed, the imaginary world of nurses and doctors becomes even more compelling. She watches an episode, and it is evident that she has seen it many times before, because she knows the dialogue by heart. As she repeats the final line, "I just know there's something special out there for me," she appears dazed; the shooting script describes her as "catatonic" (Richards and Flamberg, scene 34). The traumatized Betty now assumes the identity of a soap opera character; she heads to Los Angeles to reclaim her place as the "something special" at the hospital and in the heart of her ideal doctor, whose fiancée she once was. Her obsession is demonstrated by the fact that when she finally meets the actor who portrays the doctor, she is able to recite verbatim a long speech by the character she has assumed, from a show that aired several years before. The plot also emphasizes the seductive power of soap opera narrative, for even the two hit men who pursue her after Del's death become obsessed with the program and begin to confuse fiction and reality. This contagion of enthusiasm parallels the way in which secondary characters in *Don Quixote* become immersed in a variety of popular fictional universes as well as in the protagonist's own fantastic world.

Our current era has witnessed an explosion in visual media technology. Students will be able to use the *Don Quixote* paradigm to analyze new narrative forms, ranging from fan fiction to fan-authored and fan-filmed episodes of *Star Trek*. One example of the ever-evolving universe of narrative technologies was the 2006 *YouTube* lonely girl phenomenon, in which a video blog presented as the authentic diary of an angst-ridden young woman, lonelygirl15, gained a devoted following. When the diary was eventually revealed to be an artistic and fictional endeavor created by a group seeking to attract notice in Hollywood, viewers who had empathized with a flesh-and-blood teen felt betrayed. Like *Don Quixote* and *Nurse Betty,* the media circus surrounding the lonely girl expressed concerns about new narrative technologies and their power to elicit pathological consumption (see Foremski).

Our approach enables students to perform more sophisticated comparative analyses as they identify new media products, platforms, and devices. This work requires a reexamination of the literary and historical record in order to delineate a genealogy, a series of forebears. The continuing relevance of Cervantes's meditations on technology and immersion makes the quixotic timeless in a new way.

NOTES

Barbara Simerka wishes to thank the Professional Staff Congress at the City University of New York for a grant that supported summer research for this project.

[1] Other comparative studies of early modern Spanish textual practices with modern or postmodern film are Burningham, *Tilting*; Donnell; Simerka and Weimer, "Duplicitous Diegesis," "'Ever Want,'" "Subversive Paratexts," and "Two Characters."

[2] For other worthwhile considerations of Cervantes's manipulation of various genres, see Parr, Don Quixote: *An Anatomy*; Ardila, "Cervantes"; Flores; and Quint. On pastiche and collage as characteristic of the postmodern, see Baron; Degli-Esposti; Hutcheon, *Poetics*; and Jameson (16–31).

Seeing Quixote: Teaching *Don Quixote* in the Twenty-First Century

Rogelio Miñana

Teaching *Don Quixote* to twenty-first-century students demands a somewhat quixotic spirit. In an era of mass media and instant communication, what does a seventeenth-century Spanish text have to offer them? In my experience, underscoring *Don Quixote*'s current relevance in the cultural and sociopolitical arenas has proved to be the most effective way to engage students in the classic text. This essay explores how instructors can help students see the life this extraordinary novel has beyond its pages. Focusing on reappropriations of *Don Quixote* in modern society, I outline visual approaches that employ video and the Internet to connect *Don Quixote* to today's world.

The enormous success of Cervantes's masterpiece seems only to increase over time. In 2005, as the world commemorated the four-hundredth anniversary of the first edition of the book (1605), millions of copies of *Don Quixote* were sold or given out ("Free *Quixotes*"; "España dona"; "Especialistas"). Hundreds of cultural events, new artistic works, and academic conferences across the globe strove to bring the book to the attention of a mass audience.

Along with its literary success, Cervantes's masterpiece has filtered through to the spheres of politics and social activism. From a pedagogical standpoint, teaching Cervantes's influence today allows the instructor to tap into a pool of students whose interests lie in fields and disciplines other than classical literature. At the same time, this approach reassures literature majors that their area of interest is relevant in nonliterary ways as well.

I have researched the presence of *Don Quixote* in modern sociopolitical debates and tested in the classroom different ways to teach it. I started out dedicating only one class period before or after students read excerpts of the novel (I never assigned the book in its entirety) to probe that presence. Because of my students' enthusiastic response to this approach, I increased the number of classes devoted to the question. I paired chapters from the book with sociopolitical phenomena and texts. For instance, I connected the adventure of the windmills and the Moinho Bixiga ("the windmill of Bixiga," a neighborhood in central São Paulo), a *Quixote*-themed shelter for at-risk children designed by Gert Seewald, a Brazilian architect. To offer another example, we read the section of the cave of Montesinos in conjunction with Subcomandante Marcos's "La cueva del deseo" ("The Cave of Desire").

In the spring of 2009, I approached the text from a different angle, in a course entitled Global *Quixote*: Reading Cultural Imperialism and Resistance in Comparative Context. In my research, I have identified several organizations and public figures that situate *Don Quixote* at the heart of their activities. I grouped them into three broad movements: cultural nationalism and imperialism, leftist

revolutionary politics, and social justice community activism. My class read excerpts of the novel and considered how these groups and individuals appropriated and resignified *Don Quixote* for their political and social purposes. More
broadly, they considered how *Don Quixote* as a cultural icon was used in sociopolitical movements today.

The first section of my syllabus, "Imagined Nations," focuses on the prologue
and chapters 1 through 9 of part 1. We examine identity formation (the hidalgo's
transformation into a knight-errant) in the context of nationalistic sentiment
(Don Quixote as the embodiment of Spanish idiosyncrasy). We dissect the hero's
persona, goals, and discourse and contrast them with modern interpretations of
the knight-errant as an icon of nation-building proportions. Prime Minister José
Luis Rodríguez Zapatero's deliberate articulation of Spain's cultural and foreign
policies on the occasion of the four-hundredth anniversary of *Don Quixote* ("El
PIB") is eloquent in this respect. Nationally, Zapatero's massive state-sponsored
celebratory effort reignited the never-ending quarrels among Spanish, Basque,
and Catalan nationalists (Otero; Kortázar; Núñez Seixas; Palos; Yuste).[1] Inter-
nationally, he celebrated *Don Quixote* as the prime example of Spain's cultural
and political dominance in modern history (Rodríguez Zapatero) in a textbook
case of cultural imperialism.[2]

"Otherness as a Form of Resistance," the second part of my syllabus, centers on the Zapatista revolution in Chiapas (southern Mexico). Its best-known
spokesperson, Subcomandante Marcos, is a fervent reader and self-declared
imitator of Cervantes; he famously described *Don Quixote* as "the best book of
political theory" ever written ("Punch Card"). In addition to many references to
Don Quixote in interviews and speeches, Subcomandante Marcos wrote a number of short stories whose protagonist, Don Durito de la Lancandona, is modeled after Cervantes's knight-errant (Iffland; Vanden Berghe, "Sobre armas").
Many chapters of *Don Quixote* that deal with justice or the ability to imagine
a new reality (from the galley slaves episode to the Montesinos cave episode)
may be taught in conjunction with Marcos's folktales. I find the discussion on
otherness and the double in the prologue and first chapters of part 2 particularly
illuminating with regard to Marcos's intricate formulation of the other.[3]

"Visibility and Social Justice: The *Projeto Quixote* in Brazil," the third part of
my syllabus, introduces students to several Brazilian activist groups that utilize
Don Quixote in their work with at-risk children and youth. Four of these not-for-
profit organizations (three in São Paulo, one in Salvador de Bahia) are theater
companies that have staged socially progressive adaptations of *Don Quixote*.[4]
The fifth is the Projeto Quixote ("Quixote Project"), a São Paulo organization
founded in 1996 and coordinated by Auro Lescher in the department of psy-
chiatry at Universidade Federal de São Paulo (Federal University). Since the
Web site, videos, and some publications of this organization are translated into
English, the project offers numerous pedagogical possibilities to the instructor.

In the project's facilities, over one hundred psychiatrists, psychologists, social workers, educators, and artists employ a multidisciplinary approach to help

"transform the stories of children, adolescents, and families in situations of high social risk through integrated clinical and social care" (www.projetoquixote.org .br/the-project-quixote/). The project's main tenet is that children's discursive ability to take control of their own life narrative can save them from being, in the words of the 2006 UNICEF State of the World's Children report, tragically "excluded" and "invisible" (*Excluded*).

We discuss how Don Quixote is born out of words, how he gains visibility through deeds and discourse, and how he is seen by himself and by others: the hidalgo becomes Don Quixote (pt. 1, ch. 1), he returns home in a cage (1: 46–52), and he is defeated and dies (2: 64, 71–73). We compare Don Quixote's fight against invisibility with the struggle of the Projeto Quixote to help the "quixotinhos urbanos" 'little urban Quixotes' (Lescher and Bedoian 105), in Lescher's memorable expression, become visible in their own terms.

To demonstrate the way Cervantes's book translates into Brazilian community activism, we discuss the puzzling ending of *Don Quixote* (pt. 2, chs. 64, 71–73) in the light of *Exilados do Mundão* (*Exiles from the World*), a documentary commisioned by the Projeto Quixote to the Chilean filmmaker Daniel Rubio. We first ponder the possible meanings of Don Quixote's last-minute regression to his former self, the hidalgo Alonso Quijano, then watch and analyze the first eight minutes of *Exilados*. For his art-based social experiment, Rubio provided a video camera to six youths on their release from juvenile detention centers run by the FEBEM (Fundação do Bem-Estar do Menor ["Foundation for the Well-Being of Minors"]). The youths were given the task to document their daily lives to prove that they could develop agency over their life narrative by employing their own words and images.

In a gathering of all the prospective filmmakers, Lescher explicitly addressed the central role of *Don Quixote* in the project. He characterized the project's staff, as well as the youth involved, as Quixotes in their hunger for change, for *mudança*. To make his point, he commented on the final chapters of the book. Don Quixote, defeated by the Knight of the White Moon, returns home on the condition that he not leave his village for an entire year. Ill and demoralized, he wakes up one morning affirming his true identity and decrying Don Quixote as a product of his madness. The man's real name, as we read for the first time in more than 120 chapters, is Alonso Quijano el "Bueno" ('the Good' (2: 634 [ch. 74]; 935). The hidalgo returns to his legal place in society. He began writing his identity as a knight-errant in chapter 1, but his adventure is now over. He rewrites his life one last time (renaming himself Alonso Quijano, composing his will) and dies.

In *Exilados*, Lescher argues that Don Quixote's message is one of transformation. While we can't change society because, as he recognizes, we're not gods, we can certainly work for the collapse of the social structures that breed inequality. Awareness of the need to transform one's life narrative may lead to social change. An anthropologist named Flavia who participated in the project comments that *Exiles from the World* demonstrates the relevance of teaching children agency—that is, the ability to define themselves. Otherwise, she laments, they might simply follow the social script commonly assigned to underprivileged youth: a life of crime, punishment, and early death.

The protean ability to rewrite one's identity is best articulated in part 1, chapter 5, of *Don Quixote*. Badly hurt after Rocinante trips while charging against the Toledo merchants, Don Quixote is aided by a neighbor from his village who happens to be nearby. When addressed by the neighbor as "Señor Quijana," Don Quixote responds furiously, "Yo sé quién soy, y sé que puedo ser no sólo los que he dicho [don Rodrigo de Narváez y el Marqués de Mantua], sino todos los doce Pares de Francia, y aun todos los nueve de la Fama" 'I know who I am, and I know that I can be not only those I have mentioned [Don Rodrigo de Narváez and the Marquis of Mantua] but the twelve peers of France as well, and even all the nine paragons of Fame' (146; 43). It is precisely this affirmation of his discursive power to be whoever he wants to be that locates him outside hegemony. The term *discursive power* is important, because his social, military, and physical strengths are insufficient to allow his transformation. For Don Quixote, transformation can happen only through words. In this breach between words and things, Michel Foucault recognizes an opening to modernity: language is not subservient to matter but a force of its own ("Representing").

By focusing on the Projeto Quixote, I have sought to take *Don Quixote* out into the streets of São Paulo, a city in which youth at risk are engaged in an ongoing struggle to rewrite their life narratives before it is too late. Finding a voice, perfecting a style, attaining visibility, and developing a distinct point of view through which society can recognize their worth have become for these children and youth much more than a recreational activity—a survival tool of life-changing proportions. For those involved with the project, developing a unique, self-conscious, empowering point of view is *Don Quixote*'s most consequential message today. Seeing Don Quixote in the streets of Brazil, thanks to technology readily available in our classrooms now, may thus help our students change the way they look at the book and the world.

NOTES

The English translation of *Don Quixote* used in this essay is by Edith Grossman.

[1] My "Nación de quijotes" ("Nation of Quixotes") offers an overview of these debates at the time of the 2005 commemoration. Riera provides a detailed account of the commemoration of the three-hundredth anniversary of *Don Quixote*.

[2] The reception in Latin America of Spain's push to celebrate *Don Quixote* was strikingly positive ("Free *Quixotes*"), in sharp contast to the controversial though equally grand commemoration in 1992 of the five hundred years of the discovery of the New World. In another example of cultural imperialism in the Americas, Richard Powell's *Don Quixote, U. S. A.* offers a parodic reading of the intervention by the United States in Latin America through the creation of the Peace Corps in 1961.

3 In my seminar, I examine the concepts of self-identity and otherness in the following two Zapatista texts, both available online: "Palabras de la Comandancia General del EZLN en el Acto de Inicio del Primer Encuentro Intercontinental por la Humanidad y contra el Neoliberalismo" ("Remarks from the General Command of the EZLN in the Opening Ceremony of the First Intercontinental Meeting for Humanity and against Neoliberalism") and "Sexta declaración de la selva Lacandona" ("The Sixth Declaration of the Lacandon Jungle").

4 These groups are, in São Paulo, the Instituto Religare (historiasreligare.blogspot.com /2007/09/dom-quixote-das-ruas.html), the Circo Navegador and its "Espaço Quixotes Oficinas dos Sonhos" (www.circonavegador.com.br/index.php), and the Grupo Permanente de Pesquisa / Teatro Resurreição (www.teatroressurreicao.com.br) and, in Salvador de Bahia, the Bando de Teatro Olodum (www.teatrovilavelha.com.br/gresidentes/bando .htm#dom).

THEORETICAL APPLICATIONS

Don Quixote: A Collision of Mind-Sets

Barbara Mujica

Students confronting Don Quixote for the first time are sometimes mystified by his adherence to a worldview that diverges radically from that of other people. He strikes them as so outlandish that they miss much of the work's poignancy. It will help us elucidate his seemingly incomprehensible behavior if we point out that he represents a particular outlook, or mind-set, that has deep roots in Spanish cultural history. He is an idealist and a visionary in the tradition of Spain's great warriors and mystics — men and women motivated more by beliefs, loyalties, and intuition than by hard reason. His mind-set often pits him against mind-sets grounded in logic and empiricism. His idealism inspires a profound sense of honor, justice, and duty. These are all positive values, but so are lawfulness, order, and social stability, which are fostered by alternative mind-sets.

Novels of chivalry inform the worldview of Don Quixote, providing him with behavioral and linguistic models. Great deeds do not define him as a knight-errant, even in his own mind, as his attempts at heroism usually fall flat: giants turn out to be windmills, and great armies turn out to be herds of sheep. Instead, performance nourishes his grandiose self-image: leaving home in search of adventures, keeping vigil over his arms, paying courtesy to Maritornes, practicing self-mortification in the Sierra Morena. That is, Don Quixote consciously and deliberately performs the role of a knight-errant. Francisco LaRubia Prado argues that performance is "at the very root of subject and identity formation" (338). The anonymous hidalgo from La Mancha demonstrates his will to self-creation through performative acts that define him as Don Quixote.

His primary tool is words. His visionary zeal is evinced by his passionate, exclamatory language. When some merchants insist that they must see a portrait of Dulcinea to be sure that she is really as beautiful as Don Quixote says and that no foul fluid oozes from her eyes, he flies into a rage:

> "No le mana, canalla infame"—respondió don Quijote, encendido en cólera—; "no le mana, digo, eso que decís, sino ámbar y algalia entre algodones; y no es tuerta ni corcovada, sino más derecha que un huso de Guadarrama. Pero ¡vosotros pagaréis la grande blasfemia que habéis dicho contra tamaña beldad como es la de mi señora!" (1: 142 [ch. 4])

> "Nothing flows from her, vile rabble," replied Don Quixote, burning with rage. "Nothing flows from her, I say, but amber and delicate musk; and she is not blind or humpbacked but as upright as a peak of the Guadarramas. But you will pay for how you have blasphemed against beauty as extraordinary as that of my lady!" (40)

In comparison with the calculated irony of the merchants, Don Quixote's speech is spontaneous and impassioned.

John O'Malley's notion of the four cultures of the West is a useful tool for analyzing the interplay of mind-sets that operate not only in the narrative but also in today's world. In the *Four Cultures of the West*, O'Malley defines four distinct rhetorical styles, each of which constitutes a culture, by which he means a mode of stylistic expression. In his view, how things are said is just as important as what is said. The four cultures he identifies are the prophetic; scientific; poetic, oratorical, or statesmanlike; and artistic or performative. Each culture both reflects and nurtures a particular mind-set. Any person or fictional figure can manifest characteristics associated with more than one culture, and any given moment in history can produce all four. By identifying the dominant mode of expression associated with a person or time, we can better understand our subject's worldview.

At different moments in his career, Don Quixote displays aspects of all four cultures. Nevertheless, his dominant rhetorical modes are clearly prophetic and performative. The prophetic culture rejects the purely reasonable for the visionary:

> This is the culture that must speak out. It is the culture of alienation, of protest, of standing apart because one can do no other. . . . This is the culture of the martyr (and the fanatic). It is the culture, above all, of the reformer decrying injustice and corruption in high places. . . . This is the culture that makes the greatest purity claims and that unmasks as abomination what others welcome as the normal give-and-take of life. It cannot compromise. (O'Malley 7)

Marginalized by his idealism, his age, his appearance, and his antiquated rhetoric, Don Quixote is the perpetual outsider, the embodiment of the culture of alienation and protest. He is the reformer who interrupts the normal give-and-take of life to point out abuses and iniquities.

What Don Quixote admires about the books of chivalry is their visionary core, the utopian projection of a world in which good triumphs over evil. The very unreasonableness of their underlying design delights him:

> . . . la claridad de su prosa y aquellas intricadas razones suyas le parecían de perlas, y más cuando llegaba a leer aquellos requiebros y cartas de desafíos, donde en muchas partes hallaba escrito: La razón de la sinrazón que mi razón se hace, de tal manera mi razón enflaquece, que con razón me quejo de la vuestra fermosura.   (1: 114 [ch. 1])

> . . . the clarity of his prose and complexity of his language seemed to him more valuable than pearls, in particular when he read the declarations and missives of love, where he would often find written: The reason for the unreason to which my reason turns so weakens my reason that with reason I complain of thy beauty.   (20)

The mockery Cervantes makes of chivalric rhetoric and its disdain for reason, which it muddles beyond comprehension, illuminates his character's ideological stance.

His love for books might suggest that Don Quixote is, rather than a prophet, a product of the culture of poets. Certainly, books are his inspiration, and references not only to chivalric romances but also to sentimental, pastoral, picaresque, and Byzantine fiction abound in the novel. But he is not a literary scholar. He does not analyze layers of meaning in the books he reads. Literary culture is concerned with ambiguities, but Don Quixote's rhetoric is characterized not by the subtleties of critical thinking but by the bold assertions of the prophet. He is not interested in multiple signifying possibilities; for him, things have fixed meanings.

Michel Foucault writes that Don Quixote is himself language: "His whole being is nothing but language, text, printed pages, stories that have already been written down. He is made up of interwoven words; he is writing itself . . ." (*Order* 46). He does not stand back and look at language but, rather, absorbs it and fashions a new identity out of it.

Based on the utopian literature he reads, Don Quixote forms a worldview at odds with prevailing norms. He sets out to transform existing reality in a way that defies reason. The prophetic culture envisions perfection and gives it a name: Christ, Justice, Dulcinea. For Don Quixote, Dulcinea is the embodiment of the values he strives for: truth, beauty, righteousness. She is the emblem of his *Weltgeist*, the banner he raises as he rides into battle. The prophetic culture requires radical action. Famous prophets of Christian history such as Francis of Assisi or Ignatius of Loyola rejected material wealth to live in austerity. However, their acts of self-denial constituted not a flight from the world but a call to action. These reformers were not utterly lacking in common sense—some, like Saint Ignatius, were astute administrators—but they lived in a world of clear-cut options. Once they chose Christ, all subsequent choices had to be made in that framework.

Like them, Don Quixote is obsessive and uncompromising in his ideals. He is not content simply to dream a better world; he acts, takes risks, sallies forth into battle. It is significant that the stories of the *Golden Legend*, a widely read medieval collection of hagiographies that circulated well into the seventeenth century, were similar to chivalric novels in that they depicted heroes who forwent comfort to devote themselves to a cause, who performed great deeds to prove themselves worthy, who championed good and battled evil. Their *contemptus mundi*, like Don Quixote's, embraces a paradox: they reject the world in an attempt to reform it.

The prophet is not concerned with practical matters. Neither Saint Francis nor Amadís de Gaula cared about warm clothing. When Don Quixote ventures forth and seeks lodging in an inn, which he takes to be a castle, the innkeeper reminds him that he really must equip himself with money and clean shirts. In Don Quixote's world, such matters are insignificant.

It is an oversimplification to assert that Don Quixote is an idealist who contrasts with the realist Sancho Panza. The two characters embody different ways of seeing. Both interpret objective reality in accordance with their own worldviews. When they come across windmills, Don Quixote sees giants, because in his utopian vision giants, not windmills, play a role in the great struggle between good and evil. Sancho sees something different, not because the mechanisms with rotating blades intrinsically signify windmills but because in his experience such devices are used to grind grain. Each man comes to a conclusion based on his life experience. When Don Quixote rushes into the apparatus and is battered, instead of concluding that Sancho was right, he interprets the incident in accordance with his own worldview. The prophetic culture entertains no doubts; it does not examine its premises; it is interested not in proofs but in proclamations; it speaks in hyperboles. The prophetic culture does not scrutinize or investigate; that is the realm of the scientific culture, whose style is "analytical, questing and questioning" (O'Malley 11). Here is one example of the distance between Don Quixote and the scientific culture: before his first adventure, he assembles some armor to equip himself. He finds an ancient helmet, but it lacks a visor, so he constructs one out of pasteboard. After testing it and finding it defective, he simply repairs it and does no further testing. That is, instead of abandoning the visor, he abandons the experiments. The prophet discards—or filters out—information that invalidates his system. He rejects the very notion of dispassionate analysis.

The prophetic culture that generates Don Quixote's mind-set sees the world in terms of absolutes, of black and white, with no gray areas. Don Quixote does not debate. He sometimes pontificates in ways that seem reasonable—for example, on arms and letters or on the importance of economic stability in marriage—but he does not engage in argumentation, because the prophetic culture does not allow for alternative views. O'Malley writes, "Here lies the psychological basis for the antithetical pattern of argument—sin/grace, corruption/ goodness, with no room for anything in between" (40). Thus, when Don Quixote, who knows Catholic doctrine concerning free will, comes across a group of enchained galley slaves, he becomes indignant. For him, free will is a God-given grace and therefore not subject to contextualization: "'En resolución'—replicó don Quijote—, 'como quiera que ello sea, esta gente, aunque los llevan, van de por fuerza, y no de su voluntad'" "'In short,' replied Don Quixote, "for whatever reason, these people are being taken by force and not of their own free will"' (1: 305 [ch. 22]; 163). Sancho explains that they are being punished for their crimes, but that circumstance is insignificant to Don Quixote. His response exudes prophetic indignation.

Don Quixote goes on to interrogate the prisoners, but not in the spirit of critical inquiry, since he has already decided to set them free. The questioning reveals that even though the galley slaves have indeed broken laws, the underlying causes for their behavior are social inequity and judicial corruption. Poverty drove some to steal. Torture was used to obtain some of their confessions. One prisoner lacked money to bribe the court clerk and pay a good lawyer. Another, a pimp, was arrested for violating what Don Quixote considers unjust laws against prostitution. Ginés de Pasamonte, who is more heavily shackled and guarded than the rest, is writing his autobiography and is deemed dangerous because, as Cervantes himself knew, men of talent who question the status quo are a threat to the system. The episode exposes the corruption, persecution, economic disparity, and hopelessness rampant in seventeenth-century Spain. Rather than blind to reality, Don Quixote is acutely aware of the core social realities that are inconsonant with his utopian vision. He is indeed the reformer who "unmasks as abomination what others welcome as the normal give-and-take of life." For the prophet, it is precisely the vision of a sinful world that prompts the struggle for righteousness and redemption. Don Quixote's awareness of social injustice is what fuels his reformist furor.

After Don Quixote sets the galley slaves free, he demands that they go to El Toboso and tell Dulcinea. When they refuse, he becomes infuriated, excoriating them in the language of the prophet. He advocates humanistic values—responsible government, citizens' rights, judiciary accountability, economic fairness, and respect for artists—but although his message corresponds to the culture of statecraft, his language is that of the culture of the prophet, characterized by imperatives and exclamations. When Ginés de Pasamonte explains that it is not reasonable to expect them to travel together to El Toboso, Don Quixote erupts in fury, "'Pues ¡voto a tal!'—dijo don Quijote, ya puesto en cólera—, 'don hijo de puta, don Ginesillo de Paropillo, o cómo os llamáis, que habéis de ir vos solo, rabo entre piernas . . .'" "'Well, then, I do swear,' said Don Quixote, his wrath rising, "Don Whoreson, Don Ginesillo de Paropillo, or whatever your name is, that you will go alone, your tail between your legs . . ."' (316; 172). Although

Don Quixote finally retreats, he first asserts to Sancho his willingness to stand and face danger:

> Y no me repliques más; que en sólo pensar que me aparto y retiro de algún peligro, especialmente déste . . . estoy ya para quedarme, y para aguardar aquí solo, no solamente a la Santa Hermandad que dices y temes, sino a los hermanos de los doce tribus de Israel y a los siete Macabeos, y a Cástor y a Pólux, y aun a todos los hermanos y hermandades que hay en el mundo.   (1: 318–19 [ch. 23])

> And do not reply, for merely thinking that I am withdrawing and retreating from any danger, especially this one . . . is enough to make me want to remain and wait here alone, not only for the Holy Brotherhood which you have mentioned and fear so much, but for the brothers of the twelve tribes of Israel and the seven Maccabees, and Castor and Pollux, and all the brothers and brotherhoods that there are in the world.   (173–74)

His rhetoric is nothing if not hyperbolic.

Don Quixote's defense of humanistic values—the intrinsic worth of all human beings, the equality of all people under God, the value of art and poetry—is articulated through prophetic rhetoric. For example, in his address to the goatherds, Don Quixote defends the worth of women and argues against judicial corruption and for equality under the law, but he puts forth these tenets of Renaissance humanism in an apocalyptic style. The realization of his golden age, a mythic time when justice reigned, private property did not exist, poverty was unheard of, and all men and women were treated with respect, would require the complete destruction of his society.

Don Quixote's powerful belief system, like the Catholic faith that engendered it, requires ritual: the expression through outward signs of a profound inner experience that defies words. Don Quixote experiences a conversion in the Christian sense of a radical inner transformation. Saint Ignatius marked his conversion by giving his cape to a beggar, dressing in pilgrim's garb, and going to live in a cave, where he let his hair and nails grow long. He held a vigil modeled on that of Amadís:

> . . . because his whole mind [was] full of those things from *Amadis of Gaul* and books of that sort . . . he decided to keep a vigil of arms for a whole night, without sitting or lying down, but sometimes standing up, sometimes on his knees before the altar of Our Lady of Montserrat, where he had resolved to abandon his clothes and abandon himself in the armor of Christ.   (20)

Similarly, Don Quixote dons armor, invents a new name, and pledges allegiance to a lady. It does not matter to him that the peerless Dulcinea does not exist in tangible form, any more than it matters to Catholics that Mary does not stand before them in the flesh.

Don Quixote keeps vigil over his arms at an inn and requires the innkeeper to dub him a knight. Later, in the Sierra Morena, he withdraws among the crags to imitate Amadís and Orlando Furioso. He is clearly conscious of performing a role: "'¿Ya no te he dicho'—respondió don Quijote—'que quiero imitar a Amadís, haciendo aquí del desesperado, del sandio y del furioso . . .?'" "'Have I not told you already,' responded Don Quixote, 'that I wish to imitate Amadís, playing the part of the one who is desperate, a fool, a madman . . . ?''' (1: 344 [ch. 25]; 193). When he describes the acts of violence performed by Roland in his insane rage (344; 192), Sancho protests that such behavior is illogical and unprovoked, but Don Quixote responds that therein lies its value. Since performance requires spectators, he insists that Sancho watch him: "Por lo menos, quiero, Sancho, y porque es mensester así, quiero, digo, que me veas en cueros, y hacer una o dos docenas de locuras, que las haré en menos de media hora" 'I say I want you to see me naked and performing one or two dozen mad acts, which will take me less than half an hour . . .' (359; 203). Don Quixote not only dreams knighthood but performs knighthood and demands that an audience observe and appreciate his performance.

If Saint Ignatius and Don Quixote both engage in the same kinds of ritualistic behavior, why does Don Quixote strike readers as funny while Saint Ignatius does not? One answer is that Saint Ignatius was a prophet living in a society immersed in prophetic culture, whereas by Don Quixote's time that culture was outmoded. That is, Don Quixote speaks a language different from that of his contemporaries. Christopher Weimer notes, "The protagonist's insanity lies not in any such belief that he is truly a knight-errant out of another time, but rather in his irrational conviction that he, a rural Manchegan hidalgo of modest means and lineage, can and must assume the persona and the duties of such a knight in his own era" (71). Don Quixote is not an anachronism simply because knights-errant no longer roam the Castilian countryside but because he is the product of a different culture, a culture associated with a rhetoric that is no longer current.

Knights-errant like Amadís probably never existed, but the prophetic culture they represent is that of the great medieval and early Renaissance saints and heroes. As both Foucault (*Histoire* 33) and Johan Huizinga (*Autumn* 1–29) have pointed out, the Middle Ages made a place for extreme behaviors—madmen, visionaries, ecstatics—but Renaissance humanism and the rise of mercantilism brought a more rigid codification of conduct. By the mid–sixteenth century, the rapturous and the hyperbolic had come to be associated with groups considered unacceptable, even heretical, such as Illuminists and Lutherans. Visionaries were now highly suspect, and the authority of visionary experience, particularized and unverifiable, was losing currency. Europe was transitioning into new cultures: the culture of the philosophers and scientists, the culture of logic, evidence, and proof.

Prophets know intuitively. They know because God has spoken to them or because they have undergone an illuminating experience. For Don Quixote, as for other prophets, authority lies in the personal vision; there is no need for corroboration. When he meets some merchants on the road, he demands they accept unquestioningly the perfection of Dulcinea. But the merchants represent a different culture. They are practical men used to dealing in numbers and logic; they demand proof: ". . . mostrádnosla: que si ella fuere de tanta hermosura como significáis, de buena gana y sin apremio alguno confesaremos la verdad que por parte vuestra nos es pedida" '. . . show her to us, for if she is as beautiful as you say, we will gladly and freely confess the truth you ask of us' (1: 141 [ch. 4]; 39). Prophetic culture speaks the language of faith. Don Quixote demands that the merchants believe, precisely without seeing: "'Si os la mostrara'—replicó don Qujote—, '¿qué hiciérades vosotros en confesar una verdad tan notoria? La importancia está en que sin verla lo habéis de creer, confesar, afirmar, jurar y defender'" "'If I were to show her to you," replied Don Quixote, "where would the virtue be in your confessing so obvious a truth? The significance lies in *not* seeing her and believing, confessing, affirming, swearing, and defending that truth"' (141; 39). His exalted tone and his insistence on blind faith make him incomprehensible to the merchants, as they are to him. When one merchant continues to demand a portrait, "aunque sea tamaño como un grano de trigo" 'even if it is no larger than a grain of wheat' (141; 40), Don Quixote flies into a rage.

The merchants' demand for proof reflects a mind-set that is very much in keeping with the emerging scientific culture. The sixteenth century was an age of discovery and experimentation; age-old beliefs were being challenged. The questioning of traditional convictions about God and the universe ushered in a flourishing of philosophical and scientific inquiry. Luther was very much a prophet in his defense of the new dogma, and his challenge to the Church led to other reassessments of widely held beliefs.

Both the culture of science and the culture of poetry and philosophy are concerned with signs and their interpretation, with multiplicities of meaning. Both distrust the authority of the individual perspective and recognize that sensorial information can be misleading. Emilie L. Bergmann points to "ocularcentrism" as the stimulus for scientific and philosophical discourse in the seventeenth century, noting that "the privileging of the visual" is "a distinguishing feature of modernity" (158). Baroque pessimism stems in part from an awareness of the deceptive nature of appearances. Scientific empiricism holds the perceived object to be a potential source of knowledge but also recognizes that appearances can mislead, which is why observations must be constantly revisited and reassessed. By 1605 the new cultural perspective was ascendant. Through narrative strategies—the use of an unreliable narrator, multiple and contradictory sources, distancing, perspectivism, sudden breaks in the story line—Cervantes forces readers to doubt the text, to suspend suspension of disbelief, and to adopt a skeptical stance. He pits Don Quixote's prophetic and performative cultures and the mind-set they encourage against the mind-sets characteristic of the cultures of science and poetry.

Today we read *Don Quixote* from a perspective radically different from the protagonist's. Students have no difficulty identifying representatives of the prophetic culture in our society—Martin Luther King, Jr., for example—and explaining how they are marginalized. As for the performative culture, many past rituals have fallen by the wayside such that we no longer dress for the theater or even address each other as Mr. or Dr. In our technology- and subjectivity-driven world, Don Quixote continues to be the perpetual outsider, the product of an alien culture in which certainty is possible. Students often find this sort of idealism wonderfully attractive, and once they understand Don Quixote's cultural mind-set, they are able both to laugh at and with him and to more fully appreciate him.

NOTE

The English translation of *Don Quixote* used in this essay is by Edith Grossman.

Applying Theory of Mind to *Don Quixote*

Howard Mancing

In the first chapter of the first part of *Don Quixote*, a poor hidalgo who lives in a village of La Mancha obsessively reads romances of chivalry, comes to believe that these books describe the world as it actually is, and decides to be a knight-errant. He polishes up some old armor and then chooses new names for himself, his horse, and his lady. Next he imagines a stereotypical combat with an evil giant. He knows that the giants of the world of chivalry are inevitably evil, inhumanly large and powerful, but always beatable. He assumes that he will win this battle and that he should command the vanquished giant to visit his lady humbly and acknowledge the prowess of the man who bested him. Don Quixote knows that the giant will do this because he believes that even the worst inhabitants of the world of chivalry must keep their promises and meet their obligations. We can follow Don Quixote's thinking about how the giant will think. By the same token, we readers understand how Don Quixote thinks and assume that his thinking is natural to someone of his condition.

All these natural and commonplace cognitive processes I have just described are rarely acknowledged in literary theories. There is more discussion of the linguistic construction of subject positions than there is of literary characters as imaginative creations that we can think and talk about as if they were real people. Characters in literature, like real people, have thoughts and feelings, hopes and fears, desires and needs. Literary characters are obviously not real people, but we can understand them as if they were.

Cognitive Science

Over the last twenty years, an approach to literature grounded in cognitive science has slowly come to the fore. This approach takes its concept of language from post-Chomskyan linguistics and pragmatics, seeing language as a cognitive tool used for doing things. As Herbert Clark, a linguist, writes in his book *Using Language*, "Language is used for doing things" (3). A cognitive approach draws on contemporary biology, neuroscience, evolutionary theory, and cognitive and developmental psychology. It views human beings as evolved animals, with an imaginative mind-brain that enables each of us to be unique, individual, contextualized agents who use language as a tool in our complex social relationships. Foremost among the ways we think about ourselves and other people is a cognitive tool called theory of mind (ToM).

Theory of Mind

As described by Sanjida O'Connell in her book *Mindreading: An Investigation into How We Learn to Love and Lie*, ToM is

> the mechanism we use to understand what is going on in other people's heads. How we react to one another socially is the most important aspect of our lives. Without an understanding of what people think, what they want and what they believe about the world, it is impossible to operate in any society. Theory of Mind is the name given to this understanding of others. It is the basic necessity of humanity and is understood the same way the world over. (2)

Note O'Connell's vocabulary: *understand, think, want, believe*. We use such terms so frequently in everything we say and write that, as she suggests, "they have become invisible. We interpret people's actions using words that describe the mental states so often that we cease to think about what it is we are actually doing" (3).

ToM is an essential part of what is sometimes called folk psychology, the kind of belief-desire psychology that we use every day to guide us. It is not an infallible, scientifically based set of theories about human cognition but a heuristic that gets us by in most social circumstances. Many of our serious problems arise when we believe that we understand someone else's thinking but do not. Usually, hundreds or thousands of times a day, we read other people's minds accurately. Often we use multiple levels of ToM (what philosopher Daniel Dennett calls "levels of intentionality") when we say things like

> I *suspect* [1] that you *wonder* [2] whether I *realize* [3] how hard it is for you to *understand* [4] whether I *mean* [5] to be saying that you can *recognize* [6] that I can *believe* [7] you *want* [8] me to explain this.   (185–86)

The two major approaches to ToM are the theory theory and the simulation theory. The former proposes that as we proceed through infancy and childhood into adulthood, we develop (largely unconsciously) a theory about how other people feel and think. The latter suggests that we simulate the thoughts and feelings of others, largely on the basis of how we think we would feel and act in certain situations. Both these approaches are grounded in our experiences throughout our personal and social development.[1]

Theory of Mind and Literature

ToM gives scholars and teachers one more valuable tool to employ in their ongoing activities of reading, understanding, discussing, and writing critically about literary works. Robin Dunbar, a cognitive anthropologist, attributes to the human ToM what he calls the *"crucial ability to step back from ourselves and look at the rest of the world with an element of disinterest"* (*Grooming* 101). Like Dennett's levels of intentionality, Dunbar describes three orders of ToM: the ability to be aware of our own thoughts, the ability to understand other people's feelings, and the ability "to imagine how someone who does not actually exist might respond to particular situations" (101–02). Elaborating on this third-order ToM, Dunbar states its obvious implication: "[W]e can begin to create literature, to write stories that go beyond a simple description of events as they occurred to delve more and more deeply into why the hero should behave in the way he does, into the feelings that drive him ever onwards in his quest" (102).

William F. Allman lays out the basic premise that ToM is as essential for understanding a literary work as it is for understanding a verbal utterance or another human being's motives:

> Without our ability to form a theory of mind, human culture would not be possible. Much of the world of literature, drama, and humor relies on the supreme ability of humans not only to create theories about each character's mind but also to imagine simultaneously how each of these imaginary minds might view the minds of other characters. The tragic nature of Shakespeare's *Romeo and Juliet*, for instance, comes from a series of misconceptions among the characters that only the audience is aware of. Romeo's suicide is the result of his thinking that Juliet has died, and the audience is aware that if Romeo knew what they knew, this suicide would not have to have happened. To an audience of monkeys, however, Romeo's actions would make no sense, because they wouldn't be able to distinguish between their own beliefs and his.   (68–69)

In *Why We Read Fiction: Theory of Mind and the Novel*, Lisa Zunshine argues that a ToM "makes literature as we know it possible" (10). Her exemplary analyses of some British and American fiction illustrate the point. Dunbar agrees: "Without theory of mind—indeed, without the higher orders of theory of mind—literature and much of everyday social intercourse would be impossible" (*Human Story* 121). Other literary scholars taking a cognitive approach to literature join Zunshine in affirming that we imaginatively understand fictional characters as though they were real people and simulate their states of mind, just as we use our ToM to understand the author's intentions in the creation of the work.[2]

Theory of Mind and Don Quixote

Authors necessarily use a ToM when they contemplate their readers. Recall Cervantes's first words in the prologue to part I of *Don Quixote*: "Desocupado lector: sin juramento me podrás creer que quisiera que este libro, como hijo del entendimiento, fuera el más hermoso, el más Gallardo y más discreto que pudiera imaginarse" 'Idle reader: Without my swearing to it, you can believe that I would like this book, the child of my understanding, to be the most beautiful, the most brilliant, and the most discreet that anyone could imagine' (95; 3). Cervantes (the flesh-and-blood author) asks his readers (the flesh-and-blood readers—you and me) to believe that he wants something.

Let us turn to the character Don Quixote. It is clear that, as the novel begins, he has developed a ToM shaped decisively by his extensive reading of chivalric romances. When he first sallies forth, he uses his ToM when he simulates the thought processes of the wise enchanter who will write his history: "¿Quién duda sino que en los venideros tiempos, cuando salga a luz la verdadera historia de mis famosos hechos, que el sabio que los escribiere no ponga . . . desta manera?" 'Who can doubt that in times to come, when the true history of my famous deeds comes to light, the wise man who compiles them . . . will write in this manner?' (1: 121 [ch. 2]; 25). Throughout the chapter, he is using his chivalric-based ToM when he *invokes* Dulcinea's support, *thinks* that the ladies outside the castle are being frivolous when they laugh at him, *believes* that the lord of the castle bids him welcome, *assumes* that many *truchuelas* ("codfish") can make as fine a meal as one *trucha* ("trout"), and so forth.

Other examples in part 1 of the novel—Don Quixote's dealings with Juan Haldudo (ch. 4), with Princess Micomicona (ch. 30), with the priest and barber on the way home (chs. 47–52)—can be used to trace his gradual retreat from his chivalry-inspired models and theories. In part 2—in key scenes such as the enchantment of Dulcinea (ch. 10), the Cave of Montesinos (ch. 23), the enchanted boat (ch. 29), everything that takes place during the visit to the palace of the duke and duchess (chs. 30–62), and after his return home and death (ch. 74)—we can see how his way of understanding how and what others think, especially of him, becomes increasingly modified.

The ToM of Don Quixote is important throughout the novel, in everything he does and says. If we didn't conceive of him as a thinking, feeling, desiring human being who attributes thoughts, feelings, and desires to other characters, nothing he does or says would make sense. Because it makes sense, we are able to follow his line of thinking—and Sancho's, and Dorotea's, and Roque Guinart's, and so on. We understand all the characters, just as we understand ourselves and one another. In general, the only way to understand a literary character is to treat the character as we would a real person, as having an active ToM.

Consider what happens during the famous episode of the enchantment of Dulcinea in part 2, chapter 10:

Sancho *knows* [1] that Don Quixote *believes* [2] that evil enchanters *want* [3] to foil his *desire* [4] to gain fame as a knight-errant, therefore he (Sancho) is *sure* [5] that he can make Don Quixote *believe* [6] that a peasant woman is Dulcinea.

This is as subtle an example of the narrative presentation of a fictional mind as I have ever seen.[3]

Most interesting are those occasions in the novel when Don Quixote's thought processes are not clear. What is Don Quixote thinking, for example, when he pulls out his sword and destroys Maese Pedro's puppet show in part 2, chapter 26? He explains his actions by saying, "Ahora acabo de creer . . . lo que otras muchas veces he creído" 'Now I believe . . . what I have believed on many other occasions' (i.e., that enchanters changed the figures). He adds, "Real y verdaderamente os digo, señores que me oís, que a mí me pareció todo lo que aquí ha pasado que pasaba al pie de la letra: que Melisendra era Melisendra, don Gaiferos don Gaiferos, Marsilio Marsilio, y Carlomagno Carlomagno" 'I tell you really and truly, you gentlemen who can hear me: it seemed to me that everything that happened here was actually happening, that Melisendra was Melisendra, Don Gaiferos Don Gaiferos, Marsilio Marsilio, and Charlemagne Charlemagne' (257; 634). But can we accept this explanation as easily as we did earlier, in the encounter with the windmills in part 1, chapter 8? After all, less than a minute before his destruction of the show, Don Quixote was discussing with the puppeteer and his assistant the verisimilitude of the production, so he obviously recognized it as staged. Is he telling us the truth about believing that he was deceived by enchanters? Or do his actions have another explanation? What was he thinking, and how might we know?

This question raises another issue: our understanding of Don Quixote's ToM depends on our own. My understanding of the character's thought processes and your understanding may not always be the same; what I think that Don Quixote is thinking may not be what you think he is thinking (and neither may be what Cervantes thought he was thinking). The reader is therefore part of Dennett's levels of intentionality:

> I *think* [1] that you *believe* [2] that Don Quixote *is suspicious* [3] of Maese Pedro, who, he *believes* [4], *wants* [5] to *deceive* [6] him.

A ToM approach to literature, in other words, depends on an individualized version of reader-response criticism.

Theory of Mind in the Classroom

The last six times I taught a graduate class in *Don Quixote*, I laid out the concept of ToM and encouraged the students to think in terms of mind reading and dealing with Don Quixote, Sancho, and the other characters in the book as if they were real people. The result has been rich discussion, richer than I have experienced in my forty years of teaching *Quixote* classes at all levels. I am not suggesting that the class deals only with characters and their thoughts. We also discuss the historical and literary contexts, social and political issues, narrative technique, levels of style, the novel's brilliant metafiction, and much more.

Literary characters are imagined versions of embodied, contextualized human beings just like us, and we know them the same way that we know ourselves and others. The way we know ourselves and others in life depends on many factors: our individual brain structure, emotions, memories, mood, values, interests, and experiences; our gender, age, and social status; our social and historical context, our immediate physical context, what has recently happened in our lives, and what we think other people might be thinking. No two people ever have exactly the same understanding of anything.

In the ToM, biology and cognitive psychology have given us a new and powerful tool to understand works of literature. But in many ways this new tool is little more than the common folk psychology that human beings have used for millennia.

NOTES

The English translation of *Don Quixote* used in this essay is by Edith Grossman.

[1] The term *theory of mind* was first used by two primatologists, David Premack and Guy Woodruff, in a 1978 experiment on a chimpanzee. The idea was soon taken into child and developmental psychology and developed further with human beings in general. For an introduction to ToM, see Astington; Bartsch and Wellman; Carruthers and Smith; Goldman; Gopnik and Meltzoff; and O'Connell. Important in ToM studies is the contemporary understanding of autism, as it turns out that autistics have limitations, often severe, in understanding what other people are thinking (see Baron-Cohen; Frith). For the role of ToM in evolutionary theory, see Allman; Dunbar, *Human Story*; and Tomasello. For the importance of ToM in neuroscience, especially since the discovery of mirror neurons in the 1990s, see Iacoboni; Damasio and Damasio.

[2] Literary scholars who use embodied cognitive science in treating literary characters as if they were real people are Gerrig; Palmer; Keen; Mancing, "James' Parr's Theory" and "Sancho Panza's Theory"; Oatley; Slingerland.

[3] In my "Sancho Panza's Theory of Mind," I explore in detail the nature and implications of Sancho's ToM.

Don Quixote in the American Imaginary

Bruce R. Burningham

Over the years I occasionally have taught a general education course entitled Tales of Witches, Rogues, and Madmen in Early Modern Spain. Although students often enroll in this course expecting to read a set of macabre stories like those of Edgar Allan Poe, my purpose is to have them read *La Celestina, Lazarillo de Tormes* (among other Spanish picaresque texts), and ultimately *Don Quixote* as part of their overall undergraduate education. During the first half of the semester, the course focuses on *La Celestina* and the picaresque, at which point I assign the following topic for the midterm paper: Identify a contemporary cultural text (whether a novel, a film, a popular song, or even a video game) and articulate the ways in which this text incorporates the Spanish picaresque's caustic aesthetics, narratological structure, or inherent social critique, commenting along the way on how it updates the picaresque for modern (Anglo-American) readers and audiences. To give students an idea of what I am looking for, I walk them through a picaresque reading of the Rolling Stones' well-known song "Jumpin' Jack Flash" (a reading that eventually made its way into my book *Tilting Cervantes: Baroque Reflections on Postmodern Culture*). In the second half of the semester, the course focuses exclusively on *Don Quixote*. And while I do not explicitly assign a final paper topic that involves a Cervantine reading of a contemporary text, students often find highly innovative ways of connecting *Don Quixote* to twenty-first-century culture.

Such connections between the imaginative past and the creative present are not coincidental. A 2002 survey of contemporary authors placed Cervantes's text at the top of the list of the most influential books ever written (Chrisafis). Robert Stam traces one of the major traditions of contemporary literature and film, "reflexivity," directly back to Cervantes's pioneering narrative techniques. Scholars as diverse as David Castillo ("Literary Classics"), William Childers (*Transnational Cervantes*), Theo D'haen and Reindert Dhondt, Will McMorran, Ulla Musarra-Schroeder, Barbara Simerka and Christopher Weimer ("Duplicitous Diegesis," "'Ever Want,'" and "Two Characters"), María Stoopen, and Kristine Vanden Berghe ("*Quixote*") have all examined Cervantes's influence on world literatre and culture. (Note also the recent work of Mieke Bal, William Egginton, Angela Ndalianis, and me [*Tilting*, "David Lynch," and "Of Mad Knights"] on the neobaroque.)

On a critical level, *Don Quixote* continues to be vital to our contemporary intellectual discourse. One could argue, for instance, that French poststructuralist theory could not have developed without the creative imaginary of early modern Spain. Michel Foucault's *The Order of Things*, which begins with an examination of *Las meninas* and whose oft-cited chapter "Representing" uses *Don Quixote* as its point of departure, owes much to the work of Diego Velázquez, Cervantes, and Jorge Luis Borges (the last of whom was enormously influenced by Cervantes). In the context of Anglo-American culture, *Don Quixote* has long functioned as an important intertext for other works, from Mark Twain's *Tom Sawyer* and *Huckleberry Finn* to a *Pinky and the Brain* vignette entitled "Mouse of la Mancha" (an episode more related to Dale Wasserman's *Man of La Mancha* than Cervantes's novel). Indeed, Don Quixote has become an indispensable sign in Anglo-American culture, achieving the kind of iconicity Cervantes posits in part 2 of his novel (ironically, with regard to Don Quixote's trusty steed) when he predicts that children will point to any skinny hack they see and declare "allí va Rocinante" 'There goes Rocinante' (Cervantes, *Ingenioso hidalgo* [Murillo] 2: 64 [ch. 3]; Cervantes, *Adventures* 490). Don Quixote, like Oedipus and Faust, is one of the few characters from world literature to have engendered an English adjective: madmen and idealists are described as "quixotic."

In this regard, an article in the *Chicago Tribune* lamented what its headline called the "twilight of the blues." Commenting on the death of Hubert Sumlin, a famed Chicago bluesman, at the age of 80, the *Tribune*'s art critic, Howard Reich, cataloged the passing of a number of important bluesmen and sadly predicted that this once vibrant musical genre—central to both Chicago culture and American popular music—would soon join the ranks of the Gregorian chant, becoming a musical form "studied by academics, performed by die-hards and applauded by connoisseurs, [but] forgotten by nearly everyone else." Arguing that Chicago had largely turned its back on the blues, Reich nevertheless offered the following caveat: "Even so, a few determined souls are trying—quixotically—to give this music a future in Chicago" (5).

The *Oxford English Dictionary* defines a *Quixote* as "An enthusiastic visionary person like Don Quixote, inspired by lofty and chivalrous but false and unrealizable ideals." *Merriam-Webster's Collegiate Dictionary* defines *quixotic* as "foolishly impractical." That Reich's adverb does not conform to either definition is shown by replacing it with a word that gives the dictionary sense: "Even so, a few determined souls are trying—unrealistically—to give this music a future" or "Even so, a few determined souls are trying—impractically—to give this music a future." Consider instead this variant: "Even so, a few determined souls are trying—valiantly—to give this music a future." Such a variant is much more in line with Reich's meaning, and I would argue that his usage reveals a particularly American conception of Don Quixote.

Don Quixote has not always served as a positive emblem in American culture. In the buildup to the United States Civil War, Charles Sumner, the Republican senator from Massachusetts, delivered a fiery speech on the Senate floor entitled "The Crime against Kansas," in which he derisively compared Senators Andrew Butler (of South Carolina) and Stephen Douglas (of Illinois) with Don Quixote and Sancho, arguing that Butler's Dulcinea del Toboso was none other than "the harlot Slavery," who "though ugly to others, is always lovely to him" (9). On the other side of the Union-Confederacy divide, Adalbert John

Volck created an unflattering 1861 etching of Abraham Lincoln as Don Quixote seated in a chair and wearing pumpkin pants. The Smithsonian Institution Web site, on which this image can be found, describes Volck's etching as follows: "Lincoln, holding a quill pen, has made a list of Union defeats; his inkwell is in the shape of an artillery mortar. His foot rests irreverently on a stack of books labeled 'Constitution,' 'Law,' and 'Habeas Corpus.'"

So how did we go from Don Quixote, vile champion of the harlot Slavery, to Don Quixote, valiant defender of the Chicago blues? Wasserman's *Man of La Mancha* had a great deal to do with Don Quixote's transformation in the American imaginary. But before Wasserman there was Frank Capra, whose classic film *Mr. Smith Goes to Washington* anticipated Wasserman's notion of an "impossible dream" by two decades. Indeed, this film serves as a kind of case study of the importance of *Don Quixote* in an American master narrative that shows the defeat of a superior force at the hands of a virtuous American warrior who cheerfully fights against all odds.

Mr. Smith Goes to Washington was released by Columbia Pictures in October 1939 and was nominated for eleven Academy Awards. It tells the story of Jefferson Smith (played by James Stewart), an unknown Boy Rangers leader who is thrust into the limelight when the governor of his state (played by Guy Kibbee) appoints him as a United States senator in order to replace a longtime legislator who unexpectedly died in office. The local party boss, Jim Taylor (played by Edward Arnold), and Senator Joseph Paine (played by Claude Raines) need a seat warmer who will quietly hold office for a couple of months—not asking questions about a backroom land deal that the Taylor machine has engineered—until a suitable replacement can be sworn into office after the next election. When the naive Mr. Smith unexpectedly proposes legislation to create a national boys' camp on the site of the engineered land deal, the Taylor machine swings into action and, when it cannot persuade Smith to play ball, decides to destroy him. On more than one occasion, the film characterizes this struggle, which culminates with Smith's one-man Senate filibuster, as a David and Goliath battle.

The biblical trope, however, is incidental to the film's leitmotif of Jefferson Smith as a Don Quixote figure. For instance, in the scene immediately before the one in which Smith introduces his boys-camp legislation, his secretary, Clarissa Saunders (played by Jean Arthur), describes a pointedly Cervantine conflict for one of her journalist pals while sitting in the Senate gallery:

> Now there's the principal actor in our little play: Don Quixote Smith, man with bill. Over here, one of the supporting characters [she says while pointing to one of Taylor's Washington toadies]. . . . Ah, another prominent character in our little play: the Silver Knight [pointing to Senator Paine], soul of honor on a tightrope. . . . Don Quixote with bill will get to his feet in a minute and speak two important words: Willet Crick. When that happens, the Silver Knight will fall off his tightrope.

This is not the only reference to *Don Quixote* in the film. After Smith introduces his boys' camp legislation, Senator Paine tells him that he is "fighting windmills." In another scene, which takes place in the evening shadows of the Lincoln Memorial, Saunders tells Smith, "All the good that ever came into this world came from fools with faith."

Film scholars rarely mention Capra's intertextual dialogue with *Don Quixote*. Cervantes scholars, however, will see an abundance of connections. At the very beginning, the Boy Rangers organization functions as an ersatz chivalric order, making Smith a figure of knight-errantry even before he arrives in Washington and undergoes a kind of knighting ceremony when he takes the Senate oath of office and becomes the counterpart to Senator Paine's Silver Knight (a deliberate reference to Cervantes's Knight of the Mirrors). The ideal for which Smith ultimately fights is Lady Liberty, as he calls the statue of freedom located atop the Capitol dome. The Taylor machine against which he fights is a giant of both biblical and Cervantine proportions. And the name of Smith's loyal sidekick, Saunders, echoes "Sancho." Indeed, the film is as much about the *quijotización* of the initially cynical Saunders as it is about the *desengaño* ("disillusionment") of the idealistic Mr. Smith.

More importantly, *Mr. Smith Goes to Washington* is ultimately about arms and letters. In Capra's cinematic text, these two Cervantine elements are not contrasted, as they are in *Don Quixote*. They are made equivalent through the prominent function of writing, symbolized by the press, in the film. Smith's father, who at one time collaborated with a young Joseph Paine, was a crusading newspaperman who was shot in the back for defending in print the property rights of a single miner against a powerful mining syndicate. When Smith initiates his filibuster in order to delay his imminent expulsion from the Senate, his strategy depends on the press's disseminating his words to a home-state crowd that he hopes will rally to his defense. When the Taylor machine coopts the press in its character assassination of Smith, Smith's last hope turns out to be the Boy Rangers' newspaper that he edited before coming to Washington. When even this last lettered defense proves no match for the Taylor machine, Capra makes visually explicit in the film's climactic scene the power of letters to serve as a weapon.

In this scene, Smith's one-man filibuster has been going on for nearly twenty-four hours. Hoarse and disheveled, with dark circles under his eyes and the stubble of beard on his face, Smith has become Cervantes's Knight of the Woeful Countenance. It is at this moment of supreme weakness that Senator Paine enters the Senate chamber and delivers the coup de grâce: thousands of telegrams supposedly sent by the citizens of his state, demanding that Smith yield the floor and admit defeat. After reading through two or three random telegrams, all of which demand that he stop his filibuster, Smith wearily says:

> I guess this is just another lost cause, Mr. Paine. All you people don't know about lost causes. Mr. Paine does. He said once they were the only causes

worth fighting for. And he fought for them once. For the only reason any man ever fights for them. Because of just one plain, simple rule: love thy neighbor. And in this world today full of hatred, a man who knows that one rule has a great trust. You know that rule, Mr. Paine. And I loved you for it, just as my father did. And you know that you fight for the lost causes harder than for any others. Yes, you even die for them. Like a man we both knew, Mr. Paine. You think I'm licked. You all think I'm licked. Well, I am not licked! And I'm going to stay right here and fight for this lost cause. Even if this room gets filled with lies like these. And the Taylors and all their armies come marching into this place. Somebody will listen to me. Someb — [he collapses].

Smith's comments on lost causes in this scene recall an earlier scene in which Paine fondly remembers Smith's father. Paine says, "One look at you, and I can see him. Back at his old rolltop desk, hat and all, getting out his papers. Always kept his hat on his head so as to be ready to do battle. Clayton Smith, editor and publisher, champion of lost causes." Jefferson Smith replies, "Dad always used to say the only causes worth fighting for *were* the lost causes." Such talk is the essence of *quijotismo*, at least in a post-Unamunian world following the Generation of '98's conversion of Don Quixote into Spain's patron saint of lost causes. Had Capra's film ended with Smith's collapsing on the Senate floor after vowing to fight to the death, *Mr. Smith Goes to Washington* would have fit very well in the discourse of Miguel de Unamuno's *La vida de Don Quijote y Sancho* ("The Life of Don Quixote and Sancho"). Within such a hypothetical ending, Jefferson Smith, like Don Quixote before him, could then be read as a martyr to his ideals, defeated by a prosaic world hostile to the spiritual values embodied in this Boy Ranger, as a hero from a more innocent age.

But the film goes on for another two minutes, during which time Paine, whom we last saw quickly exiting the Senate chamber, unsuccessfully tries to commit suicide and then runs back onto the Senate floor to demand that he be expelled rather than Smith, because "every word that boy said is the truth. Every word about Taylor and me and graft and the rotten political corruption of my state. Every word of it is true." Shamed by Smith's quixotic perseverance, Paine admits defeat while the fainted Smith is carried off the Senate floor, to the cheering of the crowd in the gallery, as a conquering hero. In Capra's Cervantine encounter between Don Quixote and the Knight of the Mirrors, it is the reflective enemy who must renounce his ideology and return home in shame. Capra's Don Quixote is pointedly not the "champion of lost causes" he claims to be; instead, he is simply a champion, and hence unrelated to Unamuno's Don Quixote. Smith is an American Quixote at odds with his Spanish counterpart.

Up through the end of the nineteenth century, the Don Quixote of the Spanish imaginary and the Don Quixote of the American imaginary were basically the same: a figure of satiric ridicule. But in the wake of the Spanish-American War and with the triumph of what Anthony Close labeled "the Romantic approach to *Don Quixote*" (*Romantic Approach*), these two imaginaries diverged even as they both evolved in an idealistic direction. For Spain, 1898 marked the culmination of a long, steady, national decline; hence the Spanish Quixote became one ennobled by defeat rather than dishonored by it. For the United States, 1898 marked the beginning of what Henry Luce would later call "the American Century" (61), a golden age during which American culture could not conceive (and perhaps still cannot conceive) of anything approaching a truly lost cause. Capra's Hollywood ending in *Mr. Smith Goes to Washington* represents the epitome of this American Quixote of the eve of World War II. For Capra, Don Quixote is neither a lunatic nor a hopeless Romantic. He is an eternal optimist who sets his sights on realizing impossible dreams "not because they are easy, but because they are hard" (Kennedy 178). Thus, when Reich claims that a few determined souls are "quixotically" trying to save the Chicago blues from obscurity, he is expecting, even if only on some unconscious level, that the windmills of musical oblivion will eventually be defeated by one of these Don Quixotes of the Mississippi Delta—because in the American imaginary there simply are no impossible dreams.

Subjects, Objects, and Psychoanalysis: Lacanian Concepts as Pedagogical Approaches to *Don Quixote*

Matthew D. Stroud

The ideas and the language of psychoanalysis have so deeply penetrated the cultural vernacular that concepts such as the unconscious, the ego, overcompensation, neurosis, and oral fixation are in common usage not just in university classrooms but also in society at large. Our students are bound to be familiar with such terms even if they are a bit shaky on how the terms are used in psychoanalysis. Carroll Johnson's overview of psychoanalytic approaches to *Don Quixote* in the first edition of this volume took the model of the classroom as the scene of analysis ("Psychoanalysis"). Typical of most mid-twentieth-century Freudian criticism, his suggestions were based on the imposition of the discourse of the master, a perspective that positions the professor and the students as analysts, that is, as subjects supposed to know, and the text and the characters in it as analysands (Lacan, *Seminar* 20, 29–32, 102–06). According to Mark Bracher, who has studied Lacanian pedagogy in literary classrooms in general, this approach "foregrounds and valorizes certain identities, ideals, or values" in the search for the truths that lie in a character's unconscious (130).

It is no doubt interesting to undergraduates to look at the characters and their actions for signs of one or more psychopathologies, much as James A. Parr did in his article on Quixote's "flight from the feminine" ("Cervantes"). Unfortunately, this strategy is profoundly problematic, because few professors of literature, and fewer of their students, are trained as psychoanalysts or even psychologists or have undergone analysis themselves. The result, as Johnson himself noted, is that no one in the class knows what he or she is talking about ("Psychoanalysis" 110). Moreover, despite Henry Sullivan's arguments in support of applying the ideas and techniques of psychoanalysis to fictional protagonists ("Don Quixote"), the truth is that no literary character is a real person with a history, desires (repressed or not), an unconscious, or anything else that one associates with a living human being, as Parr also cautions ("Cervantes" 16), except those specifically and by definition artificially created for them and presented by their authors. As a result, these fictional creations cannot be questioned or speak to us in any way that might be considered authentic, nor are they going to learn anything or change, much less be cured, which invalidates both terms of Anna O.'s "talking cure" (Breuer and Freud 30). Another manifestation of the discourse of the master is equally troubling: the positioning of the professor in the role of analyst who hopes to seduce or coerce students through the process of transference to accept the opinions and interpretations of the professor—that is, the professor's desires—as their own, thus acknowledging the greatness of the professor or of the text or of some overarching signifier such as "genius" or "subversion" (Bracher 131). For Jacques Lacan, this scenario is ethically

suspect, as it forecloses a process by which students may escape "overtly au-
thoritarian literary pedagogies" (Bracher 128).

The enormous challenges presented by the incorporation of psychoanalysis
into a course on *Don Quixote* do not mean that such an approach has nothing to
offer, even at the undergraduate level. In my experience, instead of attempting
to psychoanalyze anyone (author, characters, students, professors), an attempt
that will stumble unless one wishes to make a detour of months or years to
assimilate the basic ideas of psychoanalysis on the way to understanding *Don
Quixote,* I have found that it is more rewarding, meaningful, and feasible to use
a number of Lacanian concepts and focus the discussion not on Lacan but on
Cervantes's masterpiece. The introduction of some of Lacan's more thought-
provoking notions not only allows students to read the novel through the lens of
another discipline, thus enriching and deepening the discussion, but also challenges them to place the novel in the history of ideas as well as in the context of
larger considerations of the human condition.

"What is the subject of this course?" seems a fairly innocent question, but if
we start to play around with the various meanings of the word *subject,* in just
the way that Lacan does, we find that the question becomes considerably more
interesting than one might have imagined. I have posed this very question at
different times during the semester. The first answer that students usually offer is, of course, *"Don Quixote,"* but do they mean the novel or the character?
Since we are reading and studying the book, are we not the subjects and the text
the object? Can something or someone be a subject and an object at the same
time? The class soon finds itself embroiled in issues that Cervantes built into the
very structure of his novel. Consider Don Quixote and Sancho Panza's critique
of the recently published part 1 (pt. 2, chs. 3–4), and Don Quixote's subsequent decision to change course and go to Barcelona rather than Zaragoza (525
[ch. 59]; 849) in order to differentiate himself at all costs from the rival Don
Quixote of Avellaneda's version, who may be just the fictional subject of another
novel or as real as "our" Don Quixote. After all, Álvaro Tarfe, himself a character
in the Avellaneda novel, declares that he knows this other Quixote (621 [ch. 72];
925), which means that he is at least as much of a subject-actor as Cervantes's
hero. Are truth and fiction nonoverlapping terms in a dichotomy, or is there a
sliding scale, or are there perhaps multiple levels, so that something may be true
and false simultaneously? Just as psychoanalysis must deal with the notion that
dreams and unconscious desire are as real, or even more real, than one's waking
activities and mental processes, so too does the appearance of two Quixotes in
the novel raise the questions of which one is more real and what reality is. For
the record, my students always and unanimously characterize Cervantes's Quixote as the real one—or at least more real than Avellaneda's.

Don Quixote is populated with a vast number of subjects—the principal
characters (many of whom appear in multiple guises), Cide Hamete and the
various other narrators, even Cervantes himself—but if we expand our focus
to the scene of (literary) analysis, we have to consider as well the professor,

the students, and all the authors of the secondary studies. This dizzying list of possible subjects leads seamlessly to the matter of artistic distancing, which in turn brings the class to a discussion of which of the various voices present, both in the novel and in the classroom, are the most trustworthy. That discussion highlights Lacan's assertion that the subject itself is indeterminate (*Four Fundamental Concepts* 26). In the novel, in the classroom, in the real lives of all of us, who is the "subject who is supposed to know" (230–33, 23), the source of the knowledge that will provide the answers to all our questions? On whom are we to rely in a search for understanding? The responses of my undergraduate students reveal how thoroughly they have been trained to believe that they are merely passive recipients and that the professor or the narrator or the author of a scholarly article must be the "subject supposed to know." The structure of the novel invites them to question the authority of any and all subjects, to investigate their own demand that someone else tell them what they need or want, and to look to themselves for insight and knowledge.

One of Lacan's most useful discoveries is that the subject functions in three registers, the symbolic, the imaginary, and the real. Even if one limits the discussion to the broadest possible outlines of the registers, Don Quixote presents a rich and accessible case study by means of which students can become more familiar with both how the registers work, especially the symbolic and the imaginary, and how the novel works. After I present general notions of the registers, I have the students offer examples from the literary text. On the symbolic side, the students come to understand that the protagonist is a pure creation of language: not only is the novel a work of literature but the character of Quixote himself springs from the chivalresque novels that Alonso Quijano spent too many nights reading. Quijano creates new names for himself and others and thoroughly submits to the laws of knight-errantry, patterning his actions on those he might consider his fictional fathers, Amadís and Roldán. On the imaginary side, he describes his desires in terms of a superhuman goal to rid the world of (imaginary) evils, and he creates the object of his affection, Dulcinea, almost out of whole cloth. That Dulcinea is a creation of Quijano's imaginary desire is even more evident since Aldonza Lorenzo is unaware of the role he has created for her (1: 119 [ch. 1]; 23–24).

Another fruitful approach stems from the notion of lack, in particular Lacan's concept of the human subject as structured by a missing object: the gap at the center is then filled with symbolic meanings and imaginary fantasies. The concept of the gap is a useful tool for the study of any text, as gaps abound everywhere: between professor and student, between text and meaning, between our world and the world of the novel (both the world when it was written and the world it creates). But if ever there was a work of literature marked by gaps and internal conflicts, it is *Don Quixote*. Indeed, the novel revels in its acceptance of lack and its refusal to maintain the appearance of wholeness and objectivity, and the simple request for students to identify as many gaps as they can becomes a feast of textual analysis and classroom discussion. This confrontation with lack starts on day 1, which is frequently overburdened with the discourse of the master: course requirements, dates of papers and tests, what students need to do to be successful in the course, and the like. Before they have had even one reading assignment, I like to probe their notions of a conventional reading of a novel—for example, the objective and omniscient narrator who provides us with a coherent, logical, and usually linear story populated by characters described in enough detail to allow for Samuel Coleridge's "suspension of disbelief." We then read the first paragraph of part 1, and I ask them how many of the expected conventions this one paragraph challenges. Without fail, they mention the narrator who cannot or will not give even such comforting information as where the action takes place; the lack of specificity in the description of the protagonist; the unusual, overly confident, and completely absurd assertion regarding the novel they are about to read: "basta que en la narración dél no se salga un punto de la verdad" 'in its telling there is absolutely no deviation from the truth' (114; 20). My follow-up questions deal with what one is to do with the fact that apparently no one—not the author, not Cervantes (who cannot be interrogated), not the professor, not the critics (despite their often heroic efforts), and not the students—can answer even the most basic questions regarding the action of this novel: Where exactly does it take place? What is the protagonist like beyond the scant details provided? Whom is one to believe? In other words, about twenty minutes into the course, the class has already come to appreciate that of the many subjects involved in the process of reading and studying *Don Quixote*, all of whom are supposed to know something, none can provide enough information to fill in the gaps.

By the second week, we get to the break in the narration between chapters 8 and 9 of part 1, a gap that simply cannot be overlooked because of the rupture in the fabric of the narration, the change in narrators, and the search for the rest of the text by the new voice, who not only serves as narrator of his own actions but also has apparently been a reader, along with us, of the first eight chapters. Again, the students confront a myriad of questions: How many narrators are there? Who are they? Should they be believed? As the course progresses, similar discontinuities appear in the text: What is the name of Sancho's wife? What happened to Sancho's burro, and how did it miraculously disappear and reappear (and what is one to make of Cervantes's explanation added to later editions)? How many characters take on new roles, and how do their new personas relate to their first personas? What effect does it have on the reader for Cervantes to have created Cide Hamete Benengeli, an untrustworthy narrator who, I have to remind students repeatedly, does not exist—leading to what is arguably the greatest example of intentional lack in all of literature, the episode in the Cueva de Montesinos, where even the narrative voice, untrustworthy though it may be, disappears.

One of the constant questions in Lacanian psychoanalysis involves the missing object *a* and how its lack affects the subject. In the classroom, this question can be reformulated to focus on what is missing in *Don Quixote* and how these lacks and gaps affect what happens in the text, the relation between reader and text, the differences between history and fiction, and even the classroom setting. Professors are often tempted to fill the gaps with their own analyses and opinions, but the results can be surprising and rewarding when a professor remains silent and lets students respond not only to the textual questions posed but also to larger issues—for example, the issue of why students are taking the course or, for that matter, even pursuing a university degree, and what they hope to get out of the book, the course, their educational experiences, life itself.

There are many other ways to apply Lacanian terminology to the study of *Don Quixote*. Some examples are the mirror stage (and Quixote's creation of his imaginary ego through his identifications with literary heroes); signification *après-coup* ("after the fact"), as happens with the *baciyelmo* ("basihelm") (1: 592 [ch. 44]; 390); "~~la~~ femme n'existe pas" ("~~the~~ woman does not exist"), a difficult Lacanian assertion that is made metaphorically concrete by the enchantment of the nonexistent Dulcinea.

But to return to the larger paradigmatic comparison with which we began: What is to be analyzed? Instead of taking on the role of analysts of an unresponsive (and fictional) analysand, we professors should recall Lacan's observation that when one looks at an object, the object also looks back at the viewer (*Four Fundamental Concepts* 95–96). In other words, instead of applying some master discourse to a silent text, we might invert the relation and position the text as the "subject supposed to know" and the readers (all of us, students and professors alike) as the analysands. This reversal of the relations of authority and signification allows us to discover our own master signifiers—what the text means to each of us and even what we hope to gain from the experience. It also changes what happens in the classroom.

If the novel itself is now placed in the position of the "subject supposed to know," students no longer feel pressured to have a command of the details of the text or constrained to view the professor's interpretation as the only one permitted; they need not substitute the professor's desires for their own. The novel comes alive as an agent for them to examine their own actions, demands, and desires. Is it merely a set of data to be absorbed or a task to be mastered, or are we meant to investigate and challenge both the nature of literature and the very act of reading? Are the characters no more than two-dimensional figures meant to illustrate some example or lesson, or do they invite the students into a mutual relationship? Every time I have taught the *Quixote*, I have noticed that students begin the course by maintaining a significant distance between themselves and these characters that are so foreign to their lives and to their ideas of how one should relate to a novel, but after the first few weeks, students speak of the characters as real people with real emotions and motivations (projecting, of course, their own demands onto them). Not only do they fall in love with the characters, in other words, but they end up willingly and consciously falling into the narrative traps set by Cervantes, the same kind of traps encountered by the protagonist; they begin to read fiction as though it were history. Confronting the students with their transference onto the text produces some interesting and useful discussions, as well as a lighthearted moment or two when they must confess to the loss of the distance that they as readers first tried to maintain. With the incorporation of these paradigmatic changes, the students now do most of the talking as they work through the problems they discover in the text, through their own motivations for studying *Don Quixote*, and through their responses to the classroom as the academic scene of analysis.

NOTE

The English translation of *Don Quixote* used in this essay is by Edith Grossman.

All the World's a Game: Mad about Playing

Susan Paun de García

"Life must be played."

—Johan Huizinga, *Homo Ludens*

In an age of digital media, video games, and cybernovels, we might ask ourselves how younger readers can relate to a classic work of literature like *Don Quixote*. As avid consumers of fantasy fiction and film, can they identify with the protagonist's insatiable consumption of romances of chivalry and his desire to act them out? How students relate to the main character depends on their approach to Quijano/Quixote's mind-set, to his attitude, and to his fantasies: Is he mad, or is he role-playing?

I have taught *Don Quixote* to undergraduates in Spanish, to senior Spanish majors, and in English to freshman English composition classes. My experience in teaching the novel in English has been at once risky, challenging, and illuminating. In a class entitled Inventing Yourself, Role-Playing, and Other Quixotic Endeavors, students explore the construction of identity and agency, using Alonso Quijano / Don Quixote as a mirror to examine questions related to self, identity, and role-playing.

The first goal for students of this freshman seminar is to study and practice academic writing in a variety of genres. A second and related goal is to learn to interpret a variety of texts and to experiment with different approaches to them. Students read Cervantes's masterpiece as a work of literature that bears a direct relation to their lives as independent, ethical, discerning agents in society. The principal lens through which we view the story, however, is that of fantasy role-playing, an intersection of game, narrative, and performance. We examine some theory for role-playing games as a confluence of performativity and ludology, create a game, and do some role-playing ourselves. As students read the novel, they develop avatars based on the characters they encounter, either from the fictional world of Quijano or from the metafictional realm of the romances of chivalry, work that necessitates research into the domains of their created personas. They learn about the historical, social, and literary contexts of *Don Quixote* in sixteenth- and seventeenth-century Spain and about the romances of chivalry that Quijano read, and they make up and enact a parallel narrative as they go along.

In addition to creating and performing a character in the manner of the duke and duchess, Dorotea, or Amadís of Gaul, a central question that students research, debate, analyze, write about, and perform is whether Quijano is mad or merely playing a game—specifically, a live-action role-playing game (LARP). The culminating class activity is a trial in which teams of advocates and

the novel for evidence of Quijano's madness, calling expert
; Huarte de San Juan to testify on the theory of bodily hu-
me of the trial is as varied as the roles students assume and
ımentation and persuasion.

ıdings of *Don Quixote* suggest that the protagonist cannot distinguish between his identity as Alonso Quijano, a reader of fiction, and that
of his created avatar, Don Quixote de la Mancha. The explanation offered by
the narrator is that obsessive and continual reading has dried up the brain of
Quijano, causing him to slip in and out of madness. But since the text prompts
readers to question the narrator's reliability, alternative explanations readily
arise. Perhaps Quijano is immersed in a role-playing adventure, not so much
being mad as seeming mad to those not sharing his enthusiasm. Perhaps the
difference between Quijano and Quixote could be explained by something as
simple as the difference between player and persona. Perhaps Quijano's desire
to become Quixote could be the result not of a distortion of reality but rather of
the performance of a desired, make-believe reality. Does Quijano really believe
that he is a knight-errant, or is he only pretending to believe? The question
hinges on whether he is capable of distinguishing between the role he performs
and the reality that surrounds him. In either case, it is clear that he is obsessed
with fantasy fiction and role-playing.

All role-playing games, whether live-action, tabletop, or video, feature players who make creative and consequential choices in order to develop their avatar or character. The games are popular because of the essential appeal of acting
out the dream of being a classical hero, immersing oneself in a role, and creating
a story without knowing the outcome: millions of copies are sold, received with
the same enthusiasm that players showed for the first console games of the
1970s — and with the same suspicion or rejection by nonplayers.

In order to comprehend the anachronistic fantasy narratives of today, students read about Dungeons and Dragons (D&D), a role-playing game of·the
1980s in which teenagers battled dragons and evil magicians. D&D might
seem as remote or archaic to our students as *Amadís of Gaul*, but the game
has been the model for countless role-playing games, just as *Amadís* served
as a generic forebear of chivalric fiction. Newer games, like Dragon Age, have
as many parts or sequels as any romance of chivalry did, and with versions in
other media—novels, comics, flash games, *Facebook*, anime, and Web series.
Still, they share many characteristics with the original pen-and-paper games:
developed story-telling and narrative elements, player-generated character development and complexity, and replayability and immersion. Like romances of
chivalry, these games, from the time they appeared, were distrusted, feared,
and reviled by many as dangerous to the players' (readers') mental health or
simply a waste of time (Waters). Students compare and contrast the worth
of such twentieth-century adventure games as D&D, Greyhawk, Dark Sun,
Dragonlance, or Ravenloft in much the same way that Quijano and his friends

discuss the merits of different novels of chivalry and their respective heroes' feats. This parallel throws a new light on the reading of part 1, chapter 6.

Most students are familiar with or have even participated in events such as medieval or Renaissance fairs or groups such as the Society for Creative Anachronism, whose members research and relive the life of medieval Europe, often hosting tournaments that attempt authenticity, as the bruises and contusions of those wearing padded armor and wielding real swords can testify. Like Quijano, participants strive to transport themselves into the past. But the role-playing of these societies lacks an element essential to LARPs: telling stories and creating narrative experiences (Heliö 69; Murray 42). LARP play is based on genre fiction (such as the *Lord of the Rings*), principally fantasy literature set in medieval times. Like Quijano, LARPers pursue their avatars' goals in costume and in character, interacting with one another in a physical environment appropriate to the fictive world: a forest becomes an enchanted glen, an open field turns into a battlefield, a barn morphs into a castle.

Role-playing games are essentially hybrid creatures, although the "truly defining aspect [lies] in the element of role-play over the concept of 'game' alone" (Flood 35). Daniel Mackay calls them a new performance art. But the players do not rely on scripts; they improvise as they go along. With their imaginations, they create characters that exist in a reality they construct. As Gary Alan Fine observes, they "'bracket' their 'natural' selves and enact a fantasy self [losing] themselves to the game" (4). In other words, successful or skillful players become immersed in the personas they create but can disengage themselves from play at will, since their belief in their characters and contexts is only pretended or performed.

Could Quijano be engaged in a similar activity, his sallies comparable to LARPs? This question stirs up immediate responses. Students who have enjoyed such games will defend Cervantes's hero as a skilled player; students who have no connection to them will accept the traditional view of the hero as mad. As we read, both groups gather evidence to support their position in preparation for the trial. In addition to scholarly studies centering on Quijano/Quixote's madness, we examine the character as *homo ludens*, reading theories of ludology to discover how LARPs diverge from classic games.

In classic games, rules are set before play begins; participants agree that the game will consist of certain activities in certain places at certain times. This is what Johan Huizinga termed the "magic circle," a boundary that sets a game apart from ordinary life (*Homo Ludens* 10–12). Compared with classic games, LARPs seem unbounded: boundaries exist, but the "magic circle" is expanded spatially, temporally, and socially. Games can be extended to places where they are generally not played, in the process creating disturbances for nonplayers who are unaware that a game is in progress. (We recall the confusion caused by Don Quixote's various appearances at the inn.) Games can be given no determined stop or start time or any indication that the game has ended, to the point that even the players might not know whether or not they are playing at a given moment (Montola 2.2).

A socially expanded (pervasive, in LARP terminology) game includes outsiders as game elements or as audience, and they can in turn influence and participate in the game. Bystanders, not knowing the rules or objectives, may be confused—or they may join in nevertheless. (Note that the ladies of lesser virtue in part 1 seem especially eager to play along with Don Quixote, as do the duke and duchess in part 2.) Spontaneous interaction can lead to the formation of communities (such as Dorotea's eager assumption of the role of Micomicona in the barber and priest's community of deceit, the duke and duchess's elaborate, pervasive community of role-play), but it can entail the risk of drawing unwilling persons into the game (most of those whom Don Quixote encounters).

Throughout the novel, Quijano enacts the three levels or boundaries of role-playing games: person, player, and persona (Waskul and Lust). The person and the person's normal circumstances generally operate outside the magic circle (e.g., Quijano at home). Within the boundaries of the game, the player will create a persona or character, in essence inventing another self, and use words and actions that represent what the character would say and do in situations determined by the particular diegesis. The player may move in and out of character to clarify rules or to instruct another player, or the player may momentarily revert to the person, going off-game because of pressing circumstances or an interruption. Quijano slips out of his persona as Don Quixote in order to explain to Sancho what Sancho, an uninitiated player, does not understand, but Quijano remains engaged in the game as a player. When he is immersed in the game and performing his persona, he is still conscious of his person. As a LARPer he performs belief—acts as if he believes—instead of truly believing that he is Don Quixote.

To grasp this fundamental difference, students read articles by Richard Schechner, a performance theorist; Jane McGonigal, a game theorist; and Mike Pohjola, a LARP theorist. Schechner distinguishes between "make believe," which protects the boundary between what is real and what is pretended (players pretend), and "make belief," which intentionally blurs the boundary (players pretend to believe) (42–44). This blur spurs rich discussion and writing as students read articles that attempt to explain or define *make belief*. McGonigal posits a "Pinocchio effect" that arises from an unfulfilled desire to believe for real, a "feigned and wished-for credulity" that represents a "desire to believe that life *can be* a game. . . . The more a player chooses to believe, the more (and more interesting) opportunities are revealed" (10, 13). Pohjola argues that this state is self-induced: "More than *pretending to be* the character, the player *pretends to believe she is* the character. . . . And she pretends to forget she is just pretending" (84). Could it be that Quijano wants to believe that he is not just pretending to be Don Quixote? Could that wish be the essence of his presumed madness?

If Quijano pretends to believe he lives in a magical world, he will pretend to see everyday phenomena as magical signs: all the world's a game. Those not engaged in this concentrated role-playing will consider the game madness. Even today, this view persists. McGonigal cites a colleague who dubbed immersive games "schizophrenia machines" that seem designed "for the sole purpose of turning previously sane players into paranoid, obsessive maniacs" (2). These negative reactions do not take into account what is really happening in the process of play; the question should be not to what extent players actually believe in the fictions they perform but "to what ends, and through what mechanisms, do players *pretend* to believe their own performance?" Instead of focusing on the "risks of real belief, we should investigate: What are the specific pleasures and payoffs for gamers of feigned belief in a play setting?" (3).

Perhaps these pleasures and payoffs originate in the act of reading itself, which in its own way constitutes participation in a game, the game of being caught up in a story, of finding ourselves, like Quijano, emotionally involved in a fictional world. Such transient immersion does not necessarily mean that the reader "loses touch with reality, temporarily, and actually believes in the fiction" (Walton 6). But reading is a solitary activity. LARPers, like Quijano, go beyond emotional involvement; they physically perform the fiction they create or recreate. This externalization is intimately related to acting, an aspect of *Don Quixote* that has been noted repeatedly (Van Doren; García). Role-players, like actors, function as if their emotions and thoughts were real, causing the onlooker or audience to believe in the truth, if not in the reality, of their actions. Quijano does not become a knight; he role-plays as if he were Don Quixote, immersing himself truthfully in the persona. The mistaken notion that players succumb to "a strain of madness," truly believing that the reality they create is real, has contributed to the distrust of pervasive gaming. The performed belief of pervasive gamers need not be seen as "a kind of paranoia or dangerous credulity" but rather as "a conscious decision to prolong the pleasures of the play experience" (McGonigal 22).

Does Quijano appreciate this difference? Could he be engrossed in the pleasures of play? Students explore these possibilities as they read and prepare for the trial. For defenders of Quijano as a role-player, an important feature is his total immersion in the game and his evident addiction to playing, to such a degree that he is considered to be mad by nonplayers and by players who are not so immersed. In what Quijano does, there is a clear consciousness of play, an elaborate process of character creation, and extensive knowledge of the background or history of the game world. His reading of ballads and romances gives him a ready-made supply of character traits, strengths, and feats. At first he imitates various characters of whom he has read. Later he develops his own persona, Don Quixote de la Mancha, an avatar who is independent but maintains links to the diegesis of knights-errant, to Amadís of Gaul in particular. Quijano expands the game to the real world spatially, temporally, and socially: there is no magic circle, no limited play time, and no distinction made between players and nonplayers. In part 1, he works to stay in character and tries not to revert to player or person, mistaking nonplayers for fellow LARPers. When his first objective—the knighting of his character—is accomplished, he suspends play.

As part 2 begins, the second role-playing adventure, Don Quixote has jelled as Alonso Quijano's character. Quijano's immersion in the fantasy world of the LARP is mistaken for madness by nonplayers unfamiliar with genre-based role-playing, is mocked by others, and is unwittingly validated by those whose familiarity with the romances of chivalry leads to an interaction with Don Quixote that he mistakes for participation in the game. Quijano's ability to switch among person, player, and persona is noted by friends and strangers alike, but his immersion reaches a degree in which everything becomes a clue and all persons are players or personas-characters in the LARP. In part 2, the Don Quixote LARP has become famous, and readers of part 1 are fascinated by it, although most are unaware that it is a role-playing game. Many admire Don Quixote, but many more find his adventures a ridiculous waste of time or consider him to be crazy, and they dismiss Sancho Panza as a fool. Quijano's friends, the barber, the bachelor, and the priest, see danger in his addiction to role-playing, fearing violence or self-destructive behavior. They conclude that the best way to end the role-playing is to defeat his character, thus ending that narrative thread.

Sancho, like most LARP beginners, is assigned a character at first but has no real knowledge of the role, the diegesis, or the rules of the game. He learns from off-game hints or prompts from Quijano, the designer of the LARP and the player of the character Don Quixote. A second-generation LARP is designed by Sancho when he inadvertently invents the quest (to disenchant Dulcinea), and this LARP is staged and developed by the duke and duchess, who become game masters actively directing its performance (their game manual was their reading of part 1). Both they and Sancho refer back to the initial diegesis to advance the new one. Essential conflict is supplied by the intervention of Quijano's friends, who in their attempt to stop the LARP often play characters that they hope will derail Don Quixote either by diverting his quest or by defeating him in battle, effectively killing off the character. Eventually, the defeat of Don Quixote marks the end of the game, inducing postgame depression in Quijano. With no game and no persona, his unremarkable self and circumstances are all that he has left.

For today's students, knowledge of the world and life experiences are shaped more and more by cybercommunities, social networks, and the stories generated by those digital worlds. Our virtual identities become natural extensions of our selves, expanding our sense of the nature of reality. Within us all are contradictory identities, and "[w]e construct a comforting story or 'narrative of the self' about ourselves" (Filiciak 96). In that respect, we all role-play.

Don Quixote and Political Satire:
Cervantine Lessons from Sacha Baron Cohen
and Stephen Colbert

David R. Castillo

A few years ago, I called attention to the surprising fact that Walter Benjamin, a Marxist critic, and Ernesto Giménez Caballero, a fascist ideologue, had a similar understanding of the function of humor in *Don Quixote* (*[A]Wry Views* 85–88). Both, despite their vastly divergent backgrounds and worldviews, thought of Cervantes's irony as a political tool, that is, "a weapon against stupor" ("instrumento de combate frente al estupor" [Giménez Caballero 40]). Yet, as we might expect, Benjamin and Giménez Caballero go their separate ways when it comes to assessing the political value of this Cervantine tool or weapon. Benjamin celebrates Cervantes's strategy of holding myths and counterfeit notions to the light until they turn to harmless ashes. In fact, the Marxist theorist thinks of the Cervantine style as a model of ideological critique: "The magic of true critique appears precisely when all counterfeit comes into contact with the light and melts away. What remains is the authentic: it is ashes. We laugh at it" (qtd. in Eagleton 155). By contrast, Giménez Caballero laments the destructiveness of Cervantine irony, which dealt a devastating blow to the mystical and blind pride of imperial Spain: "la soberbia—mística y ciega—de la España yugada en haz" (39). The fascist ideologue goes so far as to compare the political influence of Cervantes's work with the regrettable consequences of the Peace of Münster: "Don Quixote is the spiritual correlation of the disaster that was to come in Münster . . . the beginning of the end of all the great adventures of Spain" (my trans.).[1]

What interests me in this essay is Giménez Caballero's sense of how the author of *Don Quixote* accomplishes his demystifying goals. As Giménez Caballero writes in *Genio de España* ("The Spirit of Spain"), Cervantes boasts an excessive orthodoxy, yet we can see his irony ("alardea de excesiva ortodoxia y se le ve la ironía" [40]). I take this astute observation as a point of departure in arguing that "excessive orthodoxy" is indeed one of Cervantes's signature strategies, a form of posturing that finds fertile ground today in the political satires most familiar to our students. I sketch a comparative line of critical commentary by examining selected passages of *Don Quixote* and *Persiles* side by side with a few scenes from *Borat* (2006) and a condensed version of Stephen Colbert's 2006 roasting of President Bush. My suggestion is that students, when they see the excessive orthodoxy at work in the comedy of Sacha Baron Cohen and Colbert, may reach a deeper understanding of the mechanics of Cervantine irony and an appreciation of its political edge.

As I suggested in an online essay in which I compared Cervantes's work with some of the most popular road movies of the last four decades ("Literary

Classics"), the mock documentary directed by Larry Charles helps us reflect on matters of spectator (and reader) positioning vis-à-vis the views expressed by Borat, the eccentric character played by Cohen, and the candid opinions of those with whom he interacts as he travels across the physical and cultural landscape of the United States. I focus on two scenes that exemplify the ironizing strategy associated with excessive orthodoxy. The first takes place during a rodeo in Salem, Virginia. At the civic center there, Borat proclaims Kazakhstan's endorsement of America's war on terror. He asks the crowd to show support for "our boys in Iraq," then progressively escalates his war rhetoric, reaching a level that exposes its inherent nonsense. We can sense the crowd's growing uneasiness as Borat's images of aggression become more and more violent: "May you and they kill every single terrorist; may George Bush drink the blood of every single man, woman, and child of Iraq; may you destroy their country so that for the next thousand years not even a single lizard will survive in their desert."[2] The crowd's booing becomes deafening midway through Borat's rendition of a perverted version of the "Star-Spangled Banner," starting with the provocation, "Kazakhstan is the greatest country in the world; all other countries are run by little girls." By then, Borat has obviously blown his cover of war-time orthodoxy.

The second scene deals with our construction and propagation of mythical images of the other—in this case, the Jewish other. Borat and his producer, Azamat, arrive at a bed-and-breakfast where they plan to spend the night, only to realize that their kindly hosts are Jewish. Borat spits out the food he has been given, suspecting that it is poisoned by the Jews. He is also shown sitting up under his bedcovers holding a crucifix and a fistful of dollars for protection. Eventually he and Azamat are convinced that the Jews have turned into a pair of menacing cockroaches that are shown walking into their bedroom. At this point, the guests throw their money at the advancing insects and run for their lives.

David Marchese, in the online magazine *Salon.com*, reveals that Mariam Behar and Joseph Behar, the owners of the bed-and-breakfast, had "rented out three rooms to what they thought was a Kazakh documentarian and his film crew." Although Borat never broke character and no one in the production team let the Jewish couple in on the joke, Joseph is quoted praising the mock documentary: "Speaking on the telephone, Joseph, with Mariam chatting in the background, says they saw the film and thought it 'was not anti-Semitic at all. It was outstanding. I think [Sacha Baron Cohen] is a genius.'"

Behar's enthusiasm for the comedic craft of Cohen contrasts sharply with the response of the audience in the rodeo scene. By the time the comedian was wrapping up his ironic rant in support of America's war of terror, some in the "decidedly pro-American crowd" had resorted to a "restless kind of booing," according to John Saunders, the Salem civic center's assistant director (Marchese). Borat's twisted rendition of the "Star-Spangled Banner" did not help matters. A cohost of a local morning radio show, Robynn Jaymes, is quoted by a reporter working for the *Roanoke Times* as saying, "By then, a restless crowd had turned downright nasty. If he had been there a minute longer, I think somebody would have shot him" (Hammack).

Though admittedly anecdotal, reports of audience responses may be helpful as we compare these scenes from *Borat* with passages from *Don Quixote* and *Persiles* that reproduce mythical images of Spain's racialized other, the Morisco. In chapter 65 of part 2 of *Don Quixote*, Ricote, a Morisco, offers a seemingly straightforward justification of the expulsion of his own "poisonous kind" decreed by King Philip III, while praising the Spanish official Don Bernardino de Velasco for his diligence in carrying out His majesty's orders:

> [Bernardino de Velasco] can see that the whole body of our race is tainted and rotten, and so he applies to it the cautery that burns rather than the ointment that soothes; and thus, with wisdom, sagacity, diligence, and the fear that he inspires, he has borne upon his broad shoulders the weight of this great project and duly put it into effect; and all our tricks, stratagems, pleadings, and deceptions haven't been able to blind his Argus eyes, always on the alert so that not one of our people remains hidden from him like a root buried in the ground that later sprouts and bears poisonous fruit in a Spain now cleansed and free from the fears in which our rabble kept it.   (933)[3]

Some scholars take Ricote's words at face value, attributing his diatribe against his own kind to Cervantes's anti-Morisco sentiments. John J. Allen's judgment in *Don Quixote: Hero or Fool?* is revealing in this regard: "My reluctant conviction that Cervantes and I disagree on the issue is confirmed by my inability to identify any clues to irony in the context" (103). Yet examining this passage alongside the two scenes from *Borat* suggests that Ricote's justification is exactly the type of ironic posturing that Giménez Caballero associated with excessive orthodoxy. I read this passage in the way that the Behars interpreted the bed-and-breakfast scene, as a clever exposé of our cultural, religious, and racial fears. This defense of Spain's policy of expulsion offered by one of its victims, an exiled Morisco, seems as strange as the idea that a Jewish prisoner at a Nazi camp would praise Adolf Hitler and Adolf Eichmann for their dedication to ensure the health of the German nation (Castillo, *[A]Wry Views* 89). Ricote's passionate orthodoxy is a satire on the mythology and politics that led to the exile of hundreds of thousands of Spanish converts in 1609–14.[4]

I connect this episode of *Don Quixote* with similar passages in *Persiles*. Zenotia, a Morisca who is addressed by the narrator simply as *la española Zenotia* ("Spanish Zenotia"), denounces the unjust persecution to which she was subjected: "[P]ersecution in Spain by those known as Inquisitors tore me from my homeland, for when one is forced to leave it, one doesn't simply leave but feels torn away" (Cervantes, *Trials* 135).[5] Remarkably, Zenotia's tragic life story alludes to the widespread belief in the magical powers of the Moriscos:

> I left my homeland about four years ago fleeing the vigilance of the watchful guard dogs that keep the Catholic flock in that kingdom. I come from Mohammedan stock; my spiritual exercises are those of Zoroaster and I'm matchless in them. . . . Just ask, and in a twinkling I'll make this brightness turn to darkest night; or if by chance you'd like to see the earth tremble, the winds quarrel with each other, the sea turn rough.   (134)[6]

Obviously, her disclosure of her dark powers is incongruous with her denunciation of the persecution she and the rest of her kind suffered by the Inquisition.

Another Morisco, known as Jadraque, blames his evil race for its own punishment in a statement that is referred to by the narrator—ironically, I suspect—as a "heavenly trance" (258). Note the similarities between his words and those of Ricote in *Don Quixote*:

> Oh, noble youth! Oh, invincible King! Trample down, break through, and push aside every obstacle and leave us a pure Spain, cleaned and cleared of this evil caste of mine that so darkens and defames it! Oh counselor as wise as you are distinguished, a new Atlas supporting the weight of this monarchy, through your wise counsel help to bring about more easily this necessary migration! Let the seas be filled with your galleys loaded with the useless weight of the descendants of Hagar; may these briars, brambles, and other weeds hindering the growth of Christian fertility and abundance be flung to the opposite shore! . . . The religious orders don't harvest them, the Indies don't thin them out, wars don't draft them. They all get married and all or most of them have children. From this it follows and can be inferred that the multiplications of and additions to them will unquestionably be incalculable. So I repeat, make them go; make them go, sir, leaving the tranquil surface of the fountain of your kingdom shining like the sun and as beautiful as the sky.   (*Trials* 258)[7]

When I read the Morisco's all-out call for the persecution and exile of every single member of his "caste," I think of Borat's working of the crowd at the Salem rodeo and of his antics in the bed-and-breakfast scene. The Morisco expresses racial stereotypes in his description of the danger that his tainted kind represents for the moral health of Christian Spain—another illustration of the ironic deployment of "excessive orthodoxy" as a "weapon against stupor," to quote again Giménez Caballero.[8]

In the *Colbert Report*, Colbert poses as the neoconservative host of a late-night TV show of political commentary and interviews. The success of his act earned him an invitation to perform the traditional roasting of the president at the 2006 White House press corps dinner. His roasting of Bush became an instant *YouTube* classic due in large part to the hilarity of his "excessive ortho-doxy," which exposes the blind pride of the Bush administration in its disregard of inconvenient facts, whether we are thinking of the presence of weapons of mass destruction in Iraq or the findings of historians and scientists. I encourage students to find commonalities between the effectiveness of Colbert's brand of political satire, with which most are no doubt familiar, and the astonishing reach of Cervantine irony.

In his roasting, Colbert calls President Bush his "hero" and announces his intention to "celebrate this president," with whom he says he has so much in common. Here is part of the speech:

> Guys like us, we are not some brainiacs on the nerd patrol. We are not members of the factinista. We go straight from the gut, right sir? That's where the truth lies; right down here, in the gut. Do you know that you have more nerve endings in your gut than you have in your head? You can look it up. Now, I know that some of you are going to say, "I looked it up and that's not true." That's because you looked it up in a book. Next time look it up in your gut. I did, and my gut tells me that's how our nervous system works. Every night on my show, the *Colbert Report*, I speak straight from the gut, okay? I give people the truth unfiltered by rational argument. I call it "the no-fact zone." . . . Reality has a well-known liberal bias. . . . The greatest thing about this man is that he is steady, you know where he stands; he believes the same thing Wednesday that he believed on Monday no matter what happened Tuesday. Events can change. This man's beliefs never will.

The profile of the president foregrounded here has a marked quixotic quality: his reality-proof stance. Colbert's hero president is as immune as Don Quixote to inconvenient facts, events, physical and cultural geographies, and rational arguments.

The protagonist of Cervantes's novel does not need to change his mind about what he knows to be castles, giants, and armies just because these things look and act like inns, windmills, and herds of livestock. The knight-errant is convinced that what shines on the barber's head is Mambrino's helmet, even though, on closer inspection, the object looks and feels like a barber's basin (pt. 1, ch. 21). President Bush does not need to adjust his convictions about global warming or Iraq's weapons of mass destruction despite all the evidence to the contrary.

If, as Giménez Caballero suggested, the central tenet of empire, its defining characteristic, is "mystical and blind pride," then the real enemy of empire is not some axis of evil (empires must have an external or internal source of evil to justify their existence)[9] but the demystifying irony that Giménez Caballero and Benjamin attributed to the Cervantine legacy. This rich comedic tradition continues to hold counterfeit notions to the piercing light of truth.

NOTES

The English translation of *Don Quixote* used in this essay is by John Rutherford.

[1] "El 'Quijote' es la correlación espiritual al desastre que se fraguaría en Münster. . . . Primera despedida de toda grandeza y aventura española" (Giménez Caballero 40).

[2] The content of this video has been blocked since the quote was taken from it at the following link: http://www.youtube.com/watch?v=KbTS7320n64.

[3] "[C]omo él vee que todo el cuerpo de nuestra nación está contaminado y podrido, usa con él antes del cauterio que abrasa que del ungüento que molifica; y así, con prudencia, con sagacidad, con diligencia y con miedos que pone, ha llevado sobre sus fuertes hombros a debida ejecución el peso desta gran máquina, sin que nuestras industrias, estratagemas, solicitudes y fraudes hayan podido deslumbrar sus ojos de Argos, que contino tiene alerta, porque no se le quede ni encubra ninguno de los nuestros, que como raíz escondida, que con el tiempo venga después a brotar, y a echar frutos venenosos en España, ya limpia, ya desembarazada de los temores en que nuestra muchedumbre la tenía" (2: 524–25).

[4] I appreciate the nuanced commentary of Martínez Bonati (26–31) and William Childers (*Transnational Cervantes* 169–71) on the controversial Ricote episode and its reception but, believing in the presence of irony in the passage, come closer to the position of Márquez Villanueva (*Personajes* 234).

[5] "[L]a persecución de los que llaman inquisidores en España me arrancó de mi patria: que, cuando se sale por fuerza della, antes se puede decir arrancada que salida" (Cervantes, *Trabajos* 329).

[6] "Salí de mi patria habrá cuatro años, huyendo de la vigilancia que tienen los mastines veladores que en aquel reino tienen del católico rebaño; mi estirpe es agarena; mis ejercicios, los de Zoroastes, y en ellos soy única. . . . Pídemelo, que haré que a esta claridad suceda en un punto escura noche; o ya, si quieres ver temblar la tierra, pelear los vientos, alterarse el mar" (*Trabajos* 327).

[7] "¡Ea, mancebo generoso; ea, rey invencible, Atropella, rompe, desbarata todo género de inconvenientes, y déjanos a España tersa, limpia, y desembarazada de esta mi mala casta, que tanto la asombra y menoscaba! ¡Ea, consejero tan prudente como ilustre, nuevo Atlante del peso de esta monarquía! ¡Ayuda y facilita con tus consejos a esta necesaria transmigración; llénense estos mares de tus galeras, cargadas del inútil peso de la generación agarena; vayan arrojadas a las contrarias riberas las zarzas, las malezas, y las otras yerbas que estorban el crecimiento de la fertilidad y abundancia cristiana! Que si los propios hebreos que pasaron a Egipto multiplicaron tanto que en su salida se contaron más de seiscientas mil familias, ¿que se podrá temer de estos, que son más y viven más holgadamente? No los esquilman las religiones, no los entresacan las Indias, no los quitan las guerras; todos se casan, todos, o los más, engendran, de do se sigue que su multiplicación y aumento ha de ser innumerable. ¡Ea, pues, vuelvo a decir, vayan, vayan, señor, y deja la taza de tu reino resplandeciente como el sol y hermosa como el cielo" (*Trabajos* 558–60).

[8] This notion is consistent with Maravall's interpretation of *Don Quixote* as a "contrautopía" (*Utopía*), a term that—as Spadaccini and I argued a few years ago—might be better translated as "anti-utopia" than as "counterutopia." To be sure, Maravall is not thinking here of Erasmian humanism or other forward-looking forms of utopianism; rather, what he has in mind is the regressive utopias behind pastoral and chivalric romances. Parr may have said it best in his convincing defense of a reading of *Don Quixote*

as Menippean satire: "[T]he target or butt of the satire is often some contemporary and near-at-hand issue; as José Antonio Maravall has pointed out, that target in *Don Quixote* would seem to be utopian evasiveness, a failure properly to address and come to grips with contemporary socio-political problems, preferring instead to take refuge in the notion of a past golden age and the prospect of its resurrection" (Don Quixote: *A Touchstone* 142).

[9] In *Baroque Horrors* (esp. ch. 4), I deal with the construction of mythical enemies in connection with the politics of empire.

Don Quixote and Its Range of Audiences

Edward H. Friedman

One of the first things that we think of as teachers is how to address our presentation of materials to a particular audience. What I am talking about is not so much reader response as the other side of reader response: directed readings. As an advocate of training students to read closely and establish their own critical, analytic, and interpretive parameters, I find myself walking the tightrope of what one could call *directed spontaneity*. My goal is to lead students into readings that are not underdeveloped or uninformed but informed, logical, textually and contextually justifiable. I am giving them tools, while they are applying less a methodology than a method. I like to see this approach as a kinder and gentler version of Louis Althusser's interpellation, a kind of subconscious indoctrination whereby readers feel that they are thinking freely when their thought processes and ideological positions have been molded with calculation. My motives are neither cynical nor naive. If I bring up in introductory sessions the topics of metafiction, metatheater, metapoetry, and other terms with *meta-* prefixes and give concrete examples of such phenomena, it does not surprise me when students, in the first discussion of *Don Quixote*, part 1, for example, describe the prologue as a metaprologue, even though the word *metaprologue* was never mentioned in class or in the preparatory readings. We thus are operating in the metafictional mode from the beginning, and this technique progresses immediately to Don Quixote's appropriation of chivalric conventions and the commentary in the text on narrative composition, and subsequently to such recourses as the scrutiny of Alonso Quijano's library (ch. 6). The strategy of directed spontaneity is a staple and a common denominator of all my courses built around *Don Quixote*, but its direction varies according to the target audience.

Like many *cervantistas*, I am more than a bit quixotic. I believe that Cervantes's narrative is a treasure of literary devices and worldly wisdom and that it anticipates not only the development of the so-called modern novel of the eighteenth and nineteenth centuries but also the modernist and postmodernist responses to realism and the theoretical issues that have engaged us for the past half century. I believe that this rich and open text is profound, ironic, magnificently elusive, and highly comic. When I feel that I have successfully interested students in the intentional obscurity of baroque poetry, for example, I give myself some credit for making this difficult material accessible, if not transparent, whereas I think that one would have to make a concerted effort — to concoct a pedagogy from hell, as it were — not to animate readers of *Don Quixote*. Even so, framing the reading and discussion of it makes a difference in the classroom. In this essay, I present my objectives and approach to Cervantes's novel, in English, in three instances at Vanderbilt University: an undergraduate honors seminar for College Scholars, Vanderbilt's undergraduate elite; a course in the Master of Liberal Arts and Science program, which gives a thirty-hour general humanities degree and includes night courses for working professionals; and a summer course in the Program for Talented Youth. Despite the different audiences, I do not greatly modify the deep structure of these courses. Rather, I bring in variations on Cervantine and quixotic themes that form the basis of what I hope to convey to each group and where I hope the courses will take the students.

For me, there is something magical about *Don Quixote*, something that connects with us from the first words of the prologue. The man who becomes Don Quixote is an enthusiastic, voracious reader. Cervantes links us with him even as he creates an ironic detachment. If *Don Quixote* becomes an allegory of reading, it becomes, at the same time, an allegory of writing and storytelling, from the initial gathering of data to the discovery of the manuscript by the Arab historian Cide Hamete Benengeli and the trials of translation and transmission. Gloria Fuertes, a twentieth-century Spanish writer, wrote a beautiful and moving metapoem, "Sale caro ser poeta," whose title could be loosely rendered as "It's Tough to Be a Poet." That is one of the messages of *Don Quixote*: stories do not tell themselves; they have to be contemplated, born, polished. They generate anxiety, including the anxiety of influence (see Bloom, *Anxiety*), not to mention critical and commercial anxiety. Cervantes inserts the blood, sweat, and tears of literary construction into the frame. He surrounds the narrative action — modeled on literature — with allusions and borrowings from the genres and theoretical debates of his day. One plot has to do with adventures, the other with the fabrication of what is, in Spanish, *la historia*, which can mean both "story" and "history." This fortunate ambiguity allows Cervantes to play with fiction while calling it "true history," to examine such issues as perception and perspective, to entertain and instruct, to explore the nature and representation of reality, and, in so doing, to deconstruct the Aristotelian dichotomy of history and poetry. There is a strange psychology to Don Quixote, who seems as far as a character can be from a flesh-and-blood mortal yet who is capable of winning the sympathy of the reader on numerous occasions throughout the lengthy narrative. Cervantes investigates reality from many angles, sometimes directly, sometimes periphrastically or indirectly. His is an elaborate game, filled with humor but ultimately taken quite seriously.

In *Don Quixote*, Cervantes accentuates the limitations and strengths of the verbal sign. The narrative bears as many markers of his ingenuity as that of the knight-errant or errant knight. In my classes, I want to promote the excitement that I feel toward the novel, and I want to work mimetically rather than diegetically, by showing rather than telling, by having students adopt the roles of reader, critic, and director. I want to be their guide, their—using the parlance of narratology blended, maybe a bit facetiously, with that of Cervantes—implied second author. In other words, I want them to sense my presence while they serve as the real readers, who assume control, limited though it may be, of the analytic act. Finally, I want them to leave the course delighted with having read *Don Quixote* and armed and ready to tackle any text that comes their way.

There are three basic aims of my honors seminar, titled *Don Quixote* and the Experimental Novel: to have the students read and appreciate *Don Quixote* on a number of levels; to offer a kind of rhetoric of reading that is both comprehensible and flexible; and to identify the type of novel that is self-conscious, metafictional, calling attention to the creative process as well as to the final product. The juxtaposition of texts is not entirely obvious, because the point of contact is about mergers of form and content rather than about chivalry, literary madness, or early modern Spain or Europe. I begin in this course, as always, with fundamental background material: the concept of the golden age and its manifestations in art, history, and politics; the baroque period, as contrasted with the Renaissance; the sixteenth-century break from narrative idealism into forms of realism, from the Italian *novella* and the picaresque novel forward; the notions of metafiction and intertextuality; and aspects of the society and culture of early modern Spain. Prominent in the last category would be the Hapsburgs, the Inquisition, the Counter-Reformation, the social hierarchy, the obsession with blood purity and the division of the unified Catholic population into Old Christians and New Christians, the status of women in life and art, and the influence of the printing press. Using some very short stories as examples, I look with students at how the elements of narration—among them, voice, point of view, reliability, and irony—factor into the reading experience. I also use Diego Velázquez's *Las meninas*, which encompasses baroque expression, self-referentiality, the fusion of art and reality, and the conspicuous presence of both the maker and the consumer of the art object. It is an ideal visual analogue of *Don Quixote*.

We move to the reading and discussion of *Don Quixote*: two weeks on part 1, one week for review and selected criticism, and the same format for part 2.

The next division of the course concentrates on five experimental novels. My principal criterion for selection was a clear consciousness in the text of the task of composition per se, of a dialectics of the raw material of the plot and the intervention of an authorial figure as organizer, orchestrator. The five texts are Miguel de Unamuno's *Niebla* (*Mist*), Carlos Fuentes's *Aura*, Toni Morrison's *The Bluest Eye*, Paul Auster's *City of Glass*, and Mark Haddon's *The Curious Incident of the Dog in the Night-time*. At the end of the semester, I ask students to consider the legacy of *Don Quixote* on later fiction. I provide these tentative conclusions, tentative in that they are my personal assessment of the trajectory that we have seen:

1. Every narrative text will, in some form or another, tell a story. The input of the narrator or narrators into that story will be meaningful in itself. That is, the act of storytelling contains its own story. The reader, then, will note two processes that occur simultaneously: story and discourse, the narrative events and the form of expression that gives structure to the action. Ultimately, the two elements should be contemplated together, in a dialectical relation.

2. From the mid–sixteenth century, the Spanish picaresque novel moves realism forward, but the reader is also conscious of the act of narration, of the self-fashioning of the narrator-protagonist. This subgenre underscores the psychological progression of the lead character and also combines the intersection of realism and metafiction that will continue in the early seventeenth century in *Don Quixote* and, to greater or lesser degrees, in all forms of the developing novel.

3. *Don Quixote* makes us aware of the process of literary creation by foregrounding readers and writers. At the same time, Cervantes manages to cover such issues as history and historiography, truth, and human nature. What starts out as satire ends up as an exceedingly knowing and precocious model for the novel—specifically, for experimental narrative.

4. European realism is most associated with the eighteenth and nineteenth centuries (Richardson, Fielding, Defoe, Dickens, Austen, the Brontë sisters, Stendhal, Flaubert, Tolstoy, Dostoevsky, Pérez Galdós, Pardo Bazán, Clarín). A heightened form of realism comes to light in naturalism (associated with Zola and others). Although narrators are never totally invisible and many narrators direct messages to the reader, a goal of narrative realism and naturalism is to imitate reality in a direct way and absorb readers into the action rather than to call attention to the literary conventions at play.

5. Metafiction does precisely the opposite: as the Russian formalists say, it "lays bare its devices" (see Shklovsky) and makes the reader aware of its status as literature, as fiction.

6. The intersections of realism and metafiction are worthy of note and study. A novel such as Unamuno's *Mist*, for example, reacts against realism and

naturalism. It is metafictional, but it makes a statement about reality, perception, and human psychology. As in *Don Quixote*, its slant on reality is indirect (determinedly antithetical to the outlook of traditional realism). Unamuno invents the term *nivola* to differentiate his conception of the novel from that of his immediate predecessors.

7. In *Aura*, Fuentes plays with point of view (using the second person), together with the official history of Mexico and with questions of Latin American identity. He takes lessons from a number of masters, including Poe and others who blend realism with horror and the supernatural.

8. Morrison's *The Bluest Eye* delivers a potent message about race and class in the United States, but the novel has a prominent artistic design that adds a poetic dimension to the stark realities of the story. Over twenty years after the publication of the novel, Morrison herself questioned the imposition of art onto the story. Some may disagree with her assessment; I am one of them.

9. Auster, in *City of Glass*, seems to use a quixotic template. He shifts from chivalric romance to detective story, but his DQ (Daniel Quinn) and the author who creates him — as well as the fictionalized Auster — appear to have Cervantes (along with New York City and other matters) on their minds (*New York Trilogy* 1–158).

10. *The Curious Incident of the Dog in the Night-time* reveals character through the act (and art) of storytelling. Haddon gives himself a huge challenge: to sustain a narrative from the point of view of a fifteen-year-old with Asperger syndrome. He uses the mystery format and makes his narrator-protagonist a detective, and he creates a unique vision (in the double sense of the term).

A striking aspect of this scheme is that my conclusions are affected by the group dynamics and individual achievements in reader response. Teaching becomes about learning, whether one is at or facing the proverbial (now rarely used) blackboard.

My plan for the course *Don Quixote* and the Development of the Novel, for adult learners who in almost all cases had enrolled in the MA program out of a love of learning, was similar. Since the program requirements are ten courses in the humanities, social sciences, and natural sciences, I was less concerned with instruction in literary criticism as an end in itself than with a consideration of — and attention to — the interplay of history and poetry, realism and metafiction, and the two-pronged intertextuality of *Don Quixote*, built on and deviating from textual tradition and establishing itself as the primary intertext for what Ian Watt called, although he shortchanged the Spanish picaresque and *Don Quixote*, the rise of the novel (*Rise*). I want the class to understand the sociohistorical and cultural backdrops, the often ignored place of Spain in the literature of Shakespeare's age, the intricacies and brilliance of *Don Quixote* and its influence on the progression of the novel. By reading later novels, the students are able to see, as many scholars have said over the years, albeit more elegantly, that

Cervantes got it right. Five of the eighteen students followed the course with another on James Joyce's *Ulysses*, yet because I knew that for some of them my course would be the only one in literature, I felt pressure to bring as much into the frame as possible. I wanted to give them the training and confidence to answer two sets of questions. First: What is *Don Quixote* about? How does it reflect Spain at the beginning of the seventeenth century? How is it an example of baroque art? How does it qualify as a modern novel and as a model for the development of narrative? Second: How is literature being taught in the new millennium? How does the recent surge of theory affect the approach to the study of the novel? What are some of the basic theoretical terms and concepts that can help us feel comfortable in literary (and pseudo-literary) circles? It is fairly easy to integrate theory into a discussion of *Don Quixote*, because Cervantes does that himself, without exaggerating the topics or taking his readers out of their comfort zone.

In July 2008, I gave a three-week course on *Don Quixote* in the Vanderbilt Summer Academy to a group of seven fourteen- to sixteen-year-olds. It was a fascinating experience (and experiment) from several angles, especially given the mix of high intelligence and analytic skills with teenage sensibility. Although the reading of introductory, critical, and theoretical materials was radically abbreviated, we worked with the same concepts and contexts as I do in all my *Quixote* classes. I gave the students an extensive outline of topics, and they read a group of short stories, supplemented by other literary and critical selections in the first days, and three articles and Carroll B. Johnson's Don Quixote: *The Quest for Modern Fiction* as we read the novel. The most dedicated students saw the beauty and complexity of the novel, and they were able to present their ideas with eloquence, orally and in writing. Their critique was mature and often sophisticated. One student in particular—he was about to enter his sophomore year of high school—recalled every detail of the narrative, grasped the ironies and humor of the text, and synthesized the material with ease. Three of the young men were less interested in the novel than they were in living on a college campus, making new friends, and interacting with the college students who served as proctors. They had no trouble with the approach to *Don Quixote*, only with the time that the reading took from their social life, and they each made impressive contributions to the class. I was unable to reach everyone, but, according to the evaluations, the students had all loved being at Vanderbilt. Nonacademic distractions notwithstanding, I got them through *Don Quixote* without resorting to force. As a result, they are conversant with the novel and with concepts such as metafiction, intertextuality, the implied author, and deconstruction. And they rewarded me with an advanced course in teenage psychology.

Through the figure of Sansón Carrasco in part 2, Cervantes comments that ". . . es tan clara, que no hay cosa que dificultar en ella: los niños la manosean, los mozos la leen, los hombres la entienden y los viejos la celebran" '. . . [the book] is so clear that there is nothing in it to cause difficulty: children look at it, youths read it, men understand it, the old celebrate it' (57 [ch. 3]; 478 [trans.

Grossman]). He is conscious of the range of readers and of reader response. The novel reaches everyone, in different ways. I feel privileged to have the opportunity to teach—and to learn from—*Don Quixote* in a variety of settings and to be part of a four-hundred-plus-year process in which an exercise in anachronism seems forever mutable and forever fresh.

Advanced Placement: A Foundational Introduction to *Don Quixote*

James A. Parr

The College Board's Advanced Placement (AP) program offers a yearlong Hispanic literature and culture overview at the secondary level.[1] For 2012–13, the course included on its reading list, from *Don Quixote*, chapters 1–5 and 8–9 of part 1 and the final chapter of part 2. Also on the list from this period were four chapters of the anonymous *Lazarillo de Tormes* (1–3, 7) and the complete *Burlador de Sevilla*, featuring the original Don Juan Tenorio. Of the 17,919 students who took the exam in literature in May 2012, 33% (5,902) received scores of 4 or 5 (on a 5-point scale), which are widely accepted by colleges and universities for unit credit and sometimes for course credit. Of the test takers, 61% scored 3 or higher.

Many students who may become Spanish majors or minors in colleges and universities—some of whom will eventually become teachers or professors of Spanish—are introduced to *Don Quixote* in this foundational course. The course's importance is obvious. It has the potential to stimulate a lifelong interest in the text. It is a privilege and a great responsibility to be entrusted with such a course, and the teachers who participate in the AP program deserve our respect and admiration.

I write as a university professor who has taught the complete *Quixote* many times, lately to classes of about forty at the undergraduate level. In my department, this course is an elective, primarily for majors and minors. About 90% of my students are heritage speakers. We do a close reading of both parts, in ten weeks, which translates into a hundred pages per week, with everything in Spanish. My essay draws on my experience with this course, on my lengthy experience with the ETS segment of the operation, and on my experience with the College Board oversight committee.

A bit more time is available for *Don Quixote* since the September 2012 list revisions for the AP Hispanic literature and culture overview, yet time is still limited. It therefore might be a good strategy to begin talking about *Don Quixote* at the beginning of the course, pointing to it as special. I would definitely mention the survey of one hundred leading writers worldwide undertaken in 2002 by the Nobel Institute (http://thegreatestbooks.org/lists/28), to show that this old book continues to command respect today, not only in the Hispanic world but also universally. The poll gave the *Quixote* 50% more votes than any other title in world literature. Even the most blasé students should be impressed by this information. I would also point out that *Life* magazine included the publication of the *Quixote* on its list of the hundred most important achievements of the last thousand years, in all fields of human endeavor ("*Don Quixote de la Mancha*").

The text will be more meaningful to students if they can see that it deals with issues that are a part of their experience in the here and now. For instance, Don Quixote is very much seduced by the technology of his day, books, which were still cutting-edge though more than a hundred years had passed since the invention of the printing press (change was much slower then). Students may realize that their texting, tweeting, social media, and video games are not unlike what what Don Quixote does with books: an obsession with a medium that allows one to escape into an alternative world.

It should be made clear to students that Don Quixote is irrational only when the topic that occupies him is knight-errantry or chivalry in the broad sense. On most matters, he is quite sensible. In chapters of part 2 that the students will not read, Don Diego de Miranda and his son consider him a *cuerdo-loco* ("sane madman"). This dichotomy and a parallel binomial for Sancho (*simple-agudo* or *tontilisto* ["sharp simpleton"]) bring to mind any number of others that can help students appreciate the thematic structuring of the text. An obvious dichotomy is *pasado-presente* ("past-present"). Don Quixote's primary quest in part 1 is to revive a golden age that unfortunately never existed: it is a myth that has taken shape in his mind based on his reading. Thanks to José Antonio Maravall, a Spanish historian, we know that there was a coterie at court at the time that counseled the king to model the present and future of Spain on the past by attempting to recapture the glory days, the golden age, of Ferdinand and Isabella (*Utopía*). By showing the repeated failures of Quixote's attempts to superimpose a romanticized vision of the past on a recalcitrant present, the text suggests that a sociopolitical agenda advocating a return to past glory is a chimera.

The principal themes of part 1 are love, literature, and chivalry, but an important thematic dichotomy that brings together two of them is *armas y letras* ("arms and letters"). An ideal of the Renaissance was to combine both in one's life and person. Cervantes himself followed this model, by being a soldier and a writer, although not simultaneously, in the way that Garcilaso de la Vega or the Inca Garcilaso was able to do. The attempt of Don Quixote to combine arms and letters is a parody, since he inverts the usual order of his time, that followed by Cervantes, Lope de Vega, and Calderón de la Barca, all of whom practiced arms in their youth, then devoted themselves to letters. Alonso Quijano, well past middle age, first devotes himself to letters (passively, since he does not write); then, inspired by his reading, he takes up arms.

One antithesis that relates especially to the passages the students will read for AP is *historia y poesía* ("history vs. fiction, reality vs. fantasy"). Quijano reads fiction as though it were history, taking whatever he finds in print to be factual. Unable to distinguish between the two, he is the type of reader referred to in Cervantes's day as a *lector vulgar* ("common reader"), as opposed to a *lector discreto* ("an alert, perceptive, discerning reader"). Cervantes calls attention to Quijano's misguided manner of reading, offering him as an antimodel to the type of reader Cervantes hopes to form from among those who spend time with his book. This is an important role that Don Quixote plays, for it serves to align the author with a poetics that goes back to the Roman writer Horace and also with an expectation of the Counter-Reformation—which was in full flower at the time—that literature should play a dual function in society, offering pleasure and amusement while at the same time imparting a useful lesson. The norm was expressed in that day as *deleitar aprovechando*, which also happens to be the title of a work by Tirso de Molina, the author of *El burlador de Sevilla*. Horace's pragmatic and aesthetic *utile et dulce* was transformed by the Counter-Reformation into a moral imperative.

Strategies that have helped students succeed in my classes are keeping a list of the characters, with some identifying notes; keeping a list of the narrators and pseudo-authors; relating episodes and dialogues to the themes of love, literature, and chivalry, aware that sometimes more than one theme may be pertinent; being alert to thematic tensions (e.g., past vs. present, fantasy vs. reality); focusing on the actions of Don Quixote and whether these correspond to his view of himself, to how other characters see him, and to how he is presented by the narrators, noting especially the antithetical perspectives of the first and second pseudo-authors; finding aspects or devices that draw in readers or distance them; and deciding whether a given narrator is trustworthy or whether his authority is undermined.

As other essays in this volume point out, titles of works often tell us a great deal, and the 1605 title of *Don Quixote* is a good beginning to describe and explain Cervantine irony to students. Then the prologue should arouse curiosity in students and prepare them for the text proper. Given the limited time, I would suggest an unwavering focus throughout on Cervantes's irony, since an awareness of ironic distancing in literature makes students more competent consumers of fiction and other simulacra of reality. But the precise opposite of distancing is also important: attraction, involvement in the text. The dynamic relation in this additional dichotomy is crucial for appreciating Cervantes's skill as a writer.

The ironic treatment of the character, made explicit in the title and further developed in the prologue and the festive verses immediately preceding chapter 1, continues in the cavalier treatment accorded the story by the narrator of chapters 1–8: he does not know the name of the main character or even where he lives, but that is of no consequence, the narrator tells us, provided that all the facts given are true! In chapters 1–5 and 8–9 we meet the principal players involved in the telling and transmission of the story: a first author; a transitional editorial voice that intervenes at the end of chapter 8; a *segundo autor* ("second author") in chapter 9; then a Morisco translator contracted to render the continuation found in Toledo, a text in Arabic characters, into Spanish orthography; and finally the third and last pseudo-author, a historian named Cide Hamete Benengeli, an unbelievable construct to whom is attributed everything between the concluding segment of chapter 9 and the end of part 2, chapter 74.

We also meet several of the main characters of the mimetic plot in these early chapters: Don Quixote; Sancho, his squire (miscast, like his master); the village priest and barber, who discuss fictional characters as though they were real;

Don Quixote's housekeeper and niece; and Dulcinea, who never appears but is very much a presence nonetheless.

The beginning can profitably be contrasted with the *Lazarillo*. Rather than a life recounted from birth in the first person, in *Don Quixote* we have only a slice of life toward its end. That the text is narrated in the third person marks Cervantes's rejection of the picaresque narrative model, with the limitations inherent in pseudo-autobiography, in favor of a greater freedom—freedom to demonstrate his narrative skill and introduce a number of voices and levels, which may intrude on or undermine one another. Although the *Quixote* thus contests the picaresque, it does appropriate one important device from the *Lazarillo*: the older and wiser guide (think of Lazarillo's first master) for an innocent or naive companion.

The main character is neither a hero nor an antihero but something in between, best described as a mock hero. Programmed by his reading, he is in constant need of literary precedents on which to model his actions. His description of his initial foray, imitating the florid rhetoric of the books of chivalry, is undermined by the markedly prosaic summation of the narrator ("y era la verdad que por él caminaba" 'and in fact that's what he was doing,' then by the description of his discourse as "disparates" 'nonsense' and by the further comment that the sun was so hot that it would have melted his brains, "si algunos tuviera" 'if he had any' (25). The following episode at the inn plunges us fully into the degraded world typical of satire, a world not unlike that of the picaresque and having affinities also with that of the *Burlador de Sevilla*, despite the higher social class of many of those characters. The mock ceremony by which Don Quixote is knighted accords perfectly with the humorous tone, and it means that he is not truly a knight and now can never be, as Martín de Riquer points out (87–88). The violence Don Quixote does to the unsuspecting muledriver reminds us of his choleric nature. The next adventure, with Andrés and Juan Haldudo, shows that good intentions are not sufficient, for it leads to the lad's being whipped by his master. Andrés will reappear later and ask Don Quixote never again to meddle in his affairs.

Chapter 8 gives us the memorable windmill episode, the most iconic adventure of the entire book. Don Quixote needs an antagonist of great size and strength to prove his mettle. It is mentioned in chapter 1 that his imagination is well populated by giants, both good and bad, so this episode should not come as a surprise. It is important to note the unexpected change of narrative voice in the final paragraph of chapter 8 and the announcement by it that there will be a continuation by a second author.[2] This transition between chapters 8 and 9 provides an excellent lesson in distance and involvement: readers are distanced when attention is called to the devices of storytelling but simultaneously drawn in, curious to see what happens next.

In chapter 9, the second author begins by recounting his lucky find in Toledo, but he quickly disqualifies himself as a guide or editor for the rest of the story, because, much like Quijano, he is an undiscriminating reader, accepting everything with equal pleasure, and an obtuse reader, unaware of the irony of the first author's depiction of Don Quixote, having indeed formed an image of Don Quixote that is diametrically opposed to irony. The second author is, moreover, ethnically biased, stating that all Moors are liars. As if that were not enough to disqualify him from being taken seriously, he proceeds to tell of shepherdesses of days gone by who often went to their graves as virginal as the mothers who gave them birth! Some have identified the second author as Cervantes, which is absurd, given the obvious differences between him and this caricature of a reader. Since Cervantes does supply all the voices of the text, he is all of them but none of them in particular. The several intermediaries he inserts between himself and the represented action provide a buffer, an ironic and aesthetic distance, from everyone and everything we find in the world of his creation. His distancing of himself is a model for reader response, while his depiction of two overly involved readers, Don Quixote on the level of the represented action (showing) and the second author on the level of the narration (telling), offers models for the discreet reader to avoid.

The test that will tell whether students have internalized the concept of aesthetic distance comes in part 2, chapter 74. If they focus on the hastily contrived pathos of the deathbed scene, they are overly involved with the character and have failed to acquire the ironic distance that sets the discreet reader apart. If they appreciate the several ironies of this chapter—the misrepresentation by the narrator and Don Quixote of Don Quixote's peaceable nature; the ill-considered codicil of the will, in that it will make unlikely any marriage for his niece; the merrymaking by the mourners; the narrator's "dio su espíritu, quiero decir que se murió" '[he] gave up the ghost' followed immediately by the deflationary 'what I mean is, he died' (915)—they will receive an A for the course. If they can then decipher the suggestion of a curtain call by all the narrative voices that appeared in chapters 1–9, they will almost certainly get a 5 on the AP exam.[3]

Student response to chapter 74 will need to be guided. Their first instinct will be toward involvement, to share in the grief depicted there—as I did myself the first time I read it—but if they are shown the several ironies surrounding that scene, they will come to realize that they are being manipulated by a master puppeteer of characters, narrators, and readers.[4] I would propose to the students that the real hero of the work is Cervantes, not Don Quixote, and that it is no small achievement for an author to keep readers interested in such a character for almost a thousand pages. Careful reading of the chapters discussed here will reveal that there is an ongoing dynamic relation established in the text between distancing and involving readers. If the distancing is too great, readers may lose interest. They must be kept engaged—through humor, intriguing dialogue, unusual episodes and characters, supplementary stories and anecdotes—while at the same time reminded periodically not to become too involved.

I would relate the *Quixote* to other texts on the AP reading list, especially the *Lazarillo* and the *Burlador*, in terms of the degraded reality that typifies all three. The *Quixote* should also be contrasted with the picaresque, as a kind of countergenre to both the *Lazarillo* and the *Guzmán de Alfarache* (pts. 1 and 2). A great success at the end of the sixteenth century, the *Guzmán* loomed large on Cervantes's aesthetic horizon, although Cervantes never mentions it. The *Quixote* provides his response. In the main plot of *Don Quixote* I would concentrate on the process of characterization more than on the character. How do the narrators present Don Quixote? How does he view himself, and does that view coincide with his actions? How do other characters see him? And if there is a focus on irony and the markers that encourage the creation of aesthetic distance between text and reader, students should become more perceptive readers, and a more perceptive reader — one who will not be seduced by high-sounding rhetoric or contrived pathos — will be a more engaged and discerning person.

NOTES

The text of *Don Quixote* used in this essay is the one edited by Fajardo and Parr. All the translations are mine.

[1] The College Board contracts with a specialized agency, Educational Testing Service (ETS), for test development, administration, and scoring. Since ETS plays such a conspicuous role, on the front lines of the enterprise, many academics at all levels see it as the prime mover — erroneously.

[2] For more on telling and transmission, narrative voices, point of view, characterization, and genre, see my Don Quixote: *A Touchstone*. I revisit some of these basics from postmodern perspectives in *Don Quixote, Don Juan*.

[3] On irony in this final chapter, see Chambers; on irony in general, Muecke. On distancing, see El Saffar, *Distance*.

[4] After unprecedented deferral, the assignment of a definitive name to the main character in part 2, chapter 74 — Alonso Quijano — is doubtless in response to the name Martín Quijada, given him by the interloper Avellaneda in his spurious 1614 part 2. In this and in other interesting ways, Cervantes reclaims his intellectual property.

Don Quixote as a Great Book

Christian Michener

The pleasure that *Don Quixote* has offered to readers over the centuries and the critical attention it has received signal its value as great, but what of its status as a great book, that controversial designation by which a text is singled out as a repository of ideas and inspiration that helps define the human experience? *Don Quixote* often appears on the syllabi of great-books programs, both those that are independent majors and those, like the program in which I teach, that are part of a general education curriculum. Critical theory has long challenged the naive or even insidious nature of the humanistic confidence that first inspired the list of great books, but literary theory simultaneously reveals that the meaning of a text depends on the direction from which we approach it. A great-books model, when coupled in particular with its shared-inquiry method of instruction, provides one such direction from which to consider this complex novel, and through such a model offers readers a rare opportunity to laugh with a classic text even as it raises profound questions about perception, identity, imagination, and even interpretation itself.

In studying *Don Quixote* as a great book, which is usually taught within a two-to-three-week period of a semester alongside other great books, instructors would be wise to begin by acknowledging that time does not allow a class to cover the historical allusions, literary history, or theological controversies that the book invites one to consider. Great-books programs guided by the method of shared inquiry often do not establish historical or cultural contexts for their books, though I spend some time on topics such as the Spanish Inquisition and the history of Muslims in Spain prior to the seventeenth century. I also give a brief presentation on the genre of the novel, but otherwise I rely on the honesty of declaring the limits of our shared-inquiry approach so that we can spend our time reaping its rewards. In this pedagogical approach, students share with the instructor the responsibility of interpretation through classroom dialogue and debate, and together they inquire about the meaning and meanings of the texts they consider, relying on their interpretive abilities and the text itself rather than outside sources or experts.

Even with limited background material or with no background at all, one can almost never read all of *Don Quixote* in a great-books classroom. I have seen courses that take on only part 1, but for me this compromises too much of what I consider the innovative form of the novel, not to mention the dramatic end to the narrative. My own compromise is to read both volumes but to provide summaries of the interpolated stories and of some of the longer episodes (such as the stay at the duke's palace in part 2). In this way my students stay with Don Quixote during his physical journey, but they don't stay with Cervantes during his entire literary one.

Another significant decision to be made in including *Don Quixote* in the great-books classroom is which translation to use, a question that is raised in similar methods of studying the book, such as comparative or world literature courses. Instructors in the great-books classroom, many of whom will not be specialists, might simply decide which text to use based on which translation most appeals to them or most readily raises the questions they hope to pursue. Although I have only a rudimentary familiarity with Spanish, I let students know that we are missing much of the wit and complexity of the novel by not reading it in the original, and I choose a few brief phrases or scenes to reveal what effect different translations could have on our discussions. What kind of reader, for example, are we considered to be in the author's prologue: the "idling reader" of Samuel Putnam (Cervantes, *Don Quixote* [trans. Putnam] 11), Burton Raffel's "leisurely reader" (*Don Quijote* [trans. Raffel] 7), or an "idle reader," as Edith Grossman and Tom Lathrop each translate it (*Don Quixote* [trans. Grossman] 3; [trans. Lathrop] 3)? In a book in which the relationship of reading to reality is central to the narrative, even so small a decision as these two words has interpretive implications. Or consider the name that Don Quixote adopts during his quest. Do you prefer Raffel's intentionally prosaic but pitiful "Knight of the Sad Face" (108) or Putnam's romantically elegiac "Knight of the Mournful Countenance" (143)? Grossman chooses to call Don Quixote the "Knight of the Sorrowful Face" (139) while Lathrop provides perhaps the most idiosyncratic label, "The Woebegone Knight" (133). Each of these terms comes with its own connotations and implications, especially since Don Quixote believes that this title comes from the author of the very story in which he now presides.

Practical pedagogical questions also affect the choice of translation. Cost is of course a concern for the attentive instructor, but so is what ancillary material is available in each edition. Pure great-books programs that rely exclusively on the primary texts do not ask students to consult secondary sources, and neither does the course I have taught that has included *Don Quixote*, but curious students (and instructors like this one!) can find engaging essays provided with some editions, and their proximity encourages students to explore aspects of the novel that class discussion or assignments do not raise. I have used the Norton Critical Edition not because I consider Raffel's translation superior but because its included critical materials have allowed me to refer to appreciations of the book (to convince reluctant student-critics of the import of this odd text); examples of pure "romance" (to explain what Cervantes is emerging from and reacting against); bits of the "False Quixote" (to explain the history of the book's production); and Borges's short story of Pierre Menard (to reveal the extent of the influence of this book, plus for the pure fun of reading it). Such secondary texts are not necessary or even desired for the shared-inquiry classroom, but they can be helpful, and students on occasion find their own curiosity satisfied by what they discover there.

Whichever translation or selections the great-books teacher uses, the primary concern of the classroom is the students' inquiry into the significance of what they read. Unlike a more traditional classroom, in which the answers to interpretive questions derive in great part from the expertise of the instructor and professional critics, the source of the answers in a shared-inquiry setting is also (in theory, exclusively) the source of the questions: *Don Quixote* itself. Through shared inquiry, students are asked to develop their own questions and interpretations of what they read; in class, those readings are tested and challenged through discussion and debate, then defended or adapted as the conversation demands and the textual evidence requires. The competent shared-inquiry instructor must be willing to let the students choose which direction the conversation goes and which themes or episodes the students wish to emphasize; he or she must even let imprecise or dubious interpretations linger to see if the class can, through shared purpose, provide more legitimate and defensible readings.

The instructor, of course, cannot allow indefensible readings to proceed, but it is through appeals to the text, not to an explicit background of expertise or authority, that the instructor must correct the students—or, more accurately, must lead the students through question and quotations to discover their own misapprehensions. The competent instructor also will come equipped with numerous tactics for initiating the discussion that raises and addresses the questions to consider. A student or students may be assigned to initiate or lead discussion on a given day; the teacher may assign a reflection question to which students write a response at the beginning of class; each student may come with his or her own question on each day; or students might assemble in small groups, generate a group question, then hand that question off to another group for discussion, before the entire class reassembles. However such inquiry proceeds, it relies on a three-dimensional or non-Euclidean version of the rhetorical triangle, a kind of geodesic sphere of interpretation, where students, instructor, and text all serve as mutually supportive—and supported—foundation points of interpretation.

One practice I follow that violates this pure shared-inquiry approach is to distribute a reading guide to *Don Quixote* that combines a score of general interpretive questions with summaries of those passages we are skipping interspersed with more focused reading questions. I tell my students that they do not have to use this guide and offer it to them to use as they see fit. These questions also serve the role of teaching the students how to inquire, so that they can use them as models for their own textual considerations. Some questions help keep students focused on simple reading events (i.e., questions of plot), but others ask interpretive questions about the nature of perception, the attitudes of characters toward the knight, the relationship between Sancho and Don Quixote, or the concept of textual self-reference that we often confront in the narrative. Most of the students appreciate the questions as a way to see the kinds of inquiry they might themselves engage in, especially since most are not literature majors, but they are also savvy and proud enough to develop questions of their own as the reading continues.

In the great-books approach, which conducts itself through a seminar of shared inquiry, one cannot guarantee that any particular questions or topics will arise, even when using guided reading questions. There is no teleology of teaching in shared inquiry, which is both unnerving and invigorating. But pure great-books programs exclusively using primary texts are rare, and classroom context often shapes the conversation. Some programs employ the great-books approach but constrain it within a historical framework, so that Cervantes would be read with other works produced between the sixteenth and eighteenth centuries. Many humanities courses, though not great books courses *per se*, move chronologically through traditionally defined historical moments; there are several historically arranged textbooks available on the market, and *Don Quixote* is an excellent primary source of study in the baroque section of such a course, in which the complex but unified structure of Cervantes's novel is offered as a formal parallel to sculptural or musical compositions by Bernini or Bach.

Another kind of approach, and the one I have used most successfully, has been to design the course thematically or topically. In our program, in which we often use the term *foundational texts* along with *great books*, *Don Quixote* has been taught in a course on arts and literature that combines the study of literature, painting, and music and that, at present, is designed around the themes of art of the sacred, of ourselves, and of itself (i.e., self-referential or nonreferential art). We have read *Don Quixote* in the second unit, an "art of the self," as a novelistic depiction of a person creating his own identity, although it serves as a frequent topic in our last unit on self-referential works and could just as readily be studied there.

Obviously such an approach affects the kind of inquiry in which the class engages, but students are always curious enough, and the novel capacious enough, to allow many an intellectual digression, a practice Don Quixote himself could hardly fault. To the frequently cited dilemma of illusion versus reality in the novel, for example, we explore how one might integrate the concept of "imagination" in that debate since our course is in part about aesthetic production—and then we often, because of other texts we have read (such as *Paradise Lost* and the poetry of Wallace Stevens), consider the further relationship between imagination and religious faith, and by this route eventually find ourselves right back in la Mancha. Or we address questions about identity and agency: what does the depiction of Don Quixote's self-invented quest say about the ability of human beings to "define themselves"? What role do will and desire play in our understanding or production of who we are? How much is Don Quixote a hero, how much a fool? As the novel proceeds, and as students grapple with their uncertain and sometimes cantankerous relationship with the knight, we also consider the book's critiques of medievalism (in the way knight-errantry and its absolutes are mocked) but also modernity (in how Quixote's self-centeredness can lead one into error or absurdity), and find our way eventually into discussions of objective truth and relativism.

Such questions, of course, are not easy to uncover, especially considering the foreign nature of Cervantes's novel to many of our students. Most undergraduates probably have never used the word *quixotic* and do not understand the phrase "tilting at windmills," and many find our knight, at least at the outset, ridiculous. Inevitably the key moment early on when we are told that Don Quixote's brain suffers because he has read too much raises questions of whether he is "insane" and provides another significant opportunity for comparing translations. In all likelihood, most students will also be staggered by the sheer size of the book. Despite this challenge (not much different, after all, from *The Iliad* or *Middlemarch*), I try to get my students to see that their reading of Cervantes is itself a quixotic endeavor in today's world of texting and the Internet. The classroom thus develops two parallel adventures: that of the knight as he sallies forth on his missions, and that of the reader as he or she works in concert with the shared-inquiry classroom to experience and understand the trials of the knight and his worthy squire. In fact, one assignment I have used in the course is to have the students tell the story of their own reading (one that often moves from incredulity to sympathy).

Thankfully Cervantes makes it quite rewarding to the reader to rise to the challenge of these adventures. The work is singular in many great-books programs because rarely are they extensive enough to include Aristophanes or a Shakespeare comedy, and until Jane Austen there are few tempting choices of narrative beyond epic poetry. With his attention to the many cultures of seventeenth-century Spain, Cervantes thus gives us a break from Enlightenment philosophy or Renaissance drama: no brooding Danes here, no Greek gods to memorize, none of John Locke's dry tabula rasa. Instead we get ribaldry and lunacy, violence and confusion and slapstick and romance, the bright sun of Spain, peasants and pigs, cottage cheese on a hero's head. You mean we actually get to laugh at a great book? You mean the road to wisdom might include a stop at one of those inns?

Of course, it's not all just fun and games. Sansón Carrasco eventually unhorses our hero, and students must in the end receive a grade. As most of the consideration of *Don Quixote* in the shared-inquiry classroom is conducted through discussion, a student's oral contributions during class are a graded part of the course I teach. In the past I have also asked for a medium-length paper (five to seven pages) on the book, but I have since left that strategy behind as it encourages too many closed readings, such as the frequent theme of the changing identities of Sancho and Don Quixote. Instead, I now include all the works in the class in an ongoing series of meditations (modeled on the essays of Montaigne) in which students are asked to synthesize how several works explore shared questions or concerns. As befits a great-books course, students are required to rely only on the primary materials we have used, including *Don Quixote* itself.

Don Quixote thus works well as a great book in a classroom of shared inquiry, while it also admittedly provides great challenges. While the scholar in me worries about how much is lost, I remind myself of a situation that literature teachers such as myself often forget: if we want our students to continue to read, and read Cervantes in particular, they will have to do so on their own, without the guidance of a teacher or scholar or classroom. At some point Cervantes must stand on his own before the reader who picks his text off the library shelf (or, we might add, whoever downloads those texts). I am also consoled by the experience from several years of teaching the text by those students, very few of whom are literature or language majors, who count the reading of *Don Quixote* as one of their most memorable educational experiences.

Don Quixote in the Balance: Early Modern Studies and the Undergraduate Curriculum

Sidney Donnell

The study of early modern literature at the undergraduate level has become increasingly tenuous since the publication of *Approaches to Teaching Cervantes'* Don Quixote in 1984 (Bjornson). The curricular configurations in which we teach works like the *Quixote* have changed, and many professors and programs are adapting with difficulty. Politically, the culture wars of the late twentieth century in the United States produced a multicultural curriculum that decentered (but did not totally dislodge) the Western canon from the undergraduate curriculum. This shift resulted in the subtraction of some classic literary works and the addition of others. Today, the North American academy is experiencing a new period of compromise. Professionally minded students are turning away from certain aspects of the liberal arts. They are interested in learning about multiculturalism but only in terms of the here and now, and this limitation produces a kind of historical anemia. In this context, how does a seventeenth-century masterpiece like *Don Quixote* fare? For college instructors of Spanish, the question is further complicated by the fact that enrollment in Spanish programs has steadily risen for decades (the rise outpacing some institutions' ability to staff courses adequately) while enrollment has gradually dropped in medieval and early modern studies (the drop allowing some college administrators now to look at these subjects as unnecessary expenditures). This essay explores steps that instructors might take to make *Don Quixote* and similar texts more pertinent for the undergraduate curriculum.

In today's educational environment, the merits of a course dedicated to Cervantes are not immediately evident to students or teachers. At best, undergraduates have little notion about what to expect when they register for such a course; at worst, they feel that studying the past is a waste of time. The successful inclusion of early modern studies in the curriculum therefore requires faculty members to employ proactive administrative and pedagogical strategies. I consider the perceptions of almost three dozen faculty members about the status of Cervantes's novel in their colleges and universities in North America and draw on Janet Swaffar and Katherine Arens's multiple literacies approach to teaching a second language in order to frame the inclusion of early modern studies in the undergraduate curriculum. I maintain that, by making the *Quixote* relevant to today's students and by promoting it to them in ways that will resonate with their interests in foreign language competencies and literacies, we can create new and exciting learning opportunities. We also can build history into the curriculum and emphasize critical thinking, particularly around issues that stimulate students to develop the four language skills or modalities: reading, writing, listening, speaking.

Is Don Quixote *Hanging by a Thread?*

To gain a clear understanding of curricular dynamics and decision making about early modern studies in a variety of institutional contexts, I used what can be described loosely as an ethnographic approach.[1] I e-mailed professors at various kinds of institutions, from private colleges to public universities, from Research I institutions to teaching colleges. I asked them how the *Quixote* fits (or does not fit) into their undergraduate curriculum. I conducted follow-up interviews with eleven of the respondents, either in person or by telephone.[2] Unsurprisingly, the responses reflected the diversity of people queried as well as the particularities of their institutions and curricula.[3] Yet I learned that, across the board, courses in which the *Quixote* serves as a stand-alone topic tend not to attract students and that many institutional forces, coming after the culture wars of the late twentieth century, contribute to the subject's marginalization. Among the universities and colleges represented in my analysis, nine offer a *Quixote* seminar every year or every other year; seventeen offer a *Quixote* seminar with some regularity, usually as an elective that fulfills a distribution requirement counting toward a BA program; and eight never offer Cervantes's novel as the subject of a seminar or recently discontinued it as a course topic.

Much can be learned by taking a closer look at the schools that most frequently offer the course. Four that give a terminal MA or MEd in Spanish require familiarity with Cervantes. These programs allow advanced undergraduates to enroll, and their constituency is MA-driven. In two other schools, the *Quixote* is a requirement for a major in Spanish. Antonomasia, a professor of Spanish at Metonymy City College, confesses, "The only way to get a full class for [the *Quixote*] now is to offer it as the senior capstone seminar." Only three institutions in my study require students to take the *Quixote* as a stand-alone subject in order to graduate with a BA in Spanish, but these programs face internal resistance. According to Marcela at Pastoral State University, "it has been a point of contention whether to continue offering [*Don Quixote*] as a requirement in Spanish. Newer faculty members tend to think it shouldn't be offered; that's the trend."

The challenges instructors face in teaching the *Quixote* in the classroom go beyond programmatic concerns. One professor's students refused to read the *Quixote* in a semester-long senior capstone seminar dedicated to Cervantes's novel in its entirety. Another professor had to drum up interest in the course through a self-made marketing campaign. One department is so small that advanced classes in Spanish (including the *Quixote* course) are cross-listed and taught in both English and Spanish. Two faculty members told me that their undergraduate seminars on the *Quixote* are almost always overenrolled because they teach at public universities whose departments serve a large population of heritage speakers of Spanish. These examples confirm that instructors of the *Quixote* are working in demanding, varied, and sometimes unreceptive environments.

Programming Don Quixote: *All or Nothing?*

Decisions to include or exclude a stand-alone seminar on the *Quixote* pivot around the nature and scope of multiculturalism in a department's curriculum, I found. The stories of two professors of Spanish are instructive. Both teach at liberal arts colleges with a population of 2,000–2,500 students. (The size of the institution matters: the smaller the program, the less room for error there is when curricular revisions are made.)

Dorotea, a professor of Spanish at Saint Yelmo College, describes a program that purposefully sacrificed the *Quixote* twenty years ago, at a time during the canon wars when some second-language acquisition programs forfeited literary studies to other departments:

> Until the end of the 1980s, *Don Quixote de la Mancha* was specifically named as a course in the college curriculum. At that time a Latin Americanist and a professor of Latino studies demanded its elimination, basing their argument on the injustice of requiring all majors and minors to take a course on the *Quixote* and not, for example, on *One Hundred Years of Solitude*.

The argument that the *Quixote* has no more or less intrinsic literary value than its contemporaries or non-European counterparts is effective in getting a department to eliminate the novel as a requirement. Moreover, privileging a specific subject (e.g., early modern Peninsular studies) over a general subject (e.g., contemporary Latin American studies) involves a significant expenditure in human capital. A required seminar on the *Quixote* takes away faculty members and students from other important areas of study, some of which may be more appealing to North American undergraduates. Saint Yelmo participated actively in the canon wars, and its faculty members, instead of making the *Quixote* an elective that might not draw students, chose to cut it from the Spanish-language curriculum.

That eliminating a required course on the *Quixote* may be justified does not mean, of course, that the novel should not be taught at all. In this case, circumstances necessitated a major shift in how to teach it, and Dorotea worked with her colleagues to come up with the best ways to put it into the new curriculum. Unfortunately she received little support. On her own, Dorotea now teaches courses that include chapters from the novel as well as other literary texts from the medieval and early modern periods. But her courses hardly guarantee that the *Quixote* will be part of the curriculum at Saint Yelmo College.

Cardenio's story shows what can happen when well-intended curricular change meets with the realities of new student enrollment trends—in particular, the harm of changing a *Quixote* seminar from a requirement to an elective without attempting to resituate it in an innovative way in the curriculum. When Cardenio joined the faculty at Sierra Morena College in the mid-1990s, the Spanish Department had already started to abandon its combined literature and culture major and was about to debut two tracks so that students would have the option to specialize in either Hispanic civilization or Hispanic literature. This change had negative consequences for literature. For example, the number of matriculations in *Don Quixote* plummeted from twenty-two students [in the last year before the program was divided into two tracks] to six [in the first year of the two-track system]. Then there were three [students enrolled in the second year]. [In the third year] we canceled the course for lack of enrollment.

When given a choice of two tracks, students circumnavigated the curriculum that required the *Quixote* course and other literature courses to graduate. Cardenio reports, "Students picked the program that relied almost exclusively on introductory-level courses using journalistic and historical registers [of language]." In the end, Sierra Morena suspended the two-track system because it forfeited literature as a legitimate subject of study, and the college reinstated the *Quixote* as a requirement for all majors in Spanish. This reversal shows that a more canonical approach can sometimes prevail if pedagogical experimentation fails to meet its stated goals, but such curricular politics is a poor way to ensure the *Quixote*'s inclusion.

These two stories suggest that we need a fresh approach, one that acknowledges the new terrain of higher education and takes advantage of new pedagogies. The path I offer is labor-intensive because it requires listening to students to discover why (and there are good reasons) they don't care about *Don Quixote* in its traditional canonical setting.

Reinventing the Language Curriculum for Today's Undergraduates

Two of the greatest obstacles to the inclusion of medieval and early modern studies in new undergraduate curricula are lack of administrative support and the prevalent ideology of presentism among students. "Among early casualties of budget cuts," write Swaffar and Arens, "are often studies of premodern literatures and cultures, since students are less familiar with the materials and hence less likely to choose such courses as an elective" (178). Presentism is also common among faculty members and administrators: many are quick to assign blame to colleagues whose courses have low enrollment, and they wish to reorient the undergraduate experience away from the liberal arts and toward more narrowly vocational programs. It is true that early modern texts create challenges to teaching and learning that professors and students of more recent texts are less likely to face. When the *Quixote* or a comparable work is taught in the original Spanish, the linguistic, historical, and cultural barriers to second-language acquisition increase. So how should professors of early modern literatures contend with presentism?

Success in teaching early modern texts to advanced students of Spanish may rest, paradoxically, on the introduction of the interdisciplinary courses (principally taught in English) that have replaced more canonical approaches to teaching literature in the undergraduate curriculum. Before the mid-1980s, world literature courses were based largely on anthologies of European classics and were ubiquitous in liberal arts programs; they still exist but are usually elective rather than required. In today's multicultural curriculum, Cervantes's two-part novel is widely regarded as a text that speaks to a large and varied body of adult learners, and it lends itself well for use in interdisciplinary courses at all levels. More than half my informants indicate that all or a selection of the *Quixote* is offered in English through a variety of departments (English, comparative literature, literature in translation) and programs (first-year seminars, honors college senior seminars, and team-taught curricula). In many cases, these courses are used to fulfill a general education requirement, even though the nature of the requirement has changed from an emphasis on European classics to an emphasis on multiculturalism and critical thinking. Two professors of early modern literature paired up with colleagues in political science or history to teach a dynamic cultural studies seminar for juniors and seniors. When assignments in courses such as these are comparative, they combat presentism by encouraging students to discover, explore, and evaluate their preconceived notions about the past.

A similar approach is possible in courses that concentrate on second-language acquisition. One useful strategy is to emphasize the relevance of the *Quixote* to the language-learning curriculum. As Swaffar and Arens emphasize, it is important to place literature "alongside other complex genre formalizations of a culture . . . to form part of a language-learning curriculum" (148). The emphasis on genres in a second-language acquisition program requires a particular set of learning levels and outcomes. For example, a professor of early modern studies who is assigned a course on the novel could teach the *Quixote* as well as shorter selections from modern prose works in order to compare language, cultures, and historical periods. Courses in a vibrant multiple literacies curriculum would emphasize other points of comparison (art and visuality, speech and orality, electronic media and interactivity). My syllabus compares selections from modern genres with Cervantes's way of telling a tale. Its focus beyond the canonical helps students understand Cervantes's craft in the context of cultural production today (e.g., such adaptations of the *Quixote* as feature-length films, animated cartoons, short stories by Borges). When students find themselves liking the *Quixote*, they begin to interrogate their bias against the past.

An enormous advantage to a curriculum that focuses on discourse genres as acts of communication is the establishment of tasks for teaching cultural studies through literature. At the intermediate level, less stylized forms of poetry and advertising may be introduced to second-language learners because "both address the reader directly, who is often a specific person or interest group targeted by the message." In contrast, "longer prose forms, including nonfiction and instructional matter, introduce a narrative point of view, which readers interrogate to uncover. [A] poem or ad will signal its difference more overtly" (Swaffar and Arens 168). In a program of study consisting of a graduated sequence of learning objectives, then, an advanced course on the novel (e.g., centering around the *Quixote*) could replace the conventional survey of Peninsular Spanish literature and serve as a gateway to more challenging courses, such as a senior seminar on drama. Why teach the novel and then drama? According to Swaffar and Arens,

> [d]rama appears . . . last . . . because it is often a more consciously elite genre, lacking the additional descriptions and explanatory aids often associated with nonelite forms. Learners must be taught to read between the lines of a dialogue on the basis of what they know about time, place, staging conventions, and presumed audience for a piece. . . .   (170)

The novel and drama have dialogue in common, but, according to a pedagogical model that treats genres as acts of communication, reading drama usually requires a higher degree of cultural literacy in undergraduates.

Another strategy is to stress proficiency in the four language skills or modalities. Second-language educators often overlook reading skills in the so-called upper-division curriculum on the assumption that undergraduates have already developed sophisticated reading strategies by the time they have registered for a course required of majors. Because texts from the early modern period present special challenges (variations in usage, spelling, and grammatical structures; obsolete vocabulary; rural idiomatic expressions foreign to today's urban and suburban majority), their use in making students more proficient readers becomes apparent.[4] In my undergraduate seminar, I deemphasize formal essay-writing skills (which are the heart of much of my institution's core curriculum and BA program in Spanish) in order to approach the *Quixote* as a reading-intensive course. I think of reading in broad terms, introducing adult learners to media beyond the printed page. Teachers may choose from a large body of *Quixote*-inspired resources (film, music, illustrations) to meet a wide variety of pedagogical goals, including the development of reading as a listening skill. Many of my students use audio books to hear the *Quixote* read, an experience in keeping with the oral traditions that Cervantes deploys throughout his text.[5]

Active recruitment and advising are an important part of curricular revision. It is useful to describe innovation in the classroom, but that information needs to be integrated into the advertising for a course. As a narratological exercise in reading for the uses of dialogue, changes in narrative voice, shifts in diegesis, and so on, I ask students to adapt scenes of the *Quixote* to a computerized storyboard or comic book format. Then the director of our Language Resource Center promotes the course by posting several examples of student work on this exercise for students, parents, faculty members, and administrators. Such promotion builds a reputation for the course, and students will enroll out of interest, not because they need to fulfill a requirement. Some colleagues may consider advertisement unseemly, but the elitism and literary prestige of old mean little in an empty classroom.

New approaches to the second-language curriculum are as important as new approaches to the subjects. Spanish departments are unfortunately sometimes slower than other language programs to consider curricular reform. The increase over the past few decades in the number of undergraduates taking Spanish-language courses has allowed many Spanish departments to insulate themselves from having to implement change in their BA programs. According to Malcolm Alan Compitello, "[i]t would be easier for the head of a large department with a widely cast mission to accept the curricular and intellectual status quo" (32). Nonetheless, English departments, which are generally much larger than Spanish programs, have been relatively quicker to embrace change — introducing process writing components to course offerings, teaching against the literary canon, attempting to be inclusive of difference across the curriculum.

The German department at Georgetown University has received accolades for its multiple literacies approach to second-language learning. In part the program succeeds because students know exactly what to expect and achieve at each level. They will develop the ability to read a book after two semesters of intensive training, take college-level courses at a German-speaking university after four semesters, and communicate at the advanced level by graduation.[6] For programs that are undergoing curricular revision and that have faculty members trained in literary studies, one advantage to this task-based pedagogy is adaptability: it represents a change in approach toward course materials, not in the materials themselves. By emphasizing the incremental acquisition of target-language skills through literary-cultural studies, Georgetown's German BA program, unlike conventional second-language programs, prioritizes adult language learning over familiarity with the literary canon. One disadvantage of this emphasis is that course topics are post-eighteenth-century, and so the program encourages a presentist form of cultural literacy through second-language acquisition. This concern about presentism, however, is not a reason to reject a multiple literacies approach to language teaching.

It is encouraging that professors of medieval and early modern studies are embracing innovative pedagogies and taking on the chore of curricular revision in their departments and across disciplines. In this way, the *Quixote* and similar texts will excite interest not because they are books that deserve to be taught above others but because they can be used in a broader pedagogical approach to develop in students critical analysis and advanced language skills. Mount Holyoke College recently launched an interdisciplinary program in Spanish that promises to provide a curriculum oriented toward multiple literacies. The literary-cultural studies rubrics of the new major in second-language acquisition (e.g., studies in identities, visual cultures, concepts and practices of power, language and society) are sufficiently dynamic and flexible to allow specialists in early modern studies to reintroduce the *Quixote* in one or more of these contexts, after a hiatus that has lasted decades.

The second-language curriculum for majors in Spanish requires reinvention so that the inclusion of medieval and early modern texts makes more sense to undergraduates who are uninterested in the past and to administrators who are focused on short-term enrollment issues. Instead of an entry-level course for majors and minors that deals only with literary production in early modern Spain, or instead of a scattershot-style survey of Spanish or Latin American literature from the Middle Ages to the present, a multiple literacies approach will teach students more — linguistically, culturally, and historically. Following a single theme or set of themes (empire, love, money, power, religion, revolution, sex) will give them a steady base from which to examine cultural production and its meanings, both past and present. Instead of a canonically focused seminar on the *Quixote*, a course on the novel that is sequentially placed in a discourse-based curriculum will teach students more — contextually, comparatively, and communicatively. Even a smaller institution with limited course offerings could give a seminar on the novel almost every year by rotating professors according to their areas of expertise, covering such topics as *Don Quixote*, Isabel Allende's *The House of the Spirits*, and cybernovels.

Professors of Cervantes must get ahead of the curve and contribute to the creation of programs of study that make sense to students before they take a seat on the first day of classes. The academic road ahead is more and more interdisciplinary, and early modern literary works have a crucial role to play in the teaching of language, of culture, and of genres as acts of communication. The goal is not to sell the *Quixote* to undergraduates but to plan an entire curriculum that establishes a graduated set of educational priorities and outcomes that students, faculty members, advisers, and administrators can understand and follow. We need to design a coherent program of study from 101 through the honors thesis or even the dissertation so that early modern studies will become a necessary part of the educational offerings of our institutions.

NOTES

[1] To maintain privacy, I have assigned fictional names, often playful in their connection to *Don Quixote*, to informants and institutions.

[2] In the spring and summer of 2009, thirty-four professors of Spanish and Hispanic studies responded to my brief questionnaire "*Don Quixote* in the Undergraduate Curriculum."

[3] Eighteen state universities and sixteen private institutions of higher learning in North America are represented in the study. Most informants teach Cervantes, but I also included professors whose specialization is not the early modern period or whose institution does not offer the *Quixote*.

[4] ACTFL provides a Web site with current proficiency guidelines for speaking, writing, listening, and reading, as of 2012: www.actfl.org/publications/guidelines-and-manuals /actfl-proficiency-guidelines-2012/.

[5] The Government of Aragón's Department of Education provides Internet access to recordings of the *Quixote* in Spanish: www.educaragon.org/arboles/arbol .asp?guiaeducativa=41&strseccion=A1A68.

[6] Georgetown's German department provides detailed descriptions and a bibliography about its multiple literacies curriculum (see *Summary*).

Using an Anthology to Teach *Don Quixote*

Gregory B. Kaplan

At some institutions of higher learning, including the one I attended (the University of Texas, Austin), a course dedicated exclusively to Miguel de Cervantes's masterpiece, *Don Quixote*, is available to undergraduate majors and minors in Spanish. However, a course that focuses on only one text is frequently impractical. Creating space in an academic program for both parts of *Don Quixote* is challenging because of its length and because of the need to contextualize the work. My essay addresses this challenge by describing strategies for using an anthology to teach *Don Quixote* in an upper-division undergraduate survey course. I illustrate how an anthology can be employed as a gateway to chapters not read for class and as an effective tool for considering the artistic, historical, and social influences on *Don Quixote*. I suggest a class format for incorporating selections from the novel included in an anthology, ways to discuss and contextualize episodes not included in an anthology, and techniques for exploring the cultural milieu in which Cervantes wrote.

Structure and Methodology

I use volume 1 of *Antología de autores españoles* (edited by Antonio Sánchez-Romeralo and Fernando Ibarra) to teach *Don Quixote* at the University of Tennessee during a semester-long course focusing on a variety of medieval and Golden Age Spanish texts. The course typically meets three days a week (fifty-minute classes) and sometimes is taught twice a week (ninety-minute classes). The strategies I discuss can be adapted to either format. This course, designed to be among the first in Hispanic literature taken by majors and minors in Spanish, endeavors to develop skills that students have acquired in previous courses, in particular the ability to comprehend the Spanish text of *Don Quixote* as it is presented in *Antología de autores españoles* —the orthography is modernized, and notes explain difficult terms—and the ability to express interpretations of the work in writing in the target language.

Five fifty-minute classes or four ninety-minute classes should be sufficient for the discussion and contextualization of *Don Quixote*. Chapters of the novel, many of which are abbreviated in *Antología*, might be assigned as in figure 1.

Students should be made aware from the outset that they will be reading only a small portion of *Don Quixote*, and of course they should also be encouraged to read more of the text on their own. That an anthology is being used should not discourage instructors from devoting time to the episodes not included: the episodes can be discussed in conjunction with those that are included to give students a feel for the novel's breadth of themes and social motifs.

Day	Chapters in Fifty-Minute Class	Chapters in Ninety-Minute Class
1	part 1: 1, 2, 3, 7, 8, 16	part 1: 1, 2, 3, 7, 8, 16, 17
2	part 1: 17, 22, 25, 30, 31	part 1: 22, 25, 30, 31
		part 2: 1, 10
3	part 2: 1, 10, 17	part 2: 17, 22, 23, 43, 74
4	part 2: 22, 23, 43, 74	review
5	review	

Fig. 1. Assigning chapters of *Don Quixote* from *Antología de autores españoles*

In part 1, chapter 6 (which is not in *Antología de autores españoles*), two of Don Quixote's friends, the curate and the barber, order that most of his books of chivalry be burned in an effort to dissuade Don Quixote from continuing his adventures as a knight-errant. Even though students are not assigned chapter 6, highlighting in class the selection of books to be burned, as well as those deemed worthy to be saved, helps them, as Juan Bautista Avalle-Arce writes, "become familiar with the literary . . . [and] social . . . backgrounds on which Cervantes drew" (134).

Chapter 6 might be discussed during the first day to introduce a principal literary motif of *Don Quixote*: how Cervantes responds to the contemporary profusion of romances of chivalry. After reading chapter 1, students will have learned that Don Quixote spends so much of his time reading these romances that he becomes mentally ill. They will wonder why he is so interested in chivalry and why Cervantes argues that reading romances causes illness, especially in the light of the modern view that reading is a way to overcome a social illness: illiteracy. Students may find it ironic that literacy, associated today with professional and economic success, should be depicted as a negative thing.

In the discussion of chapter 6 to contextualize Cervantes's attitude toward romances of chivalry, I recommend Carlos Alvar's "El ideal caballeresco de Cervantes y su reflejo en *El Quijote*" ("Cervantes's Knightly Ideal and Its Representation in the *Quixote*"), although some instructors might be reluctant to assign criticism in a survey course designed to develop skills in reading primary texts. Indeed, utilizing a review of chapter 6 instead of relying on a critical piece will give students a deeper understanding of a section of *Don Quixote* that they have not actually read. Instructors might begin by outlining the corpus of literature around which Cervantes crafts his work, showing the major themes—the knight-errant's quest for adventure, his preoccupation with honor, and his unrequited and undying love for his lady—that contributed to the widespread popularity of romances of chivalry during the sixteenth century. Once students see that Don Quixote embodies the attributes common to fictional knights-errant, they can be guided through a discussion of why the same attributes form the basis of Cervantes's parody. The burning of books in chapter 6 can therefore be explained not as a rejection by Cervantes of romances of chivalry (it should be pointed out that the first such romance, Garci Rodríguez de Montalvo's *Amadís de Gaula*, is spared from the flames because of its quality) but as a condemnation of their trivialization in literature through repetition.

The idea that Cervantes is attacking not the act of reading itself but the type of material being consumed by the reading public of his day is communicated in chapter 6 through the choices made by the curate and the barber as they decide which books should be burned. Instructors might use chapter 6 also to explain the work's sociopolitical backdrop, pointing out to students the similarity between Cervantes's dislike of romances of chivalry and the attitude expressed by the Spanish monarchy, which in 1531 banned the exportation to America of those works, a proscription that two decades later was extended to their publication in America. Cervantes's view that a profusion of romances of chivalry had debased the literary genre was shared by the monarchy, whose organized campaign to restrict access to them parallels the efforts of the curate and the barber.

The literary censorship imposed by the Spanish Inquisition through its lists of prohibited books, a censorship that defined the moral boundaries of the Counter-Reformation, is a topic that complements this episode in chapter 6 and conveys the spiritual climate in which Cervantes lived and composed *Don Quixote*. Discussion of this climate might include a review of how the Spanish monarchy assumed the role of defender of the Catholic faith in the wake of the Council of Trent and how the Inquisition served as a moral police to suppress all heterodoxy.

The strategy used to present chapter 6 may be applied to other chapters from *Don Quixote* that students will not find in their anthology. An example is part 2, chapter 36: students might be asked to hand in an essay on the last day of assigned readings that considers chapter 36 in relation to the adventures of Don Quixote and Sancho at the castle of a duke and duchess. These adventures receive only brief mention in *Antología de autores españoles*, and instructors should give students a more comprehensive summary of them when the essay is assigned. This summary should contain enough information about chapter 36 — the letter that Sancho composes to his wife, the arrival of the squire of the Countess Trifaldi — to enable students to write the essay.

I suggest that instructors underscore a phrase uttered by the duchess to Sancho in chapter 36 after his reply to her that he has given himself five lashes with his hand as a manner of commencing the penance he is required to perform in order to disenchant Dulcinea: ". . . y advierta Sancho que las obras de caridad que se hacen tibia y flojamente no tienen mérito ni valen nada" '. . . be advised, Sancho, that works of charity performed in a lukewarm and halfhearted way have no merit and are worth nothing' (335; 697). In 1632, the Inquisition suppressed this phrase without offering a reason, and in the essay students can be asked to consider why an institution that was created to eradicate heresy in

Counter-Reformation Spain might expurgate wording that appeals to the notion of genuine charity (which is part of Catholic doctrine). Instructors wishing to provide more background might ask students to read Américo Castro's "Cervantes y la Inquisición" ("Cervantes and the Inquisition") and pages 333–38 from volume 7 of Francisco Rodríguez Marín's critical edition (*Ingenioso hidalgo*), each of which discusses the suppression of the phrase from chapter 36 of Cervantes's text.

Techniques for Teaching Cultural Context

In part 1, chapter 17, which is included in *Antología de autores españoles*, students will read how Don Quixote, while staying at an inn, believes it is a castle—until he is asked to pay for his lodging. This episode shows how both the knight and his squire are undergoing a transformation: Don Quixote's disenchantment begins, but the refusal of Sancho Panza to pay, on the grounds that payment would contradict the rules of chivalry, indicates that he has begun to assume the madness of his master.

This transformation is gradual and continues throughout the work, and students can follow it both in the chapters they read and in those omitted from their anthology. In part 2, chapter 10, Don Quixote is unable to see Dulcinea and her two ladies-in-waiting according to Sancho's fantastic description: he sees only three rustic peasant women. In chapter 74, the last in the work, Alonso Quijano declares before dying that he abhors romances of chivalry and that he is cured of his madness. In the same two chapters, Sancho demonstrates his quixotic transformation: in his idealistic depiction of Dulcinea and her two ladies-in-waiting and in his plea to his dying master that they return to their adventures.[1]

To provide students with a vision of the artistic milieu of *Don Quixote*, instructors might point to parallels between the novel and baroque painting. In part 1, chapter 22, which is included in the anthology, Ginés de Pasamonte, the leader of a group of prisoners liberated by Don Quixote, declares that he is writing his autobiography and that it will not be complete until his death. This declaration mirrors Cervantes's work in a way that recalls Diego de Velázquez's masterpiece, *Las meninas*, which was completed in 1656.[2] While *Las meninas* is viewed in class, an instructor might pose the question, Who is the subject of this painting? Some students may respond that the subjects are the ladies-in-waiting (*meninas*) to the infanta Margarita or perhaps the infanta herself. Others may respond that the subject is Velázquez, who appears as the painter painting. Some students may identify the subject of Velázquez's work as one that is hidden to the viewer—possibly the king and queen of Spain (Philip IV and Mariana of Austria), who appear in a mirror on the wall behind Velázquez, or even the viewer of *Las meninas*, that is, the students themselves as they consider the painting in class.

All these interpretations are valid in that they reflect a technique associated with baroque art, which emphasizes motion and multiple perspectives (in *Las meninas*, multiple perspectives are created by the movement of the viewer's eye from one possible subject to another). Instructors may include, in this comparison of art and literature, images of two sculptures, Michelangelo's *David* (1501–04) and Gian Lorenzo Bernini's *David* (1623–24). Michelangelo presents a Renaissance interpretation of the biblical figure as he stands, rock and slingshot in hand, ready to fight Goliath. In Bernini's sculpture, David is presented as he twists his body just before releasing the rock that kills Goliath, a pose that creates a sense of motion similar to that produced in *Las meninas* and chapter 22 of *Don Quixote*. Bernini invites the spectator to consider his more dynamic *David* from multiple points of view, as Velázquez invites the spectator to consider *Las meninas*. When Ginés de Pasamonte reveals that he is writing a work in which Don Quixote will appear (inasmuch as the act of being liberated by the knight will naturally constitute an episode in his autobiography), a narrative motion is created as the reader shifts from Cervantes's perspective (or from that of Cervantes's fictitious author, Cide Hamete Benengeli) to that of Ginés, who will depict his dialogue with Don Quixote and his liberation by the knight-errant from a different vantage point. Students could be asked to describe, in an essay, Don Quixote as seen through the eyes of Ginés.

Instructors might end the discussion of *Don Quixote* by broadening the focus to include some of the similarities and differences between the Renaissance and baroque periods. In many survey courses, students will read *Lazarillo de Tormes* (which immediately precedes *Don Quixote* in *Antología de autores españoles*), a Renaissance work that may be compared and contrasted with *Don Quixote*. The opportunity of this comparison demonstrates one of the benefits of using an anthology ("anthologies enable students to compare different works and to place writers in their literary, cultural, and historical contexts" [Bjornson 12]). The comparison of *Lazarillo de Tormes* and *Don Quixote* can focus on the picaresque characteristics of Lázaro and Ginés.

As a pedagogical tool for underscoring stylistic differences between *Lazarillo de Tormes* and *Don Quixote*, instructors can create a *PowerPoint* slide on which images of a Renaissance portrait such as Albrecht Dürer's *Self-Portrait* (1498) and *Las meninas* are presented. Students can then be encouraged to consider features of *Lazarillo de Tormes* and *Don Quixote* that reflect the artistic movements to which they belong. For example, Dürer's painting may be said to parallel *Lazarillo de Tormes* insofar as both are Renaissance portraits of individuals: the self-portrait invites the spectator to discern the artist's inner feelings; the adventures of the book's protagonist invites the reader to discover the reasons why he is a social outcast.

It is rarely possible to cover all of *Don Quixote* in an undergraduate course, but the strategic use of an anthology can inspire students to read the entire work, either on their own or in a graduate-level course. For most students, exposure to

Cervantes's novel will be limited to a few class periods, but hopefully the vision of it that they gain through the methods offered in this essay will provide them with a solid review of the features on which its international renown is based. Understanding the sociocultural influences on the composition of *Don Quixote* will also afford students greater opportunities to elaborate and exchange ideas in an atmosphere that furthers the development of their analytic skills.

NOTES

The English translation of *Don Quixote* used in this essay is by Edith Grossman.

[1] Among the chapters not found in *Antología de autores españoles* that illustrate this transformation is part 2, chapter 26, in which Don Quixote destroys the Moorish puppets of Maese Pedro. Although Don Quixote attributes this act to the influence of necromancers on his judgment, he acknowledges his error and agrees to pay for the damage, which indicates some awareness of reality. Another chapter not found in the anthology, part 2, chapter 41, gives an example of Sancho's transformation. Sancho claims that a spell cast on him while he rides Clavileño (a wooden horse) has allowed him to view a series of fantastic images.

[2] *Las meninas* might be viewed in class through a film such as *Velázquez: The Painter of Painters* or a slide in a *PowerPoint* presentation. I prefer using a slide, because then students may consider how a painting can be compared to a literary work without being influenced by film's interpretation, but some instructors might find the film useful to provide an overview of baroque art or to guide students toward a discussion of the baroque features of Velázquez's painting.

Pedagogy of Inclusion for *Don Quixote*

Luis Verano

When *Approaches to Teaching Cervantes' Don Quixote* was published in 1984 (Bjornson), the method I was using in my *Quixote* courses was to follow the book chapter by chapter, stopping at important places for comments and discussion. The essays in *Approaches* confirmed that my approach was fine in most respects, but they also made me realize how guilty I was of imposing my favorite topics on my students. I began to question whether my classes would be more flexible and interesting if I could lead the students to trace a wider range of topics throughout the text, even if I had to reduce the depth of those important to me personally. The question then became how to incorporate many topics into the chapter-by-chapter structure without fragmentation or confusion.

The answer came in an essay by Edward H. Friedman, "*Don Quixote* and the Act of Reading: A Multiperspectivist Approach," which tells how in his courses he spent two to three weeks preparing his students for the text by giving them guidance that would allow them to discover "the *Quixote* for themselves and to establish their own priorities regarding the mechanisms and meanings of the text" (88). Friedman explained his reasons for giving his students the background material he wanted them to explore. His essay showed the advantages of using an approach that reflected the multithematic nature of the book. It also taught me the value of preparing my students before they worked with the text, by providing the background they needed to proceed with a great variety of topics.

My first step was to compile a list of about fifty topics gathered from many books and articles about *Don Quixote*. Then, after dealing with the administrative details of the first day and explaining concisely the importance of the book, I began my courses by handing the students this list. I took several hours to explain the topics, giving enough examples so that students could determine which ones held their personal interest. This process provided a thorough preview of how we were going to proceed, and it gave everyone the information needed to read analytically and watch for the topics to appear in the text. The results were tangible. All the students felt involved in the book from the start; there was a structure to which they could adhere; and, as they read, they tracked their own topics. The preview also meant that we did not have to stop for details and explanations later as we discussed the chapters. Whenever a topic surfaced, the class identified it as an old friend and observed its progress.

Since 1984, the number of topics has nearly doubled. When I give the students the list, I indicate that some of the topics have received much critical attention while others have not. Students understand that the multiperspective approach is intended to allow them to pursue their personal interests, but they also know that more attention will be given to the topics I consider essential for understanding the text and for developing an appreciation of how critics have read *Don Quixote* over the years.

The topics lend themselves well to exam questions and essay assignments and make clear from the start the trajectory of the course. Sometimes, when introducing the topics, I indicate which might appear on an exam. Several days before the final exam, the students vote on a selection of topics, and I choose the ones that will appear on the exam. In courses where I use a combination of exams and papers, I choose the exam topics, but the students decide which to use for their papers. In this way, the important subjects are covered and recognition is given to the students' individual interests.

A Topics-Based Approach

Because this approach mirrors the multithematic quality of the text, I have chosen very diverse topics over the years. It is sometimes convenient to categorize them, but I often prefer not to, in part because some topics defy classification and in part because I want students to be open to explore other perspectives rather than be bound by the possible inflexibility of my categories.

As an example, the topic of arms and letters can be studied from a primarily literary viewpoint if one considers how the sources of Don Quixote's speech (1: 518–22 [ch. 38]; 33–34) inform the debate, but it can also be approached culturally if one discusses the interest at that time in the question of whether arms or letters provided a better career for a person. The topic can also be considered historically if one examines the attempts to harmonize the two as well as the difficulty humanism had with the earlier preeminence of arms. The instructor who wishes to cover all these aspects in a course would do well to scratch the surface only and avoid the profundities that this subject has elicited. In any case, it is impossible to put arms and letters into one category.

Here is a sample of topics arranged by category:

Methods and Techniques Used by Cervantes

use of ambiguity
use of extended allegories
narrative techniques and the role and multiplicity of narrators
juxtaposition
methods of characterization

Topics of Literary Interest

criticism of books of chivalry
difficulties in identifying the author's beliefs
role of the reader

multiplicity of styles and genres
types of humor
reality versus appearance
verisimilitude
search for self
purpose and effects of the intercalated stories
relationship between Don Quixote and Sancho
Don Quixote as the first Western novel?
concept of the hero

Topics of Historical Importance

government
religion
justice
arms and letters

Topics of Social and Cultural Interest

feminism
social hierarchies
social and cultural realities of Moriscos and conversos
concept of honor
jealousy

To prepare students for Cervantes's text, I have them read a brief but complete account of the history of Spain. This background leads to classroom discussions about Moorish Spain (711–1492), the Reconquest, and the long sixteenth century up through Cervantes's death in 1616. Spain did not participate in the Crusades because it had its own internal war with the Moors, but a few essential facts about Moorish Spain will be pertinent to our exploration of chivalry later. We discuss Isabella and Ferdinand's military victory in Granada, the arrival of Columbus in America, the expulsion of the Jews, the Inquisition, and the reigns of Charles V, Philip II, and Philip III. Emphasis is placed on the rise of Protestantism and the wars with the Ottoman Empire and France during the reign of Charles V. For the reign of Philip II, I mention Lepanto but emphasize more the Counter-Reformation, the enmity toward Elizabeth I of England, the 1588 defeat of the Armada, and the conflict with the Low Countries. I also stress Philip III's weakness as king and the 1609–14 expulsion of the Moriscos. I also dedicate some time to the Spanish Golden Age and the baroque.

All this preparation before we begin to discuss the text varies but may take as long as seven class hours. If the number of topics is reduced (I don't have to cover all in every class) and the students' background in history is already strong, the preparation could take four class hours, possibly less.

The Galley Slaves Example

The galley slaves episode (pt. 1, ch. 22) provides a good illustrati｜
thematic approach. That the episode takes place relatively early in part 1 allows me to guide students to the ideas that readers must work to penetrate the psychology behind Don Quixote's actions and must consider several apparently unrelated matters simultaneously in order to reach a conclusion. I approach the episode by focusing first on the topic of justice. The galley slaves are prisoners condemned to row in Spanish ships, and I tell the students that much of the attention of twentieth-century critics like Friedrich Schürr and James R. Browne interpreted Cervantes's ideal of justice through Don Quixote's words and actions in this episode. These critics and others sought to confirm that Cervantes defended the principles of individual freedom. But he probably did not advocate that people overrule the authority of the king and take justice into their own hands, as Don Quixote does in the episode. It is difficult to make conclusions about Cervantes's concept of justice on the basis of the text also because Don Quixote asks the galley slaves questions but does not seem to want to face the truth in their answers.

By the time we reach this point in the book, the students have learned to expect and identify ambiguity. They see that Don Quixote does not question the ambiguous answers of the prisoners and sometimes even magnifies the ambiguity. As Browne puts it, there is "a consistent factor of incomprehension on Don Quixote's part, in his conversations with [the prisoners]" (460–61). Once the students realize that as Don Quixote listens to the prisoners, he is searching for interpretations of their words that will justify their release, they see the problems that this attitude creates for the reader. Is Don Quixote adhering to his principles of justice by pretending not to understand that the prisoners are criminals? Should his incomprehension be attributed to his madness? Or is he sacrificing principles of justice for some personal reason?

These questions inevitably lead to other topics on our master list, and I try to integrate related topics into the discussion. Methods of characterization, types of humor, multiplicity of styles and genres, social hierarchies, and the concept of honor present themselves to varying degrees in Don Quixote's conversations with the prisoners, but because they are are not as central as the theme of justice, I save them to the end of our discussion.

This episode not only sheds light on Don Quixote's decision making but also leads to juxtaposition as a technique. Students will note the importance of the juxtaposition of the galley slaves episode with the conversation between Don Quixote and Sancho that begins in the previous chapter (ch. 21). There, after Don Quixote takes the basin from the barber, Sancho considers how little they are accomplishing in secluded places and suggests that Don Quixote serve a king or emperor so sthat his courage, strength, and wisdom do not go unnoticed. Don Quixote finds the idea agreeable but declares that first a knight must complete adventures to achieve renown and fame so that, by the time he arrives at court, he is known for his deeds. The thought sends him into reveries of the glorious future they can expect. When Sancho says he is excited by such prospects, Don Quixote asserts that it will all come to pass but repeats that it will require time.

At the end of chapter 21, Don Quixote reassures Sancho of his determination, but then the narrator intervenes, showing us the connection between the conversation and the galley slaves episode by saying that at that very moment the knight raised his eyes and saw what will be told in the next chapter. In the first lines of chapter 22, we are reminded how Cide Hamete said that Don Quixote, after the conversation in chapter 21, raised his eyes and saw the galley slaves.

Sancho explains that the slaves are prisoners of the king. From the moment Don Quixote hears the word "king," he ignores all Sancho's statements of the prisoners' criminal status and begins to exercise the "factor of incomprehension" that will lead to their release. His mind has been engaged in finding a deed that will reach the ears of the court, and suddenly the answer appears: if he releases the king's prisoners, the king will hear of his deed. The students understand that Don Quixote, in his release of the prisoners, may be ignoring his principles to fulfill his goal. They also understand how Cervantes leads readers to make the connection themselves (the topic of the role of the reader comes up at this time).

A passage in the text must be pointed out, as modern readers likely will overlook it. The Spanish provides a word we need to arrive at the true relation of this episode to justice. After Sancho confirms that the slaves are traveling against their will, Don Quixote says, ". . . aquí encaja la ejecución de mi oficio" '. . . here it is fitting to put into practice my profession' (1: 306; 163 [trans. Grossman]). *Encaja* is essential but hard to translate literally: *encajar* means "to fit" or "to make something fit," and Don Quixote is saying that the situation fits well his duties as knight. *Encaja* also alludes to "la ley del encaje," a term used often at the time by the people of Spain (in *Don Quixote*, it appears on 1: 195 [ch. 11]; 77 and 2: 378 [ch. 42]; 378). Roughly translated as "the law of making it fit," the word referred to the practice of judges who made crimes "fit" the sentences they had predetermined. This arbitrary mode of justice often was used with respect to prisoners assigned to the Spanish galleys. Spain, managing many enterprises around the world, had a great need for men to handle the oars. The Royal Council would then send circulars to the courts requesting prisoners for that purpose, and the judges often adjusted the seriousness of the crimes to justify the long and horribly arduous sentences.

Students begin now to understand the extent of Cervantes's literary accomplishment. When Don Quixote releases the galley slaves, he treats the king and the courts in the same way that the king and the courts have treated the accused. The judges perform the formalities of the judicial process but manipulate the evidence to justify the predetermined sentence. Don Quixote asks his questions but misunderstands the prisoners' answers to justify his predetermined decision. Cervantes does not accuse but has us consider the injustices of the king and the courts when they find themselves on the receiving end of the same unjust methods.

When I ask the students if it is possible to draw a conclusion about Cervantes's concept of justice, the topic of the difficulty in determining the author's beliefs usually comes up. As a rule, students think it safe to say that Cervantes did not approve of the justice practiced by the king and the courts. They invariably appreciate the techniques and the clues Cervantes uses to let us see what he is doing.

A multithematic approach has allowed my students to develop their own interests while also giving me the flexibility to guide them in understanding the text and appreciating the analytic work of so many who, for more than four hundred years, have endeavored to uncover the complexities and beauty of *Don Quixote.*

In every class I teach, I am gratified to see that students who begin to trace and observe the progress of a few topics end up deeply engaged with characters and situations that they might not have considered otherwise. As they follow patterns, they become adept at noticing how interrelated everything is in the book, and their horizons expand. They notice that other topics surface in the episodes they are following, and this awareness leads them to consider new convergences and connections. They find that the topics they are tracing acquire more depth when studied in conjunction with others. As students follow the new directions revealed, they come to realize that other topics, other perspectives, are at least as important as the ones they began with. The approach promotes inquisitiveness and new interests.

This topics-based approach calls for inclusivity and challenges students to shoulder a multiplicity of themes in order to be put in closer contact with Cervantes's masterpiece. They feel closer to the author and to his art. I can't think of anything more rewarding.

Helping Undergraduates Make Connections to *Don Quixote*

William Worden

The Spanish program at the University of Alabama requires all majors to take a 400-level course on Cervantes's most famous work; consequently, I teach *Don Quixote* to undergraduates every semester. A typical class has twenty-five students who are juniors or seniors, and half of them have spent a summer or semester in a Spanish-speaking country. There are few native or heritage speakers, perhaps three or four, in a normal class. Prerequisites for the course are a conversation class, an advanced grammar and composition class, and at least two survey classes in Spanish or Latin American literature. In my course, conducted entirely in Spanish, we read both parts of *Don Quixote* using Tom Lathrop's 2012 edition (*Don Quijote*, text in Spanish and introduction and notes in English) and its accompanying dictionary. Over the years I have found that my students' level of interest in the readings and in our class discussions is directly related to their ability to make connections between the text and their own lives. This essay delineates several teaching strategies and activities that I use in class to encourage students to relate what is happening in the text to the world outside it. The result of their making those connections has been increased motivation to engage with Cervantes's text both inside and outside class. The essay has three sections: introducing the work, its protagonist, and its relation to books of chivalry; encouraging students to make connections between specific moments in the work and the work as a whole; relating *Don Quixote* to the lives of today's undergraduates.

Don Quixote, *Its Protagonist, and Books of Chivalry*

In contrast to my excitement at the prospect of introducing a new class to *Don Quixote*, my students almost always seem to be thinking the following: "I know this work is considered a classic, but it's from a long time ago, probably has no relation to my life, and is most likely boring"; "This book is long, and the Spanish looks difficult. Will I really be able to understand the text?" My goals for the first day of class are to convince students that with the proper effort they can understand the text, that reading *Don Quixote* will be an enjoyable experience, and that the text will in fact have relevance to their lives.

I begin by saying that we will spend fifteen weeks reading both parts of one of the most famous works of literature ever written. Rather than offer my own appraisal of *Don Quixote*, I share with students what several celebrated writers have said of Cervantes's text, including, among others, Fyodor Dostoevsky: "In all the world there is nothing more profound and more powerful than *Don Quixote*. Further than this, it is the last and greatest word of human thought" (qtd. in Simmons 211–12); Gustave Flaubert: "I discover all my origins in the book that I knew by heart before I read it, *Don Quixote*" (qtd. in Church 61); and William Faulkner: "I read *Don Quixote* every year" (qtd. in Gwynn and Blotner 50). Finally, to emphasize how enjoyable it is to read the work, I mention what Philip III said on seeing a man reading a book and laughing hysterically: "Either that man is mad, or he is reading *Don Quixote*" (qtd. in Waite 250). My intention with these quotations is to show students that they will not simply be reading a book during the semester; they will also be joining a vast community of readers who for over four hundred years have delighted in reading *Don Quixote* and been profoundly affected by it.

Next I ask students what they already know about the work and its protagonist, thereby beginning a discussion focused on the presence of *Don Quixote* in contemporary society. Some students have been exposed to sections of the novel in previous Spanish classes, and some have read parts of the work in English translation. Most have had no direct contact with the text but have heard the word *quixotic* or the expression "tilting at windmills." During this discussion, a student or two will bring up the musical *Man of La Mancha* or the song "The Impossible Dream." Others might mention Pablo Picasso's drawing of Don Quixote and Sancho (which I then show them, as I always bring my framed copy to the first class). Either the students themselves or I will talk about other artistic production inspired by Cervantes's text, ranging from the nineteenth-century ballet to the 2000 *Don Quixote* movie starring John Lithgow as Don Quixote, Bob Hoskins as Sancho, and Vanessa Williams as Dulcinea. A reference that often comes up—perhaps most often—is a children's television show from the 1990s called *Wishbone*, in which the main character, a talking Jack Russell terrier, acts out scenes from classic literature and plays the role of Sancho Panza in one episode.

This discussion demonstrates that Cervantes's work continues to inspire writers and artists today and continues to serve as a powerful cultural reference throughout the world. Students start looking for traces of *Don Quixote* around them, and as the semester progresses, we often find references to the work or its protagonist in a range of media, including editorial cartoons, television programs, and music.

I direct students to the introduction of Lathrop's edition, which contains information on the linguistic features of seventeenth-century Spanish prose, including topics like the assimilation of consonants and the use of the future subjunctive (Introduction [2-vol. ed.]). I compare Cervantes's prose with Shakespeare's plays (pointing out that the two writers were contemporaries) and suggest that reading *Don Quixote* is not unlike reading *Hamlet* or *King Lear*. In Shakespeare, the use of "perchance," "forsooth," and similar language can be disconcerting at first, but with time the archaic language becomes easier to understand. In a similar manner, making sense of the first ten chapters of *Don Quixote* will be challenging and time-consuming for the students, but the reading gets easier as the work continues.

Before we turn to the prologue and the first chapter, I talk briefly about books of chivalry and Alonso Quijano's relation to them. I describe Amadís de Gaula as a young, noble, handsome, and valiant knight whose adventures, and those of knights like him, were wildly popular in sixteenth-century Spain. I have often found it helpful to relate books of chivalry, their magical worlds filled with enchanters, giants, and dragons, to modern works with which my students are familiar, such as *Lord of the Rings, Harry Potter,* and *Game of Thrones*.

I don't let students begin their reading of *Don Quixote* on their own, lest they become intimidated, so toward the end of the first class, we read sections of the text together. My purpose is to show them that though Cervantes's prose is indeed challenging for advanced undergraduate students in Spanish, they can understand *Don Quixote* if they are diligent. I also use this first reading together to demonstrate the helpfulness of the footnotes and vocabulary glosses that appear in the text as well as in Lathrop's Don Quijote *Dictionary*.

After we read parts of the prologue together, I ask students if in their academic writing they ever follow the advice given by the prologuist's friend: Include lots of footnotes, quote impressive authorities, use foreign languages to show how intelligent you are. They admit that sometimes those techniques do seem to impress the reader of their papers. Among the textual moments in the first chapter, I make sure to point out that Don Quixote's age is near fifty and that his armor belonged to his great-grandfather, and I ask, "Does Don Quixote seem like a worthy successor to Amadís de Gaula?" The question leads us to the notion of parody, which I define using Linda Hutcheon's description, "repetition with critical difference, which marks difference rather than similarity" (*Theory* 6). After discussing Don Quixote's obsession with books of chivalry, the dissimilarities between him and the knights who serve as his models, and Cervantes's interest in parodying the genre of books of chivalry, I suggest, "A modern-day Don Quixote would be someone who spends all his time reading Westerns and then one day puts on old cowboy boots, a ten-gallon hat, and a toy badge, walks to the center of town brandishing a rusty six-shooter, and loudly declares himself the new sheriff in town."

To explain Cervantes's literary project, I make the following comparison:

> Understanding what Cervantes is doing in *Don Quixote* is similar to understanding what Mike Myers is doing in *Austin Powers*. If you have seen a James Bond movie, you understand just how different the Austin Powers character is from the spy who serves as his model. While James Bond is handsome, debonair, serious, and successful, the Austin Powers character is strange-looking, clumsy, ridiculous, and unaware that others are laughing at him. In a similar fashion, Don Quixote serves as a degraded imitation of the chivalric models that inspire him. One can enjoy an Austin Powers film without ever having seen a James Bond film, but someone familiar with the spy genre understands more fully the humorous nature

of the Austin Powers character. Likewise, a reading of *Don Quix*
an understanding of its parodic nature are enhanced by a comprehension
of the genre of books of chivalry.

I consider a first class successful if, at certain moments in the prologue and first
chapter, students laugh. They usually do.

Relating Specific Moments in the Work to the Work as a Whole

One challenge of reading both parts of *Don Quixote* in one semester is that the
number of chapters, 126, and the proliferation of characters and adventures
can keep students from fully appreciating the arc of the story as a whole and the
themes that are essential to it. At times, the sheer quantity of pages we need to
cover in a week can lead to an overemphasis on the latest plot developments to
the detriment of reflection on how the new adventures relate to previous ones.
To slow us down as the semester progresses and with an eye toward encouraging
students to connect specific episodes in the work and *Don Quixote* as a whole, I
assign the following exercise as homework: "Find a moment in the work that in
some way comments on the whole work."

As an example, one student offered an insightful observation on the beard-
washing episode in the ducal palace, when Don Quixote is left alone covered
with soap:

> [Q]uedó don Quijote con la más estraña figura y más para hacer reír que
> se pudiera imaginar. Mirábanle todos los que presentes estaban, que eran
> muchos, y como le veían con media vara de cuello, más que mediana-
> mente moreno, los ojos cerrados y las barbas llenas de jabón, fue gran
> maravilla y mucha discreción poder disumular la risa.   (2: 300 [ch. 32])

> [D]on Quixote was left there, the strangest and most laughable figure
> that anyone could imagine. All those present, and there were many, were
> watching him, and when they saw that he had a neck half a *vara* long, and
> a complexion more than moderately dark, and closed eyes, and a beard
> full of soap, it was truly astonishing and a sign of great astuteness that they
> could hide their laughter. . . .   (669)

The student observed that the entire work could be seen in these few words. At
the very moment when the knight believes that he is nobly following chivalric
customs, he actually appears to others—both to characters in the text and to
readers outside it—as a laughable figure. Furthermore, what is metaphoric in
much of the text is literal at this moment: Don Quixote has his eyes closed and
does not see what others see.

Another exercise that helps the class consider the text as a whole relates to the adventure of the windmills and the way in which this single episode has become emblematic of the entire work. I ask students to discuss in groups this question: "Why has this episode and not another become the best known moment in the text? It is not Don Quixote's first adventure in the book, nor is it the one that is most extensively described. Yet invariably this adventure is the one most commonly depicted in artwork or mentioned by those who discuss the work. Why?" In their answer, students try to choose another episode that could equally be considered emblematic of *Don Quixote*.

Toward the end of the semester, I ask everyone in class to take ten minutes to draw any character in *Don Quixote* except the knight and his squire. Students are allowed to refer to the text, if they wish, while creating their artwork. When all the drawings are finished, I collect them and hold them up one by one in front of the class, and students guess which character is depicted in each case. When I first tried this activity in class, I feared that students might consider the exercise juvenile; experience has taught me, however, that they very much enjoy both creating their own version of a Cervantine character and deciphering which characters are depicted by their classmates.

Relating Don Quixote *to Today's Undergraduates*

The universal nature of Cervantes's text offers numerous opportunities for students to discover similarities between what is happening in *Don Quixote* and situations in their own lives. At different times during the semester, therefore, I engage in various activities designed to help students understand the novel through the lens of their personal experience. I pose questions, have students respond for ten minutes in small groups, then lead a discussion with the full class on the topic.

> Question 1: Alonso Quijano is obsessed with chivalric literature. Do you have an interest that you pursue with such passion that someone might think you are crazy?

> Student Response: Given that the University of Alabama is home to the Crimson Tide football team, which has won fifteen national championships and was coached by the legendary Paul ("Bear") Bryant, students often mention their passion for Alabama football. They might consider whether or not it is possible to be too fanatical about the team. In class I have brought up the case of a husband and wife who chose not to attend their daughter's wedding because it conflicted with an Alabama football game (described in a recent book on Alabama football fans by Warren St. John). To my question "Is it crazy to miss your daughter's wedding because of a football game?," student response has varied from "I can't

believe any parents would miss their own daughter's wedding" to "Well, it may or may not be crazy, depending on which team Alabama is playing that week."

Some students say they best understand Don Quixote's obsession with chivalric literature by relating it to the modern-day phenomenon of video games. They know people who spend an entire weekend playing video games, who prefer these games to real life, and who would spend all their time in virtual reality if they could. Other common student ideas of Don Quixote–like people are hard-core Trekkies and *Star Wars* fans.

Question 2: Did you ever enjoy reading a book so much that you wanted to live in the work and maybe even pretended to do so?

Student Response: Students, most often as children, have pretended to live in literary worlds. Popular worlds are those of the *Harry Potter* novels, of J. R. R. Tolkien, and of the *Baby-Sitters Club* books. Some students have talked about wanting to be Tarzan or to live among the characters in *Little Women*.

Question 3: What is happening in your life that makes you think of *Don Quixote*?

Student Response: Over the years, students have related Cervantes's work to their lives in a number of interesting ways. During a class discussing the vote at the inn to determine whether the barber's basin was Mambrino's helmet or not, we discussed extensively the idea of perspectivism, the various ways that different people can see the same situation, and the difficulty of determining the exact nature of reality. One student explained that she best came to understand how differently people can view the world when she met her sister's new boyfriend. To her sister, he was handsome, charming, intelligent, and funny; my student, however, saw none of these qualities in him.

I continue to teach *Don Quixote* in the conviction that it bears ongoing relevance for the students of today. I have found that the more I encourage students to relate the text to their lives, the more connections I find between *Don Quixote* and my own life. Once, after discussing in class the mania that surrounds our campus on football weekends, a student asked me if I was a fan of our team. I said that I was but not to an extreme. On reflection, however, I decided that I was not so different from many rabid fans of the Alabama football team or from Don Quixote himself. Having grown up near Boston, whose 1967 pennant-winning Red Sox team was known as the Impossible Dream Team (with reference to the song in *Man of La Mancha*), I had to admit that my interest in the team was quite fervent. Every time I teach a class on Cervantes's novel, I realize—and I hope my students do as well—that relating *Don Quixote* to our lives can help us understand not just the work but ourselves as well.

NOTE

The English translation of *Don Quixote* used in this essay is by Edith Grossman.

NOTES ON CONTRIBUTORS

David A. Boruchoff is associate professor of Hispanic studies at McGill University. In addition to numerous publications on the works of Cervantes (particularly *Don Quixote*, *Persiles*, and the *Exemplary Novels*), his research embraces a wide range of topics in the literature, historiography, and intellectual history of early modern Europe and America.

Bruce R. Burningham is professor of Hispanic studies and theater at Illinois State University and chair of the Department of Languages, Literatures, and Cultures. He is the author of *Radical Theatricality: Jongleuresque Performance on the Early Spanish Stage* (2007) and *Tilting Cervantes: Baroque Reflections on Postmodern Culture* (2008). He is the editor of *Cervantes: Bulletin of the Cervantes Society of America*.

Joan F. Cammarata is professor of Spanish at Manhattan College. Specializing in the literature of early modern Spain, she is the author of *Mythological Themes in the Works of Garcilaso de la Vega* (1983) and the editor of *Women in the Discourse of Early Modern Spain* (2003). She has published on Cervantes, Teresa of Cartagena, Garcilaso de la Vega, and Saint Teresa of Ávila.

David R. Castillo is professor of Spanish and chair of the Department of Romance Languages and Literatures at the State University of New York, Buffalo. He is the author of *Baroque Horrors: Roots of the Fantastic in the Age of Curiosities* (2010) and *(A)Wry Views: Anamorphosis, Cervantes, and the Early Picaresque* (2001). He is also coeditor of *Reason and Its Others: Italy, Spain, and the New World* (2006) and *Spectacle and Topophilia: Reading Early Modern and Postmodern Hispanic Cultures* (2012).

William Childers is associate professor of Spanish at Brooklyn College and at Graduate Center, City University of New York. He is the author of *Transnational Cervantes* (2006) as well as numerous articles on Cervantes and other aspects of Spanish baroque culture. His work typically analyzes literary texts side by side with archival documents. His current book project is "Morisco Questions: Cultural and Racial Identities in Early Modern Castile."

Frederick A. de Armas is Andrew W. Mellon Distinguished Service Professor in Humanities at the University of Chicago. His most recent books are *Cervantes, Raphael, and the Classics*; *Quixotic Frescoes: Cervantes and Italian Renaissance Art*; and *Don Quixote among the Saracens: Clashes of Civilizations and Literary Genres*.

Sidney Donnell is associate professor of Spanish at Lafayette College and head of the Department of Foreign Languages and Literatures. He is the author of *Feminizing the Enemy: Imperial Spain, Transvestite Drama, and the Crisis of Masculinity*. He is preparing the first critical edition of the seventeenth-century play *El caballero dama*, by Cristóbal de Monroy y Silva.

Salvador Fajardo is professor of Spanish at Binghamton University. He has written articles on *Don Quixote* and prepared, with James A. Parr, an edition of the book for graduate and undergraduate students. He has also directed ten NEH Summer Seminars for teachers on reading *Don Quixote*. His other field of scholarly interest is contemporary Spanish poetry.

Edward H. Friedman is Gertrude Conaway Vanderbilt Professor of Spanish and professor of comparative literature at Vanderbilt University. His primary field of research is early modern Spanish literature, with emphasis on the picaresque, Cervantes, and the *comedia*. His research also covers contemporary narrative and drama. He is the author of *Cervantes in the Middle: Realism and Reality in the Spanish Novel*.

Barbara Fuchs is professor of Spanish and English at the University of California, Los Angeles, where she also directs the Center for Seventeenth- and Eighteenth-Century Studies and William A. Clark Memorial Library. She is the author of *The Poetics of Piracy* (2013), *Exotic Nation: Maurophilia and the Construction of Early Modern Spain* (2009), *Passing for Spain: Cervantes and the Fictions of Identity* (2003), and *Mimesis and Empire: The New World, Islam, and European Identities* (2001).

Carmen García de la Rasilla is associate professor of Spanish at the University of New Hampshire. In addition to *Salvador Dalí's Literary Self-Portrait* (2009), she has published a study of twentieth-century Spanish urban history and articles and book chapters on Spanish and comparative literature and on surrealism. She is currently editing a book on the Spanish historical novel and preparing a second monograph on the work of Dalí.

Gregory B. Kaplan is professor of Spanish at the University of Tennessee, where he also holds a Lindsay Young Professorship. He is the author of *Valderredible, Cantabria (España): La cuna de la lengua española* (2009) and *The Evolution of "Converso" Literature* (2002), editor of *Sixteenth-Century Spanish Writers* (2006), and coeditor of *Marginal Voices: Studies in Converso Literature of Medieval and Golden Age Spain* (2012).

Howard Mancing is professor of Spanish at Purdue University. He is the author of *The Chivalric World of* Don Quijote (1982), *The Cervantes Encyclopedia* (2004), and *Cervantes's* Don Quixote: *A Reference Guide* (2006). He is the coeditor of *Text, Theory, and Performance: Golden Age Comedia Studies* (1994), *Theory of Mind and Literature* (2011), and *Cognitive Cervantes*, a special issue of *Cervantes* (2012).

Patricia W. Manning is associate professor of Spanish at the University of Kansas. She is the author of *Voicing Dissent in Seventeenth-Century Spain: Inquisition, Social Criticism, and Theology in the Case of El Criticón* and articles concerning seventeenth-century texts, including the *Quijote* and "El coloquio de los perros."

Christian Michener is professor of literature and creative writing and director of the Honors Program at Saint Mary's University (MN). He is the author of a short story collection titled *Numerology* and scholarly work focused on interdisciplinary arts and contemporary Irish and Irish American literature.

Rogelio Miñana is professor of Spanish in the Department of Spanish, Latina/o and Latin American Studies at Mount Holyoke College and director of the Five College Blended Learning in the Humanities Program. He is the author of *La verosimilitud en el Siglo de Oro: Cervantes y la novela corta* (2002) and *Monstruos que hablan: El discurso de la monstruosidad en Cervantes* (2008). He is working on a book entitled "Living *Quixote*: Don Quixote, Politics, and Social Justice in Twenty-First-Century Spain and the Americas."

Barbara Mujica is professor of Spanish at Georgetown University, president emerita of the Association for Hispanic Classical Theater (AHCT), and editor of *Comedia Performance,* a journal devoted to early modern Spanish theater. She is the author of *Play and Playtext* (2011); *Teresa de Ávila, Lettered Woman* (2009); and *Sister Teresa* (2007).

James A. Parr is distinguished professor of Hispanic studies at the University of California, Riverside. A founding member of the Cervantes Society of America and past president of the CSA and AATSP, he is the author of Don Quixote: *A Touchstone for Literary Criticism* and *Don Quixote, Don Juan, and Related Subjects.* He has edited the original *Don Juan* play and coedited *Don Quixote.*

Susan Paun de García is professor of Spanish and associate provost at Denison University. Her research interests lie in early modern literature, both prose and theater, but especially in the performance of the *comedia,* in Spanish and in English. She is coeditor of *The Comedia in English: Translation and Performance.*

Cory A. Reed is associate professor of Spanish at the University of Texas, Austin. His research interests include Cervantes, the drama of early modern Spain, and transatlantic studies. He is the author of *The Novelist as Playwright: Cervantes and the entremés nuevo* (1993) and articles on Cervantes's drama, the *Exemplary Novels,* and *Don Quixote.*

Barbara Simerka is professor of Spanish at Queens College, City University of New York. She is the author of *Knowing Subjects: Cognitive Cultural Studies and Early Modern Spanish Literature* (2013) and *Discourses of Empire* (2003) and coeditor of *Cognitive Cervantes,* a special issue of the *Journal of the CSA* (2012).

Matthew D. Stroud is Murchison Term Professor of Spanish at Trinity University in San Antonio. He is the author of *Fatal Union: A Pluralistic Approach to the Spanish Wife-Murder Comedias, The Play in the Mirror: Lacanian Perspectives on Spanish Baroque Theater,* and *Plot Twists and Critical Turns: Queer Approaches to Early Modern Spanish Theater.* He edited and translated Calderón's *Celos aun del aire matan,* a fully sung zarzuela whose premiere he produced in 1981.

Jonathan Thacker is faculty lecturer in Spanish and fellow of Merton College, University of Oxford. He is the author of *Role-Play and the World as Stage in the* Comedia (2002) and *A Companion to Golden Age Theatre* (2007), coeditor of *A Companion to Lope de Vega* (2008), and translator of some of Cervantes's *Novelas ejemplares* (1992).

Luis Verano is an emeritus faculty member in the Department of Romance Languages and Literatures at the University of Oregon. His specialty is Spanish Golden Age literature. He is the author of language textbooks, video scripts, video programs, and translations of and articles on pedagogy.

Lisa Vollendorf is professor of Spanish and dean of the College of Humanities and the Arts at San José State University. She is the author of *The Lives of Women: A New History of Inquisitional Spain* (2005) and the editor of *Recovering Spain's Feminist Tradition* (2001); *Literatura y feminismo en España* (2006); with Daniella Kostroun, *Women, Religion, and the Atlantic World, 1600–1800* (2009); and, with Harald Braun, *Theorising the Ibero-American Atlantic* (2013).

Christopher Weimer is professor of Spanish at Oklahoma State University. He is the coeditor, with Barbara Simerka, of *Echoes and Inscriptions: Comparative Approaches to Early Modern Spanish Literatures* (2000). He is the author of essays on early modern and contemporary Hispanic prose and theater. He is at work on a book-length study of *Don Quixote* and the European gothic novel.

William Worden is associate professor of Spanish at the University of Alabama. He specializes in Spanish literature of the sixteenth and seventeenth centuries and is the author of essays on the picaresque novel, colonial Cuban theater, and *Don Quixote*.

SURVEY PARTICIPANTS

Shifra Armon, *University of Florida*
Stacey Parker Aronson, *University of Minnesota, Morris*
David Boruchoff, *McGill University*
Keith H. Brower, *Salisbury University*
Marina S. Brownlee, *Princeton University*
Susan Byrne, *College at Oneonta, State University of New York*
Joan Cammarata, *Manhattan College*
Gwyn Campbell, *Washington and Lee University*
Anthony J. Cárdenas, *University of New Mexico*
Glen Carman, *DePaul University*
María M. Carrión, *Emory University*
Diane Chaffee-Sorace, *Loyola College, MD*
Horacio Chiong-Rivero, *Swarthmore College*
Catherine Connor, *University of Vermont*
Jennifer Cooley, *University of Northern Iowa*
Anne J. Cruz, *University of Miami*
Frederick de Armas, *University of Chicago*
Sidney Donnell, *Lafayette College*
Angelica Durán, *Purdue University*
Susan Fischer, *Bucknell University*
Edward Friedman, *Vanderbilt University*
Yolanda Gamboa, *Florida Atlantic University*
Martha García, *University of Central Florida*
Carmen García de la Rasilla, *University of New Hampshire*
Juanita Garciagodoy, *Macalester College*
Bonnie Gasior, *California State University, Long Beach*
Chad Gasta, *Iowa State University*
Margaret R. Greer, *Duke University*
Cynthia Leone Halpern, *Cabrini College*
Stephen Hessel, *State University of New York, Buffalo*
Jesus David Jérez-Gómez, *California State University, San Bernardino*
Ana Laguna, *Rutgers University*
Ignacio López, *Duke University*
Javier Lorenzo, *East Carolina University*
Katie MacLean, *Kalamazoo College*
Howard Mancing, *Purdue University*
Patricia W. Manning, *University of Kansas*
Christian Michener, *Saint Mary's University*
Rogelio Miñana, *Mount Holyoke College*
Barbara Mujica, *Georgetown University*
Susan Paun de García, *Denison University*
Shannon Polchow, *University of South Carolina, Upstate*

Cory Reed, *University of Texas, Austin*
Stacey Schlau, *West Chester University*
Barbara Simerka, *Queens College, City University of New York*
Judith Stallings-Ward, *Norwich University*
Matthew Stroud, *Trinity University*
Luz Consuelo Triana-Echeverría, *St. Cloud State University*
Roberto Veguez, *Middlebury College*
Myriam Wong, *Davis Middle School, CA*
William Worden, *University of Alabama*

WORKS CITED

Abelleira Fernández, Jesús. *Diccionario enciclopédico hermenéutico o auxiliar de lectura del* Quijote. Pozuelo de Alarcón: Abelleira, 1997. Print.

Alcalá Galán, Mercedes. *Escritura desatada: Poéticas de la representación en Cervantes*. Alcalá de Henares: Centro de Estudios Cervantinos, 2009. Print.

Allen, John J. Rev. of *The Adventures of Don Quixote de la Mancha*. By Cervantes. Trans. Smollett. *Journal of Hispanic Philology* 11 (1986): 84–86. Print.

———. *Don Quixote, Hero or Fool? A Study in Narrative Technique*. Gainesville: UP of Florida, 1969. Print.

———. "Prefacio post-centenario a la edición renovada y actualizada." Cervantes, *El ingenioso hidalgo* [Allen] 1:7–9.

———. "*Traduttori Traditori: Don Quixote* in English." *Crítica hispánica* 1 (1979): 1–13. Print.

Allen, John J., and Patricia S. Finch, eds. *Don Quijote en el arte y pensamiento de Occidente*. Madrid: Cátedra, 2004. Print.

Allman, William F. *The Stone Age Present: How Evolution Has Shaped Modern Life—From Sex, Violence, and Language to Emotions, Morals, and Communities*. New York: Simon, 1994. Print.

Alter, Robert. *Partial Magic: The Novel as a Self-Conscious Genre*. Berkeley: U of California P, 1975. Print.

Althusser, Louis. "Ideology and Ideological State Apparatuses (Notes toward an Investigation)." *Mapping Ideology*. Ed. Slavoj Žižek. London: Verso, 1994. 100–40. Print.

Alvar, Carlos. "El ideal caballeresco de Cervantes y su reflejo en *El Quijote*." *Letras* 50–51 (2004): 24–38. Print.

Ardila, John, ed. *The Cervantean Heritage: Reception and Influence of Cervantes in Britain*. Oxford: Legenda, 2009. Print.

———. "Cervantes y la Quixotic Fiction: El hibridismo genérico." *Cervantes* 21.2 (2001): 5–26. Print.

Arenal, Electa, and Stacey Schlau, eds. *Untold Sisters: Hispanic Nuns in Their Own Works*. Trans. Amanda Powell. Rev. 2nd ed. Albuquerque: U of New Mexico P, 2009. Print.

Aristotle. *Poetics. The Basic Works of Aristotle*. Trans. Richard McKeon. New York: Random, 1941. 1455–86. Print.

Arredondo, Christopher Brett. *Quixotism, the Imaginative Denial of Spain's Loss of Empire*. Albany: State U of New York P, 2005. Print.

Astington, Janet Wilde. *The Child's Discovery of the Mind*. Cambridge: Harvard UP, 1993. Print.

Auster, Paul. *The New York Trilogy: City of Glass, Ghosts, The Locked Room*. New York: Penguin, 1990. Print.

Avalle-Arce, Juan Bautista. "Background Material on *Don Quixote*." Bjornson 127–35.

———. *Las novelas y sus narradores*. Alcalá de Henares: Centro de Estudios Cervantinos, 2006. Print.

Baena, Julio. *Discordancias cervantinas*. Newark: Juan de la Cuesta, 2003. Print.

Baker, Edward. *La biblioteca de don Quijote*. Madrid: Marcial Pons, Jurídicas y Sociales, 1997. Print.

Bakhtin, Mikhail. *Problems of Dostoevsky's Poetics*. Ed. and trans. Caryl Emerson. Minneapolis: U of Minnesota P, 1984. Print.

———. *Rabelais and His World*. Trans. Hélène Iswolsky. Cambridge: MIT P, 1968. Print.

Bal, Mieke. *Quoting Caravaggio: Contemporary Art, Preposterous History*. Chicago: U of Chicago P, 1999. Print.

Bandera, Cesáreo. *The Humble Story of Don Quixote: Reflections on the Birth of the Modern Novel*. Washington: Catholic U of Amer. P, 2006. Print.

Baranda Leturio, Nieves. *Cortejo a lo prohibido: Lectoras y escritoras en la España moderna*. Madrid: Arco Libros, 2005. Print.

Barkan, Leonard. *The Gods Made Flesh: Metamorphosis and the Pursuit of Paganism*. New Haven: Yale UP, 1986. Print.

Baron, Cynthia. "*The Player*'s Parody of Hollywood." Degli-Esposti 21–43.

Baron-Cohen, Simon. *Mindblindness: An Essay on Autism and Theory of Mind*. Cambridge: MIT P, 1995. Print.

Barrio Marco, José Manuel. "Prólogo." Barrio Marco and Crespo Allué 9–13.

———. "La proyección artística y literaria de Cervantes y *Don Quijote* en la Inglaterra del siglo XVII: Los cauces de recepción en el contexto político y cultural de la época." Barrio Marco and Crespo Allué 19–72.

Barrio Marco, José Manuel, and María José Crespo Allué, eds. *La huella de Cervantes y del Quijote en la cultura anglosajona*. Valladolid: U de Valladolid, 2007. Print.

Bartsch, Karen, and Henry M. Wellman. *Children Talk about the Mind*. New York: Oxford UP, 1995. Print.

Baudrillard, Jean. "Simulacra and Simulations." *Jean Baudrillard, Selected Writings*. Ed. Mark Poster. Stanford: Stanford UP, 1988. 166–84. Print.

Beck, James. *Raphael: The Stanza della Segnatura*. New York: Braziller, 1993. Print.

Bellos, David. *Is That a Fish in Your Ear? Translation and the Meaning of Everything*. New York: Faber, 2011. Print.

Benítez Sánchez-Blanco, Rafael. "La Inquisición ante los moriscos." Pérez Villanueva and Escandell Bonet 695–736.

Bergmann, Emilie L. "Optics and Vocabularies of the Visual in Luis de Góngora and Sor Juana Inés de la Cruz." de Armas, *Writing* 151–65.

Bernis Madrazo, Carmen. *El traje y los tipos sociales en el* Quijote. Madrid: Visor, 2001. Print.

Bjornson, Richard, ed. *Approaches to Teaching Cervantes' Don Quixote*. New York: MLA, 1984. Print. Approaches to Teaching World Lit. 3.

Black, Georgina Dopico. *Perfect Wives, Other Women: Adultery and Inquisition in Early Modern Spain*. Durham: Duke UP, 2001. Print.

Black, Georgina Dopico, and Francisco Layna Ranz, eds. *USA Cervantes: 39 Cervantistas en Estados Unidos*. Madrid: CSIC; Polifemo, 2009. Print.

Blasco, Javier. *Cervantes, raro inventor*. Alcalá de Henares: Centro de Estudios Cervantinos, 2005. Print.

Blasco Pascual, Francisco J. *Cervantes: Un hombre que escribe*. Valladolid: Difácil, 2006. Print.

Bleznick, Donald W. "An Archetypal Approach to *Don Quixote*." Bjornson 96–103.

Bloom, Harold. *The Anxiety of Influence*. 2nd ed. New York: Oxford UP, 1997. Print.

———, ed. *Miguel de Cervantes*. Philadelphia: Chelsea, 2005. Print.

———. *The Western Canon: The Books and School of the Ages*. New York: Harcourt, 1994. Print.

Borat: Kazakhstan National Anthem. YouTube. YouTube, 22 Jan. 2011. Web. 7 Apr. 2013. <https://www.youtube.com/watch?v=ZLa65o1nok8>.

Borges, Jorge Luis. "Pierre Menard, Author of *Don Quixote*." Trans. Anthony Bonner. *Ficciones*. New York: Grove, 1962. 45–56. Print.

———. *Prólogos con un prólogo de prólogos*. Buenos Aires: Torres Agüero, 1975. Print.

Boruchoff, David A. "Cervantes y las leyes de reprehensión cristiana." *Hispanic Review* 63.1 (1995): 39–55. Print.

———. "Free Will, Beauty, and the Pursuit of Happiness: *Don Quijote* and the Moral Intent of Pastoral Literature." *Anuario de Estudios Cervantinos* 1 (2004): 121–35. Print.

———. "Free Will, the Picaresque, and the Exemplarity of Cervantes's *Novelas ejemplares*." *MLN* 124.2 (2009): 372–403. Print.

———. "The Poetry of History." *Colonial Latin American Review* 13.2 (2004): 275–82. Print.

Bouza, Fernando. *Corre manuscrito: Una historia cultural del Siglo de Oro*. Madrid: Marcial Pons, 2001. Print.

Bracher, Mark. "Transference, Desire, and the Ethics of Literary Pedagogy." *College Literature* 26.4 (1999): 127–46. Print.

Breuer, Josef, and Sigmund Freud. *Studies on Hysteria*. Trans. and ed. James Strachey. London: Hogarth, 1955. Print. Vol. 2 of *The Standard Edition of the Complete Psychological Works of Sigmund Freud*.

Brioso Santos, Héctor, and José Montero Reguera. *Cervantes y América*. Madrid: Marcial Pons, 2006. Print.

Broncano, Manuel. "Reading Faulkner in Spain, Reading Spain in Faulkner." *Global Faulkner*. Ed. Annete Trefzer and Ann J. Abadie. Jackson: UP of Mississippi, 2009. 99–115. Print.

Browne, James R. "Cervantes and the Galeotes Episode." *Hispania* 41 (1958): 460–64. Print.

Brownlee, Marina S. "Zoraida's White Hand and Cervantes' Rewriting of History." *Bulletin of Hispanic Studies* 82 (2005): 19–35. Print.

Burch, Alan. Rev. of *The History of That Ingenious Gentleman Don Quijote de la Mancha*, trans. Burton Raffel. *Cervantes* 17.1 (1997): 185–88. Print.

Burningham, Bruce R. "David Lynch and the Dulcineated World." *Cervantes* 30.2 (2010): 33–56. Print.

———. "Of Mad Knights and Dark Helmets: Parody and Postmodernism in *Don Quixote* and *Spaceballs*." Chicago Humanities Festival. First United Methodist Church at the Chicago Temple, Chicago. 14 Nov. 2009. Lecture.

———. *Tilting Cervantes: Baroque Reflections on Postmodern Culture*. Nashville: Vanderbilt UP, 2008. Print.

Byrne, Susan. *Law and History in Cervantes'* Don Quixote. Toronto: U of Toronto P, 2012. Print.

Byron, William. *Cervantes: A Biography*. New York: Paragon, 1988. Print.

El caballero don Quijote. Dir. Manuel Gutiérrez Aragón. Alta Films, 2002. Film.

Călinescu, Matei. *Rereading*. New Haven: Yale UP, 1993. Print.

Canavaggio, Jean. *Cervantes*. Trans. Mauro Armiño. Madrid: Espasa-Calpe, 1987. Print.

———. *Cervantes*. Trans. Joseph R. Jones. New York: Norton, 1990. Print.

———. *Cervantes entre vida y creación*. Alcalá de Henares: Centro de Estudios Cervantinos, 2000. Print.

Candler Hayes, Julie. "Eighteenth-Century English Translations of *Don Quixote*." Ardila, *Cervantean Heritage* 66–75.

Caro Baroja, Julio. *Historia de la fisiognómica: El rostro y el carácter*. Madrid: Istmo, 1988. Print.

Carpentier, Alejo. "On the Marvelous Real in America." *Magical Realism: Theory, History, Community*. Ed. Lois Parkinson Zamora and Wendy B. Faris. Durham: Duke UP, 1995. 75–88. Print.

Carruthers, Peter, and Peter K. Smith, eds. *Theories of Theories of Mind*. Cambridge: Cambridge UP, 1996. Print.

Casalduero, Joaquín. *Sentido y forma del* Quijote, *1605–1615*. Madrid: Ínsula, 1949. Print.

Cascardi, Anthony J., ed. *The Cambridge Companion to Cervantes*. Cambridge: Cambridge UP, 2002. Print.

———. *Cervantes, Literature, and the Discourse of Politics*. Toronto: U of Toronto P, 2012. Print.

Castillo, David R. *(A)Wry Views: Anamorphosis, Cervantes, and the Early Picaresque*. West Lafayette: Purdue UP, 2001. Print.

———. *Baroque Horrors: Roots of the Fantastic in the Age of Curiosities*. Ann Arbor: U of Michigan P, 2010. Print.

———. "The Literary Classics in Today's Classroom: Don Quixote and Road Movies." *Hispanic Literatures and the Question of a Liberal Education*. Ed. Nicholas Spadaccini and Luis Martín-Estudillo. *HIOL: Hispanic Issues on Line* 8 (2011): 26–41. Print.

Castillo, David R., and Nicholas Spadaccini. "El antiutopismo en *Los trabajos de Persiles y Sigismunda*: Cervantes y el cervantismo actual." *Cervantes: Bulletin of the Cervantes Society of America* 20.1 (2000): 115–31. Print.

Castro, Américo. "Cervantes y la Inquisición." *Hacia Cervantes*. 3rd ed. Madrid: Taurus, 1967. 213–21. Print.

———. *El pensamiento de Cervantes*. 1925. Ed. Julio Rodríguez-Puértolas. Barcelona: Noguer, 1972. Print.

Cátedra, Pedro M. *Invención, difusión y recepción de la literatura popular impresa (siglo XVI)*. Mérida: Regional de Extremadura, 2002. Print.

Cátedra, Pedro M., and Anastasio Rojo. *Bibliotecas y lecturas de mujeres (siglo XVI)*. Salamanca: Instituto de Historia del Libro y de la Lectura, 2004. Print.

Cejador y Frauca, Julio. *La lengua de Cervantes*. 1905–06. Ed. and rev. Delfín Carbonell Basset and James A. Parr. Barcelona: El Serbal, 2011. Print.

Cervantes Saavedra, Miguel de. *The Adventures of Don Quixote*. 1950. Trans. J. M. Cohen. Harmondsworth: Penguin, 1950. Print.

———. *Don Quijote*. Ed. Tom Lathrop. Illus. Jack Davis. Newark: European Masterpieces, 2012. Print.

———. *Don Quijote*. 1995. Trans. Burton Raffel. New York: Norton, 1999. Print.

———. *Don Quijote de la Mancha*. Ed. Francisco Rico. Barcelona: Crítica, 2001. Print.

———. *Don Quijote de la Mancha*. Ed. Francisco Rico. 4th centenary ed. Real Academia Española. Madrid: Alfaguara, 2004. Print.

———. *Don Quijote de la Mancha*. Ed. Florencio Sevilla Arroyo. Madrid: Bolchiro, 2012. EPUB 3 file.

———. *Don Quixote*. Trans. Edith Grossman. Introd. Harold Bloom. New York: Harper, 2003; London: Vintage, 2005. Print.

———. *Don Quixote*. 1742. Trans. Charles Jarvis. 2 vols. London: Oxford UP, 1907. Print.

———. *Don Quixote*. Trans. Charles Jarvis. Ed. E. C. Riley. Oxford: Oxford UP, 1992. Print.

———. *Don Quixote*. Trans. Tom Lathrop. Illus. Jack Davis. New York: Signet, 2011. Print.

———. *Don Quixote*. Trans. James H. Montgomery. Indianapolis: Hackett, 2009. Print.

———. *Don Quixote*. Trans. Samuel Putnam. New York: Viking, 1949. Print.

———. *Don Quixote*. Trans. John Rutherford. New York: Penguin, 2001. Print.

———. *Don Quixote of la Mancha*. Trans. Walter Starkie. New York: New Amer. Lib., 1964. Print.

———. *La Galatea*. Ed. Francisco López Estrada and María Teresa López García-Berdoy. Madrid: Cátedra, 1995. Print.

———. *The History and Adventures of the Renowned Don Quixote*. 1755. Trans. Tobias Smollett. New York: Modern Lib., 2001. Print.

———. *The History of Don Quixote of the Mancha*. 1612. Trans. Thomas Shelton. 2 vols. London: Navarre Soc., 1923. Print.

———. *The History of the Most Renowned Don Quixote of Mancha: And His Trusty Squire Sancho Pancha*. 1687. Trans. John Philips. London: Thomas Hodgkin, 1687. Print.

———. *El ingenioso hidalgo don Quijote de la Mancha*. Ed. John Jay Allen. 2 vols. 28th ed. Madrid: Cátedra, 2009. Print.

———. *El ingenioso hidalgo don Quijote de la Mancha*. Ed. Salvador J. Fajardo and James A. Parr. 3rd ed. 2 vols. Asheville: Pegasus; U of North Carolina, Asheville, 2009. Print.

———. *El ingenioso hidalgo don Quijote de la Mancha*. Ed. Tom Lathrop. 2 vols. 1997. 4th centenary ed. Newark: Juan de la Cuesta, 2005. Print.

———. *El ingenioso hidalgo don Quijote de la Mancha*. Ed. Luis Andrés Murillo. 5th ed. 2 vols. Madrid: Castalia, 1987. Print.

———. *El ingenioso hidalgo don Quijote de la Mancha*. Ed. Francisco Rico. Madrid: Real Academia Española, 2005. Print.

———. *El ingenioso hidalgo don Quijote de la Mancha*. Ed. Francisco Rodríguez Marín. 7 vols. Madrid: Revista de Archivos, Bibliotecas y Museos, 1927–28. Print.

———. *El ingenioso hidalgo don Quijote de la Mancha*. Ed. Florencio Sevilla Arroyo and Antonio Rey Hazas. Rev. ed. Alcalá de Henares: Centro de Estudios Cervantinos, 1994. Print.

———. *The Ingenious Gentleman Don Quixote de la Mancha*. 1885. Trans. John Ormsby. Rev. Kenneth Douglas and Joseph R. Jones. New York: Norton, 1981. Print.

———. *The Ingenious Gentleman Don Quixote de la Mancha*. 1949. Trans. Samuel Putnam. New York: Viking, 1949. Print.

———. *The Ingenious Gentleman Don Quixote of la Mancha*. 1888. Trans. Henry Edward Watts. 4 vols. London: A. and C. Black, 1895. Print.

———. *The Ingenious Knight, Don Quixote de la Mancha*. 1881. Trans. Alexander James Duffield. 3 vols. London: Kegan Paul, 1881. Print.

———. *The Life and Achievements of the Renowned Don Quixote de la Mancha*. 1700–12. Trans. Peter Motteux. 2 vols. London: Dent; New York: Dutton, 1906. Print.

———. *Novelas ejemplares*. Ed. Harry Sieber. 2 vols. Madrid: Cátedra, 1986. Print.

———. *Los trabajos de Persiles y Sigismunda*. Ed. Carlos Romero Muñoz. Madrid: Cátedra, 1997.

———. *The Trials of Persiles and Sigismunda*. Trans. Celia Richmond Weller and Clark A. Colahan. Berkeley: U of California P, 1989. Print.

Chambers, Leland. "Irony in the Final Chapter of the *Quijote*." *Romanic Review* 61 (1970): 14–22. Print.

Chartier, Roger. Introduction. *The Culture of Print: Power and the Uses of Print in Early Modern Europe*. Trans. Lydia G. Cochrane. Ed. Alain Boureau and Chartier. Princeton: Princeton UP, 1989. 1–9. Print.

Chevalier, Maxime. *Lectura y lectores en la España de los siglos XVI y XVII*. Madrid: Turner, 1976. Print.

Childers, William. "Baroque Quixote: New World Writing and the Collapse of the Heroic Ideal." *Baroque New Worlds: Representation, Transculturation, Counterconquest*. Ed. Lois Parkinson Zamora and Monika Kaup. Durham: Duke UP, 2010. 415–49. Print.

———. "*Don Quijote* en la literatura chicana y 'latina' en Estados Unidos." *La gran enciclopedia cervantina*. Vol. 10. Madrid: Castalia, forthcoming.

———. *Transnational Cervantes*. Toronto: U Toronto P, 2006. Print.

Chrisafis, Angelique. "*Don Quixote* Is the World's Best Book Say the World's Top Authors." *Guardian*. Guardian News, 8 May 2002. Web. 15 June 2014. <http://www.theguardian.com/world/2002/may/08/humanities.books>.

Church, Margaret. *Structure and Theme:* Don Quixote *to James Joyce.* Columbus: Ohio State UP, 1983. Print.

Ciallella, Louise. "Teresa Panza's Character Zone and Discourse of Domesticity in *Don Quijote.*" *Cervantes* 23.2 (2003): 275–96. Print.

Clark, Herbert H. *Using Language.* Cambridge: Cambridge UP, 1996. Print.

Close, Anthony. *A Companion to* Don Quixote. Woodbridge: Tamesis, 2008. Print.

———. *The Romantic Approach to* Don Quixote*: A Critical History of the Romantic Tradition in Quixote Criticism.* Cambridge: Cambridge UP, 1978. Print.

Cohen, J. M. *English Translators and Translations.* London: Longmans, 1962. Print.

Colahan, Clark. "Shelton and the Farcical Perception of *Don Quixote* in Seventeenth-Century Britain." Ardila, *Cervantean Heritage* 61–65.

Colbert Roasts Bush. YouTube. YouTube, 26 Aug. 2007. Web. 15 June 2014. <http://www.youtube.com/watch?v=BSE_saVX_2A>.

Compitello, Malcolm Alan. "Cultural Studies and the Undergraduate Curriculum in Spanish." *ADFL Bulletin* 40.1 (2008): 30–36. Print.

Correa-Díaz, Luis. *Cervantes y América, Cervantes en las Américas: Mapa de campo y ensayo de bibliografía razonada.* Kassel: Reichenberger, 2006. Print.

Covarrubias, Sebastian de. *Tesoro de la lengua castellana o española.* Ed. Martín de Riquer. 1943. Madrid: Turner, 1984. Print.

Cruz, Anne J. "Cervantes and His Feminist Alliances." Cruz and Johnson 134–50.

———. *Discourses of Poverty: Social Reform and the Picaresque Novel in Early Modern Spain.* Toronto: U of Toronto P, 1999. Print.

Cruz, Anne J., and Rosilie Hernández, eds. *Women's Literacy in Early Modern Spain and the New World.* Burlington: Ashgate, 2011. Print.

Cruz, Anne J., and Carroll B. Johnson, eds. *Cervantes and His Postmodern Constituencies.* New York: Garland, 1999. Print. Hispanic Issues, Garland Reference Lib. of the Humanities 17.

Damasio, Antonio, and Hanna Damasio. "Minding the Body." *Daedalus* 135.3 (2006): 15–22. Print.

de Armas, Frederick A. *Cervantes, Raphael and the Classics.* Cambridge: Cambridge UP, 1998. Print.

———. *Don Quixote among the Saracens.* Toronto: U of Toronto P, 2012. Print.

———, ed. *Ekphrasis in the Age of Cervantes.* Lewisburg: Bucknell UP, 2005. Print.

———. *Quixotic Frescoes: Cervantes and Italian Renaissance Art.* Toronto: U of Toronto P, 2006. Print.

———. "Simple Magic: Ekphrasis from Antiquity to the Age of Cervantes." de Armas, *Ekphrasis* 13–31.

———, ed. *Writing for the Eyes in the Spanish Golden Age.* Lewisburg: Bucknell UP, 2004. Print.

Defourneaux, Marcelin. *Daily Life in Spain in the Golden Age.* London: Allen, 1970. Print.

Degli-Esposti, Cristina, ed. *Postmodernism and the Cinema.* New York: Berghahn, 1998. Print.

Degrees Conferred by Sex and Race. Fast Facts. Natl. Center for Educ. Statistics, n.d. Web. 15 June 2014. <http://nces.ed.gov/FastFacts/display.asp?id=72>.

Dennett, Daniel C. "The Intentional Stance in Theory and Practice." *Machiavellian Intelligence: Social Expertise and the Evolution of Intellect in Monkeys, Apes, and Humans.* Ed. Richard W. Byrne and Andrew Whiten. Oxford: Clarendon, 1988. 180–202. Print.

Derrida, Jacques. *La vérité en peinture.* Paris: Flammarion, 1978. Print.

———. *Writing and Difference.* Trans. Alan Bass. Chicago: U of Chicago P, 1978. Print.

D'haen, Theo. "Don Quixote on the Mississippi: Twain's Modernities." D'haen and Dhondt 237–50.

D'haen, Theo, and Reindert Dhondt, eds. *International Don Quixote.* Amsterdam: Rodopi, 2009. Print.

Díaz, Junot. *The Brief Wondrous Life of Oscar Wao.* New York: Riverhead, 2007. Print.

Díaz-Plaja, Fernando. *Cervantes (la desdichada vida de un triunfador).* Barcelona: Edisven, 1969. Print.

Diccionario de autoridades. 1726–37. Facsim. ed. 3 vols. Madrid: Gredos, 1963–69. Print.

Domínguez Ortiz, Antonio. *La sociedad española en el siglo XVII.* Madrid: Consejo Superior de Investigaciones Científicas, 1963. Print.

Donnell, Sidney. "Through the Looking Glass: Reflections on the Baroque in Luis Buñuel's *The Criminal Life of Archibaldo de la Cruz.*" *Echoes and Inscriptions: Comparative Approaches to Early Modern Spanish Literatures.* Ed. Barbara Simerka and Christopher Weimer. Lewisburg: Bucknell UP, 2000. 74–97. Print.

Don Quixote. Dir. Orson Welles. El Silencio Producciones, 1992. Film.

Don Quixote. Dir. Peter Yates. TNT, 2000. Television.

"Don Quixote de la Mancha." *The Millennium.* Spec. double issue of *Life* fall 1997: 21. Print. Item 96.

"*Don Quixote* Gets Authors' Votes." *BBC News.* BBC, 7 May 2002. Web. 15 June 2014. <http://news.bbc.co.uk/2/hi/entertainment/1972609.stm>.

Doré, Gustave. *Don Quichotte.* Paris: SACELP, 1983. Print.

Dorn, Georgette Magassy, ed. *Works by Miguel de Cervantes Saavedra in the Library of Congress.* Washington: Lib. of Congress, 1994. Print.

Dudley, Edward. *The Endless Text:* Don Quijote *and the Hermeneutics of Romance.* Albany: State U of New York P, 1997. Print.

Dunbar, Robin. *Grooming, Gossip, and the Evolution of Language.* Cambridge: Harvard UP, 1996. Print.

———. *The Human Story: A New History of Mankind's Evolution.* London: Faber, 2004. Print.

Durán, Manuel. *Cervantes.* Boston: Twayne, 1974. Print.

Eagleton, Terry. *Walter Benjamin; or, Towards a Revolutionary Criticism.* London: Verso, 1981. Print.

Edwards, John. *Ferdinand and Isabella.* New York: Pearson, 2004. Print.

———. *The Spain of the Catholic Monarchs, 1474–1520.* Malden: Blackwell, 2000. Print.

Egginton, William. *The Theater of Truth: The Ideology of (Neo)Baroque Aesthetics.* Stanford: Stanford UP, 2010. Print.

Egido, Aurora. *Cervantes y las puertas del sueño: Estudios sobre la* Galatea, *el* Quijote *y el* Persiles. Barcelona: Promociones y Publicaciones Universitarias, 1994. Print.

———, ed. *Los rostros de Don Quijote: IV Centenario de la publicación de su primera parte.* Zaragoza: Ibercaja, Obra Social y Cultural, 2004. Print.

Eisenberg, Daniel. *Romances of Chivalry in the Spanish Golden Age.* Newark: Juan de la Cuesta, 1982. Print.

———. "The Text of *Don Quixote* As Seen by Its Modern English Translators." *Cervantes* 26.1-2 (2006): 103–26. Print.

Elliott, J. H. *Imperial Spain, 1469–1716.* New York: St. Martin's, 1963. Print.

El Saffar, Ruth. *Beyond Fiction: The Recovery of the Feminine in the Novels of Cervantes.* Berkeley: U of California P, 1984. Print.

———. *Distance and Control in* Don Quixote: *A Study in Narrative Technique.* Chapel Hill: U of North Carolina Studies in Romance Langs. and Lits., 1975. Print.

El Saffar, Ruth, and Diana de Armas Wilson, eds. *Quixotic Desire: Psychoanalytic Perspectives on Cervantes.* Ithaca: Cornell UP, 1993. Print.

Engels, William E. *Mapping Mortality: The Persistence of Memory and Melancholy in Early Modern England.* Amherst: U of Massachusetts P, 1995. Print.

Erlanger, Steve. "Fox News Journalists Free after Declaring Conversion on Tape." *New York Times* 28 Aug. 2006, late ed.: A3. Print.

"España dona cientos de ejemplares de *El Quijote* a Cuba." Europa Press, 22 Mar. 2005. Web. 7 Apr. 7 2014. <http://www.cubanet.org/CNews/y05/mar05/23o2.htm>.

"Especialistas de distintas áreas destacan la actualidad y universalidad del *Quijote.*" *El mundo* [Madrid] 6 Apr. 2005, Campus: 5. Print.

Excluded and Invisible: The State of the World's Children, 2006. New York: UNICEF, 2005. Print.

Exilados do Mundão. Projeto Quixote with support from Daniel Rubio, Instituto Imagem Viva, and TV UNIFESP, 2006. Film.

Fernández Álvarez, Manuel. *Cervantes visto por un historiador.* Madrid: Espasa, 2005. Print.

———. *La sociedad española en la época del Renacimiento.* Madrid: Cátedra, 1974. Print.

Fernández-Morera, Darío, and Michael Hanke, eds. *Cervantes in the English-Speaking World: New Essays.* Barcelona: Reichenberger, 2005. Print.

Feros, Antonio. *Kingship and Favoritism in the Spain of Philip III, 1598–1621.* New York: Cambridge UP, 2000. Print.

Filiciak, Miroslaw. "Hyperidentities, Postmodern Identity Patterns in Massively Multiplayer Online Role Playing Games." *The Video Game Theory Reader.* Ed. Mark J. P. Wolf and Bernard Perron. London: Routledge, 2003. 87–102. Print.

Fine, Gary Alan. *Shared Fantasy: Role Playing Games as Social Worlds.* Chicago: U of Chicago P, 1983. Print.

Fine, Ruth. *Una lectura semiótico-narratológica del* Quijote *en el contexto del siglo de oro español*. Madrid: Iberoamericana; Frankfurt: Vervuert, 2006. Print.

Finello, Dominick. *The Evolution of the Pastoral Novel in Early Modern Spain*. Tempe: Arizona Center for Medieval and Renaissance Studies, 2008. Print.

Fish, Stanley. "Rhetoric." *Critical Terms for Literary Study*. Ed. Frank Lentricchia and Thomas McLaughlin. Chicago: U of Chicago P, 1990. 203–22. Print.

Flood, Kristine. "The Theatre Connection." *Role, Play, Art: Collected Experiences of Role Playing*. Ed. Thorbiörn Fritzon and Tobias Wrigstad. Stockholm: Föreningen Knutpunkt, 2006. 35–42. Print.

Flores, R. M. "*Don Quixote* as a Genre of Genres." *Romance Quarterly* 40.4 (1993): 211–25. Print.

Foremski, Tom. "How the Secret Identity of LonelyGirl15 Was Found." *Silicon Valley Watcher*. Foremski, 12 Sept. 2006. Web. 12 June 2014. <http://www.silicon valleywatcher.com/mt/archives/2006/09/how_the_secret.php>.

Foucault, Michel. *Histoire de la folie à l'âge classique*. Paris: Gallimard, 1972. Print.

———. *The Order of Things: An Archaeology of the Human Sciences*. New York: Vintage, 1994. Print. Trans. of *Les mots et les choses*.

———. "Representing." Foucault, *Order* 46–77.

France, Peter, and Kenneth Haynes, eds. *The Oxford History of Literary Translation in English: Volume 4: 1790–1900*. Oxford: Oxford UP, 2006. Print.

"Free *Quixote*s Big Pull in Caracas." *BBC News*. BBC, 24 Mar. 2005. Web. 15 June 2014. <http://news.bbc.co.uk/go/pr/fr/-/2/hi/americas/4478007.stm>.

Friedman, Edward H. *Cervantes in the Middle: Realism and Reality in the Spanish Novel from* Lazarillo de Tormes *to* Niebla. Newark: Juan de la Cuesta Hispanic Monographs, 2006. Print.

———. "*Don Quixote* and the Act of Reading: A Multiperspectivist Approach." Bjornson 87–95.

Frith, Uta. *Autism: Explaining the Enigma*. Oxford: Blackwell, 1989. Print.

Fuchs, Barbara. *Exotic Nation: Maurophilia and the Construction of Early Modern Spain*. Philadelphia: U of Pennsylvania P, 2009. Print.

———. *Passing for Spain: Cervantes and the Fictions of Identity*. Urbana: U of Illinois P, 2003. Print.

Fuentes, Carlos. *Aura*. Trans. Lysander Kemp. Bilingual ed. New York: Farrar, 1980. Print.

Fuertes, Gloria. "Sale caro ser poeta." *Poesías incompletas*. Ed. Fuertes. 3rd ed. Madrid: Cátedra, 1977. 168–69. Print.

Garcés, María Antonia. *Cervantes in Algiers: A Captive's Tale*. Nashville: Vanderbilt UP, 2002. Print.

García, Juan José. "Visión metadramática del *Quijote*." *Cervantes, su obra y su mundo: Actas del I Congreso Internacional sobre Cervantes*. Ed. Manuel Criado de Val. Madrid: EDI-6, 1981. 509–13. Print.

García de la Rasilla, Carmen. "El *Quijote* surrealista de Salvador Dalí." *Anuario de estudios cervantinos* 2 (2005): 149–63. Print.

Genette, Gérard. *Narrative Discourse: An Essay in Method*. Trans. Jane E. Lewin. Ithaca: Cornell UP, 1980. Print.

Gerli, E. Michael. *Refiguring Authority: Reading, Writing, and Rewriting in Cervantes*. Lexington: UP of Kentucky, 1995. Print. Studies in Romance Langs. 39.

Gerrig, Richard J. *Experiencing Narrative Worlds: On the Psychological Activities of Reading*. New Haven: Yale UP, 1993. Print.

Gilman, Stephen. *The Novel according to Cervantes*. Berkeley: U of California P, 1989. Print.

———. *The Spain of Fernando de Rojas: The Intellectual and Social Landscape of* La Celestina. Princeton: Princeton UP, 1972. Print.

Giménez Caballero, Ernesto. *Genio de España: Exaltaciones a una resurrección nacional y del mundo*. Madrid: Gaceta Literaria, 1932. Print.

Ginés, Monserrat. *The Southern Inheritors of* Don Quixote. Baton Rouge: Louisiana State UP, 2000. Print.

Givanel Mas y Gaziel, Juan. *Historia gráfica de Cervantes y del* Quijote. Madrid: Plus Ultra, 1946. Print.

Goldman, Alvin I. *Simulating Minds: The Philosophy, Psychology, and Neuroscience of Mindreading*. Oxford: Oxford UP, 2006. Print.

Gómez Canseco, Luis. *El* Quijote, *de Miguel de Cervantes*. Madrid: Síntesis, 2005. Print.

González Echevarría, Roberto. "Cervantes and the Modern Latin American Narrative." *Ciberletras* 1 (1999): n. pag. Web. 15 June 2014. <http://www.lehman.cuny.edu/ciberletras/v1n1/crit_07.htm>.

———, ed. *Cervantes'* Don Quixote: *A Casebook*. Oxford: Oxford UP, 2005. Print.

———. "*Don Quijote*: Visión y Mirada." *En un lugar de la Mancha: Estudios cervantinos en honor de Manuel Durán*. Ed. José Luis de Celis. Salamanca: Almar, 1999. 109–22. Print.

———. *Love and the Law in Cervantes*. New Haven: Yale UP, 2005. Print.

González Palencia, Ángel. "Cervantes y los moriscos." *Boletín de la Real Academia Española* 27 (1947): 107–22. Print.

Gopnik, Alison, and Andrew N. Meltzoff. *Words, Thoughts, and Theories*. Cambridge: MIT P, 1997. Print.

Graf, Eric C. *Cervantes and Modernity: Four Essays on* Don Quijote. Lewisburg: Bucknell UP, 2007. Print.

———. "The Pomegranate of Don Quixote I.9." de Armas, *Writing* 42–62.

———. "When an Arab Laughs in Toledo: Cervantes's Interpellation of Early Modern Spanish Orientalism." *Diacritics* 29.2 (1999): 68–85. *Project Muse*. Web. 15 June 2014.

Greenblatt, Stephen. *Renaissance Self-Fashioning: From More to Shakespeare*. Chicago: U of Chicago P, 1980. Print.

Greene, Thomas M. *The Light in Troy: Imitation and Discovery in Renaissance Poetry*. New Haven: Yale UP, 1982. Print.

Greer, Margaret R. "Calderón de la Barca: Playwright at Court." *The Cambridge Companion to Velázquez*. Ed. Suzanne L. Stratton-Pruitt. Cambridge: Cambridge UP, 2002. 149–69. Print.

Gregory, Tobias. "Mad for Love." Rev. of Orlando Furioso: *A New Verse Translation*. *London Review of Books* 9 Sept. 2010: 23–24. Print.

Grossman, Edith. "Translator's Note to the Reader." Cervantes, *Don Quixote* [Grossman] xvii–xx.

———. *Why Translation Matters*. New Haven: Yale UP, 2010. Print.

Güntert, Georges. *Cervantes: Narrador de un mundo desintegrado*. Vigo: Academia del Hispanismo, 2007. Print.

Gwynn, Frederick L., and Joseph L. Blotner, eds. *Faulkner in the University: Class Conferences at the University of Virginia, 1957–1958*. Charlottesville: U of Virginia P, 1959. Print.

Haddon, Mark. *The Curious Incident of the Dog in the Night-time*. New York: Vintage, 2003. Print.

Haley, George. "The Narrator in *Don Quixote*: A Discarded Voice." *Estudios en honor a Ricardo Gullón*. Ed. Luis González del Valle and Darío Villanueva. Lincoln: SSSAS, 1984. 173–85. Print.

Hammack, Laurence. "Rodeo in Salem Gets Unexpected Song Rendition." *Roanoke Times*. Roanoke Times, 9 Jan. 2005. Web. 15 June 2014. <http://ww2.roanoke.com//news/roanoke/16655.html>.

Hart, Thomas R. Rev. of *The Adventures of Don Quixote de la Mancha*, by Miguel de Cervantes, trans. Tobias Smollett. *Cervantes* 8.1 (1988): 118–22. Print.

Hartt, Frederick. *Giulio Romano*. 2 vols. New Haven: Yale UP, 1958. Print.

Harvey, L. P. "The *Moro Aljamiado* Consulted by Cervantes in Toledo (*Don Quixote* I: 9)." *"Aquí se imprimen libros": Cervantine Studies in Honor of Tom Lathrop*. Ed. Mark Groundland. University: Dept. of Modern Langs., U of Mississippi, 2008. 62–71. Print. Romance Monographs.

———. *Muslims in Spain, 1500–1614*. Chicago: U of Chicago P, 2005. Print.

Hegyi, Ottmar. *Cervantes and the Turks: Historical Reality versus Literary Fiction in* La Gran Sultana *and* El amante liberal. Newark: Juan de la Cuesta, 1992. Print.

Heliö, Satu. "Role-Playing: A Narrative Experience and a Mindset." Montola and Stenros 65–74.

Hermosilla, Antonio. "Lecturas fílmicas del *Quijote*." Diss. U of Southern California, 1991. Print.

Hernández Herrero, Juan. *Léxico español para lectores de* Don Quijote de la Mancha. Barcelona: Carena, 2010. Print.

Herrero García, M. "Los rasgos físicos y el carácter según los textos españoles del siglo XVII." *Revista de filología española* 12 (1925): 157–77. Print.

Hitchcock, Richard. "Cervantes, Ricote, and the Expulsion of the *Moriscos*." *Bulletin of Spanish Studies* 81 (2004): 175–85. Print.

———. "Spanish Literature." *The Oxford History of Literary Translation in English: Volume 3, 1669–1790*. Oxford: Oxford UP, 2005. 406–15. Print.

Homer. *The Iliad of Homer*. Trans. Richard Lattimore. Chicago: U of Chicago P, 1961. Print.

Hopkins, David. "Motteux, Peter Anthony." *Oxford Dictionary of National Biography*. Oxford UP, n.d. Web. 15 June 2014. <http://www.oxforddnb.com>.

Horace. *Ars Poetica*. Satires, Epistles, *and* Ars Poetica. Cambridge: Harvard UP, 1929. 343–44. Print.

Huizinga, Johan. *The Autumn of the Middle Ages*. Trans. Rodney J. Payton and Ulrich Mammitzsch. Chicago: U of Chicago P, 1996. Print.

———. *Homo Ludens: A Study of Play Element in Culture*. 1938. London: Taylor, 1998. Print.

Huot, Sylvia. *From Song to Book: The Poetics of Writing in Old French Lyric and Lyrical Narrative Poetry*. Ithaca: Cornell UP, 1987. Print.

Hutcheon, Linda. *The Poetics of Postmodernism*. New York: Routledge, 1988. Print.

———. *A Theory of Parody: The Teachings of Twentieth-Century Art Forms*. New York: Methuen, 1985. Print.

Hutchinson, Steven. *Cervantine Journeys*. Madison: U of Wisconsin P, 1992. Print.

———. *Economía ética en Cervantes*. Alcalá de Henares: Centro de Estudios Cervantinos, 2001. Print.

Iacoboni, Marco. *Mirroring People: The New Science of How We Connect with Others*. New York: Farrar, 2008. Print.

Ife, B. W. *Reading and Fiction in Golden-Age Spain: A Platonist Critique and Some Picaresque Replies*. Cambridge: Cambridge UP, 1985. Print.

Iffland, James. "*Don Quijote* and the Dissident Intellectual: Some Thoughts on Subcomandante Marcos's *Don Durito de la Lacandona*." *Studies in Honor of James O. Crosby*. Ed. Lía Schwartz. Newark: Juan de la Cuesta, 2004. 161–79. Print.

Ignatius of Loyola. "Reminiscences." *Personal Writings*. Trans. Joseph A. Munitiz and Philip Endean. London: Penguin, 1996. 1–64. Print.

Illades, Gustavo, and James Iffland, eds. *El* Quijote *desde América*. Puebla: Benemérita U Autónoma de Puebla; El Colegio de México, 2006. Print.

Irving, Washington. *The Legend of Sleepy Hollow. Project Gutenberg*. N.p., 15 Apr. 2003. Web. 6 Mar. 2014.

Jakobson, Roman. "Closing Statement: Linguistics and Poetics." *Style and Language*. Ed. Thomas Sebeok. *Cambridge*: MIT P, 1960. 183–93. Print.

Jaksic, Iván. "Don Quijote's Encounter with Technology." *Cervantes* 14.1 (1994): 75–96. Print.

Jameson, Fredric. *Postmodernism; or, The Cultural Logic of Late Capitalism*. Durham: Duke UP, 1991. Print.

Jardine, Lisa. *Worldly Goods: A New History of the Renaissance*. New York: Talese, 1996. Print.

Jauralde Pou, Pablo, Delia Gavela, and Alique P. C. Rojo. *Diccionario filológico de literatura española: Siglo XVI*. Madrid: Castalia, 2009. Print.

———. *Diccionario filológico de literatura española: Siglo XVII*. Madrid: Castalia, 2010. Print.

Jehenson, Yvonne. "The Pastoral Episode in Cervantes' *Don Quijote*: Marcela Once Again." *Cervantes* 10.2 (1990): 15–35. *H-Cervantes*. Web. 13 Dec. 2013.

Johnson, Carroll B. *Cervantes and the Material World*. Urbana: U of Illinois P, 2000. Print. Hispanisms.

———. Don Quixote: *The Quest for Modern Fiction*. Prospect Heights: Waveland, 2000. Print.

————. *Madness and Lust: A Psychoanalytical Approach to* Don Quixote. Berkeley: U of California P, 1983. Print.

————. "Phantom Pre-texts and Fictional Authors: Sidi Hamid Benengeli, *Don Quijote*, and the Metafictional Conventions of Chivalric Romances." *Cervantes* 27.1 (2007): 179–99. Print.

————. "Psychoanalysis and *Don Quixote*." Bjornson 104–12.

————. "The Virtual *Don Quixote*: Cide Hamete Benengeli's Manuscript and *Aljamiado* Literature." Simerka and Williamsen 172–88.

Joly, Monique. "D'Alberto Naseli, di Ganasse, au comte de Benavente: Deux notes cervantines." *Bulletin hispanique* 78 (1976): 240–53. Print.

Jones, Ann Rosalind, and Peter Stallybrass. *Renaissance Clothing and the Materials of Memory*. Cambridge: Cambridge UP, 2000. Print.

Kamen, Henry. *Empire: How Spain Became a World Power, 1492–1763*. New York: Harper, 2003. Print.

————. *The Spanish Inquisition: A Historical Revision*. New Haven: Yale UP, 1998. Print.

Keen, Suzanne. *Empathy and the Novel*. Oxford: Oxford UP, 2007. Print.

Kennedy, John F. *"Let the Word Go Forth": The Speeches, Statements, and Writings of John F. Kennedy, 1947–1963*. Ed. Theodore C. Sorensen. New York: Delacorte, 1988. Print.

Knotek, Ed. "*Don Quixote* and the Modern Undergraduate Student: Making Cervantes More Accessible to the American Reader." *Cervantes* 20.1 (2000): 175–78. Print.

Kortázar, Jon. "La recepción del *Quijote* en el País Vasco." *Cuadernos de Alzate* 33 (2005): 53–64. Print.

Kramsch, Claire. *Language and Culture*. Oxford: Oxford UP, 1998. Print. Oxford Introds. to Lang. Study.

Kuhn, Thomas. *The Structure of Scientific Revolutions*. 2nd ed. Chicago: U of Chicago P, 1970. Print.

Lacan, Jacques. *Four Fundamental Concepts of Psycho-analysis*. Ed. Jacques-Alain Miller. Trans. Alan Sheridan. New York: Norton, 1978. Print.

————. *The Seminar of Jacques Lacan, Book XVII: The Other Side of Psychoanalysis*. Ed. Jacques-Alain Miller. Trans. Russell Grigg. New York: Norton, 2007. Print.

Laguna, Ana María G. *Cervantes and the Pictorial Imagination: A Study on the Power of Images and Images of Power in Works by Cervantes*. Lewisburg: Bucknell UP, 2009. Print.

Langle de Paz, Teresa. "La voz (in)divisible: Dulcinea y el feminismo en la primera parte del *Quijote*." Rubio 233–55.

LaRubia Prado, Francisco. "*Don Quijote* as Performance: The Sierra Morena Adventure." *Revista canadiense de estudios hispánicos* 33.2 (2009): 335–56. Print.

Lathrop, Thomas A. "Contradictions in the *Quijote* Explained." *Jewish Culture and the Hispanic World: Essays in Memory of Joseph H. Silverman*. Ed. Samuel G. Armistead and Mishael M. Caspi. Newark: Juan de la Cuesta, 2001. 297–301. Print.

————. Don Quijote *Dictionary*. Cervantes Project, Texas A&M U, n.d. Web. 15 June 2014. <http://cervantes.tamu.edu/V2/textos/diccionario/index.htm>.

————. "Edith Grossman's Translation of *Don Quixote*." *Cervantes* 26.1-2 (2006): 237–55. Print.

————. Rev. of *The Ingenious Hidalgo Don Quixote of La Mancha*, trans. Rutherford. *Cervantes* 22.2 (2002): 175–80. Print.

————. Introduction. *El ingenioso hidalgo don Quijote de la Mancha*. By Cervantes. Ed. Lathrop. 4th centenary, 1-vol. ed. Newark: Juan de la Cuesta, 2005. vii–xxxi. Print.

————. Introduction. Cervantes, *El ingenioso hidalgo* [Lathrop] 1: ix–xlviii.

Lehfeldt, Elizabeth A. *Religious Women in Golden Age Spain: The Permeable Cloister*. Burlington: Ashgate, 2005. Print. Women and Gender in the Early Modern World.

Lenaghan, Patrick. "A Primer in Illustration: Reading Pictures of *Don Quixote*." Urbina and Maestro 77–94.

Lescher, Auro Danny, and Graziela Bedoian, eds. *Conceitos e estratégias para o atendimento de crianças e jovens em situação de risco*. São Paulo: Projeto Quixote; Setor Ensino, 2007. Print.

López Baralt, Luce. "The Supreme Pen (*Al-Qalam al-A'lā*) of Cide Hamete Benengeli in *Don Quixote*." Trans. Marikay McCabe. *Journal of Medieval and Early Modern Studies* 30.3 (2000): 505–18. *Project Muse*. Web. 15 June 2014.

López Piñero, José María. *La introducción de la ciencia moderna a España*. Barcelona: Ariel, 1969. Print.

Lo Ré, Anthony. Introduction. *A Facsimile Edition of the First English Translations of Miguel de Cervantes Saavedra's* El Ingenioso Hidalgo Don Quixote de la Mancha *(1605–1615): Thomas Shelton, Part I, London, 1612; Leonard Digges, Part II, London, 1620*. Chapel Hill: U of North Carolina; CH Printing Services, 2002. Print.

Lost in La Mancha. Dir. Keith Fulton and Louis Pepe. Quixote Films, 2003. Film.

Luce, Henry R. "The American Century." *Life* 17 Feb. 1941: 61–65. Print.

Lucía Megías, José Manuel. *De los libros de caballerías manuscritos al* Quixote. Madrid: Sial, 2004. Print.

————. *Leer el Quijote en imágenes: Hacia una teoría de los modelos iconográficos*. Madrid: Calambur, 2006. Print.

Lukács, Georg. *The Theory of the Novel: A Historico-Philosophical Essay on the Forms of Great Epic Literature*. Trans. Anna Bostock. Cambridge: MIT P, 1971. Print.

Lynch, John. *Spain under the Habsburgs: Volume 1: Empire and Absolutism, 1516–1598*. New York: New York UP, 1984. Print.

Mackay, Daniel. *The Fantasy Role-Playing Game: A New Performing Art*. Jefferson: McFarland, 2001. Print.

Madariaga, Salvador de. Don Quixote: *An Introductory Essay in Psychology*. Trans. Constance H. M. de Madariaga and Salvador de Madariaga. Newtown: Gregynog, 1934. Print. Trans. of *Guía del lector del* Quijote. 1926.

Mallén, Enrique. "*Don Quichotte* vu par Pablo Picasso: Visual Syntax in the Iconography of *Don Quixote*." Urbina and Maestro 135–51.

Mancing, Howard. "Cervantes as Narrator of *Don Quijote*." *Cervantes* 23.1 (2003): 117–40. Print.

———, ed. *The Cervantes Encyclopedia*. 2 vols. Westport: Greenwood, 2004. Print.

———, ed. *Cervantes's* Don Quixote: *A Reference Guide*. Westport: Greenwood, 2006. Print.

———. *The Chivalric World of Don Quixote: Style, Structure, and Narrative Technique*. Columbia: U of Missouri P, 1982. Print.

———. "James Parr's Theory of Mind." Simerka and Williamsen, *Critical Reflections* 125–43.

———. "Sancho Panza's Theory of Mind." *Theory of Mind and Literature*. Ed. Paula Leverage, Mancing, Richard Schweickert, and Jennifer Marston William. West Lafayette: Purdue UP, 2011. 123–32. Print.

Maravall, José Antonio. *Culture of the Baroque: Analysis of a Historical Structure*. Trans. Terry Cochran. Minneapolis: U of Minnesota P, 1986. Print.

———. *Utopía y contrautopía en el* Quijote. Santiago de Compostela: Pico Sacro, 1976. Print.

Marchese, David. "What's Real in *Borat*?" *Salon*. Salon Media Group, 10 Nov. 2006. Web. 15 June 2014. <http://www.salon.com/2006/11/10/guide_to_borat/>.

Mariscal, George. *Contradictory Subjects: Quevedo, Cervantes, and Seventeenth-Century Spanish Culture*. Ithaca: Cornell UP, 1991. Print.

Marklein, Mary Beth. "College Gender Gap Remains Stable: 57% Women." *USA Today*. USA Today, 26 Jan. 2010. Web. 15 June 2014. <http://www.usatoday .com/news/education/2010-01-26-genderequity26_ST_N.htm>.

Márquez Villanueva, Francisco. *Fuentes literarias cervantinas*. Madrid: Gredos, 1973. Print.

———. *Moros, Moriscos y Turcos de Cervantes: Ensayos críticos*. Barcelona: Bellaterra, 2010. Print.

———. *Personajes y temas del* Quijote. Madrid: Taurus, 1975. Print.

———. "El problema historiográfico de los moriscos." *Bulletin Hispanique* 86.1–2 (1984): 61–135. Print.

Martín, Adrienne Laskier. *An Erotic Philology of Golden Age Spain*. Nashville: Vanderbilt UP, 2008. Print.

———. "Maritornes y la prostitución rural." *El* Quijote *desde América*. Ed. Gustavo Illades and James Iffland. Puebla: Benemérita U Autónoma de Puebla; El Colegio de México, 2006. 219–33. Print.

Martínez Bonati, Félix. Don Quixote *and the Poetics of the Novel*. Trans. Dian Fox. Ithaca: Cornell UP, 1992. Print.

Martínez de Bujanda, J. "Índices de libros prohibidos del siglo XVI." Pérez Villanueva and Escandell Bonet 773–828.

Martínez Mata, Emilio. *Cervantes comenta el* Quijote. Madrid: Cátedra, 2008. Print.

Martín Morán, José Manuel. *Cervantes y el* Quijote: *Hacia la novela moderna*. Alcalá de Henares: Centro de Estudios Cervantinos, 2009. Print.

————. El Quijote *en ciernes: Los descuidos de Cervantes y las fases de elaboración textual*. Torino: dell'Orso, 1990. Print.

Mayo, Arantza, and J. A. G. Ardila. "The English Translations of Cervantes's Works across the Centuries." Ardila, *Cervantean Heritage* 54–60.

McCrory, Donald P. *No Ordinary Man: The Life and Times of Miguel de Cervantes*. London: Owen, 2002. Print.

McGonigal, Jane. *A Real Little Game: The Pinocchio Effect in Pervasive Play*. Digital Games Research Assn., 1–25 Nov. 2003. Web. 15 June 2014. <http://www.digra .org/dl/db/05097.11067.pdf>.

McGrath, Michael J. Rev. of *Don Quixote*, by Cervantes, trans. Tom Lathrop. *Cervantes* 28.1 (2008): 214–16. Print.

————. Rev. of *Don Quixote*, by Cervantes, trans. James H. Montgomery. *Cervantes* 30.1 (2010): 193–99. Print.

————. "The Modern Translations of *Don Quixote* in Britain." Ardila, *Cervantean Heritage* 76–83.

————. "Tilting at Windmills: *Don Quijote* in English." *Cervantes* 26.1-2 (2006): 7–39. Print.

McKeachie, Wilbert J., and Graham Gibbs. *McKeachie's Teaching Tips: Strategies, Research, and Theory for College and University Teachers*. 10th ed. Boston: Houghton, 1999. Print.

McKendrick, Melveena. *Cervantes*. Boston: Little, 1980. Print.

McMorran, Will. "From Quixote to Caractacus: Influence, Intertextuality, and *Chitty Chitty Bang Bang*." *Journal of Popular Culture* 39.5 (2006): 756–79. Web. 15 June 2014.

Melinda and Melinda. Dir. Woody Allen. Fox Searchlight Pictures, 2004. Film.

Menéndez Pidal, Ramón. *De Cervantes y Lope de Vega*. Buenos Aires: Espasa-Calpe Argentina, 1940. Print.

Menocal, María Rosa. *The Ornament of the World: How Muslims, Jews, and Christians Created a Culture of Tolerance in Medieval Spain*. Boston: Little, 2002. Print.

Michael, Ian. "How Don Quixote Came to Oxford: The Two Bodleian Copies of *Don Quixote*, Part I (Madrid: Juan de la Cuesta, 1605)." *Culture and Society in Habsburg Spain: Studies Presented to R. W. Truman by His Pupils and Colleagues on the Occasion of His Retirement*. Ed. Nigel Griffin et al. London: Tamesis, 2001. 95–123. Print.

Miller, Stephen. "Narrar el *Quijote* I en palabras e imágenes gráficas: Cervantes, Doré y Dalí." Urbina and Maestro 95–116.

Miñana, Rogelio. "Nación de quijotes: *Don Quijote* en el discurso político contemporáneo en España." Black and Ranz 895–924.

Molina, Tirso de. *El burlador de Sevilla y convidado de piedra*. Ed. James A. Parr. Binghamton: Medieval and Renaissance Texts and Studies, 1994. Print.

Montalvo, Garci Rodríguez de. *Amadís de Gaula*. Ed. Juan Manuel Cacho Blecua. 2 vols. Madrid: Cátedra, 2001. Print.

Montero Reguera, José. *Materiales del* Quijote: *La forja de un novelista*. Vigo: Servizo de Publicacións da U de Vigo, 2006. Print.

Montgomery, James H. "Translator's Preface." Cervantes, *Don Quixote* [Montgomery] xxxix–xlii.

Montola, Markus. "Exploring the Edge of the Magic Circle: Defining Pervasive Games." IPerG, 5 Nov. 2008. Web. 15 June 2014. <http://www.pervasive-gaming.org/Publications/Exploring-the-Edge-of-the-Magic-Circle.pdf>.

Montola, Markus, and Jaakko Stenros, eds. *Beyond Role and Play: Tools, Toys, and Theory for Harnessing the Imagination*. Helsinki: Ropecon, 2004. Print.

Morón Arroyo, Ciriaco. *Para entender el* Quijote. Madrid: Rialp, 2005. Print.

Morrison, Toni. *The Bluest Eye*. New York: Vintage, 2007. Print.

"Mouse of La Mancha." *Pinky and the Brain*. Warner Bros., 25 Feb. 1996. Television.

Mr. Smith Goes to Washington. Dir. Frank Capra. Perf. James Stewart, Claude Raines, Jean Arthur, Guy Kibbee, and Edward Arnold. Columbia Pictures, 1939. Film.

Muecke, D. C. *The Compass of Irony*. London: Methuen, 1969. Print.

Mullis, V. S., et al. *PIRLS 2006 International Report*. Boston: TIMSS [Trends in Intl. Mathematics and Science Study] and PIRLS [Progress in Intl. Reading Literacy Study] Intl. Study Center, 2007. Print.

Munday, Jeremy. *Introducing Translation Studies: Theories and Applications*. London: Routledge, 2001. Print.

Murray, Janet H. *Hamlet on the Holodeck: The Future of Narrative in Cyberspace*. New York: Free, 1997. Print.

Musarra-Schroeder, Ulla. "Cervantes in Paul Auster's New York Trilogy." D'haen and Dhondt 219–35.

Nadeau, Carolyn A. *Women of the Prologue: Imitation, Myth, and Magic in* Don Quixote *I*. Lewisburg: Bucknell UP, 2002. Print.

Ndalianis, Angela. *Neo-baroque Aesthetics and Contemporary Entertainment*. Cambridge: MIT P, 2004. Print.

Nevils, René Pol, and Deborah George Hardy. *Ignatius Rising: The Life of John Kennedy Toole*. Baton Rouge: Louisiana State UP, 2001. Print.

Núñez Seixas, Xosé-Manuel. "From National-Catholic Nostalgia to Constitutional Patriotism: Conservative Spanish Nationalism since the Early 1990s." *The Politics of Contemporary Spain*. Ed. Sebastian Balfour. London: Routledge, 2005. 121–45. Print.

Nurse Betty. Dir. Neil LaBute. Gramercy Pictures, 2000. Film.

Oatley, Keith. *Such Stuff as Dreams: The Psychology of Fiction*. Malden: Wiley, 2011. Print.

O'Connell, Sanjida. *Mindreading: An Investigation into How We Learn to Love and Lie*. New York: Doubleday, 1998. Print.

Oliver, Antonio. "El morisco Ricote." *Anales cervantinos* 5 (1955–56): 249–55. Print.

O'Malley, John W. *The Four Cultures of the West*. Cambridge: Harvard UP, 2004. Print.

Ong, Walter J. *Orality and Literacy: The Technologizing of the Word*. New York: Methuen, 1982. Print.

Otero, Eloisa. "Un congreso debate el sueño antinacionalista de *El Quijote*." *El mundo* [Madrid] 20 Jan. 2005: 51. Print.

Ovid. *Metamorphoses: Books I–VIII*. Ed. G. P. Goold. Trans. Frank Justus Miller. Cambridge: Harvard UP, 2005. Print.

———. *Metamorphoses: Books IX–XV*. Ed. G. P. Goold. Trans. Frank Justus Miller. Cambridge: Harvard UP, 2005. Print.

"Palabras de la Comandancia General del EZLN en el Acto de Inicio del Primer Encuentro Intercontinental por la Humanidad y contra el Neoliberalismo." *Cartas y comunicados de EZLN*. EZLN, 27 July 1996. Web. 20 May 2014. <http://palabra.ezln.org.mx/>.

Palmer, Alan. *Fictional Minds*. Lincoln: U of Nebraska P, 2004. Print.

Palos, Manuel. "Existe una especie de rechazo al *Quijote* por parte del nacionalismo." *El correo* [Bilbao]. El Correo Digital, 21 July 2005. Web. 15 June 2014. <http://www.kultura.ejgv.euskadi.net/r464879/eu/contenidos/informacion/bibliotecas_prensa_2005/eu_bp2005/adjuntos/2005-07-21Correo.pdf>.

Parker, Geoffrey. *Philip II*. Chicago: Open Court, 2002. Print.

Parr, James A. "Cervantes Foreshadows Freud: On Don Quixote's Flight from the Feminine and the Physical." *Cervantes* 15.2 (1995): 16–25. Print.

———. Don Quixote: *An Anatomy of Subversive Discourse*. Newark: Juan de la Cuesta, 1988. Print.

———. Don Quixote: *A Touchstone for Literary Criticism*. Kassel: Reichenberger, 2005. Print. Rev. ed of Don Quixote: *An Anatomy of Subversive Discourse*.

———. *Don Quixote, Don Juan, and Related Subjects: Form and Tradition in Spanish Literature, 1330–1630*. Selinsgrove: Susquehanna UP, 2004. Print.

———. "On Narration and Theory." *Cervantes* 24.2 (2004): 119–35. Print.

Patrick, Brian D. "Metalepsis and Paradoxical Narration in Don Quixote: A Reconsideration." *Letras Hispanas* 5.2 (2008): 116–32. Web. 15 June 2014. <http://www.modlang.txstate.edu/letrashispanas/previousvolumes/vol5-2/contentParagraph/0/content_files/file7/patrick.pdf>.

Payán, Miguel Juan, ed. El Quijote *en el cine*. Madrid: Jaguar, 2005. Print.

Paz Gago, José María. *Semiótica del* Quijote: *Teoría y práctica de la ficción narrativa*. Amsterdam: Rodopi, 1995. Print.

Paz Gago, José María, and José Luis González Quirós, eds. El Quijote *y el pensamiento moderno*. 2 vols. Madrid: Sociedad Estatal de Conmemoraciones Culturales, 2005. Print.

Pérez Villanueva, Joaquín, and Bartolomé Escandell Bonet, eds. *Historia de la Inquisición en España y América*. Vol. 3. Madrid: Biblioteca de Autores Cristianos, Centro de Estudios Inquisitoriales, 2000. Print.

Perry, Mary Elizabeth. *Gender and Disorder in Early Modern Seville*. Princeton: Princeton UP, 1990. Print.

———. *The Handless Maiden: Moriscos and the Politics of Religion in Early Modern Spain*. Princeton: Princeton UP, 2005. Print.

"El PIB, Don Quijote y Zapatero." *Cinco Días* [Madrid]. Estructura Grupo de Estudios Económicos, 21 Apr. 2004. Web. 15 June 2014. <http://www.cincodias.com/articulo/opinion/PIB-Don-Quijote-Zapatero/20040421cdscdiopi_5/>.

Pohjola, Mike. "Autonomous Identities: Immersion as a Tool for Exploring, Empowering, and Emancipating Identities." Montola and Stenros 81–96.

Pollard, Kevin. *The Gender Gap in College Enrollment and Graduation.* Population Reference Bureau, Apr. 2011. Web. 7 15 June 14. <http://www.prb.org /Publications/Articles/2011/gender-gap-in-education.aspx>.

Poska, Allyson. *Women and Authority in Early Modern Spain: The Peasants of Galicia.* Oxford: Oxford UP, 2005. Print.

Powell, Richard. *Don Quixote, U. S. A.* New York: Scribner's, 1966. Print.

Premack, David, and Guy Woodruff. "Does the Chimpanzee Have a Theory of Mind?" *Behavioral and Brain Sciences* 1 (1978): 515–26. Print.

Presberg, Charles D. *Adventures in Paradox:* Don Quixote *and the Western Tradition.* University Park: Penn State UP, 2001. Print.

Prescott, William H. *History of the Reign of Ferdinand and Isabella.* New York: Heritage, 1967. Print.

Prince, Gerald. *A Dictionary of Narratology.* Rev. ed. Lincoln: U of Nebraska P, 2003. Print.

———. "The Disnarrated." *Style* 22 (1988): 1–8. Print.

Pym, Anthony, and John Style. "Spanish and Portuguese." France and Haynes 261–73.

El Quijote *de Miguel de Cervantes.* Dir. Manuel Gutiérrez Aragón. 1990. Divisa Home Video, 2012. DVD.

Quint, David. *Cervantes's Novel of Modern Times: A New Reading of* Don Quijote. Princeton: Princeton UP, 2003. Print.

"Quixote." *The Oxford English Dictionary.* 2nd ed. 1989. Print.

"Quixotic." *Merriam-Webster's Collegiate Dictionary.* 11th ed. 2003. Print.

Raffel, Burton. "Translating Cervantes: Una vez más." *Cervantes* 13.1 (1993): 5–30. Print.

Randall, Dale B. J., and Jackson C. Boswell, eds. *Cervantes in Seventeenth-Century England: The Tapestry Turned.* Oxford: Oxford UP, 2009. Print.

Redondo, Agustín, ed. *Le corps dans la société espagnole des XVIème et XVIIème siècles.* Paris: Sorbonne, 1990. Print.

———. *Otra manera de leer el* Quijote: *Historia, traduciones culturales y literatura.* Madrid: Castalia, 1998. Print.

———. "El personaje de don Quijote: Tradición folklórico-literaria, contexto histórico y elaboración cervantina." *Nueva revista de filología hispánica* 29 (1980): 36–59. Print.

———. "Tradición carnavalesca y creación literaria: Del personaje de Sancho Panza al episodio de la ínsula Barataria en el *Quijote.*" *Bulletin Hispanique* 80 (1978): 39–70. Print.

Reed, Cory A. "Ludic Revelations in the Enchanted Head Episode in *Don Quijote* (II, 62)." *Cervantes* 24.1 (2004): 189–216. Print.

Reich, Howard. "Twilight of the Blues." *Chicago Tribune* 28 Dec. 2011. Arts and Entertainment sec.: 1+. Print.

Reichenberger, Kurt. *Cervantes ¿un gran satírico? Los enigmas peligrosos del* Quijote *descifrados para el "carísimo lector."* Kassel: Reichenberger, 2005. Print.

Reiss, Timothy. "Caribbean Knights: Quijote, Galahad, and the Telling of History." *Against Autonomy: Global Dialectics of Cultural Exchange*. Stanford: Stanford UP, 2002. 360–404. Print.

Ricapito, Joseph V. *Consciousness and Truth in* Don Quijote *and Connected Essays*. Newark: Juan de la Cuesta, 2007. Print.

Richards, I. A. *The Philosophy of Rhetoric*. Oxford: Oxford UP, 1936. Print.

Richards, John C., and James Flamberg. Nurse Betty *(2000) Movie Script. Screenplays for You*. Screenplays for You, 9 Mar. 1999. Web. 12 June 2014. <http://sfy .ru/?script=nurse_betty>.

Rico, Francisco. *El texto del* Quijote: *Preliminares a una ecdótica del Siglo de Oro*. Valladolid: Centro para la Edición de los Clásicos Españoles, U de Valladolid, 2005. Print.

Riera, Carme. *El* Quijote *desde el nacionalismo catalán, en torno al Tercer Centenario*. Barcelona: Destino, 2004. Print.

Riley, Edward C. *Cervantes's Theory of the Novel*. Oxford: Clarendon, 1962. Print.

———. "*Don Quixote*: From Text to Icon." *A Celebration of Cervantes on the Fourth Centenary of* La Galatea, *1585–1985*. Ed. John J. Allen, Elias Rivers, and Harry Sieber. Spec. issue of *Cervantes* 8.3 (1988): 103–15. Print.

———. *La rara invención: Estudios sobre Cervantes y su posteridad literaria*. Barcelona: Crítica, 2001. Print.

Riquer, Martín de. *Aproximación al* Quijote. Barcelona: Teide, 1967. Print.

Ritz-Barr, Steven. *Quixote*. Classics in Miniature, 2010. DVD. Puppet vers. of *Don Quixote*, by Cervantes.

Rivero Rodríguez, Manuel. *La España de Don Quijote: Un viaje al Siglo de Oro*. Madrid: Alianza, 2005. Print.

Rodríguez Zapatero, José Luis. "*El Quijote* es la Constitución de la vida." Interview with José Luis Gutiérrez. *Leer* 158 (2004–05): 70–75. Print.

Rolling Stones. "Jumpin' Jack Flash." *Forty Licks*. ABKCO Music and Records, 2002; Virgin, 2002. CD.

Romero-Díaz, Nieves. *Nueva nobleza, nueva novela: Reescribiendo la cultura urbana del barroco*. Newark: Juan de la Cuesta, 2002. Print.

———, ed. and trans. *Warnings to the Kings and Advice on Restoring Spain*. By María de Guevara. Chicago: U of Chicago P, 2007. Print.

Rossi, Rosa. *Escuchar a Cervantes*. Valladolid: Ámbito, 1988. Print.

Rowland, Beryl. *Animals with Human Faces: A Guide to Animal Symbolism*. Knoxville: U of Tennessee P, 1973. Print.

Rubio, Fanny, ed. *El* Quijote *en clave de mujer/es*. Madrid: Complutense, 2005. Print.

Rudder, Robert S. *The Literature of Spain in English Translation: A Bibliography*. New York: Ungar, 1975. Print.

Russell, Peter E. "*Don Quixote* as a Funny Book." *Modern Language Review* 64.2 (1969): 312–26. Print.

Rutherford, John. "Brevísima historia de las traducciones de *Don Quijote*." Barrio Marco and Crespo Allué 481–98.

————. "The Dangerous Don: Translating Cervantes's Masterpiece." *In Other Words* 17 (2001): 20–33. Print.

————. Introduction. Cervantes, *Don Quixote* [Rutherford] vii–xxi.

Salazar Rincón, Javier. *El mundo social del* Quijote. Madrid: Gredos, 1986. Print.

Sánchez, Alberto. *"Don Quijote, ciudadano del mundo" y otros ensayos cervantinos*. Valencia: Institució Alfons el Magnànim, 1999. Print.

————. "Revisión del cautiverio cervantino en Argel." *Cervantes* 17.1 (1997): 7–24. Print.

Sánchez, Magdalena. *The Empress, the Queen, and the Nun: Women and Power at the Court of Philip III of Spain*. Baltimore: Johns Hopkins UP, 1998. Print.

Sánchez Ron, José Manuel, ed. *La ciencia y* El Quijote. Barcelona: Crítica, 2005. Print.

Sánchez-Romeralo, Antonio, and Fernando Ibarra, eds. *Antología de autores españoles*. 2 vols. New York: Macmillan, 1972. Print.

Sarti, Raffaella. *Europe at Home: Family and Material Culture, 1500–1800*. Trans. Allan Cameron. New Haven: Yale UP, 2002. Print.

Scaramuzza, Vidoni M., ed. *Rileggere Cervantes: Antologia della critica recente*. Milano: LED, 1994. Print.

Schechner, Richard. *Performance Studies: An Introduction*. 2nd ed. New York: Routledge, 2006. Print.

Schleiermacher, Friedrich. "On the Different Methods of Translation." *Western Translation Theory from Herodotus to Nietzsche*. Ed. and trans. D. Robinson. Manchester: Saint Jerome, 1997. 225–38. Print.

Schmidt, Rachel. *Critical Images: The Canonization of* Don Quixote *through Illustrated Editions of the Eighteenth Century*. Montreal: McGill-Queen's UP, 1999. Print.

Schürr, Friedrich. "Idea de la libertad en Cervantes." *Cuadernos hispanoamericanos* 18 (1950): 367–71. Print.

"La sexta declaración de la Selva Lacandona." *Cartas y comunicados de EZLN*. EZLN, June 2005. Web. 20 May 2014. <http://palabra.ezln.org.mx/comunicados/2005/2005_06_SEXTA.htm>.

Shapin, Steven. *The Scientific Revolution*. Chicago: U of Chicago P, 1996. Print.

Shklovsky, Victor. "Art as Technique." *Russian Formalist Criticism: Four Essays*. Trans. and introd. Lee T. Lemon and Marion J. Reis. Lincoln: U of Nebraska P, 1965. 3–24. Print.

Sicroff, Albert A. *Los estatutos de limpieza de sangre: Controversias entre los siglos XV y XVII*. Trans. Mauro Armiño. Madrid: Taurus, 1985. Print. Trans. of *The Disputes over the Purity of Blood Statutes in Spain*.

Simerka, Barbara, and Christopher B. Weimer. "Duplicitous Diegesis: *Don Quijote* and Charlie Kaufman's *Adaptation*." *Hispania* 88.1 (2005): 92–101. Print.

————. "'Ever Want to Be Someone Else?' Self-Fashioning in *Don Quijote* and *Being John Malkovich*." *Anuario de estudios cervantinos* 2 (2005): 45–54. Print.

————. "Subversive Paratexts: *Don Quixote, Lost in La Mancha* (2003), and *Looking for Richard* (1996)." Simerka and Williamsen 67–82.

————. "Two Characters Defying Their Authors: *Don Quixote* and *Stranger than Fiction.*" *Anuario de estudios cervantinos IV: Del texto del Quixote a la literatura comparada y las bellas artes*. Pontevedra: Mirabel, 2008. 281–97. Print.

Simerka, Barbara, and Amy R. Williamsen, eds. *Critical Reflections: Essays on Golden Age Spanish Literature in Honor of James A. Parr*. Lewisburg: Bucknell UP, 2006. Print.

Simmons, Ernest J. *Dostoevski: The Making of a Novelist*. London: Oxford UP, 1940. Print.

Slingerland, Edward. *What Science Offers the Humanities: Integrating Body and Culture*. Cambridge: Cambridge UP, 2008. Print.

Sliwa, Krzysztof. *Vida de Miguel de Cervantes Saavedra*. Kassel: Reichenberger, 2006. Print.

Soufas, Teresa Scott. *Melancholy and the Secular Mind in Spanish Golden Age Literature*. Columbia: U of Missouri P, 1990. Print.

Stam, Robert. *Reflexivity in Film and Literature: From* Don Quixote *to Jean Luc-Godard*. New York: Columbia UP, 1992.

Starr-LeBeau, Gretchen. *In the Shadow of the Virgin: Inquisitors, Friars, and Conversos in Guadalupe, Spain*. Princeton: Princeton UP, 2003. Print.

St. John, Warren. *Rammer Jammer Yellow Hammer: A Road Trip into the Heart of Fan Mania*. New York: Three Rivers, 2005. Print.

Stoopen, María. "Cervantine Instances of Unreliability in Ricardo Piglia's 'Assumed Name.'" D'haen and Dhondt 109–35.

Stranger than Fiction. Dir. Marc Forster. Columbia Pictures, 2006. Film.

Subcomandante Marcos. "La cueva del deseo." *Cartas y comunicados de EZLN*. EZLN, 17 Mar. 1995. Web. 20 May 2014. <http://palabra.ezln.org.mx/>.

————. "The Punch Card and the Hourglass." Interview by Gabriel García Márquez and Roberto Pombo. *New Left Review* May–June 2001. Web. 15 June 2014. <http://newleftreview.org/A2322>.

Suleiman, Susan, and Inge Crosman, eds. *The Reader in the Text: Essays on Audience and Interpretation*. Princeton: Princeton UP, 1980. Print.

Sullivan, Henry W. "Don Quixote de la Mancha: Analyzable or Unanalyzable?" *Cervantes* 18.1 (1998): 4–23. Print.

————. *Grotesque Purgatory: A Study of Cervantes's* Don Quixote, *Part II*. University Park: Pennsylvania State UP, 1996. Print.

Summary. Dept. of German, Georgetown U, July 2011. Web. 16 Feb. 2014.

Sumner, Charles. *The Crime against Kansas: Apologies for the Crime: The True Remedy*. Boston: John P. Jewett and Co., 1856. Print.

Swaffar, Janet K., and Katherine Arens. *Remapping the Foreign Language Curriculum: An Approach through Multiple Literacies*. New York: MLA, 2005. Print. Teaching Langs., Lits., and Cultures.

Terry, Arthur. "Cervantes." *The Oxford Guide to Literature in English Translation*. Ed. Peter France. Oxford: Oxford UP, 2000. 418–21. Print.

Toledo es otra historia: Ciudad patrimonio de la humanidad. Patronato Municipal de Turismo, Ayuntamiento de Toledo, n.d. Web. 15 June 2014. <http://www.toledo-turismo.com/es>.

Tomasello, Michael. *The Cultural Origins of Human Cognition*. Cambridge: Harvard UP, 1999. Print.

Toole, John Kennedy. *A Confederacy of Dunces*. Baton Rouge: Louisiana State UP, 1980. Print.

Turner, Harriet, and Adelaida López de Martínez, eds. *The Cambridge Companion to the Spanish Novel from 1600 to the Present*. Cambridge: Cambridge UP, 2003. Print.

Unamuno, Miguel de. *Mist*. Trans. Warner Fite. Urbana: U of Illinois P, 2000. Print.

———. *Vida de Don Quijote y Sancho*. 1905. Madrid: Espasa-Calpe, 1961. Print.

Urbina, Eduardo. "Visual Knowledge: Textual Iconography of the *Quixote*." Urbina and Maestro 15–37.

Urbina, Eduardo, and Jesús G. Maestro, eds. Don Quixote *Illustrated: Textual Images and Visual Readings: Iconografía del* Quijote. Pontevedra: Mirabel, 2005. Print.

Vanden Berghe, Kristine. "The *Quixote* in the Stories of Subcomandante Marcos." D'haen and Dhondt 53–69.

———. "Sobre armas y letras: El *Quijote* como intertexto en los relatos del Subcomandante Marcos." *Boletín AFEHC* 33 4 Dec. 2007: 1–11. Web. 15 June 2014. <http://afehc-historia-centroamericana.org/index.php?action=fi_aff&id=1785>.

Van Doren, Mark. *Don Quixote's Profession*. New York: Columbia UP, 1958. Print.

Velasco, Sherry. *Lesbians in Early Modern Spain*. Nashville: Vanderbilt UP, 2011. Print.

———. "*Marimachos, hombrunas, barbudas*: The Masculine Woman in Cervantes." *Cervantes* 20.1 (2000): 69–78. Print.

Velázquez: The Painter of Painters. Dir. Didier K. Baussy. Home Vision, 1991. Film.

Vélez-Sainz, Julio, and Nieves Romero-Díaz, eds. *Cervantes and/on/in the New World*. Newark: Juan de la Cuesta, 2007. Print.

Venuti, Lawrence, ed. *The Translation Studies Reader*. 2nd ed. New York: Routledge, 2004. Print.

Vidal Manzanares, César. *Diccionario del* Quijote: *La obra para entender uno de los libros esenciales de la cultura universal*. Barcelona: Planeta, 2005. Print.

———. *Enciclopedia del* Quijote. Barcelona: Planeta, 1999. Print.

Viña, Frederick, ed. *Don Quijote: Meditaciones hispanoamericanas*. Lanham: UP of Amer., 1988. Print.

Vivar, Francisco. *Don Quijote frente a los caballeros de los tiempos modernos*. Salamanca: U de Salamanca, 2009. Print.

Volck, Adalbert John. *Abraham Lincoln*. *CivilWar@Smithsonian*. Smithsonian Inst., n.d. Web. 15 June 2014. <http://www.civilwar.si.edu/lincoln_byvolck.html>.

Vollendorf, Lisa. *The Lives of Women: A New History of Inquisitional Spain*. Nashville: Vanderbilt UP, 2005. Print.

Wagschal, Steven. Rev. of Don Quijote: *A New Translation, Backgrounds, Contexts, and Criticism*, trans. Burton Raffel. *Cervantes* 21.1 (2001): 147–52. Print.

Waite, Geoffrey. "Lenin in *Las Meninas*: An Essay in Historical-Materialist Vision." *History and Theory* 25.3 (1986): 248–85. Print.

Walton, Kendall. *Mimesis as Make-Believe: On the Foundation of Representational Arts*. Cambridge: Harvard UP, 1990. Print.

Waskul, Dennis, and Matt Lust. "Role-Playing and Playing Roles: The Person, Player, and Persona in Fantasy Role-Playing." *Symbolic Interaction* 27.3 (2004): 333–56. Print.

Wasserman, Dale. *Man of La Mancha: A Musical Play*. Lyrics by Joe Darion. Music by Mitch Leigh. New York: Random, 1966. Print.

Waters, Darren. "What Happened to Dungeons and Dragons?" *BBC News Online*. BBC, 26 Apr. 2004. Web. 15 June 2014. <http://news.bbc.co.uk/2/hi/uk_news/magazine/3655627.stm>.

Watt, Ian P. *Myths of Modern Individualism*: Faust, Don Quijote, Don Juan, *and* Robinson Crusoe. Cambridge: Cambridge UP, 1996. Print.

———. *The Rise of the Novel: Studies in Defoe, Richardson, and Fielding*. Berkeley: U of California P, 1957. Print.

Weber, Alison. *Teresa of Ávila and the Rhetoric of Femininity*. Princeton: Princeton UP, 1990. Print.

Weimer, Christopher. "The Quixotic Art: Cervantes, Vasari, and Michelangelo." de Armas, *Writing* 63–84.

Weiner, Jack. "Cervantes y Don Quijote ante el ocaso de España." *Annali dell'Universita degli Studi di Napoli "L'Orientale"* 50.1 (2008): 107–44. Print.

Welsh, Alexander. "The Influence of Cervantes." Cascardi, *Cambridge Companion* 80–99.

Whalley, George. "Metaphor." *Princeton Encyclopedia of Poetry and Poetics*. Ed. Alex Preminger, Frank J. Warnke, and O. B. Hardison, Jr. Princeton: Princeton UP, 1965. Print.

Wicks, Ulrich. "The Nature of Picaresque Narrative: A Modal Approach." *PMLA* 89.2 (1974): 240–49. Print.

Williamson, Edwin. *Cervantes and the Modernists: The Question of Influence*. Woodbridge: Tamesis, 1994. Print.

Willis, Raymond. "Sancho Panza: Prototype for the Modern Novel." *Hispanic Review* 36 (1969): 207–27. Print.

Wilson, Diana de Armas. *Cervantes, the Novel, and the New World*. New York: Oxford UP, 2000. Print.

Wineburg, Sam. *Historical Thinking and Other Unnatural Acts: Charting the Future of Teaching the Past*. Philadelphia: Temple UP, 2001. Print. Critical Perspectives on the Past.

Wishbone: The Impawssible Dream. Lionsgate, 2005. DVD. Season 1, episode 11.

Worth-Stylianou, Valerie. "*Translatio* and Translation in the Renaissance: From Italy to France." *The Cambridge History of Literary Criticism, Volume III: The Renaissance*. Ed. Glyn P. Norton. Cambridge: Cambridge UP, 1999. 125–35. Print.

Yates, Frances A. *Astraea: The Imperial Theme in the Sixteenth Century*. London: Routledge, 1975. Print.

Yuste, Antonio. "El bloque cervanticida." *Diario de a bordo*. Cazurra Bit, 16 Mar. 2005. Web. 15 June 2014. <http://www.cazurrabit.com/2005/diario/03/16/index.html>. El embudo nacionalista.

Zamora Vicente, Alonso. "El cautiverio en la obra cervantina." *Homenaje a Cervantes*. Ed. Francisco Sánchez-Castañer. Valencia: Mediterráneo, 1950. 384–401. Print.

Ziolkowski, Eric J. "Don Quixote's Windmill and Fortune's Wheel." *Modern Language Review* 86.4 (1991): 885–97. Print.

Zunshine, Lisa. *Why We Read Fiction: Theory of Mind and the Novel*. Columbus: Ohio State UP, 2006. Print.

INDEX

Modern Language Association of America

Approaches to Teaching World Literature

To purchase MLA publications, visit www.mla.org/bookstore.

Conrad's "Heart of Darkness" and "The Secret Sharer." Ed. Hunt Hawkins and
    Brian W. Shaffer. 2002.

Dante's Divine Comedy. Ed. Carole Slade. 1982.

Defoe's Robinson Crusoe. Ed. Maximillian E. Novak and Carl Fisher. 2005.

DeLillo's White Noise. Ed. Tim Engles and John N. Duvall. 2006.

Dickens's Bleak House. Ed. John O. Jordan and Gordon Bigelow. 2009.

Dickens's David Copperfield. Ed. Richard J. Dunn. 1984.

Dickinson's Poetry. Ed. Robin Riley Fast and Christine Mack Gordon. 1989.

Narrative of the Life of Frederick Douglass. Ed. James C. Hall. 1999.

Works of John Dryden. Ed. Jayne Lewis and Lisa Zunshine. 2013.

Duras's Ourika. Ed. Mary Ellen Birkett and Christopher Rivers. 2009.

Early Modern Spanish Drama. Ed. Laura R. Bass and Margaret R. Greer. 2006.

Eliot's Middlemarch. Ed. Kathleen Blake. 1990.

Eliot's Poetry and Plays. Ed. Jewel Spears Brooker. 1988.

Shorter Elizabethan Poetry. Ed. Patrick Cheney and Anne Lake Prescott. 2000.

Ellison's Invisible Man. Ed. Susan Resneck Parr and Pancho Savery. 1989.

English Renaissance Drama. Ed. Karen Bamford and Alexander Leggatt. 2002.

Works of Louise Erdrich. Ed. Gregg Sarris, Connie A. Jacobs, and
    James R. Giles. 2004.

Dramas of Euripides. Ed. Robin Mitchell-Boyask. 2002.

Faulkner's As I Lay Dying. Ed. Patrick O'Donnell and Lynda Zwinger. 2011.

Faulkner's The Sound and the Fury. Ed. Stephen Hahn and Arthur F. Kinney. 1996.

Fitzgerald's The Great Gatsby. Ed. Jackson R. Bryer and Nancy P. VanArsdale. 2009.

Flaubert's Madame Bovary. Ed. Laurence M. Porter and Eugene F. Gray. 1995.

García Márquez's One Hundred Years of Solitude. Ed. María Elena de Valdés and
    Mario J. Valdés. 1990.

Gilman's "The Yellow Wall-Paper" and Herland. Ed. Denise D. Knight and
    Cynthia J. Davis. 2003.

Goethe's Faust. Ed. Douglas J. McMillan. 1987.

Gothic Fiction: The British and American Traditions. Ed. Diane Long Hoeveler
    and Tamar Heller. 2003.

Poetry of John Gower. Ed. R. F. Yeager and Brian W. Gastle. 2011.

Grass's The Tin Drum. Ed. Monika Shafi. 2008.

H.D.'s Poetry and Prose. Ed. Annette Debo and Lara Vetter. 2011.

Hebrew Bible as Literature in Translation. Ed. Barry N. Olshen and
    Yael S. Feldman. 1989.

Homer's Iliad *and* Odyssey. Ed. Kostas Myrsiades. 1987.

Hurston's Their Eyes Were Watching God *and Other Works.* Ed. John Lowe. 2009.

Ibsen's A Doll House. Ed. Yvonne Shafer. 1985.

Henry James's Daisy Miller *and* The Turn of the Screw. Ed. Kimberly C. Reed and
    Peter G. Beidler. 2005.

Works of Samuel Johnson. Ed. David R. Anderson and Gwin J. Kolb. 1993.

Joyce's Ulysses. Ed. Kathleen McCormick and Erwin R. Steinberg. 1993.
Works of Sor Juana Inés de la Cruz. Ed. Emilie L. Bergmann and Stacey Schlau. 2007.
Kafka's Short Fiction. Ed. Richard T. Gray. 1995.
Keats's Poetry. Ed. Walter H. Evert and Jack W. Rhodes. 1991.
Kingston's The Woman Warrior. Ed. Shirley Geok-lin Lim. 1991.
Lafayette's The Princess of Clèves. Ed. Faith E. Beasley and
      Katharine Ann Jensen. 1998.
Writings of Bartolomé de Las Casas. Ed. Santa Arias and Eyda M. Merediz. 2008.
Works of D. H. Lawrence. Ed. M. Elizabeth Sargent and Garry Watson. 2001.
Lazarillo de Tormes *and the Picaresque Tradition.* Ed. Anne J. Cruz. 2009.
Lessing's The Golden Notebook. Ed. Carey Kaplan and Ellen Cronan Rose. 1989.
Works of Primo Levi. Ed. Nicholas Patruno and Roberta Ricci. 2014.
Works of Naguib Mahfouz. Ed. Waïl S. Hassan and Susan Muaddi Darraj. 2011.
Mann's Death in Venice *and Other Short Fiction.* Ed. Jeffrey B. Berlin. 1992.
Marguerite de Navarre's Heptameron. Ed. Colette H. Winn. 2007.
Works of Carmen Martín Gaite. Ed. Joan L. Brown. 2013.
Medieval English Drama. Ed. Richard K. Emmerson. 1990.
Melville's Moby-Dick. Ed. Martin Bickman. 1985.
Metaphysical Poets. Ed. Sidney Gottlieb. 1990.
Miller's Death of a Salesman. Ed. Matthew C. Roudané. 1995.
Milton's Paradise Lost. First edition. Ed. Galbraith M. Crump. 1986.
Milton's Paradise Lost. Second edition. Ed. Peter C. Herman. 2012.
Milton's Shorter Poetry and Prose. Ed. Peter C. Herman. 2007.
Molière's Tartuffe *and Other Plays.* Ed. James F. Gaines and
      Michael S. Koppisch. 1995.
Momaday's The Way to Rainy Mountain. Ed. Kenneth M. Roemer. 1988.
Montaigne's Essays. Ed. Patrick Henry. 1994.
Novels of Toni Morrison. Ed. Nellie Y. McKay and Kathryn Earle. 1997.
Murasaki Shikibu's The Tale of Genji. Ed. Edward Kamens. 1993.
Nabokov's Lolita. Ed. Zoran Kuzmanovich and Galya Diment. 2008.
Works of Ngũgĩ wa Thiong'o. Ed. Oliver Lovesey. 2012.
Works of Tim O'Brien. Ed. Alex Vernon and Catherine Calloway. 2010.
Works of Ovid and the Ovidian Tradition. Ed. Barbara Weiden Boyd and
      Cora Fox. 2010.
Petrarch's Canzoniere *and the Petrarchan Tradition.* Ed. Christopher Kleinhenz
      and Andrea Dini. 2014.
Poe's Prose and Poetry. Ed. Jeffrey Andrew Weinstock and Tony Magistrale. 2008.
Pope's Poetry. Ed. Wallace Jackson and R. Paul Yoder. 1993.
Proust's Fiction and Criticism. Ed. Elyane Dezon-Jones and
      Inge Crosman Wimmers. 2003.
Puig's Kiss of the Spider Woman. Ed. Daniel Balderston and Francine Masiello. 2007.
Pynchon's The Crying of Lot 49 *and Other Works.* Ed. Thomas H. Schaub. 2008.

Works of François Rabelais. Ed. Todd W. Reeser and Floyd Gray. 2011.

Novels of Samuel Richardson. Ed. Lisa Zunshine and Jocelyn Harris. 2006.

Rousseau's Confessions *and* Reveries of the Solitary Walker. Ed. John C. O'Neal and Ourida Mostefai. 2003.

Scott's Waverley Novels. Ed. Evan Gottlieb and Ian Duncan. 2009.

Shakespeare's Hamlet. Ed. Bernice W. Kliman. 2001.

Shakespeare's King Lear. Ed. Robert H. Ray. 1986.

Shakespeare's Othello. Ed. Peter Erickson and Maurice Hunt. 2005.

Shakespeare's Romeo and Juliet. Ed. Maurice Hunt. 2000.

Shakespeare's The Taming of the Shrew. Ed. Margaret Dupuis and Grace Tiffany. 2013.

Shakespeare's The Tempest *and Other Late Romances.* Ed. Maurice Hunt. 1992.

Shelley's Frankenstein. Ed. Stephen C. Behrendt. 1990.

Shelley's Poetry. Ed. Spencer Hall. 1990.

Sir Gawain and the Green Knight. Ed. Miriam Youngerman Miller and Jane Chance. 1986.

Song of Roland. Ed. William W. Kibler and Leslie Zarker Morgan. 2006.

Spenser's Faerie Queene. Ed. David Lee Miller and Alexander Dunlop. 1994.

Stendhal's The Red and the Black. Ed. Dean de la Motte and Stirling Haig. 1999.

Sterne's Tristram Shandy. Ed. Melvyn New. 1989.

Works of Robert Louis Stevenson. Ed. Caroline McCracken-Flesher. 2013.

The Story of the Stone (Dream of the Red Chamber). Ed. Andrew Schonebaum and Tina Lu. 2012.

Stowe's Uncle Tom's Cabin. Ed. Elizabeth Ammons and Susan Belasco. 2000.

Swift's Gulliver's Travels. Ed. Edward J. Rielly. 1988.

Teresa of Ávila and the Spanish Mystics. Ed. Alison Weber. 2009.

Thoreau's Walden *and Other Works.* Ed. Richard J. Schneider. 1996.

Tolstoy's Anna Karenina. Ed. Liza Knapp and Amy Mandelker. 2003.

Vergil's Aeneid. Ed. William S. Anderson and Lorina N. Quartarone. 2002.

Voltaire's Candide. Ed. Renée Waldinger. 1987.

Whitman's Leaves of Grass. Ed. Donald D. Kummings. 1990.

Wiesel's Night. Ed. Alan Rosen. 2007.

Works of Oscar Wilde. Ed. Philip E. Smith II. 2008.

Woolf's Mrs. Dalloway. Ed. Eileen Barrett and Ruth O. Saxton. 2009.

Woolf's To the Lighthouse. Ed. Beth Rigel Daugherty and Mary Beth Pringle. 2001.

Wordsworth's Poetry. Ed. Spencer Hall, with Jonathan Ramsey. 1986.

Wright's Native Son. Ed. James A. Miller. 1997.